"Census" Department of the South
November, 1864

For
Jacksonville, Fernandina
and St. Augustine, Florida

ORDERED BY THE DEPARTMENT OF THE SOUTH
HILTON HEAD, SOUTH CAROLINA

Florida State Genealogical Society

HERITAGE BOOKS
2015

HERITAGE BOOKS
AN IMPRINT OF HERITAGE BOOKS, INC.

Books, CDs, and more—Worldwide

For our listing of thousands of titles see our website
at
www.HeritageBooks.com

Published 2015 by
HERITAGE BOOKS, INC.
Publishing Division
5810 Ruatan Street
Berwyn Heights, Md. 20740

International Standard Book Numbers
Paperbound: 978-0-7884-2008-5
Clothbound: 978-0-7884-6205-4

TABLE OF CONTENTS

FOREWARD

1864 was a pivotal time in the course of the American Civil War. The conflict had been raging for three long, bloody years, and by summer had reached a new level of intensity. The armies of Grant and Sherman pushed into Virginia and Georgia with seemingly small results in exchange for large casualty lists. Confederates fought as hard as ever in the face of increasingly long odds for success. The mood of the North was uneasy, and even President Abraham Lincoln privately doubted that he could win a second term in the White House. Only clear military victories had the power to overcome the war weariness and re-elect the president in November.

Florida was not immune to the turmoil of 1864. Although a secondary theater of operations for both sides, that year saw Jacksonville occupied yet again and a major Union ground effort in north Florida. This campaign ended in the small but sanguine battle of Olustee on February 20th. Confederate forces triumphed at Olustee, but despite their win they could not hope to evict the Union forces from their lodgments on Florida's Atlantic coast. With the fall presidential election looming, supporters of the Lincoln Administration had hopes of quickly reconstructing Florida in time to add its electoral votes to the Republican column. Presidential secretary John Hay toured Union-held Florida with the mission of signing up as many loyal Floridians as possible as voters to help win the peninsula for his White House employer. However, this scheme failed along with the Olustee campaign, and Floridians would only observe the fall canvass.

One of the forgotten legacies of this era was a special census of eastern Florida conducted on the orders of Federal military authorities. Its motivation is to this day unclear, but it seems likely to have been part of the work done to help register voters under Lincoln's "10%" reconstruction plan. African-Americans living in the region were also enumerated despite the fact that they did not yet have the legal right to vote. The number, age and gender of all "contrabands" would be of great interest to Union military men who were always on the lookout for new recruits for the growing number of United States Colored Troops regiments being formed. Thus, this special census data opens a unique window on Florida's Civil War population that has heretofore been closed.

Pamela J. Cooper and Kathleen K. Graham are to be commended for bringing this important primary source to light and making it available to both scholars of Florida and Civil War history and the public.

Robert A. Taylor
Florida Institute of Technology

INTRODUCTION

by Pamela J. Cooper & Kathleen K. Graham

According to the book: *Jacksonville's Ordeal By Fire: A Civil War History* by Richard A. Martin and Daniel L. Schafer, the Department of the South (originally called "Department of South Carolina, Georgia and Florida.") at Hilton Head, South Carolina ordered the 1864 census.

Page 244-245
"During the summer of 1864, military headquarters at Hilton Head ordered a census of Jacksonville, Fernandina and St. Augustine. The Jacksonville census was finished in September and although the record was not complete--some people known from other sources to be living in the city were not listed--it provided an index to the city's growth in the final year of the war."

The original census or documents can be found at the National Archives in Washington D.C. (Record Group #393, Item 4289.) However, the date printed at the top of each page is "November, 1864." It has not been determined exactly when this census was taken. It was never filmed and there are only four known photocopies of the original: one at the Florida State Archives, one at the Indian River County Main Library, Vero Beach, another in the Jacksonville Public Library, and the last copy is located at the St. Augustine Historical Society, all in Florida. The original census pages were not numbered, but in order to index this census, the copies located in the Indian River County Main Library were numbered in the order they were photocopied from the original pages at the National Archives.

The census was broken down as follows:

Pages 1-71 Report of the census of the colored population, Jacksonville, Florida

Pages 72-104 Report of the census of the white population, Jacksonville, Florida

Pages 105-140 Report of the census of the white population East of the St. John's River, Duval County, Florida.

Pages 141-169 Report of the census of the white population East of the St. John's River, Duval County, Florida.

Pages 170-229 Report of the census of St. Augustine, Florida

The vital information that was found in the twelve columns on each individual has been copied as it appears in the original census. Dates and cities were not recorded consistently, and not all lines in the columns were completed. In addition, as in most censuses, names and handwriting were often difficult to interpret. A question mark will be found next to the names where the interpretation was not agreed on by the proofreaders.

The five columns after each individual's name were used to record the physical characteristics of the individual including their age. The next column recorded where the individual was born, or if they were contrabands. About one-third of the individuals were born in Florida.

Birthplace State/Country	No.
Colored	67
Contraband	1767
Achaway Co	1
Alabama	12
Alogna Co FL	1
Applen Co GA	1
Arkansas	1
Baden Europe	1
Baltimore	14
Bavaria	1
Berlin, Prussia	1
Black Creek FL	2
Bladen Co NC	1
Born Free	1
Boston	1
Bristol, RI	1
Britain	2
Bronswick Co GA	1
Brooklyn NY	2
Brunswick NC	1
Bullet Co FL	1
Bulloch Co GA	4
Burlk Co GA	2
Bryan Co GA	1
Camden Co GA	34
Canada	9

Birthplace State/Country	No.
Charleston, SC	7
Clay Co FL	3
Clinch Co GA	1
Columbia Co GA	3
Connecticut	11
Crawford Co GA	1
Cuba	9
D.C.	2
Delaware	2
Duval Co FL	30
England	23
Europe	4
Fall River MA	1
Fall River NY	1
Fernandina FL	49
Florida	1593
France	13
Free	6
Georgia	358
Germany	16
Glen Co GA	2
GR?	2
Graften Co NH	1
Greece	2
Hamb'gh Europe	1
Hamilton Co FL	2

Birthplace State/Country	No.
Hanover	1
Hudson NY	2
Hungaria	1
Illinois	2
Indiana	1
Ipswich, MA	1
Ireland	106
Italy	4
Jacksonville	38
Jefferson Co FL	1
Kentucky	2
Lake City, FL	1
Lancaster PA	1
Liberty Co, GA	1
London	1
Louns Co GA	1
Lyome, CT	1
Macon, GA	1
Madison Co FL	2
Maine	36
Maderin FL	8
Marion Co FL	3
Maryland	4
Massachusetts	19
Matanzas	1
Mayport, FL	2

Birthplace State/Country	No.
McIntosh Co GA	2
Michigan	5
Milledgeville GA	1
Monticellia	1
New Hampshire	9
New Jersey	12
New York	75
New Brunswick	1
Ochaway Co	1
Nassau Co, FL	18
New Haven, CT	2
New Orleans	2
Newport RI	1
North Carolina	39
North Pitcher NY	2
Northampton MA	1
Nova Scotia	2
Onslow Co NC	1
Orange Co FL	3
Palatka FL	1
Paris	1
Pennsylvania	8
Pensacola FL	4

Birthplace State/Country	No.
Philadelphia PA	8
Picolata FL	1
Pierce Co GA	4
Poland	2
Portugese	1
Pottsfield MA	1
Prussia	3
Putnam Co FL	10
Rhode Island	4
Ridgefield CT	1
Robinson Co NC	1
Rowan NC	1
South Carolina	105
Saratoga Co NY	4
Savannah GA	2
Scotland	11
Screvin Co GA	7
Spain	2
St. Augustine	645
St. Domingo	1
St. Johns Co	9
St. Johns Bluff	1
St. Mary's GA	3

Birthplace State/Country	No.
St. Mary's River Ga	1
Stumpter Dist SC	1
Sweden	1
Switzerland	1
Talbot Island	2
Tallahassee, FL	3
Tampa Bay	1
Tatnell Co GA	1
Tennessee	2
Troy, NY	1
Union Co SC	1
Virginia	9
Vermont	3
Volusia Co	7
Waine/Wane/Wayne Co GA	15
Wales	1
West India	1
Wilmington	2
Wisconsin	3
Unknown	57
TOTAL	**5446**

Next was the column to record the last residence of the individual, which helps with the migration pattern. Next to that column shows where the individual was registered for the draft or who their former owner was if they were contrabands. The date the individual came into the department (area) is listed in the next column, and after that a column that was used to record if the individual took the oath of allegiance.

In the last column (entitled 'remarks'), the census taker recorded the occupations of some of the individuals. There was a wide range of occupations, including bricklayers, butchers, bakers, shoemakers, nuns, priests, jewelers, riverboat pilots, teachers, barbers, a governess, blacksmiths, merchants, clerks, couriers, gardeners, fishermen, wood cutters, hotel and saloon keepers, engineers, oystermen, laborers, traders, tailors, and even an artist. Many individuals were government employees.

This same column reported individuals who were destitute, old, feeble, or sick and who needed rations for support. The number of rations was determined by the Post Commander, and recorded in the preceding column. Disabilities of individuals, deserters from the Rebel Army, prisoners in the guardhouse, and some family relationships were also recorded in this column.

INDEXES:
There are two indexes. One is for every name and the other is for all owners of former slaves or contraband. Be aware that the name or person can appear on the same page more than once.

This 1864 Military Census includes much more information about an individual than any other censuses taken during the 1800's.

In Appreciation

We would like to thank the former librarian of the Jacksonville Public Library, Arden Brugger who found the citation and was interested enough to try and locate a copy of the records. She asked Pam Cooper, who was attending a National Archives class in 1993 to locate the records while in Washington DC. Along with Edie Mixon of Jacksonville and Ed Trippe of Atlanta, who also were attending the same class, they were able to locate the records with some difficulty. The Archives could not find them at first and through persistence, they were found in a back room for unknown reasons. We would like to thank Edie Mixon for making the copies available at each of the four institutions.

Special thanks to the following members of the Central Florida Genealogical Society who helped with the proof reading:

Martha Jean Burns
Nadine McCabe
Marie Santry
Betty Jo Stockton
JoAnne Telkamp

"Census". Department of the South November 1864

No	Names	Height Feet	Height in	Eyes	Complexion	Age	Where born (Contrabands)	Last Residence	Where Registered for Draft (or former Owner)	Came into the Department (Date)	Oath of Allegiance yes or no	No of Rations	Remarks
1	Alfred Baker			black	black	12	Contraband	Fernandina Fla	George Latham	=			
2	John Baker			"	"	7	"	"	"	=			
3	Henry Baker			"	"	5	"	"	"	=			
4	Martha Baker			"	"	3	"	"	"	=			
5	Charlie Dicis	5	1	"	"	25	"	"	"	=			
6	George Latham	6	1/2	Blue	Light	48	Glenn Co Ga	Camden Co Ga	—	March 10/63	Yes		
7	Hester Latham	5	5	dark	fair	5	Liberty Co Ga	"	—	"	Yes		
8	Udyz White			"	"		Ga	"	—	"			
9	Francis Latham	5	5	Blue	Light	14	"	"	—	"	Yes		
10	Thomas Holzendorf	5	9	black	black	67	Contraband	St Augustine	Francis Spains	March 2/62			
11	Jene Latham	4	11	"	"	42	"	Liberty Co Ga	George Latham	"			
12	Kate Holzendorf	4	11	"	"	25	"	"	"	"			
13	Samuel W McParr	5	9	Dark	fair	50	Penn	Lake City	—	Feb 10/64	Yes		
14	Eugine McParr	5	6	blue	light	18	Jacksonville	"	—	"	Yes		
15	Frederick W McParr			"	"	2	"	"	—	"			
16	Mary E Lassarne	4	8	"	"	16	"	Jacksonville	—	April 1/64	Yes		
17	Salena Lassarse	4	11	Dark	medium	38	Fall River Mass	"	—	"	Yes		
18	Charles H Lassarne			Grey	fair	14	Jacksonville	"	—	"			
19	Jonathan T. Turner	5	10	"	"	55	Conn	Conn	—	Nov 26/62	Yes		
20	Adalaide D Turner	5	11	blue	fair	37	"	"	—	April 9/63	Yes		
21	John T. Turner	6	11	blue	light	27	"	Atlanta Ga	—	Feb 3/64	Yes		
22	Mattie A Turner	5	11	"	fair	19	"	Conn	—	April 9/63	Yes		
23	Marvin W Turner	4	8	"	"	14	"	"	—	"			
24	Christianna Christopher	5	2	black	black	34	Contraband	Fla	John Houston	Dec 10/64			

"CENSUS" DEPARTMENT OF THE SOUTH - NOVEMBER, 1864

Pg	No	Name	Height		Eyes	Com-plexion	Age	Where born or contraband	Last residence	Where registered for draft or former owner	Date into Department	Oath of Allgn	No of Ration	Remarks
			Ft	In										
1	1	Bronson, John	5	5			55	Contraband		Summerlin, Jno			none	
1	2	Bronson, Maria	5	4			44	Contraband		Summerlin, Jno			none	
1	3	Anderson, Anne	5	5			17	Contraband		Summerlin, Jno				
1	4	Pinkney, Caroline	5	3			76	Contraband		Kirkland, Wm			none	
1	5	Paine, Anne	5	4			30	Contraband		Brooks, Eliza			none	
1	6	Paine, Ann	5	1			16	Contraband		Brooks, Eliza			none	
1	7	Paine, Sarah	4	10			12	Contraband		Brooks, Eliza			none	
1	8	Paine, Eliza					10	Contraband		Brooks, Eliza			none	
1	9	Paine, Baldwin					8	Contraband		Brooks, Eliza			none	
1	10	Paine, Clay					6	Contraband		Brooks, Eliza			none	
1	11	Paine, Wm					3	Contraband		Brooks, Eliza			none	
1	12	Smallwood, Sam	5	0			36	Contraband		Brooks, Eliza			none	
1	13	Smallwood, Josephine	5	6			50	Contraband		Brown, Henrietta			none	
1	14	Smallwood, Jno					5	Contraband		Brown, Henrietta			none	
1	15	Vanness, Geo	5	10			57	Contraband		Brushe, M.			none	
1	16	Van Ness, Lucy	5	0			50	Contraband		Brushe, M.			none	
1	17	Van Ness, Stephen	5	1			14	Contraband		Brushe, M.			none	
1	18	Van Ness, Rosa	5	0			12	Contraband		Brushe, M.			none	
1	19	Van Ness, John					10	Contraband		Brushe, M.			none	
1	20	Van Ness, Jas					8	Contraband		Brushe, M.			none	
1	21	Van Ness, Fredrik					7	Contraband		Brushe, M.			none	
1	22	Van Ness, Elizth					6	Contraband		Brushe, M.			none	
1	23	Pinckney, Morris	5	5			47	Contraband		Sanchez, Morris			none	
1	24	Pinckney, Eva	5	3			27	Contraband		Brushe, M.			none	

"CENSUS" DEPARTMENT OF THE SOUTH - NOVEMBER, 1864

Pg	No	Name	Height		Eyes	Com-plexion	Age	Where born or contraband	Last residence	Where registered for draft or former owner	Date into Department	Oath of Allgn	No of Ration	Remarks
			Ft	In										
2	25	Pinkney, Sarah					12	Contraband		Brushe, Michael			none	
2	26	Pinkney, Jos					10	Contraband		Brushe, Michael			none	
2	27	Pinkney, Morris					7	Contraband		Brushe, Michael			none	
2	28	Pinkney, Charlotte					6	Contraband		Brushe, Michael			none	
2	29	Pinkney, John					4	Contraband		Brushe, Michael			none	
2	30	Self, Eliza	5	5			34	Contraband		Weeks, Silas			none	
2	31	Self, Ellen	4	5			13	Contraband		McCrea, Dr.			none	
2	32	Danberry, Mary					12	Contraband		Prevatt, Morgan				
2	33	Danberry, Ben					9	Contraband		Prevatt, Morgan				
2	34	Craig, Absalom	5	5			25	Contraband		Sandison, J. P.				
2	35	Craig, Eliz[th]	5	3			21	Contraband		Green, Elisha				
2	36	Craig, Rachel	4	3			12	Contraband		Green, Elisha			3	By order Super[dent] Contraband
2	37	Craig, Chaney					10	Contraband		Green, Elisha				
2	38	Craig, Benj.	3	4			18	Contraband		Green, Elisha				
2	39	Craig, Robert					1	Contraband		Green, Elisha				
2	40	Collar, Charlotte	5	5			25	Contraband		Eahl, Elias				
2	41	Walker, Henry	5	5			40	Contraband		Eahl, Elias				
2	42	Walker, Elijah	5	8			41	Contraband		Eahl, Elias				
2	43	Jones, Dorcas	5	4			25	Contraband		Rhode, Wm				
2	44	Jones, Isaac					9	Contraband		Rhode, Wm				
2	45	Jones, Saml					6	Contraband		Rhode, Wm				
2	46	Jones, Harriet					13	Contraband		Rhode, Wm				
2	47	Jones, Rosa	5	4			30	Contraband		Rhode, Wm				
2	48	Jones, Isaac					11	Contraband		Rhode, Wm				

"CENSUS" DEPARTMENT OF THE SOUTH - NOVEMBER, 1864

Pg	No	Name	Height Ft	Height In	Eyes	Com-plexion	Age	Where born or contraband	Last residence	Where registered for draft or former owner	Date into Department	Oath of Allgn	No of Ration	Remarks
3	1	Dixon, Nelly					6	Contraband		Monsong, Anna				
3	2	Dixon, Geo					5	Contraband		Monsong, Anna				
3	3	Jones, Hannah	5	5			24	Contraband		McCrea, Wash.				
3	4	Jones, Ellick					7	Contraband		McCrea, Wash.				
3	5	Jones, Arthur					5	Contraband		McCrea, Wash.				
3	6	Jones, Jas					3	Contraband		McCrea, Wash.				
3	7	McCrea, Anne	5	0			25	Contraband		McCrea, Wash.				
3	9	McCrea, Robert					2	Contraband		McCrea, Wash.				
3	10	Smith, Anni	5	4			29	Contraband		GArdner, Mr.				
3	11	Little, Smith	6	2			38	Contraband		Barnhill, Gilbert				
3	12	Little, Saml					16	Contraband		Barnhill, Gilbert				
3	13	Little, Hoyt					8	Contraband		Barnhill, Gilbert				
3	14	Little, Caroline					5	Contraband		Barnhill, Gilbert				
3	15	Clarke, Anna					50	Contraband		Bernnett, Peter				
3	16	Beisbane, Eliz^th^	4	10			15	Contraband		Putnam, B. A.				
3	17	Wright, Tenah	5	1			25	Contraband		Wright, Thos				
3	18	Wright, Chester					5	Contraband		Wright, Thos				
3	19	Wright, Alice					1	Contraband		Wright, Thos				
3	20	Brown, Seiller	5	3			55	Contraband		Phummer, Jas				
3	21	Primey, Anna	5	2			21	Contraband		Phummer, Jas				
3	22	Brown, Charley	5	0			14	Contraband		Phummer, Jas				
3	23	Primey, Felicia					6	Contraband		Phummer, Jas				
3	24	Primey, Toney					4	Contraband		Phummer, Jas				

Pg	No	Name	Height Ft	Height In	Eyes	Com-plexion	Age	Where born or contraband	Last residence	Where registered for draft or former owner	Date into Department	Oath of Allgn	No of Ration	Remarks
4	25	Kelly, Dianah	5	1			16	Contraband		Phummer, Jas				
4	26	Kelly, Affey	5	4			17	Contraband		Phummer, Jas				
4	27	Crayton, Maria	5	5			16	Contraband		Phummer, Jas				
4	28	Smith, Jno	5	6			40	Contraband		Parker, Richard				
4	29	Smith, Lucy	5	4			42	Contraband		Parker, Richard				
4	30	Wilson, Mary	5	5			44	Contraband		Free Born				
4	31	Wilson, Amelia	5	5			18	Contraband		Free Born				
4	32	Wilson, Rebecca	5	2			14	Contraband		Free Born				
4	33	Wilson, Lydia	5	4			12	Contraband		Free Born				
4	34	Wilson, Nicholas					8	Contraband		Free Born				
4	35	Wilson, Saml					5	Contraband		Free Born				
4	36	Wilson, Robert					4	Contraband		Free Born				
4	37	Cook, Louisa	5	4			26	Contraband		Hemming, J. C.				
4	38	Erhl, John	5	8			50	Contraband		Erhl, Elias				
4	39	Erhl, Caroline	5	1			45	Contraband		Erhl, Elias				
4	40	Erhl, Grey					3	Contraband		Erhl, Elias				
4	41	Kelly, Winny	5	5			45	Contraband		Kelly, Wm				
4	42	Kelly, Jos	4	5			16	Contraband		Kelly, Wm				
4	43	Kelly, Clarissa					14	Contraband		Kelly, Wm				
4	44	Wiggins, Melissa	5	1			50	Contraband		Kelly, Wm				
4	45	King, Frank	5	9			52	Contraband		Ledwiter, Thos			1	Govt. Employee
4	46	Hardie, Nelly	5	3			36	Contraband		Smith, Kirby				
4	47	Mayo, Maria	5	3			46	Contraband		Hendrix, Thos				
4	48	Gray, Henry	5	5			50	Contraband		Boothe, Marcus				

Pg	No	Name	Height Ft	Height In	Eyes	Com-plexion	Age	Where born or contraband	Last residence	Where registered for draft or former owner	Date into Department	Oath of Allgn	No of Ration	Remarks
5	1	Jones, Aaron					11	Contraband		Rhode, Wm				
5	2	Sheppard, Sarah	5	4			28	Contraband		Jones, Polly Ann				
5	3	Sheppard, Danl.					11	Contraband		Jones, Polly Ann				
5	4	Sheppard, Jenkins					9	Contraband		Jones, Polly Ann				
5	5	Sheppard, Mary A					8	Contraband		Jones, Polly Ann				
5	6	Sheppard, Anninia					5	Contraband		Jones, Polly Ann				
5	7	Sheppard, Harry					3	Contraband		Jones, Polly Ann				
5	8	Mack, Ella					30	Contraband		Jones, Polly Ann				
5	9	Mack, ...ier?					28	Contraband		Jones, Polly Ann				
5	10	G.....?, Frances	5	0			24	Contraband		Perry, Starke				
5	11	Caine, Wm					1	Contraband		Perry, Starke				
5	12	Drawdy,Hernando					21	Contraband		Green, Elisha				
5	13	Reely, Jas	6	0			72	Contraband		McCrea, Wash.				
5	14	Reely, Clysa	5	0			60	Contraband		McCrea, Wash.				
5	15	Reely, Eliza	5	4			30	Contraband		McCrea, Wash.				
5	16	Reely, Henny					9	Contraband		McCrea, Wash.				
5	17	Reely, Laina					7	Contraband		McCrea, Wash.				
5	18	Reely, Sarah					3	Contraband		McCrea, Wash.				
5	19	Reely, Jack					1	Contraband		McCrea, Wash.				
5	20	Primus, Judy					35	Contraband		Tombs, Danl.				
5	21	Primus, Mimber	5	5			20	Contraband		Tombs, Danl.				
5	22	Primus, Mary					19	Contraband		Tombs, Danl.				
5	23	Primus, Toney					13	Contraband		Tombs, Danl.				
5	24	Primus, Edward					12	Contraband		Tombs, Danl.				

Pg	No	Name	Height		Eyes	Com-plexion	Age	Where born or contraband	Last residence	Where registered for draft or former owner	Date into Department	Oath of Allgn	No of Ration	Remarks
			Ft	In										
6	25	Primus, Moses					3	Contraband		Tombs, Danl.				
6	26	Richards, Jno	6	0			48	Contraband		Boston, Jno				
6	27	Lampkin, Prince	6	0			47	Contraband		Alsop, Wm				
6	28	Lenard, Cain	5	5			48	Contraband		Crosby, Wm			1	Govt Employer
6	29	Jackson, Plenty	5	8			40	Contraband		Broward, Jno			1	Govt Employer
6	30	Paine, Chas	5	5			60	Contraband		Free Born			1	Govt Employer
6	31	Brice, Edw	5	6			22	Contraband		Darby, John				
6	32	Crosby, Maria	5	5			50	Contraband		Tison, Henry				
6	33	Crosby, Cornelia					10	Contraband		Tison, Henry				
6	34	Scott, Nelly	5	2			26	Contraband		Lewis, Chas				
6	35	Scott, Susan					5	Contraband		Lewis, Chas				
6	36	Green, Wm	6	2			36	Contraband		Higginbottam, Jos				
6	37	Green, Lurena	5	4			26	Contraband		Higginbottam, Jos				
6	38	Gieger, Danl					11	Contraband		Griger, Glen				
6	39	Evans, Sarah	5	4			38	Contraband		Mosely, Gov				
6	40	Evans, Alice					4	Contraband		Mosely, Gov				
6	41	Evans, Thos					8	Contraband		Mosely, Gov				
6	42	Evans, Wm					6	Contraband		Mosely, Gov				
6	43	Sims, Emma					19	Contraband		Mosely, Gov				
6	44	Sims, Andrew					1	Contraband		Mosely, Gov				
6	45	Dixon, Ferribee	5	2			25	Contraband		Munsong, Anna				
6	46	Dixon, Patty	5	4			14	Contraband		Munsong, Anna				
6	47	Dixon, Penny					12	Contraband		Munsong, Anna				
6	48	Dixon, Maria					10	Contraband		Munsong, Anna				

Pg	No	Name	Height Ft	Height In	Eyes	Com-plexion	Age	Where born or contraband	Last residence	Where registered for draft or former owner	Date into Department	Oath of Allgn	No of Ration	Remarks
7	1	Booth, Ann	5	3			26	Contraband		Booth, Marcus				
7	2	Booth, Sylvester	4	10			11	Contraband		Booth, Marcus				
7	3	Booth, Caroline					9	Contraband		Booth, Marcus				
7	4	Booth, Mary					1	Contraband		Booth, Marcus				
7	5	Robinson, Rafila	5	3			26	Contraband		Hugons, Jro R.				
7	6	Robinson, Ruben					4	Contraband		Hugons, Jro R.				
7	7	Nesbitt, Romeo	5	6			50	Contraband		Pendarvis, Jno				
7	8	Nesbitt, Lucy	5	3			23	Contraband		Burham, Mary				
7	9	Nesbitt, Katey					12	Contraband		Burham, Mary				
7	10	Nesbitt, Eley					10	Contraband		Burham, Mary				
7	11	Nesbitt, Harriet					7	Contraband		Burham, Mary				
7	12	Nesbitt, Andrew					5	Contraband		Burham, Mary				
7	13	Jones, Moses	5	6			26	Contraband		Jones, John				
7	14	Hugin, Sarah	5	5			31	Contraband		Hugin, Nancy				
7	15	Hugin, Henry					7	Contraband		Hugin, Nancy				
7	16	Hugin, Berry					1	Contraband		Hugin, Nancy				
7	17	Mumford, Fanny					5	Contraband		Widows, Fanny				
7	18	Mumford, Hester					3	Contraband		Widows, Fanny				
7	19	May, Elizth	5	3			30	Contraband		Summerlin, Jno				
7	20	Gray, Joshua					11	Contraband		Summerlin, Jno				
7	21	Gray, Menday					9	Contraband		Summerlin, Jno				
7	22	Gray, Nath'					6	Contraband		Summerlin, Jno				
7	23	Gray, Richard					4	Contraband		Summerlin, Jno				
7	24	Gray, Moses					2	Contraband		Summerlin, Jno				

Pg	No	Name	Height Ft	Height In	Eyes	Com-plexion	Age	Where born or contraband	Last residence	Where registered for draft or former owner	Date into Department	Oath of Allgn	No of Ration	Remarks
8	25	DuPont, Flora	5	4			28	Contraband		Hening, J. C.				
8	26	Richardson, Leah	5	3			24	Contraband		Hening, J. C.				
8	27	Canady, Frances	5	4			20	Contraband		Tombs, Dan				
8	28	Deveax, Serpio	5	9			65	Contraband		Talbot, Wm				Owner in S.C.
8	29	Devenx, Maria	5	4			45	Contraband		DuPont, Ben				Owner in Fla
8	30	Wilds, Philis	5	4			45	Contraband		Tombs, Dan			3	By order Supt. Contr.
8	31	Jackson, Jane	5	2			26	Contraband		Tombs, Dan				
8	32	Boston, Scilla	5	4			24	Contraband		DuPont, B.				
8	33	Boston, Julia					10	Contraband		DuPont, B.				
8	34	Boston, Deanah					4	Contraband		DuPont, B.				
8	35	Boston, Thos					2	Contraband		DuPont, B.				
8	36	Baynard, Lucinda	5	5			40	Contraband		Howell, Henry			3	By order Supt. Contr.
8	37	Baynard, Maria	5	2			18	Contraband		Howell, Henry				
8	38	Baynard, Geo	4	8			16	Contraband		Howell, Henry				
8	39	Baynard, Rebecca					6	Contraband		Howell, Henry				
8	40	Capeis?, Rose	5	4			60	Contraband		Bouyer, C. (KeyWest)			1	By order Supt. Contr.
8	41	Williams, Mary	5	4			39	Contraband		St. Clair, Wm				Brooklin, NY
8	42	Williams, Caroline					6	Contraband		St. Clair, Wm				Brooklin, NY
8	43	Simmons, Susan	5	8			29	Contraband		Baya, A.			3	By order Supt. Contr.
8	44	Simmons, Philis					11	Contraband		Baya, A.				
8	45	Simons, Frances					6	Contraband		Baya, A.				
8	46	Simons, Alex					4	Contraband		Baya, A.				
8	47	Simons. Chas					1	Contraband		Baya, A.				
8	48	Lang, Mary	5	0			26	Contraband		St. Clair, Wm				York

Pg	No	Name	Height Ft	Height In	Eyes	Com-plexion	Age	Where born or contraband	Last residence	Where registered for draft or former owner	Date into Department	Oath of Allgn	No of Ration	Remarks
9	1	Bronson, Jno	5	5			55	Contra		Summerlin, Jno			none	
9	2	Bronson, Maria	5	4			44	Contra		Summerlin, Jno			none	
9	3	Anderon, Anne	5	5			17	Contra		Summerlin, Jno				
9	4	Lang, Johny					3	Contra		St. Clair, Wm				
9	5	Shaver, Sarah	5	6			36	Contra						Free Born
9	6	Adams, Billy	5	8			75	Contra		Carr, Jno			1	By order Supt Contr
9	7	Sanchez, Sophy					7	Contra		Carr, Jno				
9	8	Clarke, Sophy	5	2			60	Contra		Carr, Jno				
9	9	Epps, Leonora	5	0			20	Contra						Free Born
9	10	Brown, Sarah	5	0			64	Contra		Horton, Wm				
9	11	Brown, Isaac	5	6			87	Contra		Mosely, Wm				
9	12	Petty, David	6	0			52	Contra		Hory, H. H.				
9	13	Petty, Eley	5	4			49	Contra		Free Born				
9	14	Petty, Polly					12	Contra		Hopkins, Chas				
9	15	Lofton, Aleck	6	0			40	Contra		Free Born				
9	16	Lofton, Jane					8	Contra		Emery, C. S.				
9	17	Lofton, Rebeca					28	Contra		Emery, C. S.				
9	18	Lofton, Geo					3	Contra		Emery, C. S.				
9	19	Brown, John H.	5	4			30	Contra		Free Born				Boarding House
9	20	Bunday, Amanda	5	0			28	Contra		Peterman, B.				
9	21	Bushe, Wm	4	2			10	Contra		Peterman, B.				
9	22	Warfield, Charles					1	Contra		Peterman, B.				
9	23	Brown, Victoria	5	5			21	Contra		Sabol, A.				
9	24	Rose, Wm					4	Contra		Sabol, A.				

Pg	No	Name	Height		Eyes	Com-plexion	Age	Where born or contraband	Last residence	Where registered for draft or former owner	Date into Department	Oath of Allgn	No of Ration	Remarks
			Ft	In										
10	25	Pallesier, Charles	5	3			30	Contraband		Pallesie, Jas				
10	26	Lee, Wm.	5	7			37	Contraband		Mosely, Gov			1	Govt Employe
10	27	Lee, Virginia	5	4			27	Contraband		Mosely, Gov				
10	28	Lee, Eliz th					12	Contraband		Mosely, Gov				
10	29	Lee, Amelia					9	Contraband		Mosely, Gov				
10	30	Lee, Louisa					6	Contraband		Mosely, Gov				
10	31	Hagins, Genview	5	5			45	Contraband		Free Born				
10	32	Hagins, Josephine	5	5			18	Contraband		Free Born				
10	33	Hagins, Julia	5	4			21	Contraband		Free Born				
10	34	Hagins, John					12	Contraband		Free Born				
10	35	Hagins, Cahell					10	Contraband		Free Born				
10	36	Richard, Eve	5	3			100	Contraband		Rishard, Jno				
10	37	Hagins, Henry					9	Contraband		Free Born				
10	38	Hagins, Mary					6	Contraband		Free Born				
10	39	Hagins, Celia					3	Contraband		Free Born				
10	40	Miller, Rachel	5	5			37	Contraband		Clinch, Geo				
10	41	Miller, Delia					9	Contraband		Clinch, Geo				
10	42	Miller, Cyrus					7	Contraband		Clinch, Geo				
10	43	Miller, Isadore					5	Contraband		Clinch, Geo				
10	44	Miller, Thos					3	Contraband		Clinch, Geo				
10	45	Miller, Levi					1	Contraband		Clinch, Geo				
10	46	Hall, Isrial	6	0			40	Contraband		Hory, H. H.				
10	47	Hall, Eva	5	5			37	Contraband		Palmer, D. L.				
10	48	Hagins, Louisa	5	4			25	Contraband						

Pg	No	Name	Height Ft	Height In	Eyes	Com-plexion	Age	Where born or contraband	Last residence	Where registered for draft or former owner	Date into Department	Oath of Allgn	No of Ration	Remarks
11	1	Hagin, Byrd					6	Contra		Ferris, S. P.				
11	2	Mapson, Maria	5	4			25	Contra		Mosely, Wm				
11	3	Zeigler,Nelly	5	3			37	Contra		Zeigler, M.				
11	4	Zeigler, Eliza	5	2			20	Contra		Zeigler, M.				
11	5	Zeigler, Aaron	5	1			13	Contra		Zeigler, M.				
11	6	Zeigler, Beckey					11	Contra		Zeigler, M.				
11	7	Zeigler, Sarah					10	Contra		Zeigler, M.				
11	8	Zeigler, Price					9	Contra		Zeigler, M.				
11	9	Zeigler, Frank					3	Contra		Zeigler, M.				
11	10	Hill, Susan	5	4			50	Contra		Hendrix, Thos				
11	11	Tines, Jesse	6	3			52	Contra		Tines, Henry				
11	12	Tines, Mary	5	5			40	Contra		Tines, Henry				
11	13	Brown, Francis	5	3			25	Contra		Tines, Henry				
11	14	McPherson, Jas	5	2			52	Contra		Buller, Nick				
11	15	Harrison, Binah	5	2			35	Contra		Gordon, Wm				
11	16	Brown, Amy					4	Contra		Gordon, Wm				
11	17	Seymore, Henry	5	6			54	Contra		Hazel, Wm				
11	18	Mitchel, Nancy	5	0			30	Contra		Hazel, Wm				
11	19	Conyers, Peter	5	4			55	Contra		Weeks, Silas				
11	20	Tison, Rosanah	5	0			32	Contra		Tison, Henry				
11	21	Tison, Anna	5	1			16	Contra		Tison, Henry				
11	22	Bryant, Anne	5	0			34	Contra		Sains, Margt				
11	23	Conyers, Sarah	4				13	Contra		Sains, Margt				
11	24	Elizth Simons	5	4			45	Contra		Livington, W.				

"CENSUS" DEPARTMENT OF THE SOUTH - NOVEMBER, 1864

Pg	No	Name	Height		Eyes	Com-plexion	Age	Where born or contraband	Last residence	Where registered for draft or former owner	Date into Department	Oath of Allgn	No of Ration	Remarks
			Ft	In										
12	25	Riley, Robert	6	2			58	Contra		Pearson, Peyre?				
12	26	Riley, Eliz[th]	5	0			60	Contra		Holmes, T.O.				
12	27	Gambier, John					24			N. Y.	1864			Free Born
12	28	Lee, Jas A.	5	5			24			N. Y.	1864			Free Born
12	29	Livingston, Sandy	5	0			15			Broward, John				
12	30	Williams, Hester	5				14			Mosely, Wm				
12	31	Mapson, Wm					9			Mosely, Wm				
12	32	Mapson, Elleck					5			Mosely, Wm				
12	33	Mapson, Julia					3			Mosely, Wm				
12	34	Miller, Philis	5	3			55			Ferris, S. P.				
12	35	Adams, Jas					7			Ferris, S. P.				
12	36	Gordon, Maria	5	3			30			Jones, David				
12	37	Gordon, George					9			Jones, David				
12	38	Ingesol, Hagar					5			Jones, David				
12	39	Gordon, Lincoln					3			Jones, David				
12	40	Gordon, Josephine					1			Jones, David				
12	41	Crosby, Susan	5	0			34			Crosby, Wm				
12	42	Bidder, Harriet	5	6			30			Crosby, Wm				
12	43	Crayton, Maria	5	4			17			Phrinner, Jas				
12	44	May, Sarah	5	4			29			Black, John				
12	45	Young, Henry	5	4			21			Sanders, Mr.				
12	46	Young, Jane	5	3			14			Sanders, Mr.				
12	47	Wright, Clarissa					13			Black, Jno				
12	48	Wright, Dora	5	2			16			Black, Jno				

Pg	No	Name	Height Ft	Height In	Eyes	Com-plexion	Age	Where born or contraband	Last residence	Where registered for draft or former owner	Date into Department	Oath of Allgn	No of Ration	Remarks
13	1	May, Conelia					5	Contr		Black, Jno				
13	2	Macy, Mary					2	Contr		Black, Jno				
13	3	Young, Wm	5	8			50	Contr		Sanders				
13	4	Young, Lucinda	5	3			19	Contr		Church, L.				
13	5	Young, Eliza					10	Contr		Church, L.				
13	6	Young, Robt					1	Contr		Church, L.				
13	7	Lucas, Lucinda	5				25	Contr		Lucas, Jane				
13	8	Lucas, Jas					5	Contr		Lucas, Jane				
13	9	Lucas, Kitty					6	Contr		Lucas, Jane				
13	10	Lucas, Polly					4	Contr		Lucas, Jane				
13	11	Herrand, Chas					3	Contr		Lucas, Jane				
13	12	Sams, Nathan	5	4			27	Contr		Hopkins, Chas				
13	13	Sams, Eliz[th]	5	3			21	Contr		Villipegue				
13	14	Robinson, Geo					10	Contr		Villipegue				
13	15	Walker, Geo	5	3			45	Contr		Hart, J. D.				
13	16	Walker, Anne	5	3			34			Hart, J. D.				
13	17	Walker, Martha	5	3			17			Cawlk, Wm				
13	18	Walker, Sandy	4	2			13			Cawlk, Wm				
13	19	Walker, Joseph					9			Cawlk, Wm				
13	20	Walker, Jas					7			Cawlk, Wm				
13	21	King, Gandison	6	0			39			Green, Elisha				
13	22	King, Sarah	5	4			34			Green, Elisha				
13	23	King, Sarah					11			Green, Elisha				
13	24	Lussee, April	5	10			40			Pons, J. M.				

Pg	No	Name	Height Ft	Height In	Eyes	Com-plexion	Age	Where born or contraband	Last residence	Where registered for draft or former owner	Date into Department	Oath of Allgn	No of Ration	Remarks
14	26	Eubanks, Jno	5	7			55	Contr		Eubanks, S.				
14	27	Harrison, Binah	4	3			35	Contr		Gardner, E.				
14	28	Primus, Toney					11	Contr		Toms, D.				
14	29	Paine, Sarah	4				13	Contr		Brooks, Eliz				
14	30	Green, Tilmal	5	8			23	Contr		Darby, John				
14	31	Green, Anna	5	0			28	Contr		Gigers, John				
14	32	Greene, Eugene					1	Contr		Gigers, John				
14	33	Limbrick, Isabel	5	0			29	Contr		Silcox, J.				
14	34	Limbrick, Stacia?					9	Contr		Silcox, J.				
14	35	Winter, Lama	5				18	Contr		Price, Miles				
14	36	Kelly, Fanny	5				24	Contr		Kelly, Wm				
14	37	Kelly, Carvie					9	Contr		Kelly, Wm				
14	38	Kelly, Philip					4	Contr		Kelly, Wm				
14	39	Kely, Lucinda					2	Contr		Kelly, Wm				
14	40	Williams, Geo	6				50	Contr		Summerlin, Jno				
14	41	Williams, Lucinda	5	3			23	Contr		Summerlin, Jno				
14	42	Williams, Susan	5				13	Contr		Summerlin, Jno				
14	43	Williams, Eliza					7	Contr		Summerlin, Jno				
14	44	Williams, Sam					6	Contr		Summerlin, Jno				
14	45	Williams, Edwd					4	Contr		Summerlin, Jno				
14	46	Williams, Geo					1	Contr		Summerlin, Jno				
14	47	Sams, Mary					2	Contr		Hopkins				
14	48	Armstead, Geo	5	8			33	Contr		Brown, Col				

Pg	No	Name	Height Ft	Height In	Eyes	Com-plexion	Age	Where born or contraband	Last residence	Where registered for draft or former owner	Date into Department	Oath of Allgn	No of Ration	Remarks
15	1	Reese, Hannah	5	3			37	Contr		Mastey, Jos				
15	2	Reese, Isabella					7	Contr		Mastey, Jos				
15	3	Reese, Katey					3	Contr		Mastey, Jos				
15	4	Reese, Jos					1	Contr		Mastey, Jos				
15	5	McFaust, Dan'	5	8			51	Contr		McFaust, Wm				Charleston, SC
15	6	Kelly, Arthur	6	2			40	Contr		Kelly, Wm				
15	7	Kelly, Dilcy	5	3			36			Kelly, Wm				
15	8	Kelly, Isabel	4				11			Kelly, Wm				
15	9	Sidley, John					6			Kelly, Wm				
15	10	Sidley, Betsy					4			Kelly, Wm				
15	11	Roberts, Hilliard					1			Kelly, Wm				
15	12	Hicks,Gilbert	6				52			Register, John				
15	13	Hicks, Sarah	5				27			Register, John				
15	14	Hicks, Richard					7			Register, John				
15	15	Mitchel	5	0			14			Delk, Wm				
15	16	Barton, Jerome	6	0			62			Hart, T. D.				
15	17	Barton, Mary	5	0			32			Hart, T. D.				
15	18	Simons, Sarah	5	3			49			Hart, T. D.				
15	19	Smith, Dinah	5	4			50			Hart, T. D.				
15	20	Raphile, John	5	8			20			Roberts, John				
15	21	Murdock, Matt	5	6			49			Haddock, Jno				
15	22	Sumerlin, Joe	5	8			48			Sumerlin, Jno				
15	23	Smith, Mary					2			Sumerlin, Jno				
15	24	Spearing, Sam	5	9			16			Green, Elisha				

Pg	No	Name	Height Ft	Height In	Eyes	Com-plexion	Age	Where born or contraband	Last residence	Where registered for draft or former owner	Date into Department	Oath of Allgn	No of Ration	Remarks
16	25	Spearing, Maria					11			Green, Elisha				
16	26	Spearing, Geo					6			Green, Elisha				
16	27	Green, Caroline					2			Green, Elisha				
16	28	Sinny?, Sarah	5	3			50			Hart, T. D.				
16	29	Robinson, Peter	6	0			59			Pons, Jno				
16	30	Eubanks, Rosa	5				40			Eubanks, Steven				
16	31	Eubanks, Morgan	4	3			21			Eubanks, Steven				
16	32	Eubanks, Fanny	5				19			Eubanks, Steven				
16	33	Eubanks, Eliz[th]	4	4			16			Eubanks, Steven				
16	34	Eubanks, Lewis	4				13			Eubanks, Steven				
16	35	Eubanks, Cornelia	4	1			12			Eubanks, Steven				
16	36	Eubanks, Peter					7			Eubanks, Steven				
16	37	Bryant, Cyrus	6				70			Bryant, Milton				
16	38	Bryant, Felix	5	6			35			Hopkins, B.				
16	39	Bryant, Binah	5	4			36			Heming, J. C.				
16	40	Bryant, Rebecca					10			Heming, J. C.				
16	41	Bryant, Lucious					9			Heming, J. C.				
16	42	Sams. Angelina					1			Heming, J. C.				
16	43	Small, Eugenia	5	2			26			Garnie, J. V.				
16	44	Small, Ellinor					10			Garnie, J. V.				
16	45	Callahan, Emma					5			Garnie, J. V.				
16	46	Mick, Chas	4	3			13			Presston, Wm				
16	47	Jenkins, Peggie	5				50			Heming, J. C.				
16	48	Simons, Jesse					4			Heming, J. C.				

Pg	No	Name	Height		Eyes	Com-plexion	Age	Where born or contraband	Last residence	Where registered for draft or former owner	Date into Department	Oath of Allgn	No of Ration	Remarks
			Ft	In										
17	1	Wicklif, Fredrick	5	6			37	Contraband		Downs, Jas				
17	2	Wicklif, Susan	5	0			32	Contraband		Downs, Jas				
17	3	Wicklif, Thos					5	Contraband		Downs, Jas				
17	4	Wicklif, May					4	Contraband		Downs, Jas				
17	5	Wicklif, Sarah					1	Contraband		Downs, Jas				
17	6	L'Engler, Gunter	5	4			80	Contraband		L'Engle, Jno				
17	7	Andey, Hannah	5	4			40	Contraband		Toms, Danl.				
17	8	Anders, Marg^{t}	4	3			13	Contraband		Toms, Danl.				
17	9	Andrews, Jas	4				10	Contraband		Toms, Danl.				
17	10	Anders, Susan					8	Contraband		Toms, Danl.				
17	11	Anders, Katie					6	Contraband		Toms, Danl.				
17	12	Murray, Fanny	5	2			35	Contraband		Johnson, Jack				
17	13	Murray, Mary	4	10			15	Contraband		Johnson, Jack				
17	14	Murray, Saul	4	6			14	Contraband		Johnson, Jack				
17	15	Murray, Fanny	4				12	Contraband		Johnson, Jack				
17	16	Murray, Charley					7	Contraband		Johnson, Jack				
17	17	Williams, Alonzo	5	5			30	Contraband		Sammig, J. S.				
17	18	Williams, Julia	5	2			26	Contraband		Sammig, J. S.				
17	19	Williams, Molly	5	3			36	Contraband		Sammig, J. S.				
17	20	Williams, Sarah					5	Contraband		Sammig, J. S.				
17	21	Williams, Mary	5	3			24	Contraband		Sammig, J. S.				
17	22	Williams, Mary					1	Contraband			Free Born			
17	23	Williams, Maria	5	4			47	Contraband		Houston, Ed				
17	24	Green, Hannah	5	3			21	Contraband		Stone, Geo				

"CENSUS" DEPARTMENT OF THE SOUTH - NOVEMBER, 1864

Pg	No	Name	Height Ft	Height In	Eyes	Com-plexion	Age	Where born or contraband	Last residence	Where registered for draft or former owner	Date into Department	Oath of Allgn	No of Ration	Remarks
18	25	Williams, Andrew	4				13	Contraband		Houston, Ed				
18	26	Dixon, Mortin	5	6			40	Contraband		Holmer, T. O.				
18	27	Butter, Jim	5	6			60	Contraband		Butter, Lee				
18	28	Purrear, Charles	5	4			26	Contraband		Roux, Lewis				
18	29	Sanchez, Morris	5	9			45	Contraband		Sanchez, V.				
18	30	Sumeral, Margt	5	2			40	Contraband		Sumeral, J.				
18	31	Sumeral, Jim	4				13	Contraband		Sumeral, J.				
18	32	Sumeral, Jane					10	Contraband		Sumeral, J.				
18	33	Sumeral, Susan					8	Contraband		Sumeral, J.				
18	34	Spearing, Priscilla	5	3			48	Contraband		Green, Elisha				
18	35	Leonard, Mary	5	5			25	Contraband		St.Clair, Wm				New York
18	36	Smith, Lucy	5	5			25	Contraband		Hening, J. C.				
18	37	Floyd, Lucy	5	3			24	Contraband		Fleming, Lewis				
18	38	Montgomery, Maria	5	3			36	Contraband		Prevatt, R.				
18	39	Sanders, Jas	5	6			27	Contraband		Hanson, Col.				
18	40	Rivers, Stephen	5	4			15	Contraband		Hanson, Col.				
18	41	Turner, Richard	5	4			14	Contraband		Hanson, Col.				
18	42	Walker, Sandy	4	8			12	Contraband		Caulk, Wm				
18	43	Reddish, Thos	5	2			15	Contraband		Caulk, Wm				

Pg	No	Name	Height Ft	In	Eyes	Com-plexion	Age	Where born or contraband	Last residence	Where registered for draft or former owner	Date into Department	Oath of Allgn	No of Ration	Remarks
19	1	Fanelley, Charlotte			black	black	5	Contraband	St.Marys, Ga	Cozn?, Mrs.	Feb. 20/61			
19	2	Fanelley, Phillip			black	black	3	Contraband	St.Marys, Ga	Cozn?, Mrs.	Feb. 20/61			
19	3	Fanelley, John			black	black	2	Contraband	St.Marys, Ga	Cozn?, Mrs.	Feb. 20/61			
19	4	Young, William			black	black	1M.	Fernandina						
19	5	Dahn, Mery	5	4	black	black	79	Contraband	Ga	Johntson, Mr.	March 20/61			
19	6	Walker, Lusia	5	6	black	black	30	Contraband	Fla	Dahn, John D.	March 13/63			
19	7	Walker, Samuel			black	black	8	Contraband	Fla	Dahn, John D.	March 13/63			
19	8	Popelia, Nancy	4	10	black	black	20	Contraband	Jacksonville	Gidding, Elias	March13/61		1	Sick & Destitute: by order Lt. Loveridge Comdg Post
19	9	Popalia, Lucinda			black	black	1	Fernandina						
19	10	Coopper, Cumes	5	1	black	black	85	Contraband	Jacksonville	Saddler, Henry	Feb. 20/64		1	Old & Feeble by order Lt. Loveridge Comdg Post
19	11	Byin, Phillis	5	6	black	black	47	Contraband	Jacksonville	Hart, Isaac	Feb20/64			
19	12	Evans, Richard	5	7	black	black	56	Contraband	Fla	Mosley, William	Oct 17/62			
19	13	Evans, Silia	5	7	black	black	49	Contraband	Fla	Mosley, William	March 17/61			
19	14	Evans, Zumas			black	black	9	Contraband	Fla	Mosley, William	March 17/61			
19	15	Evans, Maywood?			black	black	4	Contraband	Fla	Mosley, William	March 17/61			
19	16	Simmons, Peter			black	black	5	Contraband	Fla	Mosley, William	March17/61			
19	17	Smith, Betsey	5	4	black	black	16	Contraband	Lake City, Fla	Smart, Peter	Aug. 9/64			
19	18	Field, Prince	5	7	black	black	49	Contraband	Lake City, Fla	Brock, J. B.	March 5/62			
19	19	Finley, Sthepen	5	5	black	black	76	Contraband	Lake City, Fla	McGill, William	April 2/61			
19	20	Finley, Hannah	5	1	black	black	70	Contraband	Lake City, Fla	McGill, William	April 2/61			
19	21	Higgins, Susan	5	6	black	dark	38	Fla.	Jacksonville		Feb. 5/61			
19	22	Higgins, Martha	5	2	black	dark	17	Jacksonville	Jacksonville		Feb. 5/61			
19	23	Higgins, Allice	5	2	black	dark	15	Jacksonville	Jacksonville		Feb. 5/61			
19	24	Higgins, Julia			black	dark	12	Jacksonville	Jacksonville		Feb. 5/61			

Pg	No	Name	Height Ft	Height In	Eyes	Com-plexion	Age	Where born or contraband	Last residence	Where registered for draft or former owner	Date into Department	Oath of Allgn	No of Ration	Remarks
20	25	Higgins, Isabelle			black	black	10	Jacksonville	Jacksonville		Feb. 5/61			
20	26	Higgins, Jane	5	7	black	black	60	Ga	Jacksonville		Feb. 5/61			
20	27	Hubert, John	5	10	black	black	56	Contraband	Ga	Napse?, Calvin	March 17/61			
20	28	Hubert, Ann	5	2	black	black	58	Contraband	Ga	Napse?, Calvin	March 17/61			
20	29	Hubert, Robert			black	black	11	Contraband	Ga	Napse?, Calvin	March 17/61			
20	30	Hubert, Richard			black	black	7	Contraband	Ga	Napse?, Calvin	March 17/61			
20	31	Anderson, Joseph	5	9	black	black	57	Contraband	Ga	Napse?, Calvin	March17/61			
20	32	Delana, Sam	4	9	black	black	76	Contraband	Ga	Delance, Mrs.	Sept.17/63		1	Old & sick: by order of Lt. Loveridge comd'g Post
20	33	Stafford, Edward			black	black	14	Contraband	Cumberland	Stafford, Robert	April 3/62			
20	34	King, Harriette	4	11	black	black	42	Contraband	Fla	Barat, Julias	March10/61			
20	35	King, Port			black	black	13	Contraband	Fla	Barat, Julias	March10/61			
20	36	Hunter, Wallace	5	5	black	black	35	Fernandina	Fla	Barat, Julias	March10/61			
20	37	Hunter, Jenney	5	7	black	black	22	Contraband	Mayport, Fla	Braddock, Spizer	April 1/62			
20	38	Hunter, Willa			black	black	1	Contraband						
20	39	Hicks, Barrack	5	4	black	black	45	Contraband	Fla	Sampson, John	April 30/62			
20	40	Hicks, Caroline	5	4	black	black	45	Contraband	Fla	Sampson, John	April 30/62			
20	41	Hicks, Nancy	5	2	black	black	16	Contraband	Fla	Sampson, John	April 30/62			
20	42	Hicks, Cira			black	black	14	Contraband	Fla	Sampson, John	April 30/62			
20	43	Hicks, Maurice			black	black	9	Contraband	Fla	Sampson, John	April 30/62			
20	44	Hicks, Henry			black	black	11	Contraband	Fla	Sampson, John	April 30/62			
20	45	Hicks, Rebecca			black	black	6	Contraband	Fla	Sampson, John	April 30/62			
20	46	Hicks, Anna			black	black	7	Contraband	Fla	Sampson, John	April 30/62			
20	47	Hicks, Lewis			black	black	3	Contraband	Fla	Sampson, John	April 30/62			
20	48	Lunkins, Major	5	5	black	black	68	Contraband	Fla	Brocks, J. B.	March 5/62			

Pg	No	Name	Height Ft	Height In	Eyes	Com-plexion	Age	Where born or contraband	Last residence	Where registered for draft or former owner	Date into Department	Oath of Allgn	No of Ration	Remarks
21	1	Jenkins, Charlotte	5	5	blk	blk	41	Contraband	Jacksonville	Philips, Albert	Nov.11/62			1 ration for 2 destitute children: issued by order of Lt. Loveridge Comd'g Post
21	2	Jenkins, Harry			blk	blk	7	Contraband	Jacksonville	Philips, Albert	Nov.11/62		1/2	
21	3	Jenkins, Charles P.			blk	blk	6m	Contraband		Born Free	June 6/64		1/2	
21	4	Bradock, Marguerit	5	3	blk	blk	18	Contraband	Nassau Co., Fla	Bradock, W. M.	Feb.6/64		1/2	2 rations for 4 destitute children: by order of Lt. Loveridge, 3rd U.S.C.T. Commanding Post
21	5	Bradock, Mariah			blk	blk	12	Contraband	Nassau Co., Fla	Bradock, W. M.	Feb.6/64		1/2	
21	6	Smith, Abraham			blk	blk	9	Contraband	Nassau Co., Fla	Bradock, W. M.	Feb. 6/64		1/2	
21	7	Smith, Phibee			blk	blk	7	Contraband	Nassau Co., Fla	Bradock, W. M.	Feb.6/64		1/2	
21	8	Smith, Eve			blk	blk	5	Contraband	Nassau Co., Fla	Bradock, W. M.	Feb. 6/64			
21	9	Smith, Adam			blk	blk	5	Contraband	Nassau Co., Fla	Bradock, W. M.	Feb. 6/64			
21	10	Smith, Henry			blk	blk	4	Contraband	Nassau Co., Fla	Bradock, W. M.	Feb. 6/64			
21	11	Haddick, Elizabeth	5	4	blk	blk	27	Contraband	Duval Co. Fla	Hickenbodem, L.	July 5/63			
21	12	Johnson, Sarah	5	7	blk	blk	80	Contraband	Jacksonville	Smaris, Tom	May 16/64		1	Old & Feeble by order of Lt. Loveridge, Comd'g Post
21	13	Polite, Nana	5		blk	blk	68	Contraband	Alachua Co., Fla	Pharrom, Levon	Augt. 1/62			
21	14	Auston, Nancy	5	2	blk	blk	72	Contraband	Nassau Co., Fla	Acosta, Mr.	March 7/62			
21	15	Watson, Berry	5	6	blk	blk	50	Contraband	St. Augustine	Stark, I.	April 9/62			
21	16	Little, Emma	5	5	blk	blk	19	Contraband	Duval Co. Fla	Eubanks,Wm	April 9/62			
21	17	Little, Charles			blk	blk	5m	Contraband		Born Free	July 16/64			
21	18	Robinson, Jacob			blk	blk	8yrs	Contraband	Duval Co. Fla	Eubanks,Wm	April 9/62			
21	19	Williams, Saml	5	7 1/2	blk	blk	44	Contraband	St. Augustine	Born Free	April 9/62			
21	20	Williams, Marguerit	5	5	blk	blk	38	Contraband	St. Augustine	Delopus, Domingo	April 9/62			
21	21	Hills, Flora	5	3	blk	blk	19	Contraband	St. Augustine	Delopus, Domingo	April 9/62			
21	22	Williams, Theodor			blk	blk	14	Contraband	St. Augustine	Delopus, Domingo	April 9/62			
21	23	Williams, Augustina			blk	blk	10	Contraband	St. Augustine	Delopus, Domingo	April 9/62			
21	24	Williams, Comillia			blk	blk	8	Contraband	St. Augustine	Delopus, Domingo	April 9/62			
21	25	Williams, Saprena			blk	blk	8	Contraband	St. Augustine	Delopus, Domingo	April 9/62			

"CENSUS" DEPARTMENT OF THE SOUTH - NOVEMBER, 1864

Pg	No	Name	Height Ft	Height In	Eyes	Com-plexion	Age	Where born or contraband	Last residence	Where registered for draft or former owner	Date into Department	Oath of Allgn	No of Ration	Remarks
22	26	Wilson, W. J.	5	8	brwn	fair	20	Nassau Co., Fl	Nassau Co., Fl		Sept. 5/64	yes		Deserter from Rebel Army
22	27	Wilson, D. B.	5	8	brwn	dark	24	Nassau Co., Fl	Nassau Co., Fl		Sept. 5/64	yes		Deserter from Rebel Army
22	28	Hills, Charles	5	9	blk	bk	48	Contraband	Jacksonville	Alsop, William	March 10/62			
22	29	Young, Anna	5	6	blk	bk	28	Contraband	Florida	Bradick, David	March 10/62			1 1/2 rations for 3 destitute children:
22	30	Young, Abraham			blk	bk	6	Contraband	Florida	Bradick, David	March 10/62		1/2	issued by order of Lt. Loveridge 3
22	31	Young, Jessenton?			blk	bk	4	Contraband	Florida	Bradick, David	March 10/62		1/2	U.S.C.T. Comd'g Post
22	32	Young, Susana			blk	bk	2	Contraband		Born Free	Nov. 4/62		1/2	
22	33	Albert, Linda	5	4	blk	bk	78	Contraband	Florida	Rau?, Lewis	April 14/62		1	Od & feeble: by order of Lt Loveridge Comd'g Post
22	34	Brooks, Victoria	5	2	blk	bk	23	Contraband	Nassau Co.,FL	Storry, Marg	April 14/62			
22	35	Albert, Silva			blk	bk	3	Contraband	Nassau Co., Fl	Storry, Marg	April 14/62			
22	36	Brooks, Marrietta			blk	bk	2m	Contraband		Born Free	Oct. 6/64			
22	37	Albert, Randel	5	5	blk	bk	53	Contraband	Nassau Co., Fl	Storry, Marg	April 14/62			
22	38	Albert, Linda	5	0	blk	bk	17	Contraband	Nassau Co., Fl	Storry, Marg	April 14/62			
22	39	Albert, Amelia	4	8	blk	bk	15	Contraband	Nassau Co., Fl	Storry, Marg	April 14/62			
22	40	Albert, Charlotte	4	10	blk	bk	22	Contraband	Nassau Co., Fl	Storry, Marg	Sept. 9/62			1 ration for 2 destitute children:
22	41	Albert, Prince			blk	bk	3	Contraband	Nassau Co., Fl	Storry, Marg	Sept. 9/62		1/2	issued by order of Lt. Loveridge 3rd
22	42	Albert, Robert			blk	bk	10m	Contraband		Born Free	Feb. 15/64		1/2	USCT Comd'g Post
22	43	Jinkens, Thomas	5	3	blk	bk	53	Contraband	Cumberland Isl. GA	Downs, Mrs.	March 8/63			
22	44	Kinsley, Rose	5	7	blk	bk	48	Contraband	Mandrin, Fla	Plumer, James	March 8/63			
22	45	Kinsley, Catherina	5	3	blk	bk	15	Contraband	Mandrin, Fla	Plumer, James	March 8/63			
22	46	Kinsley, Hauet			blk	bk	10	Contraband	Mandrin, Fla	Plumer, James	March 8/63			
22	47	Robinson, Jane	5	2	blk	bk	29	Contraband	Mandrin, Fla	Plumer, James	March 8/63			
22	48	Robinson, Thomas			blk	bk	8	Contraband	Mandrin, Fla	Plumer, James	March 8/63			

Pg	No	Name	Height Ft	Height In	Eyes	Complexion	Age	Where born or contraband	Last residence	Where registered for draft or former owner	Date into Department	Oath of Allgn	No of Ration	Remarks
23	1	Lang, Tab	4	10	blk	blk	13	Contraband	Nassau Co., Fla	Bradrick, Wm	Feb. 28/64			
23	2	Lang, Ella	5	4	blk	blk	35	Contraband	Nassau Co., Fla	Bradrick, Wm	Feb. 28/64			
23	3	Anderson, Jacob			blk	blk	9	Contraband	Mandrin, Fla	Plumer, James	March 16/63			
23	4	Young, Latisha	5	0	blk	blk	24	Contraband	Mandrin, Fla	Plumer, James	March 16/63			
23	5	Young, Alice			blk	blk	4	Contraband	Mandrin, Fla	Plumer, James	March 16/63			
23	6	Young, Allen			blk	blk	3m	Contraband		Born Free	Augt. 28/64			
23	7	Craton, Phebie	5	5	blk	blk	38	Contraband	Mandrin, Fla	Plumer, James	March 16/63			
23	8	Conada, Elsy	5	2	blk	blk	22	Contraband	Mandrin, Fla	Plumer, James	March 16/63			
23	9	Craton, Patience	4	11	blk	blk	16	Contraband	Mandrin, Fla	Plumer, James	March 16/63			
23	10	Craton, Hariette			blk	blk	11	Contraband	Mandrin, Fla	Plumer, James	March 16/63			
23	11	Craton, Andrew			blk	blk	8	Contraband	Mandrin, Fla	Plumer, James	March 16/63			
23	12	Craton, Sarah Ann			blk	blk	7	Contraband	Mandrin, Fla	Plumer, James	March 16/63			
23	13	Sam, Sarah	5	5	blk	blk	58	Contraband	Mandrin, Fla	Plumer, James	March 16/63			
23	14	Kinsley, Clara	5	5	blk	blk	35	Contraband	Mandrin, Fla	Plumer, James	March 16/63			
23	15	Williams, Hanna	5	3	blk	blk	47	Contraband	Jacksonville	Sauder, Daniel	April 1863		1	Old & feeble: by order of Lt. Loveridge Comd'g Post
23	16	Finnigan, Harry	5	4	blk	blk	93	Contraband	Beaufort SC	Firnnigan, Gen'l	March 18/62			
23	17	Floyd, Charles	5	6	blk	blk	44	Contraband	Jacksonville	Papus, Andrew	April 13/63			
23	18	Floyd, Nancy	5	5	blk	blk	41	Contraband	Jacksonville	Papus, Andrew	April 13/63			
23	19	Lotery, Lirus	5	8	blk	blk	37	Contraband	Talbot Isl., Fla	Houston?, Sam	March 16/63			
23	20	Lotery, Julia	5	5	blk	blk	34	Contraband	Nassau Co., Fla	Eubanks,Wm	March 9/62			
23	21	Lotery, Sophie			blk	blk	6	Contraband	Nassau Co., Fla	Eubanks,Wm	March 9/62			
23	22	Lotery, Lilla			blk	blk	4	Contraband	Nassau Co., Fla	Eubanks,Wm	March 9/62			
23	23	Lotery, Nickles			blk	blk	3	Contraband	Nassau Co., Fla	Eubanks,Wm	March 9/62			
23	24	Hall, Adam	5	8	blk	blk	41	Contraband	Jacksonville	Ferris, Mrs.	Augt. 24/62			
23	25	Hall, Nancy	5	2	blk	blk	33	Contraband	Jacksonville	Hallowday, Mr.	Augt 24/62			

Pg	No	Name	Height Ft	Height In	Eyes	Com-plexion	Age	Where born or contraband	Last residence	Where registered for draft or former owner	Date into Department	Oath of Allgn	No of Ration	Remarks
24	26	Moeri, Thomas			blk	blk	11	Contraband	Jacksonville	Hallowday, Mr.	Augt. 24/62			
24	27	Moeri, Ellick			blk	blk	9	Contraband	Jacksonville	Hallowday, Mr.	Augt. 24/62			
24	28	Moeri, Paul			blk	blk	8	Contraband	Jacksonville	Hallowday, Mr.	Augt. 24/62			
24	29	Hall, Charles			blk	blk	4	Contraband	Jacksonville	Hallowday, Mr.	Augt 24/62			
24	30	Robinson, Daniel			blk	blk	7	Contraband	GAinesville, Fla	Sparkman, P.	Sept 6/64			
24	31	Kinne, Ansel	5	10 1/2	blue	fair	44	New York	New York	Fernandina	Jany 13/64	no		
24	32	Kinne, Emma	5	3	blck	fair	35	New York	New York		Oct. 10/64	no		
24	33	Kinne, Charles W.	4	6	blue	fair	12	New York	New York		Oct. 10/64	no		
24	34	Kinne, Lucius M.			dark	fair	9	New York	New York		Oct. 10/64	no		
24	35	Kinne, Mary A.			blue	fair	4	New York	New York		Oct. 10/64	no		
24	36	Kinne, Kitty E.			blue	fair	2	New York	New York		Oct. 10/64	no		
24	37	Burch, Mary E.	5	2	gray	Fair	28	New York	New York		Oct 10/64	no		
24	38	Burch, Abbie	5	5	brwn	Fair	26	New York	New York		Oct 10/64	no		
24	39	Merrideth, George W.			brwn	dark	13	Alabama	Beaufort, SC		Oct. 10/64	no	1/2	5 Rations for 10 Asylum Children, in charge of Mr. A. Kinne Supt: Rations issued by order Lt. Loveridge 3rd U. S. C. T. Comd'g Post
24	40	Merrideth, Mary			gray	Fair	9	Jacksonville	Beaufort, SC		Feb. 1863		1/2	
24	41	Mashow, Henry			gray	Fair	12	North Carolina	Beaufort, SC		Feb. 1863		1/2	
24	42	Mashow, Marion			gray	Fair	10	S Carolina	Beaufort, SC		Feb. 1863		1/2	
24	43	Duglad?, Fred			blk	blk	13	Contraband	Florida	Hickenbodem, L.	Jan 1864		1/2	
24	44	Johnson, Abraham			blk	blk	13	Contraband	Georgia	Todd, Robert	Oct. 1863		1/2	
24	45	Haywood, Ellen			blk	blk	12	Contraband	Jacksonville	Burten, G.	March 1862		1/2	
24	46	Lola, Lullen			blk	blk	10	Contraband	Jacksonville	Sauder, Daniel	March 1862		1/2	
24	47	Kinsley, Thomas			blk	blk	8	Contraband	Marion Co., Fla	Sauder, Daniel	March 1862		1/2	
24	48	Ross, Wm.			blk	blk	7	Contraband	Jacksonville	Sadler, Wm	Feb. 1864		1/2	

Pg	No	Name	Height Ft	Height In	Eyes	Com-plexion	Age	Where born or contraband	Last residence	Where registered for draft or former owner	Date into Department	Oath of Allgn	No of Ration	Remarks
25	1	Discon?, Adelaine			blk	blk	14	Contraband	Duval Co., Fla	Grissom, Jesse	April 9/62			
25	2	Williams, Sarah			blk	blk	5	Contraband	Duval Co., Fla	Grissom, Jesse	April 9/62			
25	3	Williams, Marian			blk	blk	4	Contraband	Duval Co., Fla	Grissom, Jesse	April 9/62			
25	4	Robinson, Susan			blk	blk	4	Contraband	Duval Co., Fla	Grissom, Jesse	April 9/62			
25	5	Cook, Remilia	5	4	blk	blk	38	Contraband	Duval Co., Fla	Grissom, Jesse	April 9/62			
25	6	Williams, Jane	5	6	blk	blk	16	Contraband	Duval Co., Fla	Grissom, Jesse	April 9/62			
25	7	Kader, Patta	5	5	blk	blk	68	Contraband	Jacksonville	Hart, Major	Mar. 10/63		1	Old & feeble: by order of Lt. Loveridge Comd'g Post
25	8	Young, Marguerit	5	5	blk	blk	35	Contraband	St. Marys, GA	Harlow, Col.	March 10/63			
25	9	Young, Henry	5	9	blk	blk	52	Contraband	St. Marys, GA	Harlow, Col.	March 13/62			
25	10	Young, Patta	5	3	blk	blk	22	Contraband	Palatka, Fla	Sap, James	Augt. 2/64			
25	11	Young, Saml.			blk	blk	7	Contraband	Palatka, Fla	Sap, James	Augt. 2/64			
25	12	Young, Nancy			blk	blk	5	Contraband	Palatka, Fla	Sap, James	Augt. 2/64			
25	13	Josiah, Iras?	5	10	blk	blk	56	Contraband	Jacksonville	Gedon, Elias	April 1/64			
25	14	Josiah, Sarah	5	6	blk	blk	52	Contraband	Duval Co., Fla	Grissom, Jesse	April 14/62			
25	15	Brill?, Fred			blk	blk	13	Contraband	Duval Co.,, Fla	Grissom, Jesse	April 14/62			
25	16	Harisson, Wm			blk	blk	14	Contraband	Duval Co., Fla	Grissom, Jesse	April 14/62			
25	17	Lutisha, Sarah			blk	blk	4	Contraband	Duval Co., Fla	Grissom, Jesse	April 14/62			
25	18	Dilap, Catherina	5	1	dark	dark	31	Mass.	New York		March 13/60	yes		
25	19	Parsira?, Carolina J.			gray	light	11	New Orleans	New York		Mar. 13/60	no		
25	20	Forester, Apha	5	5	blk	blk	40	Contraband	Magnolia, Fla	Born Free	Jan. 9/63			
25	21	Forester, Louis Franklin			blk	blk	10	Contraband	Magnolia, Fla	Born Free	Jan. 9/63			
25	22	Forester, Barbara			blk	blk	8	Contraband	Magnolia, Fla	Born Free	Jan. 9/63			
25	23	Forester, Anna Jane			blk	blk	6	Contraband	Magnolia, Fla	Born Free	Jan. 9/63			
25	24	Forester, Susan			blk	blk	4	Contraband	Magnolia, Fla	Born Free	Jan. 9/63			
25	25	Forester, David A.			blk	blk	3	Contraband	Magnolia, Fla	Born Free	Jan. 9/63			

"CENSUS" DEPARTMENT OF THE SOUTH - NOVEMBER, 1864

Pg	No	Name	Height Ft	Height In	Eyes	Com-plexion	Age	Where born or contraband	Last residence	Where registered for draft or former owner	Date into Department	Oath of Allgn	No of Ration	Remarks
26	26	Robinson, Letty	4	11	blk	blk	28	Contraband	Duval Co., Fla	Bradley, N.	July 22/62			2 Rations for 4 children in destitute
26	27	Robinson, Thomas			blk	blk	11	Contraband	Duval Co., Fla	Bradley, N.	July 22/62		1/2	circumstances: by order of Lt.
26	28	Robinson, Wietti			blk	blk	10	Contraband	Duval Co., Fla	Bradley, N.	July 22/62		1/2	Loveridge 3rd U. S. C. T. Comd'g
26	29	Robinson, Steven			blk	blk	8	Contraband	Duval Co., Fla	Bradley, N.	July 22/62		1/2	Post
26	30	Robinson, Rocilla			blk	blk	3	Contraband	Duval Co., Fla	Bradley, N.	July 22/62		1/2	
26	31	Carney, Hester	5	5	blk	blk	78	Contraband	Nassau Co., Fla	Bradick, Wm	Feb. 25/64			1 Ration fior 2 childrn:by order of Lt.
26	32	Carney, Lola			blk	blk	8	Contraband	Nassau Co., Fla	Bradick, Wm	Feb. 25/64		1/2	Loveridge 3rd U. S. C. T. Comd'g
26	33	Carney, Hariette			blk	blk	7	Contraband	Nassau Co., Fla	Bradick, Wm	Feb. 25/64		1/2	Post
26	34	Carney, Clara	5	6	blk	blk	17	Contraband	Nassau Co., Fla	Bradick, Wm	Feb. 25/64			
26	35	Long, Marian	5	5	blk	blk	26	Contraband	Jacksonville, Fla	Born Free	April 1862			1 Ration for 2 destitite children: by
26	36	Long, Hanna			blk	blk	6	Contraband	Jacksonville, Fla	Born Free	April 1862		1/2	order of Lt. Loveridge 3rd U. S. C. T.
26	37	Long, Nalla			blk	blk	5	Contraband	Jacksonville, Fla	Born Free	April 1862		1/2	Comd'g Post
26	38	Helper, H. H.	6	00	blue	dark	43	Rovan, NC	Illinois		Jan. 1862	yes		Discharged from U.S. Service for disability
26	39	Helper, Anna S.	5	4 1/2	blk	fair	29	Virginia	Illinois		Jan. 1862	yes		
26	40	Helper, Mattie			blue	fair	4	Illinois	Illinois		Jan. 1862	no		
26	41	Helper, Maggie			blue	fair	1	Fernandina			Dec. 19/63	no		
26	42	Wests, Mary S.	5	2 1/2	grey	fair	45	New York	New York		Oct. 15/64	yes		Could not produce certification
26	43	Jones, Mariah	5	00	blk	blk	48	Contraband	Amelia Isl. Fla	Lee, Levi	June 21/64			
26	44	Craton, Lueie	4	10	blk	blk	14	Contraband	Jacksonville	Plumer, Mr.	March 15/63			
26	45	Sutton, Catherina	5	2	blk	blk	45	Contraband	St. Marys, GA	Hickenbodem,Jos	March 15/64			
26	46	Sutton, Rose	5	3	blk	blk	16	Contraband	Jacksonville	Geger, Land	Sept. 9/64			
26	47	Sutton, Robert	5	0	blk	blk	15	Contraband	St. Marys, GA	Coster, C.	March 19/64			
26	48	Mitchel, Benjamin			blk	blk	6	Contraband	St. Marys, GA	Coster, C.	March 19/64			

Pg	No	Name	Height Ft	Height In	Eyes	Com-plexion	Age	Where born or contraband	Last residence	Where registered for draft or former owner	Date into Department	Oath of Allgn	No of Ration	Remarks
27	1	Gibson, Rebecca	5	4	blue	fair	59	South Carolina	Jacksonville		April 11/62	yes	1	Old & feeble: by order of Lt. Loveridge Comd'g Post
27	2	Valana, Dalla	5	4	brwn	fair	14	Jacksonville	Jacksonville		April 11/62	yes		
27	3	De Forest, J. A.	5	9	brwn	fair	28	Pennsylvania	Haverhill,Mass		Feb. 12/64	yes		Reverend
27	4	Fidell, Lacrisha	5	5	blue	fair	31	Mass.	New York		Feb. 2/64	no		
27	5	Reed, Juliette B.	5	5	blue	light	23	Wisconsin	Wisconsin		Oct. 15/64	no		
27	6	Fiddell, Sam'l T	5	10	black	light	32	Vermont	New York	Vermont	Oct. 7/63	yes		
27	7	Whitfield, Valitia	5	5	blk	blk	23	Contraband	Jacksonville	Plumer, James	March 31/63			
27	8	Floyed, Adilia	5	5	blk	blk	21	Contraband	Duval Co., Fla	Grissom, E.	March 15/62			
27	9	Frisbie, Sarah	5	3 3/4	hazel	fair	40	North Carolina	Maine		Augt. 5/57	yes		
27	10	Frisbie, James F.	5	9	blue	light	39	Maine	Maine	Fernandina, Fla	Augt. 5/57	yes		
27	11	Harisson, Nancy	5	6	black	black	27	Contraband	Duval Co., Fla	Barn, Steven	March 7/62			
27	12	Harisson, Evan			black	black	12	Contraband	Duval Co., Fla	Barn, Steven	March 7/62		1/2	2 rations: Destitute Family by order of Lt. Loveridge Comd'g Post
27	13	Harisson, Ann			black	black	9	Contraband	Duval Co., Fla	Barn, Steven	March 7/62		1/2	
27	14	Harisson, Phillip			black	black	8	Contraband	Duval Co., Fla	Barn, Steven	March 7/62		1/2	
27	15	Harisson, Wm J.			black	black	2	Contraband		Born Free	Oct. 9/62		1/2	
27	16	Young, Vina	5	00	black	black	24	Contraband	South Carolina	Hickenbodem, J.	July 20/64			
27	17	Crosher, Jenda	5	3	black	black	58	Contraband	Nassau Co., Fl	Crosher, James	June 9/62			
27	18	Wood, Susana	5	2	black	black	23	Contraband	May Port, Fla	Bradick. O.	Nov. 9/62			
27	19	Wood, James			black	black	5	Contraband	May Port, Fla	Bradick. O.	Nov. 9/62			
27	20	Sachus, Roma	5	4	black	black	60	Contraband	Duval Co., Fla	Barn, Steven	March 1863			
27	21	Sadler, Lipiel?	5	6	black	black	78	Contraband	Duval Co., Fla	Sadler, Henry	Oct. 3/62			
27	22	Cooper, Charles	5	5	black	black	80	Contraband	Amelia Isl. Fla	Cooper, James	Mar.7/62		1	Old & feeble by order of Lt. Loveridge Comd'g Post
27	23	McCall, Charles	5	8	blue	fair	67	Georgia	Jacksonville		Feb. 12/64	yes		Refugee from Rebel lines
27	24	McDemot, Sarah	5	4	brwn	light	21	Georgia	Jacksonville		Feb. 12/64	yes	2	1 women & 2 children sick & destitute: by order of Lt. Loveridge Comd'g Post
27	25	McCall, Christian			brwn	light	10	Georgia	Jacksonville		Feb. 12/64	no		

"CENSUS" DEPARTMENT OF THE SOUTH - NOVEMBER, 1864

Pg	No	Name	Height Ft	Height In	Eyes	Com-plexion	Age	Where born or contraband	Last residence	Where registered for draft or former owner	Date into Department	Oath of Allgn	No of Ration	Remarks
28	26	Lee, John					4	Florida	Jacksonville		Feb. 16/64	no		
28	27	Wilds, T. W.	5	7	gray	fair	27	Florida	Nassau Co., Fla		Sept. 8/64	yes	1	Refugee & Destitute: by order of Lt Loveridge comd'g
28	28	Wilds, Charlotte	5	5	blue	fair	26	Florida	Nassau Co., Fla		Oct. 15/64	yes		
28	29	Wilds, Elizabeth					2	Florida	Nassau Co., Fla		Oct. 15/64	no		
28	30	Wilds, Georgiana					4	Florida	Nassau Co., Fla		Oct. 15/64	no		
28	31	Hall, Henry	5	10	blk	blk	64	Contraband	Talbot Isl. Fla	Houston, John C.	May 15/62			
28	32	Hall, Emma			blk	blk	13	Contraband	Talbot Isl. Fla	Grissom, J.	May 15/62			
28	33	Hall, Henry			blk	blk	8	Contraband	Talbot Isl. Fla	Grissom, J.	May 15/62			
28	34	Hall, Paul			blk	blk	4	Contraband	Talbot Isl. Fla	Grissom, J.	May 15/62			
28	35	Hall, Sam'l			blk	blk	3	Contraband	Talbot Isl. Fla	Grissom, J.	May 15/62			
28	36	Prascott, Thomas	5	7 1/2	blue	dark	54	Bullet Co., Fla	Camden Co., GA		Oct. 21/64	yes		Refugee from Rebel lines
28	37	Prascott, Sarah	5	7	blue	light	56	Tatnell Co., GA	Camden Co., GA		Oct. 21/64	yes	1	5 Rations: 1 woman & 6 children
28	38	Prascott, Wm. F.	5	8	brwn	light	20	Byran Co., GA	Camden Co., GA		Oct. 21/64	yes	1/2	very sick & destitute: by order of Lt.
28	39	Prascott, Thomas C.	5	6 1/2	blue	dark	18	ColumbiaCo., GA	Camden Co., GA		Oct. 21/64	yes	1/2	Loveridge U.S.C.T. Comd'g Post
28	40	Prascott, Sarah T.	5	3	blue	dark	16	ColumbiaCo., GA	Camden Co., GA		Oct. 21/64	no	1/2	
28	41	Prascott, Virginia					14	ColumbiaCoGA	Camden Co., GA		Oct. 21/64	no	1/2	
28	42	Prascott, Minnie Jos.					12	Camden Co., GA	Camden Co., GA		Oct. 21/64	no	1/2	
28	43	Prascott, Alender					10	Camden Co., GA	Camden Co., GA		Oct. 21/64	no	1/2	
28	44	Prascott, Adelaine					7	Camden Co., GA	Camden Co., GA		Oct. 21/64	no	1/2	
28	45	Prascott, Mary					4	Camden Co., GA	Camden Co., GA		Oct. 21/64	no	1/2	
28	46	Hase, Louisa	5	6	blk	blk	43	Contraband	Duval Co. Fla	Grisson, Jessie	April 9/62			
28	47	Benjamin, Catherina	5	4	blk	blk	23	Contraband	Duval Co. Fla	Grisson, Jessie	April 9/62			
28	48	Benjamin, Mariah	5	6	blk	blk	25	Contraband	Duval Co. Fla	Grisson, Jessie	April 9/62			

"CENSUS" DEPARTMENT OF THE SOUTH - NOVEMBER, 1864

Pg	No	Name	Height Ft	Height In	Eyes	Com-plexion	Age	Where born or contraband	Last residence	Where registered for draft or former owner	Date into Department	Oath of Allgn	No of Ration	Remarks
29	1	Cole, Emma V.	5	7	gray	light	19	St. Augustine	Jacksonville		April 9/63	yes		
29	2	Wrightman, Larana M.	5 1/2	5	gray	light	21	St. Augustine	Jacksonville		April 9/63	yes		
29	3	Cole, Marguerit	5	5	gray	light	38	St. Augustine	Jacksonville		April 9/63	yes		
29	4	Thomas, Sarah	5	4	blk	blk	24	Contraband	St. Marys, GA	Albridge, J.	April 11/62			
29	5	King, Joseph			blk	blk	7	Contraband	St. Marys, GA	Albridge, J.	April 11/62			
29	6	King, Charles			blk	blk	6	Contraband	St. Marys, GA	Albridge, J.	April 11/62			
29	7	King, Willy			blk	blk	4	Contraband	St. Marys, GA	Albridge, J.	April 11/62			
29	8	Simmons, Mary	5	5	blk	blk	34	Contraband	St. Marys, GA	De Fort, M.	April 11/62			
29	9	Simmons, Charles	5	4	blk	blk	14	Contraband	St. Marys, GA	De Fort, M.	April 11/62			
29	10	Simmons, Lisabella	5	5	blk	blk	20	Contraband	St. Marys, GA	De Fort, M.	April 11/62			
29	11	Hepperd, James	5	6	blk	blk	72	Contraband	St. Marys, GA	Hoak, Mrs.	March 1862			
29	12	Williams, Toba	5	6	blk	blk	48	Contraband	Woodstock,FL	Throng?, Siras	Feb. 13/63			
29	13	Williams, Sophie	5	5	blk	blk	51	Contraband	Marine, GA	Mallets,Gidson	Feb. 13/63			
29	14	Williams, Martha	5	5	blk	blk	17	Contraband	Woodstock, Fla	Throng?, Siras	Feb. 13/63			
29	15	Williams, Rina	4	8	blk	blk	15	Contraband	Woodstock, Fla	Throng?, Siras	Feb. 13/63			
29	16	Abraham. Jacob	5	9	blk	blk	78	Contraband	Jacksonville	Born Free	March 1861		1	Old & feeble by order of Lt. Loveridge comd'g Post
29	17	Abraham, Anna	5	7	blk	blk	65	Contraband	Jacksonville,	Johnson, John	March 1861		1	Old & feeble by order of Lt. Loveridge comd'g Post
29	18	Moeri?, Anna			blk	blk	11	Contraband	Jacksonville	Johnson, John	March 1861			
29	19	Long, James	5	6	blk	blk	84	Contraband	Tabot Isl., Fla	Christopher, Mr	May 9/1863			
29	20	Long, Susan	5	4	blk	blk	80	Contraband	Tabot Isl., Fla	Christopher, Mr	May 9/1863			
29	21	Cooner, John	5	7	blue	dark	30	BullochCo., GA	Camden Co., GA		June 19/64	yes		Refugee from Rebel Lines
29	22	Cooner, Mariah	5	5	gray	light	19	Camden Co., GA	Camden Co., GA		June 19/64	no		Refugee from Rebel Lines
29	23	Cooner, Francis			gray	light	5	Camden Co., GA	Camden Co., GA		June 19/64	no		Refugee from Rebel Lines
29	24	Williams, Steven	6	00	gray	light	35	Clinch Co. GA	Camden Co., GA		Oct. 15/64	yes		Refugee from Rebel Lines
29	25	Williams, Nancy	5	6	blue	fair	27	RobinsonCo.NC	Camden Co., GA		Oct. 15/64	yes		Refugee from Rebel Lines

Pg	No	Name	Height Ft	Height In	Eyes	Com-plexion	Age	Where born or contraband	Last residence	Where registered for draft or former owner	Date into Department	Oath of Allgn	No of Ration	Remarks
30	26	Bronson, Sarah T.	5	4	blue	fair	33	Connecticut	South Carolina		March 23/59	yes		
30	27	Bronson, Catherina	5	8	hazel	fair	63	Connecticut	South Carolina		March 23/59	yes		
30	28	Bronson, Mary M.			blue	fair	6	South Carolina	South Carolina		March 23/59	no		
30	29	Anderson, Richard	5	6	black	black	46	Contraband	Cumberland Is., GA	Stafford, R.	March 7/62		1	Lame, by order of Lt Loveridge 3rd U.S.C.T. Comd't Post
30	30	Anderson, Lizzie	5	3	black	black	37	Contraband	Cumberland Is.,GA	Stafford, R.	March 7/62			
30	31	Anderson, Dalsa	5	2	black	black	15	Contraband	Cumberland Is.,GA	Stafford, R.	March 7/62			
30	32	Anderson, Samson			black	black	9	Contraband	Cumberland Is.,GA	Stafford, R.	March 7/62			
30	33	Anderson, Emely			black	black	7	Contraband	Cumberland Is.,GA	Stafford, R.	March 7/62			
30	34	Anderson, Luinia			black	black	2	Contraband		Born Free	Dec. 17/62			
30	35	Heppard, Lizzy	5	5	black	black	21	Contraband	Amelia Isl. Fla	Arosta, Mr.	May 29/62			
30	36	Middleton, Samuel	5	10	black	black	55	Contraband	Jacksonville	Fritt, D.	April 1862			
30	37	Middleton, Richel	5	4	black	black	33	Contraband	Jacksonville	Summers, Ch.	April 1862			
30	38	James, Steven			black	black	13	Contraband	Duval Co. Fla	Hickenbodem, L.	May 13/64			
30	39	Low, Alex	5	8	black	black	68	Contraband	JacksonvilleFL	Stone, G.	Nov. 21/62			
30	40	Sammes, Batta	5	5	black	black	85	Contraband	Jacksonville	Sammis, Col.	Nov. 21/62		1	Old & destitute: order of Lt. Loveridge 3rd USCT Comd'g Pst
30	41	Lisamore, Rosa	5	6	black	black	21	Contraband	Cumberland Is., GA	Staffores, R.	March 7/62			
30	42	Lisamore, Samuel			black	black	11	Contraband	Cumberland Is., GA	Staffores, R.	March 7/62			
30	43	Ivers, Barbara	5	3	brwn	dark	40	St. Augustine	Jacksonville		April 11/62	yes		
30	44	Ivers, Mary	5	4	gray	dark	19	St. Augustine	Jacksonville		April 11/62	yes		
30	45	Ivers, Julie	5	6	brwn	dark	16	Jacksonville	Jacksonville		April 11/62	yes		
30	46	Ivers, John			brwn	dark	14	Jacksonville	Jacksonville		April 11/62	no		
30	47	Ivers, William			brwn	dark	11	Jacksonville	Jacksonville		April 11/62	no		
30	48	Ivers, Andrew			brwn	dark	9	Jacksonville	Jacksonville		April 11/62	no		

Pg	No	Name	Height Ft	Height In	Eyes	Com-plexion	Age	Where born or contraband	Last residence	Where registered for draft or former owner	Date into Department	Oath of Allgn	No of Ration	Remarks
31	1	Jumane, Charity	5	00	blk	blk	28	Contraband	Cumberland Isl., GA	Stafford, R.	April 6/62			
31	2	Jumane, Mariah			blk	blk	12	Contraband	Cumberland Isl., GA	Stafford, R.	April 6/62			
31	3	Jumane, Suset			blk	blk	8	Contraband	Cumberland Isl., GA	Stafford, R.	April 6/62			
31	4	Stafford, Batza	5	4	blk	blk	26	Contraband	Cumberland Isl., GA	Stafford, R.	Oct. 9/63			
31	5	Stafford, Louie			blk	blk	12	Contraband	Cumberland Isl., GA	Stafford, R.	Oct. 9/63			
31	6	Wilds, Solon	5	8	blk	blk	49	Contraband	Nassau Co., Fla	Wilds, Phamel?	May 13,/64			
31	7	Wilds, Elizabeth	5	6	blk	blk	48	Contraband	Nassau Co., Fla	Hickenbodem, Joseph	Jan. 21/64			
31	8	Wilds, Chrishana			blk	blk	14	Contraband	Nassau Co., Fla	Johnson, John	Jan. 21/64			
31	9	Johnson, Mary			blk	blk	7	Contraband	Nassau Co., Fla	Johnson, Prince	Jan. 21/64		1/2	2 Rations for 4 Asylum children: by
31	10	Johnson, Batza			blk	blk	6	Contraband	Nassau Co., Fla	Johnson, Prince	Jan. 21/64		1/2	order of Lt. Loveridge,3rd....
31	11	Johnson, Jane			blk	blk	4	Contraband	Nassau Co., Fla	Johnson, Prince	Jan. 21/64		1/2	
31	12	Wilds, John			blk	blk	5	Contraband	Nassau Co., Fla	Hickenbodem, Joseph	Jan. 21/64			
31	13	Johnson, Prince			blk	blk	6	Contraband	Nassau Co., Fla	Johnson, Prince	Jan. 21/64		1/2	....(con't) U.S.C.T .Comd'g Post
31	14	Wilds, Marick			blk	blk	9	Contraband	Nassau Co., Fla	Hickenbodem, Joseph	Jan. 21/64			
31	15	Lopez, Catherina	5	2	brown	fair	25	St. Augustine	Jacksonville		April 8/62	yes		
31	16	Lopez, Jane	5	0	blk	dark	48	St. Augustine	Jacksonville		April 8/62	yes		
31	17	Lopez, Peter	4	8	blk	fair	14	St. Augustine	Jacksonville		April 8/62	no		
31	18	Lopez, Josephine			blk	fair	8	Jacksonville	Jacksonville		April 8/62	no		
31	19	Lopez, Joseph			blk	fair	4	Jacksonville	Jacksonville		April 8/62	no		
31	20	Fenamore, Janiet	5	5	hazel	dark	40	Scottland	Jacksonville		July 15/63	yes		
31	21	King, Plato	5	6	blk	blk	58	Contraband	Amelia Isl. Fla	Waughn, D.	March 7/62			
31	22	King, Clara	5	6	blk	blk	45	Contraband	Amelia Isl. Fla	Waughn, D.	March 7/62			
31	23	King, Ida	5	6	blk	blk	26	Contraband	Amelia Isl. Fla	Waughn, D.	March 7/62			
31	24	King, Amelia			blk	blk	12	Contraband	Amelia Isl. Fla	Waughn, D.	March 7/62			
31	25	King, Florence			blk	blk	10	Contraband	Amelia Isl. Fla	Waughn, D.	March 7/62			

"CENSUS" DEPARTMENT OF THE SOUTH - NOVEMBER, 1864

Pg	No	Name	Height Ft	Height In	Eyes	Com- plexion	Age	Where born or contraband	Last residence	Where registered for draft or former owner	Date into Department	Oath of Allgn	No of Ration	Remarks
32	26	King, Clarenda			blk	blk	3	Contraband	Amelia Isl. Fla	Waughn, D.	March 7/62			
32	27	Anderson, Charlotte	5	2	blk	blk	65	Contraband	St. Johns Co. Fla	Brian, Steven	June 3/62			
32	28	Albert, Luginia			blk	blk	10	Contraband	St. Johns Co. Fla	Brian, Steven	Oct. 13/62			
32	29	King, Jane	5	5	blk	blk	30	Contraband	Jacksonville	Mitchel, Niel	Nov. 17/62		1	Paralized: by order Lt. Loveridge 3rd USCT Comd'g Post
32	30	Mills, Jane			blk	blk	30	Contraband	Palatki, Fla	Mills, Mrs.	Mar. 14/63			
32	31	Williams, Mathilda	5	5	blk	blk	59	Contraband	Jacksonville	Harrison, S.	June 3/62			
32	32	Whilan, Joseph			blk	blk	3	Contraband	Jacksonville	Harrison, S.	June 3/62			
32	33	Green, Julia	5	0	blk	blk	29	Contraband	Jacksonville	Born Free	June 3/62			
32	34	Green, Charlotte			blk	blk	11	Contraband	Jacksonville	Born Free	June 3/62			
32	35	Green, Charles H.			blk	blk	8	Contraband	Jacksonville	Born Free	June 3/62			
32	36	Green, George			blk	blk	7	Contraband	Jacksonville	Born Free	June 3/62			
32	37	Green, Mary Catharina			blk	blk	3	Contraband	Jacksonville	Born Free	June 3/62			
32	38	Jeffis, Harry	5	9	blk	blk	24	Contraband	Savannah, GA	Jones, G. W.	Feb. 12/62			
32	39	Curtis, Catherinia	5	6	blue	fair	38	Brunswick NC	Jacksonville		Dec. 8/1859			
32	40	Curtis, Richard	5	10	hazel	?	59	North Carolina	Jacksonville	Fernandina, Fla	Dec. 8/1859	yes		
32	41	Rosket, Edward	5	8	blk	blk	39	Contraband	Sanderson, Fla	Williams, Sam'l	Jan. 12/63	yes		
32	42	Rosket, Rosa	5	5	blk	blk	32	Contraband	Sanderson, Fla	Williams, Sam'l	Jan. 12/63			
32	43	Rosket, Spencer			blk	blk	6	Contraband	Jacksonville, Fla	Holmes, Alexs?	Oct. 5/1862			
32	44	Steven, Munan	5	6	blk	blk	58	Contraband	Savannah, GA	Houster, Patrick	June 15/62			
32	45	Steven, John	5	8	blk	blk	52	Contraband	Makanopa, FL	Gager, Washington	March 5/62			
32	46	Jackson, Emma			blk	blk	3	Contraband	Savannah, GA	Houster, Patrick	June 15/62			
32	47	Paria, Lucenda	5	6	blk	blk	35	Contraband	St. Augustine	Palsier?, James	June 15/63			
32	48	Paria, Lucie			blk	blk	4	Contraband	St. Augustine	Palsier?, James	June 15/63			

Pg	No	Name	Height Ft	In	Eyes	Com-plexion	Age	Where born or contraband	Last residence	Where registered for draft or former owner	Date into Department	Oath of Allgn	No of Ration	Remarks
33	1	Forrester, Chas			black	black	15	Contraband	Fla	Narlly?, Nathainel	April 6/ 63			
33	2	Forrester, Phebe			black	black	13	Contraband	Fla	Narlly?, Nathainel	April 6/ 63			
33	3	Forrester, Fanny			black	black	11	Contraband	Fla	Narlly?, Nathainel	April 6/ 63			
33	4	Forrester, Lena?			black	black	9	Contraband	Fla	Narlly?, Nathainel	April 6/ 63			
33	5	Forrester, Banard			black	black	3	Contraband	Fla	Narlly?, Nathainel	April 6/ 63			
33	6	Travis, Jane	4	11	black	black	35	Jacksonville	Jacksonville		April 6/62			
33	7	Travis, Micheal	5	9	black	black	46	Contraband	Jacksonville	Saddler, William	April 6/62			
33	8	Evans, Isreal	5	5	black	black	48	Contraband	Palatka, Fla	Mosley, William	April 9/62			
33	9	Evans, Sarah	5	1	black	black	32	Contraband	Palatka, Fla	Grag, Henry	April 9/62			
33	10	Evans, Richard	5	3	black	black	80	Contraband	Palatka, Fla	Mosley, William	March 10/62		1	Old: by order of Lt.Loveridge Comd'g Post
33	11	Thomas, James	5	8	black	black	55	Contraband	Amelia Isl.	Cahn?, Richard	March 10/62			
33	12	Thomas, Ema	5	2	black	black	47	Contraband	Amelia Isl.	Cahn?, Richard	March 10/62			
33	13	Thomas, Jane	5	3	black	black	20	Contraband	Amelia Isl.	Cahn?, Richard	March 10/62			
33	14	Thomas, William			black	black	12	Contraband	Amelia Isl.	Cahn?, Richard	March 10/62			
33	15	Thomas, James			black	black	3	Contraband	Amelia Isl.	Cahn?, Richard	March 10/62			
33	16	Armstrong, Nega	5	4	black	black	50	Contraband	Amelia Isl.	Cahn?, Richard	March 10/62			
33	17	Armstrong, Charlotte	5	2	black	black	95	Contraband	Amelia Isl.	Cahn?, Richard	March 10/62			
33	18	Aberdeen, James	5	?	black	black	35	Contraband	Jacksonville, Fla	Kinsley, M.	Aug. 17/62			
33	19	Aberdeen, Rebecca	5	4	black	black	34	Contraband	Jacksonville, Fla	Kinsley, M.	Aug. 17/62			
33	20	Aberdeen, Emma	5	5	black	black	15	Contraband	Jacksonville, Fla	Kinsley, M.	Aug. 17/62			
33	21	Peeples, Juha	5		blue	fair	20	Bulloch Co., GA	Camden Co., Ga		Aug. 5/64	yes		
33	22	Peeples, James			blue	fair	5	Camden Co.,GA	Camden Co., Ga		Aug. 5/64			
33	23	Tillman, George	5	2	black	black	82	Contraband	Jacksonville	Hammer, Charles	Feb. 12/64			
33	24	Tillman, Dolly	5	7	black	black	73	Contraband	Jacksonville	Hammer, Charles	Feb. 12/64			

Pg	No	Name	Height Ft	Height In	Eyes	Com-plexion	Age	Where born or contraband	Last residence	Where registered for draft or former owner	Date into Department	Oath of Allgn	No of Ration	Remarks
34	25	Tillman, Nancy	5	2	black	black	32	Contraband	Jacksonville, Fla	Hammer, Charles	Feb. 12/64			
34	26	Tillman, Louisa			black	black	4	Contraband	Jacksonville, Fla	Hammer, Charles	Feb. 12/64			
34	27	Tillman, George			black	black	2	Contraband	Jacksonville, Fla	Hammer, Charles	Feb. 12/64			
34	28	Tillman, Lovina			black	black	1m	Fernandina						
34	29	Scott, Dilsa	5	5	black	black	41	Contraband	GA	Lynch, Charles	April 2/64			
34	30	Pettie, Susan	5	2	black	black	16	Contraband	GA	Lynch, Charles	April 2/64			
34	31	Gardener. Sarah	5	4	black	black	25	Contraband	GA	Lynch, Charles	April 2/64			
34	32	Gardener, Mary			black	black	2m	Fernandina						
34	33	Doray, Smart	5	6	black	black	49	Contraband	St, Marys, GA	Debose, John	Jan. 10/64			
34	34	Doray, Catharine	5	2	black	black	47	Contraband	St, Marys, GA	Elbott, Mrs.	Jan. 10/64			
34	35	McFola,Cezar	5	9	black	black	48	Contraband	Cumberland Island	Stafford, Robert	Oct. 5/62			
34	36	McFola, Arbagan	5	2	black	black	33	Contraband	Cumberland Island	Stafford, Robert	Oct. 5/62			
34	37	McFola, Elias			black	black	13	Contraband	Cumberland Island	Stafford, Robert	Oct. 5/62			
34	38	McFola, Andrew			black	black	8	Contraband	Cumberland Island	Stafford, Robert	Oct. 5/62			
34	39	Hooper, Moses	5	10	black	black	30	Contraband	Duval Co., Fla	Joubanks?, Wm	April 15/62			
34	40	Hooper, Laura	5	6	black	black	28	Contraband	Nassau Co. Fla	Stennick, Marjarette	April 15/62			
34	41	Hooper, Francis			black	black	12	Contraband	Nassau Co. Fla	Stennick, Marjarette	April 15/62			
34	42	Hooper, James			black	black	10	Contraband	Nassau Co. Fla	Stennick, Marjarette	April 15/62			
34	43	Hooper, Josephine			black	black	9	Contraband	Nassau Co. Fla	Stennick, Marjarette	April 15/62			
34	44	Hooper, Moses			black	black	7	Contraband	Nassau Co. Fla	Stennick, Marjarette	April 15/62			
34	45	Hooper, Laura			black	black	6	Contraband	Nassau Co. Fla	Stennick, Marjarette	April 15/62			
34	46	Hooper, Samuel			black	black	7m	Fernandina						
34	47	Williams, Dolley	5	4	black	black	25	Contraband	Talbott Island	Houston, Marj.	June 15/62			
34	48	Williams, James			black	black	9	Contraband	Talbott Island	Houston, Marj.	June 15/62			

Pg	No	Name	Height Ft	Height In	Eyes	Com-plexion	Age	Where born or contraband	Last residence	Where registered for draft or former owner	Date into Department	Oath of Allgn	No of Ration	Remarks
35	1	Paria, Mary Jane			blk	blk	11m	Contraband		Born Free	Jan.13/64			
35	2	Rivers, Ellen	5	4	blk	blk	27	Contraband	Jacksonville	Born Free	April 9/62			
35	3	Rivers, Elizabeth			blk	blk	7	Contraband	Jacksonville	Born Free	April 9/62			
35	4	Rivers, Mary			blk	blk	4	Contraband	Jacksonville	Born Free	April 9/62			
35	5	Rivers, Laura			blk	blk	2-Nov	Contraband	Jacksonville	Born Free	May 26/63			
35	6	Rivers, Elsa	5	2	blk	blk	17	Contraband	Jacksonville	Born Free	April 9/62			
35	7	Williams, John	5	5	blk	blk	29	Contraband	Alabama	Livingston, Lewis	April 9/64			
35	8	Williams, Francis	5	4	blk	blk	24	Contraband	Alabama	Rinfrose, John	April 9/64			
35	9	Turknot, Clorissa	5	0	blk	blk	92	Contraband	Jacksonville	Triknot, W.	Nov. 21/62		1	Very feeble: by order of Lt.Loveridge Comd'g Post
35	10	Seapus?, Dia?	5	4	blk	blk	13	Contraband	Jacksonville	Fairbank, L.	Nov. 21/62			
35	11	Smith, Richard	5	5	blk	blk	48	Contraband	Jacksonville	Picket, Seymour	Nov. 21/62			
35	12	Smith, Julia	4	11	blk	blk	25	Contraband	Jacksonville	Picket, Seymour	Non. 21/62			
35	13	Smith, Sarah Jane			blk	blk	6	Contraband	Jacksonville	Picket, Seymour	Nov. 21/62			
35	14	Smith, Washington			blk	blk	5	Contraband	Jacksonville	Picket, Seymour	Nov. 21/62			
35	15	Smith, Benjamin			blk	blk	3	Contraband	Jacksonville	Picket, Seymour	Nov. 21/62			
35	16	Smith, Susan			blk	blk	6m	Contraband	born at this place	Born Free	June 14/64			
35	17	Jordon, Prive?	5	6	blk	blk	62	Contraband	Jacksonville	Sanderson, John	April 9/62			
35	18	Jordon, Catherina	5	7	blk	blk	59	Contraband	Jacksonville	Broach, Capt.	Nov. 14/62			
35	19	Forester, Patience?	4	11	blk	blk	30	Contraband	Columbia SC	Highed, Dr.	March 7/62			
35	20	Simmon, James	6	0	blk	blk	42	Contraband	Columbia SC	Highed, Dr.	March 7/62			
35	21	Braker. Gibon	5	5	blk	blk	29	Contraband	Jacksonville	Hart, Idee	June 20/62			
35	22	Braker, Elisabella	5	5	blk	blk	27	Contraband	Jacksonville	Siliox, James	May 30/64			
35	23	Baker, Lusima F. R.			blk	blk	11	Contraband	Jacksonville	Siliox, James	May 30/64			
35	24	Hart, Lewis	5	6	blk	blk	106	Contraband	Jacksonville	Hart, Idee	April 9/62		1	Blind: by order of Lt. Loveridge Comd/g Post
35	25	Lewis, Tina	5	4	blk	blk	49	Contraband	Jacksonville	Hart, Idee	April 9/62		1	Old & sick: by order of Lt. Loveridge Comd'g Post

Pg	No	Name	Height Ft	Height In	Eyes	Com-plexion	Age	Where born or contraband	Last residence	Where registered for draft or former owner	Date into Department	Oath of Allgn	No of Ration	Remarks
36	26	Hills, Thomas	5	8	blk	blk	34	Contraband	Jacksonville	Olsup, W.	April 7/1862		1	One leg: by order of Lt. Loveridge Comd'g Post
36	27	Hills, Priscilla	5	6	blk	blk	30	Contraband	Jacksonville	Born Free	April 7/1862		1/2	Distributed by order of Lt. Loveridge Comd'g Post
36	28	Hills, Refilia			blk	blk	14	Contraband	Jacksonville	Born Free	April 7/1862		1/2	Distributed by order of Lt. Loveridge Comd'g Post
36	29	Henry, Charles			blk	blk	10	Contraband	Jacksonville	Born Free	April 7/1862		1/2	Distributed by order of Lt. Loveridge Comd'g Post
36	30	Edward, James			blk	blk	5	Contraband	Jacksonville	Born Free	April 7/1862			
36	31	Robinson, Jane	5	6	blk	blk	45	Contraband	Duval Co., FL	Brian, Col.	June 18/62			
36	32	Gibson, George	5	5	blk	blk	49	Contraband	Duval Co., FL	Hart, Idee	June 18/62			
36	33	Robbin, Tina			blk	blk	12	Contraband	Duval Co., FL	Brian, Col.	June 18/62			
36	34	Robinson, Elizabeth			blk	blk	13	Contraband	Duval Co., FL	Brian, Col.	June 18/62			
36	35	Goodwell, Marguerit	5	0	blk	blk	60	Contraband	Duval Co., FL	Walker, Mr.	Nov. 18/63			
36	36	Goodwell, John	5	5	blk	blk	63	Contraband	Duval Co., FL	Walker, Mr.	Nov. 18/63			
36	37	Bradick, Louise	5	0	blk	blk	70	Contraband	Nassau Co., Fl	Bradick, Mr.	July 1864		1	Old & Feeble: by order of Lt. Loveridge Comd'g Post
36	38	Clauser, Sophie	5	2	hazel	fair	39	Europe	Charleston, SC		June 1859	yes		
36	39	Clauser, Sophie			brwn	dark	14	New York	Charleston, SC		June 1859	no		
36	40	Clauser, William			blue	fair	7	Charleston, SC	Charleston, SC		June 1859	no		
36	41	Clauser, Carolina			blue	fair	5	Fernandina			Oct. 1859	no		
36	42	Clauser, Hermine			blue	fair	3	Fernandina			Dec. 1861	no		
36	43	Stark, Gustave	5	8	blue	fair	32	Switzerland	Thomasville, GA	Fernandina	Sept. 1857	yes		
36	44	Stark, Mary B.	5	5	blue	fair	31	Bavaria	Mount Moris, NY		Oct. 1860	yes		
36	45	Stark, Julius			blue	fair	10	New York	Mount Moris, NY		Oct. 1860	no		
36	46	Stark, Wm J.			blue	fair	7	Wisconsin	Mount Moris, NY		Oct. 1860	no		
36	47	Stark, Charles Marion			blue	fair	3m	Fernandina			Augt. 15/64	no		
36	48	Annau, Fanny	5	6	blk	blk	94	Contraband	St. Marys, GA	Anau, Joseph	Oct. 18/63		1	Old & Feeble: by order of Lt. Loveridge Comd'g Post

Pg	No	Name	Height Ft	Height In	Eyes	Com-plexion	Age	Where born or contraband	Last residence	Where registered for draft or former owner	Date into Department	Oath of Allgn	No of Ration	Remarks
37	1	Quinland?, Thomas	6	1	blue	fair	31	Ireland	Brookland, Mass		Oct. 15/64			Has taken aliens oath
37	2	Ouinland?, Michael	5	3	blue	fair	16	Ireland	Brookland, Mass		Oct. 15/64			Has taken aliens oath
37	3	Ragan, Patrick	5	6	brwn	dark	55?	Ireland	Boston		Oct. 15/64	yes		
37	4	Ronnan, Phillip	5	5	blue	fair	18	Ireland	Boston		Oct. 15/64			Has taken aliens oath
37	5	Rehards, Charles	5	5	black	black	35	Contraband	Fla	Baxter, Mrs.	Nov. 12/63			
37	6	Robinson, George	5	10	black	black	48	Contraband	Jacksonville	GArnel, Bsadise?	Nov. 12/63			
37	7	Sullivan, Daniel	5	6	grey	dark	40	Ireland	Boston		Oct. 15/64			Has taken aliens oath
37	8	Sullivan, Patrick	5	7	blue	fair	37	Ireland	Boston		Oct. 15/64			Has taken aliens oath
37	9	Sheehan, Daniel	5	5	grey	dark	48	Ireland	Boston		Oct. 15/64	yes		
37	10	Stafford, Dnash?	5	8	black	black	49	Contraband	Cumberland	Stafford, Robert	Nov. 15/64			
37	11	Stafford, Alonza	5	3	black	black	29	Contraband	Cumberland	Stafford, Robert	Oct. 1/64			
37	12	Scott, Joseph	5	5	black	black	60	Contraband	St Augustine	Lance, Martin	April 15/61			
37	13	Scott, Alexander			black	black	12	Contraband	Fla	Lance, Martin	April 15/61			
37	14	Simmons, Charles			black	black	14	Contraband	GA	Defo, Alonzo	May 13/64			
37	15	Sweet, Isacc	5	6	black	black	50	Contraband	GA	Depaunt, Mrs.	June 15/64			
37	16	Scarlet, Aaun			black	black	14	Contraband	GA	Depaunt, Mrs.	June 15/64			
37	17	Simmons, James	5	7	black	black	56	Contraband	Jacksonville	Allsip, William	March 5/64			
37	18	Thompson, William	5	8	dark	fair	27	Georgia	New York		April 20/63	yes		
37	19	Tagne?, Charles	5	5	grey	fair	18	Boston	Boston		Oct. 15/64	yes		
37	20	Trumps, Jacob	5	6	grey	fair	16	Savannah, GA	GA		March 3/64	yes		
37	21	Trei?, Julius	5	8	black	dark	19	Fernandina	Fernandina	Fernandina	March 3/64			
37	22	Virgil?, Elexander	6	11	black	black	35	Contraband	Fla	Henderson	July 15/63			
37	23	Woods, Charles	5	6	dark	dark	26	Ireland	New York		Nov. 25/63	yes		
37	24	Williams, Dudley?	5	8	black	black	30	Contraband	Cumberlance?	Stafford, Robert	March 15/64			

Pg	No	Name	Height Ft	Height In	Eyes	Com-plexion	Age	Where born or contraband	Last residence	Where registered for draft or former owner	Date into Department	Oath of Allgn	No of Ration	Remarks
38	25	Williams, Peter	5	8	black	black	25	Contraband	GA	Linch, Charles	Nov.19/62			
38	26	Williams, Adam	5	6	black	black	61	Contraband	Fla.	Flemming, Lewis	Feb. 15/64			
38	27	Lynes, Samuel	5	5	brwn	fair	20	Ga	GA		July 28/64	yes		
38	28	St. Embry, Thomas	5	6	blue	dark	40	England	Jacksonville	Jacksonville	Aug.12/63	yes		
38	29	Werplank, Hilenrd?	5	8	brwn	fair	46	New York	New Jersey	New Jersey	Oct. 5/63	yes		
38	30	Smith, James	5	8	grey	fair	26	Ireland	NewYork	New York	July 15/64	yes		
38	31	Dounds?, Samuel S.	5	7	grey	fair	27	KY	New York	New York	July 15/64	yes		
38	32	Graham, John	5	3	brwn	fair	22	London	New York	New York	July 15/64	yes		
38	33	McNeal, Michael	5	10	brwn	fair	27	Novia Scotia	Boston		July 15/64	yes		
38	34	Cirran, Thomas	5	7	brwn	fair	52	Ireland	New York		Aug.24/64	yes		
38	35	Greely John D.	5	8	blue	fair	63	New Hamp?	Boston		April 1/64	yes		
38	36	Ward?, E.	5	7	blue	fair	22	Ireland	Savannah, Ga		Feb. 1/64	yes		
38	37	Mohern, Edward	5	9	blue	fair	20	Ireland	N. J.		Sept. 15/64	yes		
38	38	Brozel, David	5	10	grey	dark	31	Ga	GA		June 2/ 64	yes		
38	39	Brown, Crawford	5	10	dark	fair	19	Ga	GA		Oct. 8/64	yes		
38	40	Richardson, John	5	8	grey	fair	16	Duval Fla	Fla		May 29/64	yes		
38	41	Williams, S.	6	0	blue	dark	35	Ga	GA		Oct. 8/64	yes		
38	42	Smart, Daniel	5	5	black	black	49	Contraband	Fla	Debose, John	Feb. 15/63			
38	43	Herculos, George	5	9	black	black	61	Contraband	GA	Harlow, Miles	March 11/62			
38	44	Harler, Aron	5	9	black	black	28	Contraband	GA	Davis, Allen	May 18/64			
38	45	Dick, Richard	5	10	black	black	60	Contraband	GA	Houston, Patrick	May 15/63			
38	46	Crews, Harley	5	11	blue	medium	23	Fla	Jacksonville		Aug. 11/64	yes		
38	47	Kelley, Daniel	5	8	blue	dark	35	Ireland	Jacksonville		March 9/64	yes		
38	48	Miller, Nathaniel	5	8	blue	dark	50	Conn.	Jacksonville		July 15/64	yes		

Pg	No	Name	Height Ft	Height In	Eyes	Complexion	Age	Where born or contraband	Last residence	Where registered for draft or former owner	Date into Department	Oath of Allgn	No of Ration	Remarks
39	1	Williams, Laura	5	4	black	black	22	Contraband	Yellow Bluff,Fla	Housten, David	April 15/62			
39	2	Williams, Hannah			black	black	4	Contraband	Yellow Bluff,Fla	Housten, David	April 15/62			
39	3	Wright, Francis	5	2	black	black	21	Contraband	Nassau Co., Fla	Joubanks, William	April 15/62			
39	4	Wright, Mary			black	black	5m	Fernandina						
39	5	King, Polly	5	4	black	black	21	Contraband	Jacksonville	Baxter, Martha	April 15/62			1 Ration for 2 children: by order of Lt. Loveridge 3rd U.S.C.T. Comd'g Post
39	6	King, George			black	black	4	Contraband	Jacksonville	Baxter, Martha	April 15/62		1/2	
39	7	King, Lissadive?			black	black	1	Fernandina					1/2	
39	8	Robinson, Rosa			black	black	6	Contraband	Nassau Co., Fla	Joubanks, William	Jan 15/63			
39	9	Jones, Edward	5	10	blue	dark	43	England	Nassau Co., Fla		March 15/64	yes	1	Sick and destitute family 4 Rations by order of Lt. Loveridge Comd'g Post
39	10	Jones, Marg	5	1	dark	fair	29	Screvin Co., GA	Nassau Co., Fla		March 15/64	yes	1	
39	11	Jones, Richard			blue	fair	9	Screvin Co., GA	Nassau Co., Fla		March 15/64	yes	1/2	
39	12	Jones, Edward			dark	fair	6	Screvin Co., GA	Nassau Co., Fla		March 15/64		1/2	
39	13	Jones, William			dark	fair	4	Nassau Co., FL	Nassau Co., Fla		March 15/64		1/2	
39	14	Jones, Henry			dark	fair	1	Nassau Co., FL	Nassau Co., Fla		March 15/64		1/2	
39	15	Roberts, Elliott	6	0	blue	dark	23	S.C.	St. Marys, GA		Aug. 23/64	yes		
39	16	Roberts, Angeline	5	4	grey	fair	21	Camden Co., GA	Camden Co., GA		Sept. 13/64	yes		
39	17	GAil, John	5	0	brwn	fair	16	Camden Co., GA	Camden Co., GA		Sept. 13/64	yes		
39	18	Roberts, William H.			grey	fair	6	Camden Co., GA	Camden Co., GA		Sept. 13/64			
39	19	Freeman, Alfred	6	0	grey	fair	47	GA	GA		Feb. 27/64	yes		
39	20	Freeman, Mary	5	3	blue	light	33	Screvin Co., GA	Nassau Co., FL		Feb. 27/64	yes		
39	21	Freeman, Florence			grey	light	11	Jefferson Co., FL	Nassau Co., Fl		Feb. 27/64			
39	22	Freeman, Louisa			grey	light	8	Nassau Co., FL	Nassau Co., Fl		Feb. 27/64			
39	23	Freeman, Georgia			grey	light	2	Nassau Co., FL	Nassau Co., Fl		Feb. 27/64			
39	24	Sanders, Mana	5	4	black	black	35	Contraband	Jacksonville	Elmory, Doctor	Oct. 15/63		1	sick and distitute:by order of Lt. Loveridge Comd'g

"CENSUS" DEPARTMENT OF THE SOUTH - NOVEMBER, 1864

Pg	No	Name	Height Ft	Height In	Eyes	Com-plexion	Age	Where born or contraband	Last residence	Where registered for draft or former owner	Date into Department	Oath of Allgn	No of Ration	Remarks
40	25	Lewis, G. L.	5	7	blue	light	30	North Carolina	Baldwin, Fla		June 6/64	yes		
40	26	Lewis, Catherine	5	3	brwn	fair	26	North Carolina	Nassau Co., Fla		July 5/64	yes		
40	27	Lewis, John			blue	fair	7	North Carolina	Nassau Co., Fla		July 5/64			
40	28	Lewis, Sarah			blue	fair	4	North Carolina	Nassau Co., Fla		July 5/64			
40	29	Lewis, Amelia			blue	fair	5	Fla	Nassau Co., Fla		July 5/64			
40	30	Gail, Joseph			blue	fair	12	Camden Co., GA	Camden Co., GA		Sept. 28/64			
40	31	Peeples, Randolph	5	6	brwn	dark	19	Camden Co., GA	Camden Co., Ga		Sept. 28/64	yes		
40	32	Peeples, Jane	5	4	grey	fair	20	Camden Co., GA	Camden Co., Ga		Sept. 28/64	yes		
40	33	Peeples, Robert			blue	fair	1	Camden Co., GA	Camden Co., Ga		Sept. 28/64			
40	34	Gordon, Andrew	5	3	black	black	23	Contraband	Fla	Perry,Stark	March 15/64			
40	35	Delanee, Thomas S.	6	0	black	black	56	Fernandina	St. Marys	Fernandina	Oct. 8/63			
40	36	Delanee, Sarah	5	3	black	black	53	Contraband	St. Marys	Mork?, J. A.	Oct. 8/63			
40	37	Batties, Sophia			black	black	12	Contraband	St. Marys	Mork?, J. A.	Sept. 9/62			
40	38	Batties, Mary Jane			black	black	8	Contraband	St. Marys	Mork?, J. A.	Sept. 9/62			
40	39	Batties, William			black	black	6	Contraband	St. Marys	Mork?, J. A.	Sept. 9/62			
40	40	Batties, Daniel			black	black	2	Contraband	St. Marys	Mork?, J. A.	Sept. 9/62			
40	41	Cotton, Eliza	4	10	black	black	28	Contraband	St. Marys	Mork?, J. A.	Sept. 9/62			
40	42	Cordelia, Sarah			black	black	10	Contraband	St. Marys	Mork?, J. A.	Sept. 9/62			
40	43	Delanee, Laura	5	3	black	black	24	Contraband	St. Marys	Mork?, J. A.	Sept. 9/62			
40	44	Delanee, Mary	5	2	black	black	22	Contraband	St. Marys	Mork?, J. A.	Sept. 9/62			
40	45	Delanee, Thomas			black	black	13	Contraband	St. Marys	Mork?, J. A.	Sept. 9/62			
40	46	Delanee, William			black	black	12	Contraband	St. Marys	Mork?, J. A.	Sept. 9/62			
40	47	Delanee, James			black	black	10	Contraband	St. Marys	Mork?, J. A.	Sept. 9/62			
40	48	Delanee, Henry			black	black	8	Contraband	St. Marys	Mork?, J. A.	Sept. 9/62			

Pg	No	Name	Height Ft	Height In	Eyes	Com-plexion	Age	Where born or contraband	Last residence	Where registered for draft or former owner	Date into Department	Oath of Allgn	No of Ration	Remarks
41	1	Madaugh, James E.	5	8	Hazel	brwn	36	N.J.	N.J.	Fernandina Fla.	Jan. 22/62	yes		
41	2	Benjamin, Catherine	5	4	black	black	27	Contraband	Fla.	Cressin, James	April 2/63			
41	3	Mooney, John H.	5	8	dark	dark	42	Scotland	Charleston		Feb. 5/57	yes		
41	4	Mooney, Loucisa	5	1	Hazel	dark	41	Phil. PA	Charleston		Feb. 5/57	yes		
41	5	Mooney,Deborah			dark	fair	12	Charleston	Charleston		Feb. 5/57			
41	6	Mooney, John			dark	fair	9	Charleston	Charleston		Feb. 5/57			
41	7	Mooney, James			dark	fair	6	Fernandina, Fla						
41	8	Mooney, Florence			dark	fair	2	Fernandina, Fla						
41	9	Fonres?, Cyrus	5	8	dark	black	94	Contraband	Fla.	Clinch, Duncan	Nov.6/63			
41	10	Sherrit,Sam'l	5	2	dark	black	84	Contraband	Fla.	Sherrit, Mrs.	March 7/62		1	Old & feeble: by order of Lt. Loveridge Comd'g Post

"CENSUS" DEPARTMENT OF THE SOUTH - NOVEMBER, 1864

Pg	No	Name	Height Ft	Height In	Eyes	Com-plexion	Age	Where born or contraband	Last residence	Where registered for draft or former owner	Date into Department	Oath of Allgn	No of Ration	Remarks
42	1	Hatchet, Maanorva	5	4	blk	blk	41	Contraband	Pilatka	Mosley, Gov.	March 1862			
42	2	Wright, Nalla	5	6	blk	blk	26	Contraband	Florida	Debause, Mary	March 1862			
42	3	Wright, Elizabeth			blk	blk	9	Contraband	Florida	Debause, Mary	March 1862			
42	4	Wright, Louise			blk	blk	7	Contraband	Florida	Debause, Mary	March 1862			1 Ration for 2 children: by order of
42	5	Wright, Adeline			blk	blk	2m	Contraband		Born Free	Sept. 24/64		1/2	Lt. Loveridge, 3rd U. S. C. T.
42	6	Wright, Marguerit			blk	blk	2yr	Contraband		Born Free	Jan. 6/63		1/2	Comd'g Post
42	7	Harrison, Burel	5	8	blk	blk	51	Contraband	Lake City, Fla	Meyers, W^{m}	July 6/64			
42	8	Hobbard, John	5	10	blk	blk	47	Contraband	Florida	Hobbard, H.	Jan. 9/63			
42	9	Sharr, Marion	5	5	blk	blk	38	Contraband	Georgia	Holgendorf,J.	March 9/62			
42	10	Watt, James	5	9	blk	blk	52	Contraband	Greenfield, Fla	Watt, Joseph	Jan. 2/63			
42	11	Weeks, Catherina	5	1 1/4	blue	fair	27	England	North Carolina		May 6/58	yes		
42	12	Weeks, Mary			blue	fair	11	New York	North Carolina		May 6/58	no		
42	13	Weeks, Josephine			blue	fair	71/2	North Carolina	North Carolina		May 6/58	no		
42	14	Weeks, Lovely Luginia?			blue	fair	61/2	North Carolina	North Carolina		May 6/58	no		
42	15	Weeks, Laura Jane			blue	fair	5	Fernandina			Jan. 9/60	no		
42	16	Sanford, V. A.	4	10	blue	light	30	New York	New York		Nov. 10/64	yes		
42	17	Sanford, H. P.	5	6	blue	light	35	Philadelphia	New York		Nov. 10/64	yes		Discharged from U.S. Service
42	18	Williams, Julia	4	11	blk	blk	48	Contraband	Putnam Co., Fla	Sauder, Daniel	April 1/63			
42	19	Gibs, Jesse			blk	blk	10	Contraband	Putnam Co., Fla	Sauder, Daniel	April 1/63			
42	20	Williams, Harriette			blk	blk	6	Contraband	Putnam Co., Fla	Sauder, Daniel	April 1/63			
42	21	Ross, Charles	5	10	blue	fair	52	New Jersey	Maryland	Fernandina	Jan. 1858	yes		
42	22	P?rwn, Mary	5	3	brwn	light	40	Ireland	Philadelphia		Oct. 10/60	yes		
42	23	Washington, Nancy	5	2	blk	blk	75	Contraband	South Carolina	Pharron, Steven	March 9/62			
42	24	Sams, Elizabeth	5	1	blk	blk	26	Contraband	Florida	Plumer, James	April 14/63			
42	25	Kinsley, Hager	5	2	blk	blk	28	Contraband	Florida	Plumer, James	April 14/63			

Pg	No	Name	Height Ft	Height In	Eyes	Complexion	Age	Where born or contraband	Last residence	Where registered for draft or former owner	Date into Department	Oath of Allgn	No of Ration	Remarks
43	26	Kinsley, Clara			blk	blk	5	Contraband	Florida	Plumer, James	April 14/63			
43	27	Jones, Catherina	5	7	blk	blk	38	Contraband	Hilton Head, SC	Kayvida?, Mr.	Sept. 6/63			
43	28	Jones, Sarah			blk	blk	12	Contraband	Hilton Head, SC	Kayvida?, Mr.	Sept. 6/63			
43	29	Morse, Jane Rebecca	5	4	dark	medm	21	Fernandina				yes		
43	30	Latham, Georgia	5	9	blue	fair	28	St. Marys, GA	St. Marys, GA		April 1843	yes		
43	31	Morse, Marguerit			dark	fair	4	Fernandina			Sept. 1861	no		
43	32	Morse, Marian			blue	fair	3	Fernandina			Oct. 1862	no		
43	33	Morse, Florida					4m	Fernandina			July 21/64	no		
43	34	Dimarachy?, Manuela	5	7	browr	medium	59	St.Augustine			1814	yes		
43	35	Brown, Lourisha?	4	10	blk	blk	17	Contraband	Amelia Isl	Capt. Latham	March 17/62			
43	36	Hebbard, Felisha	4	9	blk	blk	14	Contraband	Cumberland Isl	Stafford, R.	March 17/62			
43	37	Williams, Louisa	5	0	blk	blk	28	Contraband	Geo	Born Free	March 17/62			
43	38	Williams, Lina			blk	blk	7	Contraband		Born Free	born in Dept.			
43	39	Williams, Alex			blk	blk	5	Contraband		Born Free	born in Dept.			
43	40	Williams, Dorcet			blk	blk	4	Contraband		Born Free	born in Dept.			
43	41	Williams, Calvin			blk	blk	2	Contraband		Born Free	born in Dept.			
43	42	Richard, Marguerit	5	2	blk	blk	23	Contraband	Jacksonville	Backster, Martha	Augt. 28/62			
43	43	Richard, Peter			blk	blk	5	Contraband	Jacksonville	Backster, Martha	Augt. 28/62			
43	44	Longwood, Lisa	5	7	blk	blk	26	Contraband	Amelia Isl	Born Free	March 7/62			
43	45	Longwood, Francis			blk	blk	4	Contraband	Amelia Isl	Born Free	March 7/62			
43	46	Lang, Rose	5	3	blk	blk	35	Contraband	Amelia Isl	Born Free	March 7/62			
43	47	Lang, Charles			blk	blk	11	Contraband	Amelia Isl	Born Free	March 7/62			
43	48	Lang, James	5	6	blk	blk	70	Contraband	Amelia Isl	Born Free	March 7/62			

Pg	No	Name	Height Ft	Height In	Eyes	Com-plexion	Age	Where born or contraband	Last residence	Where registered for draft or former owner	Date into Department	Oath of Allgn	No of Ration	Remarks
44	1	Johnson, Susan	5	3	blk	blk	34	Contraband	Amelia Island	Waughn, Harris	March 7/62			
44	2	Johnson, Simon L.			blk	blk	9	Contraband	Amelia Island	Waughn, Harris	March 7/62			
44	3	Frei?, Rosina	5	5	blk	blk	40	Contraband	Amelia Island	Born Free	March 7/62			
44	4	Frei?, Nancy	5	5	blk	blk	17	Contraband	Amelia Island	Born Free	March 7/62			
44	5	Frei?, Winson			blk	blk	12	Contraband	Amelia Island	Born Free	March 7/62			
44	6	Danagole, Mary			blk	blk	12	Contraband	South Carolina	Born Free	Jan. 3/64			
44	7	Lee, Lucy	5	5	blk	blk	26	Contraband	St. Augustine	Harron, Nichols	March 7/62			
44	8	Sharp, Manuel			blk	blk	8m	Contraband		Born Free	March 18/64			
44	9	Capo, Patricia	5	3	hazel	medm	32	Fernandina	Fernandina		born in dept.	yes	1	3 rations Stopped since11/20/1864:
44	10	Capo, Hethusas	5	1	blue	light	50	St. Augustine	St. Augustine		born in dept.	yes	1	by ordr Lt. Loveridge, 3rd U. S. C. T.
44	11	Capo, John	5	7	hazel	light	66	Fernandina	Fernandina		born in dept.	yes	1	Comd'g Post
44	12	Mitchel, Georgiana	5	0	blk	blk	28	Contraband	Amelia Island	Capo, John	March 7/62			
44	13	Mitchel, Clarenda			blk	blk	8	Contraband	Amelia Island	Capo, John	March 7/62			
44	14	Mitchel, Joseph			blk	blk	1	Contraband	Amelia Island	Born Free	Dec. 3/63			
44	15	Lonson?, Victoria	5	1	blk	blk	22	Contraband	Amelia Island	Capo, John	March 7/62			
44	16	Frei?, Francis			blk	blk	2m	Contraband	Amelia Island	Born Free	Oct. 4/64			
44	17	Boatwright, Civility?	5	6	brwn	dark	25	Burk Co, GA.	Georgia		Aug. 28/64	yes		
44	18	Boatwright, Washington			blue	fair	12	South Carolina	Georgia		Aug. 28/64	no		
44	19	Boatwright, Elmer			blue	fair	9	Georgia	Georgia		Aug. 28/64	no		
44	20	Boatwright, Daniel			dark	fair	7	Burk Co, GA.	Georgia		Aug. 28/64	no		
44	21	Boatwright, Rophin			dark	fair	5	Sribbon Co., GA	Georgia		Aug. 28/64	no		
44	22	Boatwright, Marian			dark	fair	4	Wayne Co., GA	Georgia		Aug. 28/64	no		
44	23	Boatwright, Jordan Monroe			dark	fair	3	Applen Co., GA	Georgia		Aug. 28/64	no		
44	24	Cook, Lisa	5	3	blk	blk	37	Contraband	Georgia	Bazard, John	March 7/62	no		
44	25	Cook, Joseph?	5	6	blk	blk	43?	Contraband	Georgia	Bazard, John	March 7/62	no		

Pg	No	Name	Height Ft	Height In	Eyes	Com-plexion	Age	Where born or contraband	Last residence	Where registered for draft or former owner	Date into Department	Oath of Allgn	No of Ration	Remarks
45	26	Acosta, Domingo	5	8	hazel	dark	77	St. Augustine	St. Augustine		born in dept.	yes	1	2 Rations stopped since Nov.
45	27	Acosta, Jane Y.	4	8	blue	medm	56	St. Augustine	St. Augustine		born in dept.	yes	1	20/1864:by order Lt. Loveridge 3rd
45	28	Baker, Alvera	5	2	blk	blk	50	Contraband	Amelia Isl. Fla.	Capo, John	March 7/ 62			
45	29	Frazer, Sophia	5	7	brwn	light	42	Maine	Nassau Co., Fla		Oct. 21/64	yes		
45	30	Frazer, Ella	5	3	blue	light	15	Maine	Nassau Co., Fla		Oct. 21/64	no		
45	31	William, Erran	5	0	blk	blk	15	Contraband	Talbot Island	Houston, S.	Nov. 9/62			
45	32	Whitemore, Martin	5	5	brwn	light	53	Camden Co., GA	Nassau Co., Fla		Feb. 28/64	yes		
45	33	Whitemore, Anna	5	3	blue	light	39	NassauCo., Fla	Nassau Co., Fla		Feb. 28/64	yes		
45	34	Whitemore, Mary C.			brwn	light	15	NassauCo., Fla	Nassau Co., Fla		Feb. 28/64	no		
45	35	Whitemore, James G.			brwn	light	13	NassauCo., Fla	Nassau Co., Fla		Feb. 28/64	no		
45	36	Whitemore, John H.			brwn	light	10	NassauCo., Fla	Nassau Co., Fla		Feb. 28/64	no		
45	37	Whitemore, Wm A.			brwn	light	8	NassauCo., Fla	Nassau Co., Fla		Feb. 28/64	no		
45	38	Whitemore, June			brwn	light	6	NassauCo., Fla	Nassau Co., Fla		Feb. 28/64	no		
45	39	Whitemore, Samuel P.			brwn	light	5	NassauCo., Fla	Nassau Co., Fla		Feb. 28/64	no		
45	40	Whitemore, Jeff. Davis			brwn	light	3	Alogna Co., Fla	Nassau Co., Fla		Feb. 28/64	no		
45	41	Whitemore, Francis M.			brwn	light	1	Nassau Co., Fla	Nassau Co., Fla		Feb. 28/64	no		
45	42	Miller, Solomon	6	0	blk	blk	57	Contraband	Hilton Head, SC	Chud, D.	Augt.9/62			
45	43	Parker, James	5	5	gray	dark	46	Philadelphia	Amelia Isl.		Jany. 1864	yes		Discharged from U.S. Army
45	44	Sawadskey?, Mary	5	5	gray	fair	35	Florida	Jacksonville		April 7/62	yes		
45	45	Sawadskey?, Julia E.			gray	fair	12	Florida	Jacksonville		April 7/62	no		
45	46	Sawadskey?, Mary			blue	light	7	Florida	Jacksonville		April 7/62	no		
45	47	Sawadskey?, William			blue	light	4	Florida	Jacksonville		April 7/62	no		
45	48	Sawadskey?, Lida			blue	light	1	Fernandina			Nov. 6/63	no		

Pg	No	Name	Height Ft	Height In	Eyes	Com-plexion	Age	Where born or contraband	Last residence	Where registered for draft or former owner	Date into Department	Oath of Allgn	No of Ration	Remarks
46	1	Sears, Augusta B.	5	2	blue	light	36	Massachusetts	New Jersey		Nov. 9/62	yes		
46	2	Sears, Alfred L.			blue	light	12	N. Carolina	New Jersey		Nov. 9/62	no		
46	3	Sears, Mary L.			black	dark	8	New York	New Jersey		Nov. 9/62	no		
46	4	Hill, Laura P.	5	4	blue	light	21	New Jersey	New Jersey		Oct. 15/64	yes		
46	5	Parsons, Lunt W.	5	7 1/2	gray	light	27	Massachusetts	Massachusetts	Massachusetts	Oct. 15/64	yes		
46	6	Sipfert, George	5	11	gray	fair	45	Europe	New Jersey		Feb. 7/64	yes		
46	7	Frazer, John	5	9 1/2	blue	dark	47	Nova Scotia	Florida		May 5/64	yes		
46	8	Bready, Gilbert	5	4	blue	medm	36	New York	New York	Fernandina	May 16/62	yes		
46	9	Dunham, John W.	5	7	blue	light	41	England	New York	Fernandina	Aug. 8/64	yes		
46	10	Sharp, William	5	7	gray	medm	45	England	Maine	Fernandina	Nov. 25/62	yes		
46	11	Woodrow, James	5	5	gray	light	39	Delaware	Waldo	Fernandina	June 23/62	yes		
46	12	Lawadski, John	5	8	blue	light	52	Poland	Jacksonville		March 9/63	yes		
46	13	Arthur, John I.	5	7	gray	fair	24	Ireland	Massachusetts		Oct. 15/64	yes		
46	14	Boyle, Arthur	5	7	gray	dark	47	Ireland	New York		Oct. 15/64	yes		
46	15	Collins, Lawrence	5	9	gray	dark	24	Illinois	New York		Oct. 15/64	yes		
46	16	Conner, Brian	5	9	blue	fair	33	Ireland	Massachusetts		Oct. 15/64			Has taken aliens oath
46	17	Dinand, John	5	4	gray	dark	22	Ireland	Massachusetts		Oct. 15/64			Has taken aliens oath
46	18	Freeman, H.	5	6	blue	fair	36	Ireland	New York		Oct. 15/64	yes		
46	19	Finnermore, Joshua	5	2	gray	medm	65	New Jersey	Philadelphia		March 31/63	yes		
46	20	GArtland, Peter W.	5	8	gray	fair	28	Ireland	Massachusetts		Oct.15/64			Has taken aliens oath
46	21	Gibbon, Abraham	5	6 1/2	blue	light	30	Canada	Massachusetts	Massachusetts	Oct. 15/64			Has taken aliens oath
46	22	Gillan, Abraham	5	6	gray	fair	28	Ireland	Tenessee		Nov. 15/64	yes		
46	23	Keymes, Saml	5	8	gray	fair	22	British subj.	Massachusetts		Oct. 15/64			Has taken aliens oath
46	24	Lopez, Pauline	5	5 1/2	brwn	dark	28	St. Augustine	Jacksonville	Fernandina	April 25/62	yes		
46	25	Lopez, Joseph	5	11 1/2	brwn	dark	52	St. Augustine	Jacksonville	Fernandina	April 25/62	yes		

Pg	No	Name	Height Ft	Height In	Eyes	Complexion	Age	Where born or contraband	Last residence	Where registered for draft or former owner	Date into Department	Oath of Allgn	No of Ration	Remarks
47	26	Quinland, Thomas	5	11	blue	dark	46	Ireland	Massachusetts		Oct. 15/64			Has taken aliens oath
47	27	Robinson, Robert F.	5	5	gray	medm	28	England	Massachusetts		Oct. 15/64			Has taken aliens oath
47	28	Redman, Thomas	5	5	blue	?	26	Ireland	New York		Oct. 15/64			Has taken aliens oath
47	29	Small, Joseph	5	6	blue	light	24	Ireland	New York		July 25/62			Has taken aliens oath
47	30	Sullivan, John	5	5	blue	dark	38	England	Massachusetts		Oct. 15/64	yes		
47	31	Thomson, Thomas L.	5	8	blue	medm	33	Ireland	New York		Oct. 15/64	yes		Discharged from U.S.Army
47	32	Lassire, Eugene	5	2	blue	fair	52	Savannah	Jacksonville		April 1/63	yes		
47	33	Dago, Henry	5	8	blk	blk	37	Contraband	Jacksonville	Born Free	April 4/62			
47	34	Dalana, Daniel	5	10	blk	blk	24	Contraband	St Mary's Geo.	Moak, John A.	Oct. 9/63			
47	35	Ratigan, Thomas	5	8	gray	light	24	Ireland	New Jersey	New York	Nov. 21/64	yes		
47	36	Boatwright, Jordon	5	6	brwn	fair	46	North Carolina	Georgia		Aug. 28/64	yes		Refugee from Rebel lines
47	37	McClellan, W. B.	5	8	gray	dark	47	Georgia	Florida		Feb. 27/64	yes		Refugee from Rebel lines
47	38	Rudderham, W. E.	6	1	gray	medm	33	Britain	Massachusetts		Oct. 15/64	yes		Discharged from U.S.Army
47	39	Bronson, Norman	5	7	gray	fair	41	Vermont	South Carolina	Fernandina	March 31/59	yes		
47	40	Blackwood, Sam'l	5	1	hazel	dark	51	Philadelphia	Jacksonville		April 19/63	yes		
47	41	Brady, John	5	5	blue	fair	19	Ireland	Cumberland Isl, GA		May 10/61	yes		
47	42	Buckley, John	5	6	gray	dark	30	Ireland	Massachusetts		Oct. 15/64			Has taken aliens oath
47	43	Bunnen, Michael	5	4	brwn	fair	18	?						
47	44	Baker, Cesar	5	4	blk	blk	34	Contraband	Jacksonville	Johnson, John	April 21/62			
47	45	Baker, Fredrick	5	3	blk	blk	19	Contraband	Jacksonville	Capo, John	March 4/62			
47	46	Brown, Sam'l	5	10	blk	blk	40	Contraband	South Carolina	Ludnick, James	April 17/62			
47	47	Boatwright, Wm			blue	light	13	South Carolina	Georgia		Aug. 28/64	no		
47	48	Cary, Thomas	5	10	blue	light	20	Ireland	Massachusetts		Oct. 15/64			Has taken aliens oath

Pg	No	Name	Height Ft	Height In	Eyes	Com-plexion	Age	Where born or contraband	Last residence	Where registered for draft or former owner	Date into Department	Oath of Allgn	No of Ration	Remarks
48	1	Wanton, Charles	5	8	brwn	dark	62	St. John's Co., Fl	Alachua Co., Fla	Fernandina, Fla.	Oct. 17/64	yes		
48	2	Hokins, Lisa	5	5	blk	blk	35	Contraband	Georgia	Wingate, W.	Aug. 15/62			
48	3	Griffen, Frank	5	6	blk	blk	59	Contraband	Georgia	Miller, D.	Jan. 15/63			
48	4	Hopkins, Daniel	5	5	blk	blk	52	Contraband	Georgia	Patman, Benj.	July 1, 1863			
48	5	Hopkins, Luginia	4	6	blk	blk	41	Contraband	St. Augustine	Harlom, Miller	April 30/62			
48	6	Jones, Charity	5	4	blk	blk	23	Contraband	Georgia	Bradick, Otto	Sept. 9/64		1	1 ration for one? adult: by order Lt. Loveridge Comd'g Post
48	7	Jones, Mariah			blk	blk	5m	Contraband	Georgia	Bradick, Otto	Sept. 9/64			
48	8	Jones, Harriet			blk	blk	5	Contraband	Georgia	Bradick, Otto	Sept. 9/64			
48	9	Buit, John	5	9	blue	fair	48	Europe	New Orleans	Fernandina, Fla.	Oct.18/1858	yes		
48	10	Buit, Barbara	4	11	blue	fair	41	France	New Orleans		Oct.18/1858			Has taken aliens oath
48	11	Peterson, Henry	5	6	blue	fair	48	Hamb'gh Europe	Moniety, Fla.	Fernandina	March 16/59	yes		
48	12	Pidell?, Henry	5	7	blue	dark	23	StateVermont	Bemington, VT.	Merington, Vermont	Nov. 13/63	yes		
48	13	Dalana, Ray	5	9	blk	blk	19	Contraband	Georgia	Moak, Julia	Sept. 8/63			
48	14	Bram, Emma	5	4	blk	blk	36	Contraband	Georgia	Phillips, Albert	Nov. 15/62			
48	15	Sams, Georgiana	5	5	blk	blk	19	Contraband	Georgia	Hoag?, Alstead	March 28/64			
48	16	Marie, Albert	5	8	blk	blk	52	Contraband	Georgia	Hickenbodem, Th.	Nov. 5/64			
48	17	Bram, Sarah	4	11	blk	blk	56	Contraband	St. Augustine	FitzPatrick, W.	Feb. 6/64			
48	18	Colby, Wm.	5	7	blk	blk	50	Contraband	Georgia	Mazell, O. K.	Dec. 26/62			
48	19	FitzPatrick, W. H.	5	11	blue	fair	68	Duval Co., Fla.	Duval Co., Fla.	Jacksonville	Feb. 7/64	yes		
48	20	Davis, Nancy	5	5	blk	blk	32	Contraband	Georgia	Hadick, Thomas	Feb. 18/64			
48	21	Davis, Mariah	5	5	blk	blk	18	Contraband	Georgia	Hadick, Thomas	Feb. 18/64			
48	22	Davis, Priscilla			blk	blk	11	Contraband	Georgia	Hadick, Thomas	Feb. 18/64			
48	23	Davis, Rosa			blk	blk	6	Contraband	Georgia	Hadick, Thomas	Feb. 18/64			
48	24	Davis, David			blk	blk	4	Contraband	Georgia	Hadick, Thomas	Feb. 18/64			

Pg	No	Name	Height Ft	Height In	Eyes	Com-plexion	Age	Where born or contraband	Last residence	Where registered for draft or former owner	Date into Department	Oath of Allgn	No of Ration	Remarks
49	25	Davis, Jacob			blk	blk	1	Contraband	Georgia	Hadick, Thomas	Feb. 19/64			
49	26	Davis, William			blk	blk	1	Contraband	Georgia	Hadick, Thomas	Feb. 19/64			
49	27	Phelan, William	5	6	blue	fair	51	Ireland	Marion Co., Fla	Fernandina,Fla	May 1/60	yes		
49	28	McDia, Dina	5	4	blk	blk	23	Contraband	Georgia	Wahn?, Dicke	June 25/64			
49	29	McDia, John			blk	blk	4	Contraband	Georgia	Wahn?, Dicke	June 25/64		1/2	1 ration for 2 children by order of Lt.
49	30	McDia, Louisa			blk	blk	2	Contraband	Georgia	Wahn?, Dicke	June 25/64		1/2	Loveridge, 3rd U.S.C.T. Comd'g
49	31	Thompson, Martha	5	3	blk	blk	25	Contraband	Georgia	Fiders, Henry	July 20/63			
49	32	Thompson, Jane			blk	blk	6m	born free			June 13/64			
49	33	Einstein, Jane	5	5	brwn	fair	22	Camden Co., GA	Camden Co., GA		Sept. 23/64	yes		
49	34	Einstein, Mary					8	Camden Co., GA	Camden Co., GA		Sept. 23/64	no		
49	35	Einstein, Josephine					4	Camden Co., GA	Camden Co., GA		Sept. 23/64			
49	36	Einstein, Emma					2	Camden Co., GA	Camden Co., GA		Sept. 23/64			
49	37	Alvers, Isaac	5	6	blk	blk	64	Contraband	St.Augustine	Alvers, Isaac	March 15/62			
49	38	Langley, Marguerit	5	5	blk	blk	24	Contraband	Lake City	Lanchus, V.	April 1/63			
49	39	Purkins, Robert			blk	blk	12	Contraband	Lake City	Lanchus, V.	April 1/63			
49	40	Rogers, Charlotte	5	3	blk	blk	28	Contraband	Jacksonville	Fairbanks, L.	April 20/62			
49	41	Richard, Lizzie	4	10	blk	blk	16	Contraband	Jacksonville	Sutton, Mrs.	April 20/62			
49	42	Rosket, Lisa	5	4	blk	blk	24	Contraband	Jacksonville	Sutton, Mrs.	Oct. 15/62			
49	43	Rosket, Henry	5	5	blk	blk	35	Contraband	Jacksonville	Williams, Sam'l	Jan.12/63			
49	44	Rosket, Amanda			blk	blk	4	Contraband	Jacksonville	Sutton, Mrs.	Oct. 15/62			
49	45	Rosket, Caroline			blk	blk	3	Contraband	Jacksonville	Sutton, Mrs.	Oct. 15/62			
49	46	Johnson, Pamelia L.	5	8	blk	blk	62	Contraband	Jacksonville	Huron, Michael	Oct. 7/62		1	Old & feeble: by order of Lt. Loveridge Comd'g Post
49	47	Johnson, Albert L.	5	9	blk	blk	28	Contraband	Jacksonville	Huron, Michael	Oct. 7/62		1	Idiot: by order of Lt Loveridge Comd'g Post
49	48	GArdner, Dalla	5	2	blk	blk	18	Contraband	Jacksonville	Born Free	Oct. 7/62			

"CENSUS" DEPARTMENT OF THE SOUTH - NOVEMBER, 1864

Pg	No	Name	Height Ft	Height In	Eyes	Com-plexion	Age	Where born or contraband	Last residence	Where registered for draft or former owner	Date into Department	Oath of Allgn	No of Ration	Remarks
50	1	Clark, Agnes	5	4	blk	blk	29	Contraband	St. Augustine	Alvers, A.	March 15/62			
50	2	Robinson, Mary	5	4	blk	blk	45	Contraband	Beaufort, S. C.	Foreman, Dr.	Oct. 18/62			
50	3	Delia, Lucrisha	5	6	blk	blk	63	Contraband	St. Mary's, GA	King, Thomas	Nov. 3/62		1	Old & feeble: by order of Lt Loveridge Comd'g Post
50	4	Robinson, Priscilla	5	5	blk	blk	104	Contraband	St. Mary's, GA	King, Thomas	Nov. 3/62		1	Old &feeble: by order of Lt Loveridge Comd'g Post
50	5	Harlow, Dorcus	5	2	blk	blk	48	Contraband	St. Mary's, GA	Harlow, Col.	March 15/62			
50	6	Harlow, Lisa	5	1	blk	blk	15	Contraband	St. Mary's, GA	Harlow, Col.	March 15/62			
50	7	Harlow, Manta			blk	blk	3	Contraband	St. Mary's, GA	Harlow, Col.	March 15/62			
50	8	Harlow, Lewis	5	4	blk	blk	45	Contraband	St. Mary's, GA	Harlow, Col.	March 15/62			
50	9	Harlow, Lagusta			blk	blk	6 wks			Born Free	Oct. 10/64			
50	10	Burns, William	5	6	blk	blk	52	Contraband	St. Mary's, GA	Burns, L.	March 7/62			
50	11	Burns, Agnes	5	4	blk	blk	45	Contraband	St. Mary's, GA	Harlow, Col.	March 7/62			
50	12	Burns, Harriet			blk	blk	6	Contraband	St. Mary's, GA	Harlow, Col.	March 7/62			
50	13	Burns, Emma			blk	blk	5	Contraband	St. Mary's, GA	Harlow, Col.	March 7/62			
50	14	Burns, Paga	5	4	blk	blk	96	Contraband	Jacksonville	Gidon, L.	March 7/62			
50	15	Stafford, Emma	5	5	blk	blk	55	Contraband	Cumberland Isl., GA	Stafford, R.	Dec. 2/62			
50	16	Stafford, Richel?			blk	blk	6	Contraband	Cumberland Isl., GA	Stafford, R.	Dec. 2/62			
50	17	Stafford, Warren			blk	blk	5	Contraband	Cumberland Isl., GA	Stafford, R.	Dec. 2/62			
50	18	Stafford, Tina			blk	blk	4	Contraband	Cumberland Isl., GA	Stafford, R.	Dec. 2/62			
50	19	Stafford, Marietta	5	4	blk	blk	43	Contraband	Cumberland Isl., GA	Stafford, R.	Sept. 14/62			
50	20	Mitchel, Amenda	5	6	blk	blk	24	Contraband	Cumberland Isl., GA	Stafford, R.	March 7/62			
50	21	Mitchel, Catherina			blk	blk	5	Contraband	Cumberland Isl., GA	Stafford, R.	March 7/62			
50	22	Mitchel, Dority			blk	blk	8	Contraband	Cumberland Isl., GA	Stafford, R.	March 7/62			
50	23	Ellwood, Jane	5	6	blk	blk	46	Contraband	Cumberland Isl., GA	Stafford, R.	March 16/60?			
50	24	Ellwood, Dorcus			blk	blk	3	Contraband	Cumberland Isl., GA	Stafford, R.	March 16/60?			
50	25	Ellwood, James			blk	blk	1m	Contraband	Cumberland Isl., GA	Born Free	Oct. 27/64			

Pg	No	Name	Height Ft	Height In	Eyes	Complexion	Age	Where born or contraband	Last residence	Where registered for draft or former owner	Date into Department	Oath of Allgn	No of Ration	Remarks
51	26	Ellwood, John	5	6	blk	blk	28	Contraband	Cumberland Isl., GA	Stafford, R.	March 7/62			
51	27	Mitchel, Eve	5	5	blk	blk	26	Contraband	Cumberland Isl., GA	Stafford, R.	March 7/62			
51	28	Mitchel, Stapna			blk	blk	7	Contraband	Cumberland Isl., GA	Stafford, R.	March 7/62			
51	29	Mitchel, Julia			blk	blk	6	Contraband	Cumberland Isl., GA	Stafford, R.	March 7/62			
51	30	Mitchel, Lark			blk	blk	4	Contraband	Cumberland Isl., GA	Stafford, R.	March 7/62			
51	31	Mitchel, Paris			blk	blk	3	Contraband	Cumberland Isl., GA	Stafford, R.	March 7/62			
51	32	Mitchel, Lizzie			blk	blk	6m	Contraband		Born Free	June 3/64			
51	33	Stafford, Stapna	5	8	blk	blk	60	Contraband	Cumberland Isl.	Stafford, R.	Dec. 10/62		1	Old & sick by order of Lt. Loveridge Comd'g Post
51	34	Stafford, Bella	5	6	blk	blk	46	Contraband	Cumberland Isl.	Stafford, R.	Dec. 10/62			
51	35	Stafford, Wm			blk	blk	4	Contraband	Cumberland Isl.	Stafford, R.	Dec. 10/62			
51	36	Stafford, Louisa			blk	blk	14	Contraband	Cumberland Isl.	Stafford, R.	Dec. 10/62			
51	37	Lissamore, Clisha	5	5	blk	blk	26	Contraband	Cumberland Isl.	Stafford, R.	Dec. 10/62			
51	38	Lissamore, Molla			blk	blk	6	Contraband	Cumberland Isl.	Stafford, R.	Dec. 10/62			
51	39	Lissamore, Fanny			blk	blk	1 1/2			Born Free	June 16/63			
51	40	Davis, Tilla	5	3	blk	blk	45	Contraband	Camden Co., Geo	Hickenbodem,Lewis	Feb. 5/64			
51	41	Davis, Sophia	5	4	blk	blk	18	Contraband	Camden Co., Geo	Hickenbodem,Lewis	Feb. 5/64			
51	42	Davis, Frank			blk	blk	9	Contraband	Camden Co., Geo	Hickenbodem,Lewis	Feb. 5/64			
51	43	Davis, John			blk	blk	8	Contraband	Camden Co., Geo	Hickenbodem,Lewis	Feb. 5/64			
51	44	Davis, Peter			blk	blk	7	Contraband	Camden Co., Geo	Hickenbodem,Lewis	Feb. 5/64			
51	45	Davis, Lucie			blk	blk	2m			Born Free	Sept. 29/64			
51	46	Stafford, Marguerit	5	3	blk	blk	27	Contraband	Cumberland Isl., GA	Stafford, R.	Dec. 10/62			
51	47	Stafford, Lipis?			blk	blk	11	Contraband	Cumberland Isl., GA	Stafford, R.	Dec. 10/62			
51	48	Stafford, Angeline			blk	blk	5	Contraband	Cumberland Isl., GA	Stafford, R.	Dec. 10/62			

Pg	No	Name	Height Ft	Height In	Eyes	Com-plexion	Age	Where born or contraband	Last residence	Where registered for draft or former owner	Date into Department	Oath of Allgn	No of Ration	Remarks
52	1	Beard, Emma?	5	0	blk	blk	30	Contraband	St, Marys, GA	Mork?, Z. A.	Sept. 9/62			
52	2	Beard, Nancy			blk	blk	9	Contraband	St, Marys, GA	Mork?, Z. A.	Sept. 9/62		1/2	1 Ration by order of Lt. Loveridge
52	3	Beard, Laura			blk	blk	7	Contraband	St, Marys, GA	Mork?, Z. A.	Sept. 9/62		1/2	Comd'g Post
52	4	McQuinn, Joseph	5	6	blk	blk	57	Contraband	Fernandina	Costo, Domingo	Sept. 9/62			
52	5	McQuinn, Eliza	5	1	blk	blk	17	Contraband	Fernandina	Costo, Domingo	Sept. 9/62			
52	6	McQuinn, Sarah	5	6	blk	blk	46	Contraband	Fernandina	Costo, Domingo	Sept. 9/62			
52	7	McQuinn, Antonio	5	5	blk	blk	28	Contraband	Fernandina	Costo, Domingo	Sept. 9/62			
52	8	McQuinn, Sarah			blk	blk	12	Contraband	Fernandina	Costo, Domingo	Sept. 9/62			
52	9	McQuinn, Dora			blk	blk	6	Contraband	Fernandina	Costo, Domingo	Sept. 9/62			
52	10	McQuinn, Marj.			blk	blk	5	Contraband	Fernandina	Costo, Domingo	Sept. 9/62			
52	11	McQuinn, Thomas			blk	blk	2	Contraband	Fernandina	Costo, Domingo	Sept. 9/62			
52	12	Williams, Jane			blk	blk	14	Contraband	S. C	Tanner, William	May 6/56			
52	13	Floyd, Mary			blk	blk	2m	Fernandina						
52	14	Taylor, Phebe	5	3	blk	blk	45	Contraband	Jacksonville	Tersis, Davius	April 2/62			
52	15	Taylor, Anna			blk	blk	9	Contraband	Jacksonville	Joubanks, James	April 2/62		1/2	One child: by order of Lt Loveridge Comd'g Post
52	16	Razor, China	5	2	blk	blk	40	Contraband	Jacksonville	Turner, Rending?	March 18/62			
52	17	Bomas, Marj	5	5	blk	blk	46	Contraband	Jacksonville	Turner, Rending?	March 18/62			
52	18	King, Joseph			blk	blk	13	Contraband	Jacksonville	Turner, Rending?	March 18/62			
52	19	King, James			blk	blk	11	Contraband	Jacksonville	Turner, Rending?	Mrch 18/62			
52	20	Steward, Louisa	5	2	blk	blk	19	Contraband	Jacksonville	Turner, Rending?	March 18/62			
52	21	Travis, Anthony	5	7	blk	blk	60	Contraband	Jacksonville	Swan, Sam	March 15/62			
52	22	McIntosh, Thomas	5	9	blk	blk	51?	Contraband	GA	McIntosh, George	March 15/63			
52	23	McIntosh, Magdelana	5	2	blk	blk	58	Contraband	GA	Fishhook, Frank	March 15/63			
52	24	McIntosh, Rebecca			blk	blk	7	Contraband	GA	Fishhook, Frank	March 15/63			

Pg	No	Name	Height Ft	Height In	Eyes	Complexion	Age	Where born or contraband	Last residence	Where registered for draft or former owner	Date into Department	Oath of Allgn	No of Ration	Remarks
53	25	Forrester, Dorcus	5	2	blk	blk	60	Contraband	Fla	Clinch, Duncan	Nov. 6/63		1	Old: by order of Lt. Loveridge Comd'g Post
53	26	Forrester, Matilda	5	3	blk	blk	19	Contraband	Fla	Clinch, Duncan	Nov. 6/63			
53	27	Forrester, Charley			blk	blk	7	Contraband	Fla	Clinch, Duncan	Nov. 6/63			
53	28	Stafford,Rogers	5	5	blk	blk	45	Contraband	Cumberland Island	Stafford, Robert	March 19/62			
53	29	Stafford, Ellen	5	3	blk	blk	39	Contraband	Cumberland Island	Stafford, Robert	March 19/62			
53	30	Stafford, William?			blk	blk	1m	Fernandina	Cumberland Island					
53	31	Stafford, Charlette	5	3	blk	blk	34	Contraband	Cumberland Island	Stafford, Robert	March 19/62			
53	32	Stafford, Belle			blk	blk	3	Contraband	Cumberland Island	Stafford, Robert	March 19/62			
53	33	Hoglap, George	5	7	blk	blk	90	Contraband	St. Mary's	Harlow?, Miller	Mrch 19/62			
53	34	Hoglap, Lucy	5	6	blk	blk	40	Contraband	St. Mary's	Harlow?, Miller	March 19/62			
53	35	Adams, Dublin			blk	blk	8	Contraband	St. Mary's	Harlow?, Miller	March 19/62		1/2	Sick:1 Ration by order of Lt. Loveridge, Comd'g Post
53	36	Adams, Louisa			blk	blk	10	Contraband	St. Mary's	Harlow?, Miller	March 19/62		1/2	
53	37	Abota, Sarah	5	5	blk	blk	27	Contraband	Cumberland	Stafford, Robert	March 19/62			
53	38	Abota, Simon?			blk	blk	9	Contraband	Cumberland	Stafford, Robert	March 19/62			
53	39	Abota, Hattie			blk	blk	3?	Contraband	Cumberland	Stafford, Robert	March 19/62			
53	40	Daymond, Sallie	5	2	blk	blk	105	Contraband	Duval Co., Fla.	Albota, Mr.	June 20/64		1	Old & destitute: by order Lt. Loveridge Comd'g Post
53	41	Williams, Hettie	5	3	blk	blk	47	Contraband	Duval Co., Fla.	Houston, David	March 20/64			
53	42	Williams, Martha	5	2	blk	blk	18	Contraband	Duval Co., Fla.	Houston, David	March 20/64			
53	43	Williams, Rebecca	5	3	blk	blk	17	Contraband	Duval Co., Fla.	Houston, David	March 20/64			
53	44	Williams, Charles			blk	blk	7	Contraband	Duval Co., Fla.	Houston, David	March 20/64			
53	45	Robinson, Ellen	5	2	blk	blk	23	Contraband	Nassau Co., Fla	Joubanks, William	Jan. 15/63			
53	46	Robinson, Phillis			blk	blk	10	Contraband	Nassau Co., Fla	Joubanks, William	Jan. 15/63		1/2	1 1/2 ration by order of Lt. Loveridge Comd'g Post
53	47	Robinson, Sarah			blk	blk	6	Contraband	Nassau Co., Fla	Joubanks, William	Jan. 15/63		1/2	
53	48	Robinson, Lewis			blk	blk	4	Contraband	Nassau Co., Fla	Joubanks, William	Jan. 15/63		1/2	

Pg	No	Name	Height Ft	Height In	Eyes	Complexion	Age	Where born or contraband	Last residence	Where registered for draft or former owner	Date into Department	Oath of Allgn	No of Ration	Remarks
54	1	Baker, Alfred			black	black	12	Contraband	Fernandina, Fla	Latham, George				
54	2	Baker, John			black	black	7	Contraband	Fernandina, Fla	Latham, George				
54	3	Baker, Henry			black	black	5	Contraband	Fernandina, Fla	Latham, George				
54	4	Baker, Martha			black	black	3	Contraband	Fernandina, Fla	Latham, George				
54	5	Dias, Charita	5	1	black	black	25	Contraband	Fernandina, Fla	Latham, George				
54	6	Latham, George	6	1	blue	light	48	Glenn Co. GA	Camden Co., GA		March 15/63	yes		
54	7	Latham, Hester	5	5	dark	fair	5	Liberty Co., GA	Camden Co., GA		March 15/63	yes		
54	8	White, Ndxy?			dark	fair		Georgia	Camden Co., GA		March 15/63			
54	9	Latham, Francis	5	5	blue	light	14	Georgia	Camden Co., GA		March 15/63	yes		
54	10	Holzendorf, Thomas	5	9	black	black	67	Contraband	St. Augustine	Spans, Francis	March 2/62			
54	11	Latham, Lena	4	11	black	black	42	Contraband	Liberty Co., GA	Latham, George	March 2/62			
54	12	Holzendorf, Kate	4	10	black	black	25	Contraband	Liberty Co., GA	Latham, George	March 2/62			
54	13	McCarr, Samuel W.	5	9	dark	fair	30	Penn.	Lake City		Feb. 10/64	yes		
54	14	McCarr, Eugine	5	6	blue	light	18	Jacksonville	Lake City		Feb. 10/64	yes		
54	15	McCarr, Frederick W.			blue	light	2	Jacksonville	Lake City		Feb. 10/64			
54	16	Lassarse?, Mary E.	4	8	blue	light	16	Jacksonville	Jacksonville		April 1/64	yes		
54	17	Lassarse?, Salena	4	11	dark	medm	38	Fall River, Mass	Jacksonville		April 1/64	yes		
54	18	Lassarse?, Charles H.			gray	fair	14	Jacksonville	Jacksonville		April 1/64			
54	19	Turner, Jonathan T.	5	10	gray	fair	55	Conn	Conn.		Nov. 26/62	yes		
54	20	Turner, Adalade D.	5	0	blue	fair	37	Conn	Conn.		April 9/63	yes		
54	21	Turner, John T.	6	0	blue	light	27	Conn	Atlanta, GA		Feb. 5/64	yes		
54	22	Turner, Hattie A.	5	0	blue	fair	19	Conn	Conn.		April 9/63	yes		
54	23	Turner, Marvin W.	4	8	blue	fair	14	Conn	Conn.		April 9/63			
54	24	Christopher, Christianna	5	2	black	black	34	Contraband	Fla	Houston, John	Dec. 15/64			

Pg	No	Name	Height Ft	In	Eyes	Com-plexion	Age	Where born or contraband	Last residence	Where registered for draft or former owner	Date into Department	Oath of Allgn	No of Ration	Remarks
55	25	Williams, Dilsa	5	2	black	black	30	Contraband	St Mary, GA	Defo, John	March 15/62			
55	26	King, John	5	7	black	black	41	Contraband	GA	Dound, Mrs.	Sept. 2/64			
55	27	King, Harriette	5	3	black	black	35	Contraband	GA	Holder, Mrs.	Sept. 2/64			
55	28	Minns?, William M.	5	10	gray	dark	43	Del.	Del.		Oct. 6/62	yes		
55	29	Merrick, Peter	5	5	gray	dark	44	Hungaria	GA		March 14/64	yes		
55	30	Murray, James	5	10	blue	fair	21	Ireland	Boston		Oct. 15/64			
55	31	Murphey, Timithy	5	8	blue	fair	68	Ireland	Boston		Oct. 15/64			Has taken aliens oath
55	32	McGill, David	5	8	gray	fair	19	Ireland	Boston		Oct. 15/64			Has taken aliens oath
55	33	Mulheron, Luke	5	7	gray	fair	57	Ireland	Boston		Oct. 15/64			Has taken aliens oath
55	34	Mulheron, Michael	5	9	brwn	dark	21	Ireland	Boston		Oct. 15/64			Has taken aliens oath
55	35	McMannan, Francis	5	7	gray	dark	39	Ireland	Boston		Oct. 15/64	yes		
55	36	Meaghan, Martin	5	6	brwn	ruddy	21	Ireland	Boston		Oct. 15/64			Has taken aliens oath
55	37	Murray, Bartley	5	9	gray	fair	26	Ireland	Boston		Oct. 15/64			Has taken aliens oath
55	38	Mitchel, Abner	5	10	black	black	22	Contraband	St. Mary's	Annew, Peter	March 15/63			
55	39	McDonald, Obaid?	5	8	black	black	34	Contraband	Jacksonville	Fanns?, John	April 12/62			
55	40	McDonald, Robert	5	8	black	black	16	Contraband	Georgia	Hahn, H.	Feb. 29/64			
55	41	McFarland, Elias			black	black	12	Contraband	Cumberland	Stafford, Robert	March 9/63			
55	42	Napier, William	5	4	blue	fair	44	England	Cumberland		Dec. 4/63			Has taken aliens oath
55	43	Nightingale, Bulter	5	10	black	black	68	Contraband	Cumberland	Nighingale, T. M.	March 4/64			
55	44	Nab, Charles	5	11	black	black	47	Contraband	GA	Hahn, John	March 3/62			
55	45	Aniel?, John	5	7	blue	fair	23	England	Boston	Boston	Oct. 15/64	yes		
55	46	Peeples, J. H.	5	8	blue	dark	25	Camden Co., GA	Camden Co., GA		Aug. 1/64	yes		
55	47	Palmer, Thomas	5	8	gray	fair	20	Ireland	New Hamp.		Oct. 15/64			Has taken aliens oath
55	48	Papelia, Lewis	5	4	black	black	40	Contraband	Jacksonville, Fla	Juding, Elias	April 1/62			

Pg	No	Name	Height Ft	Height In	Eyes	Com-plexion	Age	Where born or contraband	Last residence	Where registered for draft or former owner	Date into Department	Oath of Allgn	No of Ration	Remarks
56	1	Nape, Louisa			black	black	6	Contraband	Jacksonville	Palmer, David L.	Oct. 5/62			
56	2	King, Maria			black	black	8m	Ferrandina						
56	3	Samms, Joseph	5	6	black	black	15	Contraband	Jacksonville	Palmer, David L.	Oct. 5/62			
56	4	Armstrong, Rachel	5	1	black	black	41	St. Mary, GA	Jacksonville		Oct. 20/62			
56	5	Cole, John Henry			black	black	10	Jacksonville	Jacksonville		Oct. 20/62			
56	6	Cole, Florida			black	black	8	Jacksonville	Jacksonville		Oct. 20/62			
56	7	McFall, Benjamin			black	black	8	Jacksonville	Jacksonville		Oct. 20/62			
56	8	Mason, Georgia			black	black	3	Jacksonville	Jacksonville		Oct. 20/62			
56	9	Cooner, Erven	5	7	black	dark	18	GA	GA		Sept. 23/64	yes		
56	10	Holzendorf, Henry	5	5	black	black	29	Contraband	St. Mary's, GA	Swarenger?, Sam	May 29/62			
56	11	Holzendorf, Louisa	5	4	black	black	35	Contraband	St. Mary's, GA	Swarenger?, Wayne	May 29/62			
56	12	Holzendorf, Henry			black	black	8	Contraband	St. Mary's, GA	Swarenger?, Wayne	May 29/62			
56	13	Holzendorf, Frank			black	black	5	Contraband	St. Mary's, GA	Swarenger?, Wayne	May 29/62			
56	14	Holzendorf, Mary Ann			black	black	2	Contraband	St. Mary's, GA	Swarenger?, Wayne	May 29/62			
56	15	Holzendorf, Harriett	5	4	black	black	28	Contraband	St. Mary's, GA	Swarenger?, Wayne	May 29/62			
56	16	Holzendorf, Satiro?			black	black	8	Contraband	St. Mary's, GA	Swarenger?, Wayne	May 29/62			
56	17	Holzendorf, Susan			black	black	7	Contraband	St. Mary's, GA	Swarenger?, Wayne	May 29/62			
56	18	Shingleton, Prince	5	10	black	black	45	Contraband	St. Mary's, GA	Hickenbottem, Eligh?	Feb. 10/63			
56	19	Baker, Mary Ann	5	4	black	black	25	Jacksonville	Jacksonville		April 15/62			
56	20	Baker, Julia			black	black	3	Jacksonville	Jacksonville		April 15/62			
56	21	Baker, William			black	black	1	Fernandina						
56	22	McDonald, Marj.	5	1	black	black	29	Jacksonville	Jacksonville		April 11/63			
56	23	McDonald, James			black	black	10	Jacksonville	Jacksonville		April 11/63			
56	24	McDonald, Francis			black	black	7	Jacksonville	Jacksonville		April 11/63			

Pg	No	Name	Height		Eyes	Com-plexion	Age	Where born or contraband	Last residence	Where registered for draft or former owner	Date into Department	Oath of Allgn	No of Ration	Remarks
			Ft	In										
57	25	McDonald, Renolda			black	black	5	Jacksonville	Jacksonville, Fla		April 11/63			
57	26	McDonald, Henry			black	black	1	Fernandina						
57	27	Long, Rosa	5	5	black	black	21	Contraband	Fla	Braddock, Spicer	May 3/63			
57	28	Long, Charlotte			black	black	?	Contraband	Fla	Braddock, Spicer	May 3/63			
57	29	Tousend, Molley	4	11	black	black	25	Contraband	Fla	Braddock, Spicer	May 3/63			
57	30	Anderson, Dianna	4	10	black	black	18	Contraband	Fla	Braddock, Spicer	May 3/63			
57	31	Donham, Simon			black	black	9	Contraband	Fla	Braddock, Spicer	May 3/63			
57	32	Anderson, Mila			black	black	1	Contraband	Fla	Braddock, Spicer	May 3/63			
57	33	McClellan, Elizabeth	5	2	brwn	fair	31	Scuvin Co., GA	Nassau Co., Fla		March 21/64	yes		
57	34	McClellan, Daniel			brwn	fair	9	Nassau Co., Fla	Nassau Co., Fla		March 21/64			
57	35	McClellan, Opheila			gray	fair	4m	Fernandina						
57	36	Stafford, Phebe	5	1	black	black	55	Contraband	Cumberland Island	Stafford, Robert	March 19/62			
57	37	Stafford, Easter	5	2	black	black	29	Contraband	Cumberland Island	Stafford, Robert	March 19/62			
57	38	Stafford, Betsey	4	10	black	black	19	Contraband	Cumberland Island	Stafford, Robert	March 19/62			
57	39	Stafford, Jenny	4	8	black	black	15	Contraband	Cumberland Island	Stafford, Robert	March 19/62			
57	40	Stafford, Shepherd			black	black	7	Contraband	Cumberland Island	Stafford, Robert	March 19/62			
57	41	Stafford, Mila			black	black	6	Contraband	Cumberland Island	Stafford, Robert	March 19/62			
57	42	Stafford, Barbara			black	black	3	Contraband	Cumberland Island	Stafford, Robert	March 19/62			
57	43	Stafford, Isaac			black	black	12	Contraband	Cumberland Island	Stafford, Robert	March 19/62			
57	44	Stafford, Peter			black	black	5	Contraband	Cumberland Island	Stafford, Robert	March 19/62			
57	45	Stafford, Jonas			black	black	5	Contraband	Cumberland Island	Stafford, Robert	March 19/62			
57	46	Stafford, Jane			black	black	4	Contraband	Cumberland Island	Stafford, Robert	March 19/62			
57	47	Baker, Anna	4	10	black	black	35	Contraband	Fernandina	Latham, George				
57	48	Baker, Virginia			black	black	15	Contraband	Fernandina	Latham, George				

Pg	No	Name	Height Ft	Height In	Eyes	Com-plexion	Age	Where born or contraband	Last residence	Where registered for draft or former owner	Date into Department	Oath of Allgn	No of Ration	Remarks
58	1	Robinson, Lovince			black	black	2	Contraband	Nassau, Fla	Joubanks, Wm	Jan. 15/63		1/2	By order of Lt. Loveridge Comd'g Post
58	2	Albott, Nellie	5	2	black	black	42	Contraband	Nassau, Fla	Richardson, John	March 15/63			
58	3	Albott, Christianna			black	black	10	Contraband	Nassau, Fla	Richardson, John	March 15/63			
58	4	Albott, Easter			black	black	12	Contraband	Nassau, Fla	Richardson, John	March 15/63			
58	5	Albott, Martin			black	black	7	Contraband	Nassau, Fla	Richardson, John	March 15/63			
58	6	_____,John			black	black	1m	Fernandina						
58	7	Albert, Prince	5	3	black	black	40	Contraband	Fla	Wilds, Nat	March 12/63			
58	8	Travis?, Polodire			black	black	9	Contraband	Fla	Braddick, Harlow	March 12/63			
58	9	Hooper, Sam	5	6	black	black	100	Contraband	Fla	Joubanks, Wm	March 12/63			
58	10	Jones, Jim	5	7	black	black	40	Contraband	Fla	Joubanks, Wm	March 12/63			
58	11	Bacus, Jim	5	8	black	black	43	Contraband	Fla	Joubanks, Wm	March 12/63			
58	12	Robinson, Charles	5	9	black	black	34	Contraband	Fla	Oneal, James	March 7/62			
58	13	Wingate. Nathaniel	5	10	gray	light	35	NassauCo., Fla	Nassau Co., Fla		June 24/64	yes		
58	14	Wingate, Macilla	5	3	dark	fair	23	NassauCo., Fla	Nassau Co., Fla		June 24/64	yes		
58	15	Robinson, Robert	5	4	black	black	67	Contraband	Nassau Co., Fla	Joubanks, Wm	Mrch 15/62			
58	16	Costa, Peter	5	9	black	black	76	Contraband	Nassau Co., Fla	Costo, Domingo	March 15/62			
58	17	Hartley, Lelana	5	1	black	black	15	Contraband	Nassau Co., Fla	Joubanks, Wm	Mrch 15/62			
58	18	Hartley, Emeiline			black	black	8	Contraband	Nassau Co., Fla	Joubanks, Wm	MArch 15/62			
58	19	Costa, Flora			black	black	10	Contraband	Nassau Co., Fla	Joubanks, Wm	March 15/62			
58	20	Williams, Sarah	5	1	black	black	16	Jacksonville	Jacksonville		March 15/62			
58	21	Williams, Lewis			black	black	12	Jacksonville	Jacksonville		March 15/62			
58	22	Blue, Mary	5	3	black	black	26	Contraband	Duval Co., Fla.	Denison, Mrs.	June 6/62			
58	23	Blue, Jane			black	black	13	Contraband	Duval Co., Fla.	Denison, Mrs.	June 6/62			
58	24	Blue, John			black	black	11	Contraband	Duval Co., Fla.	Denison, Mrs.	June 6/62			

Pg	No	Name	Height		Eyes	Com-plexion	Age	Where born or contraband	Last residence	Where registered for draft or former owner	Date into Department	Oath of Allgn	No of Ration	Remarks
			Ft	In										
59	26	Blue, William			black	black	9	Contraband	Duval Co., Fla.	Denison, Mrs.	June 6/62			
59	27	Blue, Elek			black	black	7	Contraband	Duval Co., Fla.	Denison, Mrs.	June 6/62			
59	28	Johnston, Calvin			black	black	14	Contraband	Duval Co., Fla.	Ogelsby?, Elizabeth	March 5/64?			
59	29	Dago, John	5	9	black	black	82	Contraband	St.Johns Co., Fla	Jenk, Edward	June 17/62		1	Old & destitute, by order of Lt. Loveridge, Comd'g
59	30	Dago, Rose	5	4	black	black	75	Contraband	St.Johns Co., Fla	Jenk, Edward	June 17/62		1	Old & destitute, by order of Lt. Loveridge, Comd'g
59	31	Johntson, Edell	5	2	black	black	26	Contraband	Jacksonville	Fraser, Phillip	Feb. 6/62			
59	32	Robinson, Hester	5	0	black	black	16	Contraband	Jacksonville	Fraser, Phillip	Feb. 6/62			
59	33	Johntson, Rosella			black	black	9	Contraband	Jacksonville	Fraser, Phillip	Feb. 6/62			
59	34	Johntson, Rufas			black	black	6	Contraband	Jacksonville	Fraser, Phillip	Feb. 6/62			
59	35	Johntson, Edgar			black	black	5	Contraband	Jacksonville	Fraser, Phillip	Feb. 6/62			
59	36	Miller, Elizabeth	5	7	black	black	30	Contraband	Jacksonville	Bathone, Franklin	March 15/62			
59	37	Miller, Joshua			black	black	12	Contraband	Jacksonville	Bathone, Franklin	March 15/62			
59	38	Reddy, Jane	5	3	black	black	55	Contraband	Jacksonville	Bathone, Franklin	March 15/62			
59	39	Reddy, Eliza			black	black	8	Contraband	Jacksonville	Bathone, Franklin	March 15/62			
59	40	Reddy, Anthony	5	7	black	black	24	Contraband	Jacksonville	Bathone, Franklin	March 15/62			
59	41	Reddy, George	5	8	black	black	72	Contraband	Jacksonville	Hart?, Isaha	Oct. 29/64			
59	42	Harrisson, Martha			black	black	14	Contraband	Jacksonville	Hart?, Isaha	Oct. 29/64			
59	43	Walker, James			black	black	5	Contraband	Jacksonville	Hart?, Isaha	Oct. 29/64			
59	44	Tillman, Henry			black	black	4	Contraband	Jacksonville	Hart?, Isaha	Oct. 29/64			
59	45	Palmer, Rodwell	4	11	black	black	75	Contraband	Jacksonville	Palmer, David L.	Oct. 5/62			
59	46	Palmer, Ann	4	10	black	black	83	Contraband	Jacksonville	Palmer, David L.	Oct. 5/62			
59	47	King, Rebecca	5	1	black	black	27	Contraband	Jacksonville	Palmer, David L.	Oct. 5/62			
59	48	Hayse?, Anna			black	black	9	Contraband	Jacksonville	Palmer, David L.	Oct. 5/62			

Pg	No	Name	Height Ft	Height In	Eyes	Complexion	Age	Where born or contraband	Last residence	Where registered for draft or former owner	Date into Department	Oath of Allgn	No of Ration	Remarks
60	1	Freeman, Anna			black	black	4	Contraband	Jacksonville	Geiger, James	June 30/64		1/2	Destitute; by order of Lt. Loveridge Comd'g Post
60	2	Thompson, Amanda	4	10	black	black	30	Contraband	Jacksonville	Price, Miles	Aug. 15/63			
60	3	Thompson, Hester			black	black	7	Contraband	Jacksonville	Price, Miles	Aug. 15/63			
60	4	Josie, Jane	5	7	black	black	31	Contraband	Censusville, GA	Costa, Amingo	Dec. 6/57			
60	5	Josie, William			black	black	9	Contraband	Censusville, GA	Costa, Amingo	Dec. 6/57			
60	6	Josie, David			black	black	8	Contraband	Censusville, GA	Costa, Amingo	Dec. 6/57			
60	7	Josie, Lucy			black	black	5	Fernandina						
60	8	Ferndes, Clve?	5	2	black	black	70	Contraband	Fernandina	Fernandes,Domingo			1	Old & destitute: order of Lt. Loveridge Comd'g Post
60	9	Napolian, Lewis	5	6	black	black	25	Contraband	Fla	Stone, George	Nov. 27/61			
60	10	Lane, William	5	8	gray	fair	58	GA	GA		Sept. 24/64	yes		
60	11	Lycurcus, Neattie	5	3	black	dark	17	Contraband	Jacksonville		June 15/62			
60	12	Magill, Hannah	5	6	black	black	42	Contraband	Jacksonville	Nightingale, P. M.	April 22/62			
60	13	Mott, Adolphus	5	9	black	dark	57	France	Washington	Washington D. C.	Nov. 4/64	yes		
60	14	Morill, William	5	10	blue	fair	32	Maine	Maine	Fernandina	June 11/63	yes		
60	15	Holmes, Arthur	5	4	blue	fair	35	Maine	Maine	Frankfort, Maine	March 7/64	yes		
60	16	Girvin, Martha	5	2	blue	fair	35	Ireland	Charleston, SC		May 15/57	yes		
60	17	Girvin, Anna	5	3	brwn	dark	17	Ireland	Charleston, SC		May 15/57	yes		
60	18	Girvin, John			blue	fair	13	Charleston, SC	Charleston, SC		May 15/57			
60	19	Girvin, Jane			gray	fair	11	Charleston, SC	Charleston, SC		May 15/57			
60	20	Girvin, Mary Elisa			blue	fair	5	Fernandina, Fla	Fernandina					
60	21	Girvin, Martha			blue	fair	1	Fernandina, Fla	Fernandina					
60	22	Miller, Jacob	5	7	gray	fair	54	Germany	Fla	Fernandina	Aug. 25/58	yes		
60	23	Rich, Anna	5	4	black	black	22	Contraband	GA	Braddock, Spicer	May 29/62			
60	24	Rich, Robert			black	black	18m	Contraband	GA	Braddock, Spicer				

Pg	No	Name	Height		Eyes	Com-plexion	Age	Where born or contraband	Last residence	Where registered for draft or former owner	Date into Department	Oath of Allgn	No of Ration	Remarks
			Ft	In										
61	25	Major, Jane	5	3	black	black	20	Contraband	Fla	Hickenbottem, Elijah	July 15/63			
61	26	Jenkins, Sarah	5	2	black	black	25	Contraband	Fla	Braddock, Spicer	May 15/64			
61	27	Jenkins, Thomas			black	black	9	Contraband	Fla	Upchurch, Nathaniel	July 18/64			
61	28	Sweet, Cornelius	5	4	black	black	20	Contraband	GA	Christopher, J. L.	Oct. 9/62			
61	29	King, Olliver	5	7	black	black	70	Contraband	Fla	Christopher, J. L.	Oct. 11/62			
61	30	King, Sophia	5	5	black	black	40	Contraband	Fla	Christopher, J. L.	Oct. 11/62		1/2	One destitute child: by order of Lt. Loveridge Comd'g. Post
61	31	Christopher, Martin	5	6	black	black	80	Contraband	Fla	Christopher, J. L.	Oct. 11/62		1	Old & destitute by order Lt. Loveridge Comd'g Post
61	32	Housten, Pracilla	5	6	black	black	30	Contraband	Fla					
61	33	McClue, Lucilla	5	5	black	black	21	Contraband	Fla	Sanders, Felix	Feb. 29/64			
61	34	Housten, Angeline			black	black	6	Contraband	Fla	Christopher, J. L.	Feb. 29/64			
61	35	Housten, Sophia			black	black	5	Contraband	Fla	Christopher, J. L.	Feb. 29/64			
61	36	Christopher, Julia	4	10	black	black	16	Contraband	Fla	Christopher, J. L.	Feb. 29/64			
61	37	Daivy?, Joseph	5	7	black	black	37	Contraband	Fla	Joubanks, Wm	Nov. 12/61			
61	38	Daivy?, Deta	5	5	black	black	34	Contraband	Fla	Housten, Samuel	Nov. 12/61			
61	39	Daivy?, Amanata			black	black	8	Contraband	Fla	Housten, Samuel	Nov. 12/61			
61	40	Daivy?, Daniel			black	black	6	Contraband	Fla	Housten, Samuel	Nov. 12/61			
61	41	Falana, Joseph	5	2	brwn	dark	44	Fla	Jacksonville	Fernandina	April 1/63	yes		
61	42	Falana, Susan	5	1	blue	light	30	GA	Jacksonville		April 1/63	yes		
61	43	Falana, Joseph			brwn	fair	11	GA	Jacksonville		April 1/63			
61	44	McIntosh, Gilbert	5	6	black	black	30	Contraband	St. Mary's, GA	Harlow, Col.	March 20/61			
61	45	McIntosh, Charlotte	5	4	black	black	28	Contraband	St. Mary's, GA	Dilworth?, John	March 20/61			
61	46	McIntosh, Thomas			black	black	7	Contraband	St. Mary's, GA	Dilworth?, John	March 20/61			
61	47	Lynes, Selana	4	8	brwn	fair	17	S. C.	GA		July 28/64	yes		
61	48	Evans, Andrew	5	7	black	black	62	Contraband	Fla	Mosley, William	Oct. 1/64			

Pg	No	Name	Height Ft	Height In	Eyes	Complexion	Age	Where born or contraband	Last residence	Where registered for draft or former owner	Date into Department	Oath of Allgn	No of Ration	Remarks
62	1	Crozer, Susan	5	2	black	black	14	Contraband	Nassau Co., Fla	Jones, Jack	May 17/63		1/2	Destitute family 3 Rations: by order
62	2	Crozer, Ellanora			black	black	12	Contraband	Nassau Co., Fla	Jones, Jack	May 17/63		1/2	of Lt. Loveridge Comd'gPost
62	3	Crozer, Tobias			black	black	10	Contraband	Nassau Co., Fla	Jones, Jack	May 17/63		1/2	
62	4	Crozer, David			black	black	8	Contraband	Nassau Co., Fla	Jones, Jack	May 17/63		1/2	
62	5	Crozer, Daniel			black	black	6	Contraband	Nassau Co., Fla	Jones, Jack	May 17/63		1/2	
62	6	Crozer, William			black	black	4	Contraband	Nassau Co., Fla	Jones, Jack	May 17/63		1/2	
62	7	Rannels, Albert	6	10	black	dark	32	Contraband	Key West Fla	Fernandina, Fla.	Jan. 2/63			
62	8	Rannels, Sarah	5	3	black	black	29	Contraband	Fernandina	Fernandina, Fla.	Jan. 2/63			
62	9	Rannels, Romine			black	black	12	Contraband	Fernandina					
62	10	Rannels, Rosena			black	black	7	Contraband	Fernandina					
62	11	Rannels, Samuel			black	black	4	Contraband	Fernandina					
62	12	Lyon, Phillis			black	black	12	Contraband	Fernandina					
62	13	Mott, Henry L.	5	11	gray	fair	20	Paris	Washington DC	Fernandina	Aug. 8/64	yes		
62	14	Masi, W, M.	5	8	black	dark	21	Washington DC	Washington DC	Fernandina	June 15/63	yes		
62	15	Hill, Fortune	5	8	black	black	41	Contraband	Magnolia, Fla	Sumlin, John	March 3/62			
62	16	Ready?, Samuel	5	5	black	black	15	Contraband	Jacksonville	Bathone, Judge	Aug. 5/63			
62	17	Cohrt, E. L.	5	8	brwn	fair	31	Germany	Savannah, GA		March 8/58			Took Alien's Oath
62	18	Hackel, William	5	9	brwn	fair	29	Germany	Jacksonville Fla	Fernandina, Fla.	May 14/60			Took Neutral Oath
62	19	Thomas, Hannah	5	1	black	black	34	Contraband	Jacksonville Fla	Jacks, Robert	Nov. 6/62			
62	20	Elliott, Hester	4	10	black	black	30	Contraband	Jacksonville Fla	Phillips, Albert	Nov. 6/62			
62	21	Elliott, Maria			black	black	10	Contraband	Jacksonville Fla	Phillips, Albert	Nov. 6/62			
62	22	Elliott, Nancy			black	black	7	Contraband	Jacksonville Fla	Phillips, Albert	Nov. 6/62			
62	23	Elliott, Sammy			black	black	5	Contraband	Jacksonville Fla	Phillips, Albert	Nov. 6/62			
62	24	Elliott, Sarah			black	black	2	Contraband	Jacksonville Fla	Phillips, Albert	Nov. 6/62			

Pg	No	Name	Height Ft	Height In	Eyes	Com-plexion	Age	Where born or contraband	Last residence	Where registered for draft or former owner	Date into Department	Oath of Allgn	No of Ration	Remarks
63	25	Donaly, Joseph	5	10	gray	fair	46	Lascaster, PA	Charleston, SC	Fernandina, Fla.	Aug. 20/60	yes		Artist
63	26	Donaly, Jane M.	5	9	blue	fair	52	Glen Co., GA	St. Mary's, GA		Nov. 2/57	yes		
63	27	Propemodin?, Lewis	5	9	brwn	fair	34	France	Charleston, SC	Fernandina, Fla.	July 28/57			Barber:Took Neutral Oath
63	28	Pohite, Patsey	5	4	black	black	45	Contraband	St. Mary's, GA	Proctor, William	March 10/61			
63	29	Ribron, Peter F.	5	7	brwn	dark	47	Camden Co., GA	Hilton Head SC		Aug. 3/64	yes		Working in Engineer Dept.
63	30	Ribron, Mary	5	2	blue	fair	40	Camden Co., GA	Hilton Head SC		Aug. 3/64	yes		
63	31	Ribron, Henry	5	4	blue	fair	16	Camden Co., GA	Hilton Head SC		Aug. 3/64	yes		
63	32	Ribron, Anna Delila	4	10	brwn	fair	13	Camden Co., GA	Hilton Head SC		Aug. 3/64	yes		
63	33	Ribron, David			blue	fair	11	Camden Co., GA	Hilton Head SC		Aug. 3/64			
63	34	Robron, Peter			blue	fair	9	Camden Co., GA	Hilton Head SC		Aug. 3/64			
63	35	Robron, Jacob			blue	fair	7	Camden Co., GA	Hilton Head SC		Aug. 3/64			
63	36	Ribron, George			blue	fair	5	Camden Co., GA	Hilton Head SC		Aug. 3/64			
63	37	Bunkley, James	5	9	blue	fair	30	Bullock Co., GA	Camden Co., GA		Aug. 19/64	yes		Working in Q. M. Dept.
63	38	Bunkley, Charity	5	4	blue	fair	28	Camden Co., GA	Camden Co., GA		Aug. 19/64	yes		
63	39	Bunkley, David			blue	fair	6	Camden Co., GA	Camden Co., GA		Aug. 19/64			
63	40	Bunkley, John			blue	fair	4	Camden Co., GA	Camden Co., GA		Aug. 19/64			
63	41	Bunkley, James			blue	fair	3	Camden Co., GA	Camden Co., GA		Aug. 19/64			
63	42	Bunkley. Allen?			blue	fair	6m	Camden Co., GA	Camden Co., GA		Aug. 19/64			
63	43	Bunkley, Martin	6	1	blue	fair	24	Bullock Co., GA	Camden Co., GA		Feb. 20/64	yes		Working in Q. M. Dept.
63	44	Head, William	5	4	brwn	fair	17	Wayne Co., GA	Wayne Co., GA		Aug. 31/64	yes		Working in Q. M. Dept.
63	45	Brown, Miss E. P.	5	4	brwn	fair	46	Ipswich, Mass	Charleston, SC		Aug. 28/56	yes		
63	46	Freman, Patsy	5	6	black	black	45	Contraband	Jacksonville	Geiger, James	June 30/64			
63	47	Freman, Mitchel			black	black	9	Contraband	Jacksonville	Geiger, James	June 30/64		1/2	Destitute family1 Ration: by order of
63	48	Freman, Joshua			black	black	6	Contraband	Jacksonville	Geiger, James	June 30/64		1/2	Lt loveridge Comd'g Post

"CENSUS" DEPARTMENT OF THE SOUTH - NOVEMBER, 1864

Pg	No	Name	Height		Eyes	Com-plexion	Age	Where born or contraband	Last residence	Where registered for draft or former owner	Date into Department	Oath of Allgn	No of Ration	Remarks
			Ft	In										
64	1	Curran, Henry	5	10	blue	light	33	Ireland	Massachusetts		Oct. 15/64			Has Taken Aliens Oath
64	2	Curran, Patrick	5	5	brwn	fair	40	Ireland	Massachusetts		Oct. 15/64			Has Taken Aliens Oath
64	3	Curley, Thomas	5	7	blue	dark	42	Ireland	Massachusetts		Oct. 15/64			Has Taken Aliens Oath
64	4	Cristopher, Moody	5	3	black	black	63	Contraband	Savannah, GA	Cristopher, Lewis	March 4/62			
64	5	Commodore, Henry			black	black	12	Contraband	Cumberland Isl., GA	Stafford, R.	Nov. 9/63			
64	6	Cristopher, Jane	5	9	black	black	35	Contraband	Talbot Isl., Fla	Christopher	Nov. 4/62			
64	7	Dunavan, David	5	10	blue	dark	30	Ireland	Massachusetts		Oct. 15/64			Has Taken Aliens Oath
64	8	Davis, David	5	10	black	black	37	Contraband	Nassau Co., Fla		Feb. 15/64			
64	9	Einstein, Joseph	5	5	brwn	dark	35	Europe	Camden Co., GA		Sept. 23/64			Has Taken Aliens Oath
64	10	Flemming, John	5	7	gray	med.	21	Ireland	Massachusetts		Oct. 15/64			Has Taken Aliens Oath
64	11	Fuller, Benjamin	5	1	black	black	38	Contraband	Florida	Jones, John	July 3/64			
64	12	Floyed. Sandy	5	6	black	black	63	Contraband	Georgia	Floyed, Gen't	Dec. 15/63			
64	13	Gleeson, Michael	5	2	blue	med.	49	Ireland	Massachusetts		Oct. 15/64	no		Sick: Aliens oath could not be administered to him
64	14	Holly, John	5	8	dark	dark	50	Ireland	Massachusetts		Oct. 15/64			Has Taken Aliens Oath
64	15	Hukley?, Jerry	5	7	blue	med.	37	Ireland	Massachusetts		Oct. 15/64			Has Taken Aliens Oath
64	16	Halloran, James	5	7	blue	fair	25	Ireland	Massachusetts		Oct. 15/64			Has Taken Aliens Oath
64	17	Haughey, Michael	5	8	gray	dark	56	Ireland	Massachusetts		Oct. 15/64	yes		
64	18	Hally, Lue	5	2	gray	med.	16	Ireland	Massachusetts		Oct. 15/64			Has taken Aliens Oath
64	19	Holligan, David	5	4	gray	med.	52	Ireland	Massachusetts		Oct. 15/64			Has taken Aliens Oath
64	20	Houston, Charles	5	4	blk	blk	55	Contraband	Florida	Cristopher	April 20/64			
64	21	Hubbard, Robert			blk	blk	12	Contraband	St. Mary's, GA	Hase, Mr.	March 7/62			
64	22	Henry, Wm			blk	blk	14	Contraband	St. Mary's, GA	Coster, D.	March 7/62			
64	23	Hubbard, Joseph			blk	blk	12	Contraband	Cumberland Isl., GA	Stafford, R.	Aug. 10/63			
64	24	Jermain, S..?			blk	blk	12	Contraband	Cumberland Isl., GA	Stafford, R.	Nov. 9/62			
64	25	James, Steven			blk	blk	14	Contraband	Duval Co., Fla.	Hickenbodem, L.	July 7/64			

Pg	No	Name	Height Ft	Height In	Eyes	Com-plexion	Age	Where born or contraband	Last residence	Where registered for draft or former owner	Date into Department	Oath of Allgn	No of Ration	Remarks
65	26	Kneeland, James	5	7	blue	med.	18	Ireland	Massachusetts		Oct 15/64			Has taken Aliens Oath
65	27	Kane, Richard	5	8	blk	blk	39	Contraband	Florida	Marina, Dr.	Oct. 15/62			
65	28	King, Port			blk	blk	13	Contraband	St. Mary's, GA	Barrat, Mr.	March 7/62			
65	29	Lopez, Andrew	5	4	brwn	dark	68?	St. Augustine	Jacksonville, FL		Nov. 13/63	yes		
65	30	Lynch, Patrick	5	8	gray	dark	28	Ireland	Massachusetts		Oct. 15/64			Has taken Aliens Oath
65	31	Long, Phalis	5	5	blk	blk	33	Contraband	Talbot Isl., Fla	Cristopher, I.	June 19/62			
65	32	Longworth, Joseph	5	9	blk	blk	52	Contraband	Savannah, GA	Hamilton, Ed	March 4/62			
65	33	Leonard, John	5	5	blk	blk	40	Contraband	Georgia	Locket, Abner	Sept. 17/64			
65	34	Lisamore, Stephen	4	8	blk	blk	15	Contraband	Cumberland Isl.	Stafford, R.	May 7/64			
65	35	Robinson, J. C.	5	6	gray	dark	24	Massachusetts	PhiladelphiaPA	Philadelphia, PA	Aug. 1/64	yes		Discharged from U.S. Service
65	36	Wilson, Robert	5	7	blue	dark	47	Ireland	South Carolina		Feb. 19/64	yes		
65	37	Kinsley, William	5	8	black	black	70	Contraband	Jacksonville	Kinsley, J.	Feb.21/63			
65	38	Dormbergh?, Albin	5	7	blue	fair	22	Sweden	Amelia Island		March 7/62	yes		
65	39	Cole, Jacob	5	9	gray	fair	16	St. Augustine	Jacksonville		April 9/63	yes		
65	40	Miller, Regina	5	4	dark	fair	24	BadenEurope	New York		Aug. 24/64	yes		
65	41	Pettit, John	5	4	blue	fair	18	Ireland	Massachusetts		Oct. 15/64			Has Taken Aliens Oath
65	42	Archy, A.	5	8	blk	blk	22	Contraband	Macon, GA	Locket, Abner	Sept. 2/64			
65	43	Mitchel, Jack	5	2	blk	blk	75	Contraband	Jacksonville	Mitchel, Dr.	Feb. 1863		1	Old & feeble: by order of Lt. Loveridge Comd'g. Post

"CENSUS" DEPARTMENT OF THE SOUTH - NOVEMBER, 1864

Pg	No	Name	Height Ft	Height In	Eyes	Com-plexion	Age	Where born or contraband	Last residence	Where registered for draft or former owner	Date into Department	Oath of Allgn	No of Ration	Remarks
66	1	Evans, Mary	4	8	black	black	27	Contraband	Florida	Mosley, William	Oct. 1/64			
66	2	Evans, Jane			black	black	12	Contraband	Florida	Mosley, William	Oct. 1/64			
66	3	Evans, Racheal			black	black	8	Contraband	Florida	Mosley, William	Oct. 1/64			
66	4	Evans, Adalade			black	black	7	Contraband	Florida	Mosley, William	Oct. 1/64			
66	5	Evans, Margarette			black	black	5	Contraband	Florida	Mosley, William	Oct. 1/64			
66	6	Walton, Carolina	5	5	black	black	75	Contraband	Georgia	Defo, John	June 15/62			
66	7	Walton, Margarett	5	4	black	black	46	Contraband	Talbot Isl., Fla	Housten, Spencer	Nov. 9/63			
66	8	Williams, Martha	5	4	black	black	19	Contraband	Talbot Isl., Fla	Housten, Spencer	Nov. 9/63			
66	9	Wright, Elizabeth			black	black	13	Contraband	Talbot Isl., Fla	Housten, Spencer	Nov. 9/63			
66	10	Wright, Lelana			black	black	5	Contraband	Talbot Isl., Fla	Housten, Spencer	Nov. 9/63			
66	11	Wright, Eliza			black	black	2	Contraband	Talbot Isl., Fla	Housten, Spencer	Nov. 9/63			
66	12	Smith, Maria			black	black	12	Contraband	Florida	Braddock, William	Feb. 1/64			
66	13	Smith, Abram			black	black	10	Contraband	Florida	Braddock, William	Feb. 1/64			
66	14	Smith, Henry			black	black	5	Contraband	Florida	Braddock, William	Feb. 1/64			
66	15	Anthony, John	5	5	brwn	fair	55	Portugese	GA		Oct. 20/64	yes		
66	16	Nix, Beuford	5	9	brwn	fair	35	GA	GA		Oct. 18/64	yes		
66	17	Nix, Sarah	5	5	brwn	fair	27	GA	GA		Oct. 18/64	yes		
66	18	Nix, Preston			brwn	fair	8	GA	GA		Oct. 18/64			
66	19	Nix, Ella			brwn	fair	5	GA	GA		Oct. 18/64			
66	20	Nix, Susan			brwn	fair	3	GA	GA		Oct. 18/64			
66	21	Nix, Mary			brwn	fair	1	GA	GA		Oct. 18/64			
66	22	Benjamin, Bristo	5	7	black	black	80	Contraband	Defo, John		March 1/61			
66	23	Benjamin, Arga	5	4	black	black	59	Contraband	Defo, John		March 1/61			
66	24	Benjamin, Elexander			black	black	2	Contraband	Defo, John		March 1/61			

Pg	No	Name	Height Ft	Height In	Eyes	Com-plexion	Age	Where born or contraband	Last residence	Where registered for draft or former owner	Date into Department	Oath of Allgn	No of Ration	Remarks
67	25	Benjamin, Robert			black	black	7	Contraband	GA or La?	Defo, John	March 29/61			
67	26	Wass, J. M.	5	8	brwn	fair	41	Germany	Tallehasse, Fla	Fernandina, Fla	June 2/58	yes		
67	27	Wass, Henry			brwn	fair	14	Tallehasse Fla	Tallehasse, Fla		June 2/58			
67	28	Wass, Alfred N.			brwn	fair	12	Tallehasse Fla	Tallehasse, Fla		June 2/58			
67	29	Wass, Benjamin			brwn	fair	10?	Tallehasse Fla	Tallehasse, Fla		June 2/58			
67	30	Wass, Maria Louisa			brwn	fair	5	Fernandina	Fernandina, Fla					
67	31	Polite, Hannah	5	1	black	black	43	Contraband	Fa	Broddick, Malto	July 18/64			
67	32	Polite, Fanning	5	3	black	black	19	Contraband	Fa	Broddick, Malto	July 18/64		1/2	Destitute family 1 Ration by order Lt.
67	33	Polite, Hector			black	black	6m	Contraband	Fa	Broddick, Malto	July 18/64		1/2	Loveridge Comd'g Post
67	34	Young, Henry	5	6	black	black	30	Contraband	Fa	Pleasant, John	March 5/61			
67	35	Talbot, Betsey	5	0	black	black	50	Contraband	Jacksonville	?ambus?, M.	Sept. 10/64			
67	36	Talbot, Laura	5	2	black	black	16	Contraband	Jacksonville	?ambus?, M.	Sept. 10/64			
67	37	Talbot, Alisha			black	black	10	Contraband	Jacksonville	?ambus?, M.	Sept. 10/64			
67	38	Young, Henry			black	black	11	Contraband	St. Mary's, GA	Church, Miss	March 5/61			
67	39	Young, Margaret			black	black	3	Contraband	St. Mary's, GA	Church, Miss	March 5/61			
67	40	Mauris, Martha	5	5	hazel	light	32	GA	GA		March 17/64	yes		
67	41	Mauris, William H.	5	2	hazel	light	14	GA	GA		March 17/64	yes		
67	42	McKendre, Mark	6	0	gray	ruddy	35	S. C.	GA		Oct. 8/64	yes		
67	43	McKendre, Jane	5	4	blue	fair	19	S. C.	GA		Sept. 28/64	yes		
67	44	Butler, William	6	1	dark	dark	27	GA	GA		Aug. 17/64	yes		
67	45	Butler, Anna	5	2	blue	fair	22	GA	GA		Aug. 11/64	yes		
67	46	Butler, Ellen			blue	fair	4m	GA	GA		Aug. 11/64			
67	47	Young, Adam	5	9	black	black	78	Contraband	St. Augustine	Verunh?, Daniel	March 18/61			
67	48	Young, Georgia	4	11	black	black	30	Contraband	St. Augustine	Verunh?, Daniel	March 18/61			

"CENSUS" DEPARTMENT OF THE SOUTH - NOVEMBER, 1864

Pg	No	Name	Height Ft	Height In	Eyes	Com-plexion	Age	Where born or contraband	Last residence	Where registered for draft or former owner	Date into Department	Oath of Allgn	No of Ration	Remarks
68	1	Simmons, Paris	5	11	black	black	54?	Contraband	St. Mary's, GA	Bezard, John	March 10/62			
68	2	Simmons, Molley	5	2	black	black	44	Contraband	St. Mary's, GA	Debos, Mrs.	March 10/62			
68	3	Williamson, Sarah	5	3	black	black	16	Contraband	St. Mary's, GA	Debos, Mrs.	March 10/62			
68	4	Dorrell, Jack	5	7	black	black	73	Contraband	Nassau Co., FL	Debos, Mrs.	Feb. 5/63			
68	5	Dorrell, Lucinda	5	6	black	black	60	Contraband	Cumberland Island	Nightingale, Miller	Feb. 5/63			
68	6	Nightingale, Sila	5	5	black	black	100	Contraband	Cumberland Island	Nightingale, Miller	Feb. 5/63		1	Old & Feeble: by order Lt. Loveridge Comd'g. Post
68	7	Andrew, Jacob	5	3	black	black	95	Contraband	Cumberland Island	St. Mary's GA	Bassler, John	Nov.4/64		
68	8	Edwards, Rose	5	7	black	black	23	Contraband	Jacksonville, FL	Felix, Stephen	March 16/62			
68	9	Robinson, William			black	black	9	Contraband	Jacksonville, FL	Felix, Stephen	March 16/62			
68	10	Spade, Carlton			black	black	5	Contraband	Jacksonville, FL	Felix, Stephen	March 16/62			
68	11	Floyd, Charlotte	5	9	black	black	46	Contraband	Jacksonville, FL	Felix, Stephen	March 16/62			
68	12	Depena, Emanuel	5	9	black	black	49	Contraband	Jacksonville, FL	Hartman, Frank	April 17/62			
68	13	Jenkins, Easter	5	4	black	black	60	Contraband	Talbot Isl., Fla	Housten, John	Nov. 5/61		1	Old & destitute: by order Lt. Loveridge Comd'g Post
68	14	Dees?, Nancy	5	4	black	black	65	Contraband	Jacksonville, FL	Paince?, John	April 6/62			
68	15	Baker, Ellanera			black	black	8	Contraband	Jacksonville, FL	Buffenten, Col.	April 6/62			
68	16	Baker, Nancy			black	black	5	Contraband	Jacksonville, FL	Buffenten, Col.	April 6/62			
68	17	Moore, Anna			black	black	12	Contraband	Jacksonville, FL	Buffenten, Col.	April 6/62			
68	18	Harrisson, Sarah	5	2	black	black	28	Contraband	Talbot Isl., Fla	Housten, John	Nov. 3/63			
68	19	Grissen, William			black	black	3	Contraband	Talbot Isl., Fla	Housten, John	Nov. 3/63			
68	20	Grissen, Madelana			black	black	2	Contraband	Talbot Isl., Fla	Housten, John	Nov. 3/63			
68	21	Christopher, John			black	black	5	Contraband	Talbot Isl., Fla	Housten, John	Nov. 3/63			
68	22	Sams, Hannah	5	3	black	black	90	Contraband	Jacksonville, FL	Sams, John	Aug. 2/62		1	Old & destitute; by order Lt. Loveridge Comd'g Post
68	23	Price, Marice	5	1	black	black	35?	Contraband	Jacksonville, FL	Kinsley, Mr.	Aug. 2/62			
68	24	Samms, Sarah	5	4	black	black	21	Contraband	Jacksonville, FL	Kinsley, Mr.	Aug. 2/62			

Pg	No	Name	Height Ft	Height In	Eyes	Complexion	Age	Where born or contraband	Last residence	Where registered for draft or former owner	Date into Department	Oath of Allgn	No of Ration	Remarks
69	25	Price, Dora			black	black	10	Contraband	Jacksonville	Kinsley, Mr.	Aug. 2/62			
69	26	Price, Roselena			black	black	8	Contraband	Jacksonville	Kinsley, Mr.	Aug. 2/62			
69	27	Copp, Rachel	5	3	blue	dark	50	Contraband	St. Mary's, GA	Creighton, Mrs.	Dec. 30/62			
69	28	Copp, Anthm			blue	dark	8	Contraband	St. Mary's, GA	Creighton, Mrs.	Dec. 30/62			
69	29	Hebert. Londen	5	7	black	black	43	Contraband	Cumberland	Stafford, Robert	March 19/62			
69	30	Hebert. Rachel	5	6	black	black	37	Contraband	Cumberland	Stafford, Robert	March 19/62			
69	31	Hebert, Sukey	4	10	black	black	16	Contraband	Cumberland	Stafford, Robert	March 19/62			
69	32	Hebert, Joe			black	black	10	Contraband	Cumberland	Stafford, Robert	March 19/62			
69	33	Hebert, Cumber?			black	black	5	Contraband	Cumberland	Stafford, Robert	March 19/62			
69	34	Hebert, Lewis			black	black	3	Contraband	Cumberland	Stafford, Robert	March 19/62			
69	35	Hebert, Jim			black	black	1	Contraband	Cumberland	Stafford, Robert	March 19/62			
69	36	Towsend, William	5	10	black	black	52	Contraband	S. C.	Baker, Jackson	Dec. 15/59			
69	37	Flood, Richard	5	9	black	black	53	Contraband	GA	Housten, Patrick	Aug. 10/63			
69	38	Joubanks, Hannah	4	10	black	black	54	Contraband	Fla	Joubanks, William	Nov.15/62		1	Old & Feeble: by order Lt. Loveridge Comd'g Post
69	39	Joubanks, Patty			black	black	10	Contraband	Fla	Joubanks, William	Nov.15/62			
69	40	Joubanks, Kelley?			black	black	14	Contraband	Fla	Joubanks, William	Nov.15/62			
69	41	Acka, Ann	6	0	black	black	32	Contraband	Fla	Davis, K.	May 16/64			
69	42	Acka, Sophia?	5	6	black	black	25	Contraband	Fla	Hatrick, Joe	Feb. 9/64			
69	43	Acka, Jack			black	black	10	Contraband	Fla	Hatrick, Joe	Feb. 9/64		1/2	Destitute family 3 Rations by order Lt. Loveridge Comd'g Post
69	44	Acka, Aaron			black	black	8	Contraband	Fla	Hatrick, Joe	Feb. 9/64		1/2	
69	45	Acka, Charlotte			black	black	6	Contraband	Fla	Hatrick, Joe	Feb. 9/64		1/2	
69	46	Acka, Ella			black	black	4	Contraband	Fla	Hatrick, Joe	Feb. 9/64		1/2	
69	47	Acka, Mila			black	black	2	Contraband	Fla	Hatrick, Joe	Feb. 9/64		1/2	
69	48	Acka, Hearnette			black	black	1	Contraband	Fla	Hatrick, Joe	Feb. 9/64		1/2	

Pg	No	Name	Height Ft	Height In	Eyes	Complexion	Age	Where born or contraband	Last residence	Where registered for draft or former owner	Date into Department	Oath of Allgn	No of Ration	Remarks
70	1	Jackson, Sophia	4	11	black	black	24	Contraband	Savannah, GA	Housten, Patrick	March 10/62			
70	2	Jackson, Emma			black	black	3	Contraband	Savannah, GA	Housten, Patrick	March 10/62			
70	3	Hampton, Adam	5	10	black	black	30	Contraband	Jacksonville, Fl	Sadeller, Henry	Sept. 19/62			
70	4	Hampton, Willey	5	6	black	black	57	Contraband	Jacksonville, Fl	Shull?, John	Sept. 19/62			
70	5	GAskin, Elsa			black	black	12	Contraband	Jacksonville, Fl	Shull?, John	Sept. 19/62			
70	6	GAskin, Emma			black	black	8	Contraband	Jacksonville, Fl	Shull?, John	Sept. 19/62			
70	7	GAskin, Lydia			black	black	7	Contraband	Jacksonville, Fl	Shull?, John	Sept. 19/62			
70	8	Prisler, Noah	5	8	blue	light	26	North Carolina	GA		Aug. 3/64	yes		
70	9	Prisler, Emily	5	4	dark	fair	35	GA	GA		Aug. 3/64	yes		
70	10	Bruzzer?, Resella			gray	fair	5	GA	GA		Feb. 13/64			
70	11	Miller, Jack	5	9	black	black	102	Contraband	St. Mary's, GA	Miller, Robert	March 10/62		1	Old & destitute: order of Lt. Loveridge Comd'g Post
70	12	Miller, Easter	4	10	black	black	101	Contraband	St. Mary's, GA	Miller, Robert	March 10/62		1	Old & destitute: order of Lt. Loveridge Comd'g Post
70	13	White, Jacob	5	7	black	black	65	Contraband	St. Mary's, GA	Haddock, Joe	March 10/64			
70	14	White, Flira	5	2	black	black	80	Contraband	St. Mary's, GA	Morrisson, Joe	March 10/64			
70	15	Clark, George	5	6	black	black	76	Contraband	Jacksonville	Byant, Stephen	June 17/63			
70	16	Clark, Harnette	4	11	black	black	82	Contraband	Jacksonville	Byant, Stephen	June 17/63			
70	17	Young, George	5	5	black	black	75	Contraband	St Mary's, GA	Albota, Edwin	March 10/64			
70	18	Young, Harriette	5	2	black	black	67	Contraband	St. Mary's, GA	Saddler, Mrs.	March 10/64			
70	19	Williams, Jane	5	1	black	black	36	Contraband	Jacksonville	Saddler, Henry	April 12/63			
70	20	Williams, Phebe			black	black	12	Contraband	Jacksonville	Saddler, Henry	April 12/63			
70	21	Williams, Lizzie			black	black	9	Contraband	Jacksonville	Saddler, Henry	April 12/63		1/2	Destitute family 2 Rations: by order Lt. Loveridge Comd'g Post
70	22	Williams, Andrew			black	black	7	Contraband	Jacksonville	Saddler, Henry	April 12/63		1/2	
70	23	Williams, Nancy			black	black	4	Contraband	Jacksonville	Saddler, Henry	April 12/63		1/2	
70	24	Williams, William			black	black	2	Contraband	Jacksonville	Saddler, Henry	April 12/63		1/2	

Pg	No	Name	Height Ft	Height In	Eyes	Com-plexion	Age	Where born or contraband	Last residence	Where registered for draft or former owner	Date into Department	Oath of Allgn	No of Ration	Remarks
71	25	Nightingale, Belle	5	5	black	black	80	Contraband	Cumberland Island	Nightingale, Miller	April 12/62		1	Old 1Ration by order of Lt. Loveridge Comd'g Post
71	26	Housten, Anna	5	7	black	black	22	Jacksonville	Jacksonville, Fl		March 15/62			
71	27	Housten, Alana			black	black	3m	Fernandina						
71	28	Honten, Julia			black	black	13	Jacksonville	Jacksonville Fl		March 15/62			
71	29	Floyd, Angelina	5	8	black	black	29	Talbott Island	Talbot Island Fla		Feb. 19/63			
71	30	Floyd, John			black	black	9	Talbott Island	Talbot Island Fla					
71	31	Curtis, Lousia	4	8	black	black	16	Contraband	Talbot Island Fla	Houston, John				
71	32	Curtis, Jane	5	7	black	black	40	Contraband	Talbot Island Fla	Houston, John				
71	33	Curtis, Josephine			black	black	7	Contraband	Talbot Island Fla	Houston, John				
71	34	Curtis, James			black	black	2	Contraband	Talbot Island Fla	Houston, John				
71	35	Williams, Susan	5	9	black	black	36	Contraband	Jacksonville	Housten, Sam	April 9/62			
71	36	Williams, Emma			black	black	7	Contraband	Jacksonville	Housten, Sam	April 9/62			
71	37	Jenkins, Malber	5	9	black	black	75	Contraband	Nassau Co., Fla	Youbanks, John	Sept. 29/62			
71	38	Robinson, Rachel	5	8	black	black	38	Contraband	Nassau Co., Fla	Wilson, Jim	May 1/62			
71	39	Floyd, Charles	5	10	black	black	24	Contraband	Nassau Co., Fla	Wilson, Jim	May 1/62			
71	40	Knat, Lucinda	5	6	black	black	45	GA	GA		April 2/34			
71	41	Knat, Margarette			black	black	12	Contraband	Fla	Johntson, Fin	March 15/62			
71	42	Knat, Emaline			black	black	8	Contraband	Fla	Johntson, Fin	March 15/62			
71	43	Knat, Flira			black	black	6	Contraband	Fla	Johntson, Fin	March 15/62			
71	44	Knat, Sarah			black	black	4	Contraband	Fla	Johntson, Fin	March 15/62			
71	45	Forrester, Elek	5	8	black	black	60	Contraband	Mandrine, Fla	Samaule, Jack	April 6/63			
71	46	Forrester, Louisa	5	4	black	black	37	Contraband	Mandrine, Fla	Hartley, Nathaniel	April 6/63			
71	47	Forrester, Amelia	4	10	black	black	19	Contraband	Mandrine, Fla	Hartley, Nathaniel	April 6/63			
71	48	Forrester, Mary	4	11	black	black	17	Contraband	Mandrine, Fla	Hartley, Nathaniel	April 6/63			

Pg	No	Name	Height		Eyes	Com-plexion	Age	Where born or contraband	Last residence	Where registered for draft or former owner	Date into Department	Oath of Allgn	No of Ration	Remarks
			Ft	In										
72	1	Sedgewick, Jno	5	6	dk	dk	51	N Y	Fla	never	1840	yes	none	Cripple
72	2	Sedgewick, Wm	5	7	blue	F	47	N Y	Fla	never	1840	yes	none	Blacksmith
72	3	Sedgewick, Martha	5	4	blue	F	40	S. C.	Fla		1845	yes	non	
72	4	Sedgewick, Lizzie	5	4	blue	F	18	Fla	Fla		native	yes	non	
72	5	Sedgewick, Wm			blue	F	7	Fla	Fla		native	no	non	
72	6	Sedgewick, Lucy			blue	F	4	Fla	Fla		native	no	non	
72	7	Prevatt, Elizabeth	5	5	blue	F	66	S. C.	Fla		1845	no	non	
72	8	French, Alf.	5	6	dk	dk	27	Canada	Fla	never	1864	yes	none	Unemployed
72	9	French, Augusta	5	3	dk	dk	21	Fla	Fla		native	yes	non	
72	10	French, Martha			dk	dk	1	Fla	Fla		native	no	non	
72	11	Capella, Lorenzo	5	6	dk	dk	46	Fla	Fla	never	native	yes	none	ShopKeeper
72	12	Capella, Gorate?	5	4	dk	dk	47	Fla	Fla		native	yes	non	
72	13	Capella, Joe			dk	dk	7	Fla	Fla		native	no	non	
72	14	Ortagus, Prudencia?	5	5	blk	dk	35	Fla	Fla	never	native	yes	non	
72	15	Ortagus, Edwalda	5	4	blk	dk	21	Fla	Fla		native	yes	non	
72	16	Ortagus, Francis	4	8	blk	dk	11	Fla	Fla		native	no	non	
72	17	Ortagus, Jerome	4	6	blk	dk	23	Fla	Fla	never	native	yes	none	Segar? Maker
72	18	Andreau, Stancia	5	0	blk	dk	19	Fla	Fla		native	yes	non	
72	19	Lucas, Bartolo	5	4	blk	dk	46	Italy	Fla	never	1854	yes	non	
72	20	Lucas, Catherine	5	0	blk	dk	44	Italy	Fla	never	1854	yes	non	
72	21	Lucas, Mary	5	2	blk	dk	15	Mass	Fla		1854	yes	non	
72	22	Lucas, Elizabeth			blk	dk	6	Fla	Fla			no	non	
72	23	Lucas, Thomas			blk	dk	5	Fla	Fla			no	non	
72	24	Lucas, Phiolmena			blk	dk	3	Fla	Fla			no	non	

Pg	No	Name	Height Ft	Height In	Eyes	Com-plexion	Age	Where born or contraband	Last residence	Where registered for draft or former owner	Date into Department	Oath of Allgn	No of Ration	Remarks
73	25	Smith, Oswald	5	7	blk	dk	47	Scotland	N Y	never	1864	yes	none	Storekeeper
73	26	Myers, Theo G.	5	5	Blue	f	46	Ger	Fla	never	1844	yes	none	Oyster Saloon
73	27	Myers, Louisa	5	4	blk	dk	48	GA	Fla		1844	yes	non	
73	28	Myers, Eveline	5	0	blk	dk	15	Fla	Fla			yes	non	
73	29	Myers, Ureka	4	6	blk	dk	12	Fla	Fla			no	non	
73	30	Myers, Geo J.	4	0	blk	dk	11	Fla	Fla			no	non	
73	31	Maulden, Eli	5	10	blk	dk	24	GA	Fla	never	1863	yes	none	ShopKeeper
73	32	Maulden, Jesse	5	10	blue	f	26	GA	Fla		1863	yes	none	ShopKeeper
73	33	Maulden, Nancy	5	4	blue	f	25	GA	Fla		1863	yes	non	
73	34	Driver, John	5	10	blue	f	56	SC	Fla	never	184_	yes	non	
73	35	Driver, Margaret	5	4	blue	f	41	SC	Fla		1864	yes	non	
73	36	Driver, Jas. M.	4	8	blue	f	14	Fla	Fla	never		no	non	
73	37	Hernandiz, Jos	5	7	dk	dk	29	Fla	Fla	never		yes	none	Deserter from Rebel Army
73	38	Watson, Robert B.	5	11	dk	dk	34	Me	Me	never	1864	yes	none	Clerk in a store
73	39	Ingersoll?, Nathaniel	5	10	dk	dk	25	Me	Me	Lincoln, Me	1864	no	none	Storekeeper
73	40	Iugersoll, Augustas	6	0	blue	f	24	Me	Me	Holton, Me	1864	no	none	Storekeeper
73	41	Thrilling, Solomon	5	6	blue	f	30	Poland	N Y	never	1864	yes	none	Storekeeper
73	42	Ingersoll, Daniel	5	9	blue	f	24	Me	Me	Lincoln, Me	1864	no	none	Sutler for 34th U.S.C.T
73	43	Thompson, Thos	5	8	blue	dk	25	Pen	Pen		1864	no	none	Late Captain in US Army
73	44	Stoddart, Morgan	5	11	dk	dk	38	N Y	Fla	never	1860	yes	none	Storekeeper
73	45	Thompson,Cutahain?	5	4	dk	dk	28	Fla	Fla			yes	non	
73	46	Thompson, Jennie			dk	dk	2	Fla	Fla			no	non	
73	47	Rector, Lizzie	5	0	dk	dk	18	Fla	Fla			no	non	
73	48	Dean, Maggie	5	4	dk	dk	18	Fla	Fla			yes	non	

Pg	No	Name	Height Ft	Height In	Eyes	Complexion	Age	Where born or contraband	Last residence	Where registered for draft or former owner	Date into Department	Oath of Allgn	No of Ration	Remarks
74	1	Martin,Wm H.	5	8	blu	f	23	N J	N J	never	1863	no	none	Clerk for C. A. Stevenson
74	2	Herthern, Chas. H.	5	9	blu	dk	50	Eng^{d}	N Y	never	1864	yes	none	Tailor (Merchant)
74	3	Ornsby, Robert	5	6	blu	dk	32	Ireland	N Y	never	1864	yes	none	Deserter from Rebel Army
74	4	Price, Jno W.	5	8	blu	f	38	GA	Fla	never	1848	yes	none	Storekeeper
74	5	Mott, Jno. C.	5	4	blu	dk	16	Fla	Fla	never		yes	none	Clerk for Price
74	6	Jones, Deury	5	10	blu	dk	26	Fla	Fla		native	yes	none	Clerk for Robinson
74	7	Msina, Dominego	5	3	dk	dk	19	Fla	Fla	never	native	yes	none	Clerk for C. Slager
74	8	Dylinski, Morris	5	7	dk	dk	23	Prussia	Fla	never	1850	yes	none	Clerk for C. Slager
74	9	McKinlay, Wm	5	3	blu	f	21	Pen	Pen	never	1864	no	none	Clerk for C. Slager
74	10	Almstead, Frank	5	4	blk	dk	24	Fla	Fla	never	native	yes	none	Deserter from Rebel Army
74	11	Strobel, Wash^{g}	5	11	blu	f	22	S C	Fla	never	1862	yes	none	Deserter from Rebel Army
74	12	Day, Saml L.	5	8	blk	dk	36	Va	Fla	never	1856	yes	none	Refugee
74	13	Andrew, Ignacio	5	7	grey	f	29	Fla	Fla	never	native	yes	none	Deserter
74	14	Case, Caleb A.	5	4	dk	dk	31	N Y	N Y	never	1864	yes	none	Jeweler in Pecks Store
74	15	Tomlinson, Mark	5	8	blu	f	32	Conn	Conn	never	1864	yes	none	Sutler for 3rd U.S.C.T
74	16	Tomlinson, Lizzie	5	4	blu	f	26	Conn	Conn		1864	no	non	
74	17	Tomlinson, Jennie			blu	f	4	Conn	Conn		1864	no	non	
74	18	Goode, Thos	5	6	blu	f	17	Fla	Fla	never	native	yes	none	Clerk for Tomlinson
74	19	Bruce, Elizha	5	9	blu	f	29	NH	NH	never	1864	yes	none	Clerk
74	20	Bruce, Rafila	5	4	blu	f	28	Fla	Fla		native	yes	non	
74	21	Turner, Jno. A.	5	6	blk	dk	39	Me	Me	never	1864	no	none	Clerk for Tomlinson
74	22	Manning, Geo	5	8	blu	f	22	Germ	N Y	never	1864	yes	none	Clerk for Tomlinson
74	23	Moore, Jno	5	8	dk	dk	55	Maine	Me	never	1864	yes	none	Store Keeper
74	24	Roberts, Warren S.	5	10	blu	dk	40	Me	Fla	never	1850	yes	none	Clerk ~~for Moore~~

Pg	No	Name	Height Ft	Height In	Eyes	Complexion	Age	Where born or contraband	Last residence	Where registered for draft or former owner	Date into Department	Oath of Allgn	No of Ration	Remarks
75	25	Henry, Edward	5	7	blue	f	28	Scotland	N York	never	1864	yes	1	Govt. Employee
75	26	Fraser, Geo. W.	5	0	blue	f	17	Fla	Fla	never		yes	1	Conney? Clerk
75	27	Powers, Jim	6	2	blue	f	32	Ireland	N Y	never	1864	yes	1	Govt. Employee
75	28	Penny, Jas.	5	11	dk	dk	48	Fla	Key West	never	1864	yes	1	Govt. Employee
75	29	Bicsney?, M.	5	5	blue	f	21	Ireland	N Y	never	1864	yes	1	Govt. Employee
75	30	Brady, Jas.	5	9	blue	f	30	Ireland	N Y	never	1864	yes	1	Govt. Employee
75	31	Murray, Romeo					40	Contr		Willy, Chas.			1	River Pilot
75	32	Burton, Canto					55	Contr		Willy, Chas.			1	River Pilot
75	33	Sheppard, Wm F.	5	8	blue	f	38	Me	Me	never			1	Govt Employee
75	34	Peterson, Mike	6	0	blue	f	23	Fla	Fla	never			1	Govt Employee
75	35	Wilson, Rebecca	5	4	blue	f	33	Fla	Fla		1864	yes	none	
75	36	Wilson, Lucinda			blue	f	8	Fla	Fla		1864		no	
75	37	Wilson, Mary			blue	fair	4	Fla	Fla				no	

"CENSUS" DEPARTMENT OF THE SOUTH - NOVEMBER, 1864

Pg	No	Name	Height Ft	Height In	Eyes	Com-plexion	Age	Where born or contraband	Last residence	Where registered for draft or former owner	Date into Department	Oath of Allgn	No of Ration	Remarks
76	1	Franklin, Francis	5	11	dark	dark	45	Mass.	Mass	Boston	1864	yes	none	
76	2	Boyd, John A.	5	10	dark	dark	24	N J	S C	never	1864	yes	none	Clerk for Howard
76	3	Abrams, John H.	5	4	dark	dark	16	N Y	N Y	never	1864	no	none	Clerk for Howard
76	4	Richard, Clinton	5	4	dark	dark	16	Fla	Fla	never	native	yes	none	Clerk for Howard
76	5	Sharer, Bernard	5	8	dark	dark	40	Ger	N Y	never	1864	yes	none	Baker
76	6	Holinever, Ditmer	5	10	Blue	fair	19	Ger	Baltimore	never	1864	yes	none	Baker
76	7	Loach, Wm	4	10	Blue	fair	38	Eng^d	Fla	never	1856	yes	none	ShopKeeper
76	8	Loach, Rachel	5	4	Blue	fair	22	Fla	Fla		native	yes	none	
76	9	Jones, Henry			Blue	fair	8	Fla	Fla		native	no	none	
76	10	Eilbeek, Wm	5	6	Blue	fair	39	Eng^d	Fla	never	1851	yes	none	ShopKeeper
76	11	Tracey, John			Blue	fair	10	Fla	Fla			no	none	
76	12	Eilbeek, Danl			Blue	fair	6	Fla	Fla			no	none	
76	13	Bele, John	5	8	Blue	fair	73	Scotland	Fla		1832	yes	none	Invalid
76	14	Porter, Jos.	5	10	Blue	fair	47	NY	Fla	never	1836	yes	none	Govt. Employee
76	15	Sammies?, Jno. S.	5	10	blue	dark	58	N Y	Fla	never	1830	yes	none	Store Keeper
76	16	Sammies?, Ezmo	5	10	dark	dark	28	Fla	Fla	never	native	yes	none	Clerk
76	17	Sammies?, Egbert	5	6	dark	dark	17	Fla	Fla	never	native	yes	none	Clerk
76	18	Damiani, Damiano	5	10	Blue	fair	44	Italy	Fla	never	1856	no	none	Alien-restaurant
76	19	Damiani, Cath^en	5	4	Blue	fair	30	France	Fla	never	1856	yes	none	
76	20	Damiani, Sophy			dark	dark	1	Fla	Fla	never		no	none	
76	21	Scott, David	5	9	dark	dark	23	N Y	N Y	never	1863	no	none	Cook in restaurant
76	22	Chase, Benj. K.	5	10	dark	dark	32	Mass.	Mass.	never	1864	yes	none	Eatery Saloon
76	23	Nicholas,Constantine	5	8	dark	dark	49	Greece	Fla	never	1858	yes	none	Eatery Saloon
76	24	Doutes, Robt.	5	11	dark	dark	54	Mass.	Mass.	never	1864	yes	none	Cook in Saloon

Pg	No	Name	Height Ft	Height In	Eyes	Com-plexion	Age	Where born or contraband	Last residence	Where registered for draft or former owner	Date into Department	Oath of Allgn	No of Ration	Remarks
77	25	Witchen, Clause	5	9	blue	f	38	Ger.	Fla	never	1844	yes	none	ShopKeeper
77	26	Howard, Frank	5	10	blue	f	31	Me	Me	never	1864	yes	none	Sutter for 107th Ohio Vols.
77	27	Seiley?, Harry	5	8	dk	dk	24	N Y	N Y	never	1864	no	none	Engineer
77	28	Driggs, John S.	5	8	blue	f	37	N Y	Fla.	never	1864	no	none	Store Keeper
77	29	Alley, Reuben	5	8	blue	f	56	Mass.	Fla.	never	1854	no	none	Machinist
77	30	Purt, Robert	5	9	blue	f	52	Scotland	N Y	never	1864	no	none	Govt Employee
77	31	Savage, Jesse L.	6	0	blue	f	45	Me	Con	never	1864	yes	none	Sutler for "Yellow Bluff"
77	32	Courier, Edw[d]	5	10	dk	dk	43	Mass.	Mass.	never	1864	yes	none	Sutler 4th Mass. Cavalry
77	33	Robinson, Isaac	5	9	blue	f	51	N Y	N Y	never	1864	yes	none	Clerk in a store
77	34	Mitchell, Edw[d]	5	6	blue	f	50	England	Fla		1839	yes	none	Unemployed
77	35	Mitchell, Cath[en]	5	4	blue	f	41	Ireland	Fla		1839	yes	none	
77	36	Messman?, Marg[t]	5	4	blue	f	35	Fla	Fla			yes	none	
77	37	Messman?, Jas.	4	7	blue	f	13	Fla	Fla			no	none	
77	38	Messman?, Emma	4	4	blue	f	11	Fla	Fla			no	none	
77	39	Messman?, Sarah			blue	f	8	Fla	Fla			no	none	
77	40	Osteen, Leonard	5	8	blue	f	45	Fla	Fla	never		yes	1	Government Employee
77	41	Osteen, Scillah	5	4	blue	f	38	Fla	Fla			yes	none	
77	42	Osteen, Margaret	5	3	blue	f	22	Fla	Fla			yes	none	
77	43	Osteen, Lelitia	5	4	blue	f	18	Fla	Fla			yes	none	
77	44	Osteen, Berry	4	8	blue	f	16	Fla	Fla			no	none	
77	45	Osteen, Nancy	4	4	blue	f	12	Fla	Fla			no	none	
77	46	Osteen, Noah			blue	f	10	Fla	Fla			no	none	
77	47	Osteen, Elias			blue	f	7	Fla	Fla			no	none	
77	48	Molphus, Lydia	5	4	blue	f	38	Fla	Fla			yes	none	

"CENSUS" DEPARTMENT OF THE SOUTH - NOVEMBER, 1864

Pg	No	Name	Height Ft	Height In	Eyes	Com-plexion	Age	Where born or contraband	Last residence	Where registered for draft or former owner	Date into Department	Oath of Allgn	No of Ration	Remarks
78	1	Molphus, Ezekiel			blue	fair	10	Fla	Fla			no	none	
78	2	Molphus, Danl			blue	fair	7	Fla	Fla			no	none	
78	3	Molphus, Isham			blue	fair	5	Fla	Fla			no	none	
78	4	Smith, Jas	5	10	blue	fair	33	GA	Fla	never	1858	yes	1	Govt. Employee
78	5	Smith, Olive	5	8	blue	fair	28	GA	Fla		1858	yes	none	
78	6	Smith, Wm			blue	fair	6	Fla	Fla			no	none	
78	7	Smith, John			blue	fair	4	Fla	Fla			no	none	
78	8	Smith, Mary			blue	fair	2	Fla	Fla			no	none	
78	9	Ault, Harriet	5	4	blue	fair	35	Fla	Fla			no	none	
78	10	Ault, Drucity?	5	0	blue	fair	16	Fla	Fla			no	none	
78	11	Ault, Georgian	4	8	blue	fair	13	Fla	Fla			no	none	
78	12	Ault, Harriet	4	4	blue	fair	11	Fla	Fla			no	none	
78	13	Ault, Infant			blue	fair	1	Fla	Fla			no	none	
78	14	Taylor, Edith	5	4	blue	fair	29	Fla	Fla			yes	none	
78	15	Capps, Michael	5	10	blue	fair	38	GA	Fla	never	1857	yes	1	Govt. Employee
78	16	Capps, Eliz[th]	5	4	blue	fair	29	GA	Fla		1857	yes	none	compus mentis?
78	17	Capps, Henry	4	8	blue	fair	13	GA	Fla	never	1857	no	none	
78	18	Shad, Susan			blue	fair	4	Fla	Fla			no	none	
78	19	Shad, Robert			blue	fair	3	Fla	Fla			no	none	
78	20	Bairden, Howell	6	0	blue	fair	42	SC	Fla		1852	yes	none	unemployed
78	21	Bairden, Lizzie	5	4	blk	dk	25	GA	Fla		1859	no	none	
78	23	Holmes, Caroline J.	5	3	blue	fair	24	Mass.	Fla		1861	yes	none	
78	24	Jones, Peter	5	11	blue	dk	33	N Y	N Y	N York	1863	no	none	Capt.Sh- "Wyoming"

Pg	No	Name	Height Ft	Height In	Eyes	Com-plexion	Age	Where born or contraband	Last residence	Where registered for draft or former owner	Date into Department	Oath of Allgn	No of Ration	Remarks
79	25	Mainard, Abel	5	7	blue	f	61	NC	Fla	never	1859	yes	no	Unemployed
79	26	Mainard, Jas.	5	8	blue	f	38	NC	Fla	never	1854	yes	no	Preparing to Farm
79	27	Mainard, Sarah F.	5	4	blue	f	28	Fla	Fla			yes	no	
79	28	Mainard, Mary A.			blue	f	6	Fla	Fla			no	no	
79	29	Mainard, Ella S.			blue	f	4	Fla	Fla			no	no	
79	30	Register, Maria	5	4	blk	dk	39	GA	Fla		1844	yes	no	
79	31	Register, Mary A.	5	4	blk	dk	16	Fla	Fla			yes	no	
79	32	Register, Moses	4	6	blk	dk	12	Fla	Fla			no	no	
79	33	Lee, Charlotte	5	4	blk	dk	22	GA	Fla		1864	yes	no	
79	34	Oliver, Chas.	5	7	blue	f	76	GA	Fla		1831	yes	21/2	Cripple
79	35	Oliver, Mary	5	4	blue	f	62	GA	Fla		1831	yes	none	
79	36	Oliver, Thos	5	6	blue	f	19	Fla	Fla	never		yes	none	
79	37	Oliver, Mary	5	4	blue	f	17	Fla	Fla			yes	none	
79	38	Oliver, Chapman	4	6	blue	f	13	Fla	Fla	never		yes	none	
79	39	Summers, Sarah	5	4	blue	f	36	Fla	Fla			yes	none	
79	40	Summers, Mary	5	4	blue	f	16	Fla	Fla			yes	none	
79	41	Summers, Charley	4	10	blue	f	15	Fla	Fla	never		no	none	
79	42	Summers, Fanny			blue	f	12	Fla	Fla	never		no	none	
79	43	Summers, Michael			blue	f	8	Fla	Fla			no	none	
79	44	Summers, Owen			blue	f	5	Fla	Fla			no	none	
79	45	Toms, Sarah	5	4	blue	f	18	Fla	Fla			no	none	
79	46	McCrea, Geo	5	9	blue	f	17	Fla	Fla	never		yes	none	Unemployed
79	47	Diggins, W^{m}	5	10	dk	dk	43	GA	Fla	never	1853	yes	none	Unemployed
79	48	Diggins, Jack	4	8	dk	dk	46	GA	Fla	never	1853	no	none	Unemployed

Pg	No	Name	Height Ft	Height In	Eyes	Com-plexion	Age	Where born or contraband	Last residence	Where registered for draft or former owner	Date into Department	Oath of Allgn	No of Ration	Remarks
80	1	Barker, Charlotte	5	4	blue	f	28	Fla	Fla		native	no	none	Non compus mentis?
80	2	Bardin, Mary E.	5	4	blue	f	28	Ireland	Fla		1848	yes	none	Keeps Boarding House
80	3	Bardin, Mary C.	4	8	blue	f	13	Fla	Fla			no	none	
80	4	Bardin, Jos.			blue	f	9	Fla	Fla			no	none	
80	5	Bardin, Wm			blue	f	3	Fla	Fla			no	none	
80	6	Coburn, Henry	5	9	blue	f	32	Me	Me	Lincoln	1864	no	none	Trader
80	7	Rogers, Washington	6	0	blue	f	47	Ala	Fla	never	1859	yes	none	Hotel Keeper
80	8	Rogers, Rebecca	5	4	blue	f	49	GA	Fla		1859	yes	none	
80	9	Rogers, Geo. W.	5	6	blue	f	17	GA	Fla	never	1859	yes	none	
80	10	Rogers, Henry S.	5	2	blue	f	15	Fla	Fla	never		yes	none	
80	11	Brooks, Lizzie	5	5	blue	f	24	GA	Fla		1859	yes	none	School Teacher
80	12	Goode?, Florida V.	5	4	dk	dk	19	Fla	Fla			yes	none	School Teacher
80	13	DaCosta, Aaron W.	6	0	blue	f	41	S.C.	Fla	never	1850	yes	none	
80	14	DaCosta, Mary M.	5	4	blue	f	43	S.C.	Fla		1850	yes	none	Custodian of Public records of Duval County late Clerk of Circuit Court
80	15	DaCosta, Jennie E.	5	4	blue	f	18	S.C.	Fla		1850	yes	none	
80	16	DaCosta, Maggie J.	5	5	blue	f	16	S.C.	Fla		1850	yes	none	
80	17	DaCosta, Aaron J.	4	10	blue	f	13	Fla	Fla			yes	none	
80	18	DaCosta, Charles W.			blue	f	8	Fla	Fla			no	none	
80	19	Craig, Carrie M.	5	4	dk	dk	27	N Y	Fla		1859	yes	none	
80	20	Craig, Charley			blue	f	2	Fla	Fla			no	none	
80	21	Roberts, Wm. P.	5	8	blue	f	24	GA	Fla	never	1844	yes	none	unemployed
80	22	Causey, Geo.	5	11	blue	f	52	Pen	Fla	never	1833	yes	none	Ship Carpenter
80	23	Gordon, Kessiah	5	4	blue	f	30	Fla	Fla			yes	none	
80	24	Gordon, Sarah	3	2	dk	dk	15	Fla	Fla			no	none	

Pg	No	Name	Height Ft	Height In	Eyes	Complexion	Age	Where born or contraband	Last residence	Where registered for draft or former owner	Date into Department	Oath of Allgn	No of Ration	Remarks
81	25	Flinn, Murian			blue	f	9	Fla	Fla			no	none	
81	26	Clarke, Wm.	5	7	blue	dk	47	Scotland	Fla	never	1850	yes	none	Unemployed
81	27	Clarke, Margaret	5	3	blue	dk	30	Scotland	Fla		1850	yes	none	
81	28	Mahoney, Mathew			blue	dk	6	Fla	Fla		1850	no	none	
81	29	Mahoney, Cath[m]	5	4	blue	dk	28	Ireland	Fla		1850	yes	none	
81	30	Mahoney, Marg[t]			blue	dk	4	Fla	Fla			no	none	
81	31	Mahoney, Patrick			blue	dk	3	Fla	Fla			no	none	
81	32	Dunn, Geo			blue	dk	9	Fla	Fla			no	none	
81	33	Hutchings, Thos	5	8	dk	dk	31	Me	Fla	never	1864	no	none	Store Keeper
81	34	Hutchings, Sarah	5	2	blue	f	28	Ireland	Fla		1864	yes	none	
81	35	Hutchings, Mary			blue	f	5	Fla	Fla		1864	no	none	
81	36	Marthel, Margaret	5	4	blue	f	24	Canada	Fla		1864	no	none	
81	37	Monroe, Mary	5	3	blue	f	27	Ireland	Fla		1864	yes	none	
81	38	Hern, Dinnah	5	5	blk	dk	25	Ireland	Fla		1864	yes	none	
81	39	Clark, Asa	5	11	blue	f	30	Fla	Fla	never		yes	none	Shop Keeper
81	40	Lyson, Wm. O.	5	8	blue	f	29	Fla	Fla	never			none	Shop Keeper
81	41	Stickney, John K.	5	9	blue	f	36	Vt	Vt.	never	1864	yes	none	Local Special Treasury Agent
81	42	Stickney, Mary	5	0	blue	f	26	Mich.	Vt.		1864	no	none	
81	43	Stickney,Clementine			blue	f	6	Mich.	Vt.		1864	no	none	
81	44	Stickney, Lilian			blue	f	3	Mich.	Vt.		1864	no	none	
81	45	Stickney, Sidney			blue	f	2	Mich.	Vt.		1864	no	none	
81	46	Othello, Mary	5	3	blue	f	30	Va.	Fla		1858	yes	none	
81	47	Othello, Charles			blue	f	6	Fla	Fla			no	none	
81	48	Linton, Maria	5	3	blue	f	48	Fla	Fla			yes	none	

Pg	No	Name	Height Ft	Height In	Eyes	Com-plexion	Age	Where born or contraband	Last residence	Where registered for draft or former owner	Date into Department	Oath of Allgn	No of Ration	Remarks
82	1	Linton, Isabella	5	3	blue	f	19	Fla	Fla			yes	none	
82	2	Linton, Wm. G.	5	0	blue	f	17	Fla	Fla			yes	none	
82	3	Linton, Fanny E.	5	0	blue	f	15	Fla	Fla			no	none	
82	4	Linton, John H.	4	6	blue	f	12	Fla	Fla			no	none	
82	5	Oak, Calvin	5	8	blue	f	58	Vt	Fla	never	1850	yes	none	Clerk for C. L. Robinson
82	6	Oak, Eliza. A.	5	2	blue	f	57	Mass.	Fla		1850	yes	none	
82	7	Peterson, Cath^{m}	5	4	blue	f	22	GA	Fla		1863	yes	none	
82	8	Peterson, Louisa			blue	f	6	Fla	Fla			no	none	
82	9	Peterson, Alfreo			blue	f	4	Fla	Fla			no	none	
82	10	Peterson, Henry			blue	f	1	Fla	Fla			no	none	
82	11	Henry, Howell	5	5	blue	f	55	GA	Fla		1840	yes	none	Invalid
82	12	Biggs, Pamlia	5	5	dk	dk	38	GA	Fla		1840	yes	none	
82	13	Biggs, Wm. H.			dk	dk	3	Fla	Fla			no	none	
82	14	Biggs, Sarah A.			dk	dk	8	Fla	Fla			no	none	
82	15	Howell, Cimenthy	4	3	blue	f	13	Fla	Fla			no	none	
82	16	Dartis, Robt.	5	6	blk	dk	50	Fla	Fla	never	1859	yes	none	Laborer
82	17	Dartis, Mary	5	2	blk	dk	40	Fla	Fla		1859	yes	none	
82	18	Dartis, Robert	4	4	blk	dk	15	Fla	Fla		1859	no	none	
82	19	Dartis, Peter	4	3	blk	dk	15	Fla	Fla		1859	no	none	
82	20	Dartis, John	3	10	blk	dk	12	Fla	Fla			no	none	
82	21	Dartis, Thos.			blk	dk	7	Fla	Fla			no	none	
82	22	Poinsett, Cath^{m}	5	6	blk	dk	45	Fla	Fla			yes	none	
82	23	Poinsett, Mary L	5	3	blk	dk	27	Fla	Fla			yes	none	
82	24	Rivas, Joseph	5	5	blk	dk	30	Spain	Fla		1858	yes	none	Baker

Pg	No	Name	Height		Eyes	Com-plexion	Age	Where born or contraband	Last residence	Where registered for draft or former owner	Date into Department	Oath of Allgn	No of Ration	Remarks
			Ft	In										
83	25	Cole, Chas.	5	4	blk	dk	19	Fla	Fla	never		yes	none	
83	26	Koopman, Henry	5	3	blue	f	40	Hanover	Fla	never	1845	yes	none	Baker
83	27	Parr, Mary A.	5	4	blue	f	42	S.C.	Fla		1864	yes	none	
83	28	Parr, Miller	5	5	blue	f	18	S.C.	Fla		1864	yes	none	
83	29	Lowe, Wesley	5	7	blue	dk	23	Fla	Fla	never	1848	yes	none	Laborer
83	30	Lowe, Harriet	5	2	blue	dk	20	Fla	Fla			yes	none	
83	31	Lowe, Wm.			blue	dk	3	Fla	Fla			no	none	
83	32	Parr, Christopher			blue	dk	10	Fla	Fla			no	none	
83	33	Hall, Wm. J.	6	0	blk	dk	45	N. C.	Fla	never	1845	yes	1	Govt. Employee
83	34	Hall, Mary Ann	5	5	blue	f	37	GA	Fla		1845	yes	none	
83	35	Hall, Jas. H.	5	3	blue	f	16	Fla	Fla	never		yes	none	
83	36	Hall, Alexander			blue	f	8	Fla	Fla			no	none	
83	37	Hall, Captolia			blue	f	6	Fla	Fla			no	none	
83	38	Hall, Leton	.		blue	f	3	Fla	Fla			no	none	
83	39	Hall, Rocksy Ann			blue	f	1	Fla	Fla			no	none	
83	40	Hughes, Sarah	5	0	grey	f	50	GA	Fla		1835	no	none	
83	41	Hughes, Reuben	5	2	grey	f	25	Fla	Fla	never		yes	none	Unemployed
83	42	Hall, Sarah M.	5	0	grey	f	17	Fla	Fla			yes	none	
83	43	Hughes, Geo. W.	5	1	grey	f	16	Fla	Fla	never		yes	none	
83	44	Kelly, Jas.	5	5	grey	f	30	Fla	Fla	never		yes	none	
83	45	Kelly, Elizabeth	5	0	grey	f	14	Fla	Fla			yes	none	
83	46	Kelly, Lucy	4	6	grey	f	13	Fla	Fla			no	none	
83	47	Kelly, Mary			grey	f	8	Fla	Fla			no	none	
83	48	Hodges, Marg	5	5	grey	f	39	Fla	Fla			no	none	

Pg	No	Name	Height Ft	Height In	Eyes	Com-plexion	Age	Where born or contraband	Last residence	Where registered for draft or former owner	Date into Department	Oath of Allgn	No of Ration	Remarks
84	1	Chapel, Robert	5	3	blue	f	36	England	Fla	never	1854	no	none	Unemployed
84	2	Chapel, Ellen	5	2	blue	f	35	England	Fla		1854	yes	none	
84	3	Chapel, Wm.			blue	f	8	Fla	Fla		1854	no	none	
84	4	Chapel, John			blue	f	4	Fla	Fla			no	none	
84	5	Chapel, Edw[d]			blue	f	1	Fla	Fla			no	none	
84	6	Baya, Jos	5	7	blue	f	50	Fla	Fla	never	native	yes	none	Drayman
84	7	Baya, Catharine	5	4	blue	f	48	Fla	Fla			yes	none	
84	8	Baya, Constanein	5	3	blue	f	22	Fla	Fla			yes	none	
84	9	Baya, Christina	5	4	blue	f	20	Fla	Fla			yes	none	
84	10	Baya, Oliver	4	5	blue	f	14	Fla	Fla			no	none	
84	11	Baya, Philip	4	0	blue	f	11	Fla	Fla			no	none	
84	12	Baya, Mary			blue	f	8	Fla	Fla			no	none	
84	13	Leonardy, Mercella	5	3	blue	f	24	Fla	Fla			no	none	
84	14	Leonardy, Rosa			blue	f	4	Fla	Fla			no	none	
84	15	Boatwright, W[m.]			blk	dk	3	Fla	Fla			no	none	
84	16	Boatwright, Eliz[th]	5	2	blk	dk	25	Fla	Fla			yes	none	
84	17	Boatwright, John			blk	dk	5	Fla	Fla			no	none	
84	18	Bowen, Clementine	5	0	blue	f	36	GA	Fla		1864	no	4	By order of Pro. Marshal
84	19	Bowen, Richard	4	2	blue	f	15	GA	Fla		1864	no	none	By order of Pro. Marshal
84	20	Bowen, Wright	4	3	blue	f	14	GA	Fla		1864	no	none	By order of Pro. Marshal
84	21	Bowen, Sarah	4	0	blue	f	13	GA	Fla		1864	no	none	By order of Pro. Marshal
84	22	Bowen, Abner			blue	f	8	GA	Fla		1864	no	none	By order of Pro. Marshal
84	23	Bowen, Jas.			blue	f	6	GA	Fla		1864	no	none	By order of Pro. Marshal
84	24	Bowen, Benj			blue	f	4	GA	Fla		1864	no	none	By order of Pro. Marshal

Pg	No	Name	Height Ft	Height In	Eyes	Com-plexion	Age	Where born or contraband	Last residence	Where registered for draft or former owner	Date into Department	Oath of Allgn	No of Ration	Remarks
85	25	Youngblood, Nancy	5	4	blk	dk	39	GA	Fla		1848	yes	3	Pro. Marshal's order
85	26	Youngblood, John	4	0	blk	dk	11	Fla	Fla			no		
85	27	Youngblood, Eliza			blk	dk	13	Fla	Fla			no		
85	28	Ferrand, John L.	5	4	blk	dk	34	N. C.	Fla		1856	yes	1	Govt. Employee
85	29	Ferrand, Mary Ann	5	4	blk	dk	24	Fla	Fla			yes	none	
85	30	Ferrand, Stephen	5	6	blk	dk	25	N. C.	Fla		1856	yes	1	Govt. Employee
85	31	Ferrand, Mary J.	5	4	blue	f	25	Fla	Fla			yes	none	
85	32	Ferrand, Julia			blue	f	4	Fla	Fla			no	none	
85	33	Lacourse, Jos.	5	0	blue	f	44	Canada	Fla		1858	yes	1	Govt. Employee
85	34	Lacourse, Lucy	5	4	dk	dk	40	S.C.	Fla		1858	yes	none	
85	35	Lacourse, Emma	4	10	dk	dk	14	GA	Fla		1858	no	none	
85	36	Lacourse, Mary Ann	4	8	dk	dk	12	GA	Fla		1858	no	none	
85	37	Lacourse, Jos.			dk	dk	7	Fla	Fla			no	none	
85	38	Lacourse, Elmira			dk	dk	3	Fla	Fla			no	none	
85	39	Cooper, Mary	5	4	dk	dk	43	Fla	Fla			yes	none	
85	40	Cooper, Margaret	5	2	blue	f	18	GA	Fla		1858	yes	none	
85	41	Cooper, Charles	5	3	dk	f	15	N Y	Fla		1858	yes	none	
85	42	Cooper, Isaac			dk	f	10	N Y	Fla		1858	no	none	
85	43	Thebout, Bartolo	6	0	dk	dk	42	Fla	Fla	never		yes	1	Superintendent Mill Govt. Employee
85	44	Thebout, Mary	5	4	dk	dk	38	Fla	Fla	never		yes	none	
85	45	Pupaul, Oscar	5	3	dk	dk	20	Fla	Fla	never		yes	none	
85	46	Pupaul, Foreman	5	3	dk	dk	18	Fla	Fla	never		yes	none	
85	47	Thebout, Bartolo	4	0	dk	dk	10	Fla	Fla			no	none	
85	48	Thebout, Josh			dk	dk	10	Fla	Fla			no	none	

Pg	No	Name	Height Ft	Height In	Eyes	Com-plexion	Age	Where born or contraband	Last residence	Where registered for draft or former owner	Date into Department	Oath of Allgn	No of Ration	Remarks
86	1	Thebout, Mary			blue	f	6	Fla	Fla			no	none	
86	2	Thebout, Wm. R.			blue	f	1	Fla	Fla			no	none	
86	3	Andrew, Ignacio	5	6	blue	dk	28	Fla	Fla			yes	none	Unemployed
86	4	Andrew, Magdalene	5	0	dark	dk	24	Fla	Fla			yes	none	
86	5	Andrew, John			blue	f	7	Fla	Fla			no	none	
86	6	Andrew, Rafile			blue	f	3	Fla	Fla			no	none	
86	7	Andrew, Ignacio			blue	f	1	Fla	Fla			no	none	
86	8	Hermandez, Mary	5	3	blue	f	48	Fla	Fla			no	none	
86	9	Hermandez, Theodocia	4	11	blue	f	15	Fla	Fla			no	none	
86	10	Shad, Mary E.	5	4	blue	f	36	Fla	Fla			no	none	Boarding House Keeper
86	11	Shad, Soloman F.	4	8	blue	f	14	Fla	Fla			no	none	
86	12	Shad, Anninous?			blue	f	10	Fla	Fla			no	none	
86	13	Shad, Florida			blue	f	9	Fla	Fla			no	none	
86	14	Shad, Henry			blue	f	7	Fla	Fla			no	none	
86	15	Ponce, Mary	5	4	dk	dk	51	Fla	Fla			yes	none	
86	16	Ponce, Espranza	4	11	dk	dk	24	Fla	Fla			yes	none	
86	17	Ponce, Joseph	4	8	dk	dk	14	Fla	Fla			no	none	
86	18	Ponce, Virginia	4	3	dk	dk	13	Fla	Fla			no	none	
86	19	Ponce, John	5	5	dk	dk	50	Fla	Fla			yes	none	
86	20	Santo, Jose	5	0	dk	dk	50	Fla	Fla			yes	none	
86	21	Barry, Morris	5	3	blue	f	48	Ireland	Fla		1840	yes	none	
86	22	Ortagus, Marg[t]			blue	f	8	Fla	Fla			no	none	
86	23	Ortagus, John A.			blue	f	5	Fla	Fla			no	none	
86	24	Ortagus, Leron D.			blue	f	2	Fla	Fla			no	none	

Pg	No	Name	Height Ft	Height In	Eyes	Com-plexion	Age	Where born or contraband	Last residence	Where registered for draft or former owner	Date into Department	Oath of Allgn	No of Ration	Remarks
87	25	Hernandez, Jos	5	5	dk	dk	25	Fla	Fla	never	native	yes	none	Boot and shoe maker
87	26	Asino, Mingo	5	5	dk	dk	20	Fla	Fla	never	native	yes	none	Clerk for Slager
87	27	Slager, Chas.	5	8	dk	dk	43	Ger.	Fla	never	1851	no	none	Store Keeper
87	28	Segue?, Ellen	5	0	blk	dk	19	Fla	Fla			no	none	
87	29	Fatis, Rebecca S.	5	4	blk	dk	18	Fla	Fla			no	none	
87	30	Gilbert, Mary	5	0	blk	dk	19	Fla	Fla			yes	none	
87	31	Gilbert, Jno. S.	6	0	blue	f	40	Fla	Fla	never		yes	none	Farmer
87	32	Wingate, Mary	5	2	blk	dk	32	Fla	Fla			yes	none	
87	33	Wingate, Wm	4	8	blk	dk	13	Fla	Fla			no	none	
87	34	Wingate, Susan	4	4	blk	dk	10	Fla	Fla			no	none	
87	35	Wingate, George			blk	dk	6	Fla	Fla			no	none	
87	36	Wingate, Alice			blk	dk	4	Fla	Fla			no	none	
87	37	Wingate, Martha	5	0	blk	dk	16	Fla	Fla			no	none	
87	38	Land, Catherine	5	3	blk	f	35	GA	GA		1850	yes	3	By order Pro. Marshal
87	39	Land, Cornelia			blk	dk	12	Fla	Fla		1850	no		
87	40	Land, Constance			blk	dk	9	Fla	Fla			no		
87	41	Land, Susan			blk	dk	7	Fla	Fla			no		
87	42	Land, Frances			blk	dk	5	Fla	Fla			no		
87	43	Falany, Emanuel	5	8	blk	dk	39	Fla	Fla			yes	1	Govt. Employee
87	44	Falany, Virginia	5	4	blk	dk	21	Fla	Fla			yes		
87	45	Falany, Geo.			blk	dk	9	Fla	Fla			no		
87	46	Genevar, Sabastian	5	7	blk	dk	48	Fla	Fla			yes	1	Govt. Employee
87	47	Genevar, Mary	5	4	blk	dk	46	Fla	Fla			yes		
87	48	Genevar, Francis	5	2	blk	dk	19	Fla	Fla			yes	none	

Pg	No	Name	Height Ft	Height In	Eyes	Com-plexion	Age	Where born or contraband	Last residence	Where registered for draft or former owner	Date into Department	Oath of Allgn	No of Ration	Remarks
88	1	Genevar, Franklin	5	0	blk	dk	17	Fla	Fla	never		yes	none	
88	2	Genevar, Peter	5	0	blk	dk	15	Fla	Fla			yes	none	
88	3	Genevar, Mary	4	0	blk	dk	11	Fla	Fla			no	none	
88	4	Genevar, Wm.			blk	dk	8	Fla	Fla			no	none	
88	5	Tyler, Marg[t]	5	0	blue	f	47	S.C.	Fla		1845	yes	none	Keeps Boarding House
88	6	Tyler, Mary W.			blue	f	25	S.C.	Fla		1845	yes	none	School Teacher
88	7	Tyler, Orville	4	6	blue	f	13	Fla	Fla			no	none	
88	8	Tyler, Franklin			blue	f	9	Fla	Fla			no	none	
88	9	Kerwick, Ellenor	5	5	dk	dk	65	Canada	Fla		1853	yes	none	School Teacher
88	10	Moody, Paran	5	9	dk	dk	55	Me.	Fla	never	1845	yes	none	
88	11	Moody, Mary L.	5	4	blue	f	35	Fla	Fla			yes	none	
88	12	Moody, Mary A.			blue	f	10	Fla	Fla			no	none	
88	13	Moody, Hattie			blue	f	7	Fla	Fla			no	none	
88	14	Moody, Lucy			blue	f	5	Fla	Fla			no	none	
88	15	Doggett, Maria	5	0	dk	dk	53	Mass.	Fla		1835	yes	none	
88	16	Doggett, John L.	5	9	dk	dk	37	Fla	Fla	never		yes	none	Deserter from Rebel Army
88	17	Doggett, Maria C.	4	10	dk	dk	22	Fla	Fla			yes	none	
88	18	Hanford, Alfred M.	6	0	dk	dk	27	Fla	Fla	never		yes	none	Carpenter
88	19	Hanford, Josephin	5	0	dk	dk	26	NC	Fla		1859	yes	none	
88	20	Hanford, Wm. L			dk	dk	3	Fla	Fla			no	none	
88	21	Douglas, Hannah	4	10	dk	dk	66	Con.	Fla		1840	yes	none	Wife of late Hon.Thos.Douglas
88	22	Burrett, Lucy A.	5	4	dk	dk	48	Con.	Fla		1840	yes	none	Wife of Judge Burrett
88	23	Shields, Rosannah	5	2	blue	fair	29	Ireland	N Y		1864	yes	none	
88	24	Shields, Timothy	5	8	blue	fair	40	Ireland	N Y	never	1864	yes	1	Govt. Employee

Pg	No	Name	Height Ft	Height In	Eyes	Com-plexion	Age	Where born or contraband	Last residence	Where registered for draft or former owner	Date into Department	Oath of Allgn	No of Ration	Remarks
89	25	Ochus, Carroll	5	2	dk	dk	2	Fla	Fla	never	native	yes	none	
89	26	Ochus, Kate	4	10	dk	dk	13	Fla	Fla		native	no	none	
89	27	Ochus, Andrew J.	4	5	dk	dk	11	Fla	Fla		native	no	none	
89	28	Ochus, Gustave			dk	dk	9	Fla	Fla		native	no	none	
89	29	Ochus, Lula			dk	dk	7	Fla	Fla		native	no	none	
89	30	Taylor, Catharine	5	0	dk	dk	69	Fla	Fla		native	yes	none	Keeps "Taylor House"
89	31	McFaddle, Anna	5	0	dk	dk	35	Ireland	Fla		1864	yes	none	Servant
89	32	Reed, Edward	5	10	blue	f	22	Wis.	Fla	never	1864	yes	none	Post Master
89	33	Reed, Helen	4	11	black	f	20	N Y	Fla		1864	no	none	
89	34	Clements, D. G.	5	8	blue	f	21	GA	Fla	never	1864	yes	none	
89	35	Clements, Lucinda	4	7	blue	f	14	Fla	Fla			no	none	
89	36	Silcox, Mary	5	?	blk	dk	22	Fla	Fla			yes	none	
89	37	Hammond, Sarah	5	3	blk	dk	32	Fla	Fla			yes	none	
89	38	Hammond, Cimenthy	4	8	blk	dk	11	Fla	Fla			no	none	
89	39	Hammond, Lavinia			blk	dk	8	Fla	Fla			no	none	
89	40	Hammond, Wm. D.			blk	dk	6	Fla	Fla			no	none	
89	41	Hammond, Mary			blk	dk	3	Fla	Fla			no	none	
89	42	Revels, John	6	0	blk	dk	21	Fla	Fla	never		yes	none	Farmer
89	43	Enfinger, Laura C.	5	0	blue	f	19	Fla	Fla			yes	none	
89	44	Enfinger, Geo.			blue	f	2	Fla	Fla			no	none	
89	45	Revels, Wm. R.	5	8	blk	dk	24	Fla	Fla	never		yes	1	Govt. Employee
89	46	Woodward, Mary C.	5	5	blue	f	23	S.C.	S.C.		1864	yes	none	Refugee
89	47	McCormick, John	5	6	blk	dk	46	S.C.	Fla	never	1860	yes	none	Oysterman
89	48	McCormick, Liza	5	0	blk	dk	43	Fla	Fla			yes	none	

Pg	No	Name	Height Ft	Height In	Eyes	Com-plexion	Age	Where born or contraband	Last residence	Where registered for draft or former owner	Date into Department	Oath of Allgn	No of Ration	Remarks
90	1	McCormick, Eliza A.	5	0	blue	f	16	Fla	Fla	never		no	none	
90	2	McCormick, John	4	4	blue	f	15	Fla	Fla			no	none	
90	3	McCormick, Seborn			blue	f	10	Fla	Fla			no	none	
90	4	McCormick, Thos			blue	f	9	Fla	Fla			no	none	
90	5	Limbrick, Jos	5	6	bk	dk	51	Fla	Fla	never		yes	none	Invalid
90	6	Townsend, Marg[t]	5	0	blue	f	45	Scotland	Fla		1845	no	none	
90	7	Townsend, Aut[d]	4	5	blue	f	12	Fla	Fla			no	none	
90	8	Boothe, Rich[d]	5	8	blue	f	54	Eng[d]	Fla		1845	yes	none	Drayman
90	9	Hudson, Jas.	6	0	blue	f	31	GA	Fla	never	1864	yes	none	Unemployed refugee
90	10	Hudson, Penelope	5	0	bk	f	27	GA	Fla		1864	yes	none	
90	11	Hudson, Jno. M.			bk	f	10	GA	Fla		1864	no	none	
90	12	Hudson, Andrew			bk	f	8	GA	Fla		1864	no	none	
90	13	Hudson, Emma			bk	f	4	GA	Fla		1864	no	none	
90	14	Hudson, Jas.			bk	f	1	GA	Fla		1864	no	none	
90	15	Kelly, Frances	5	10	bk	dk	30	Ireland	N Y	never	1864	yes	none	Laborer
90	16	Barnes, John	5	9	blue	f	44	Ireland	N Y	never	1864	yes	none	Laborer
90	17	Barnes, James	5	2	blue	f	42	Ireland	N Y	never	1864	yes	none	Laborer
90	18	Bennett, Jno.			blue	f	9	Fla	Fla			no	none	
90	19	Canova, Bartolo	5	3	blue	f	28	Fla	Fla			yes	none	Bricklayer
90	20	Canova, Chas	5	0	dk	dk	20	Fla	Fla			yes	none	
90	21	Canova, Victoria			dk	dk	6	Fla	Fla			no	none	
90	22	Canova, Bartolo			dk	dk	4	Fla	Fla			no	none	
90	23	Clarke, E. M.	5	2	blue	f	23	S. C.	Fla		1844	yes	none	
90	24	Brown, Thos. B.			blue	f	3		Fla			no	none	

Pg	No	Name	Height Ft	Height In	Eyes	Com-plexion	Age	Where born or contraband	Last residence	Where registered for draft or former owner	Date into Department	Oath of Allgn	No of Ration	Remarks
91	25	Robinson, Rebecca	5	4	dk	f	25	Fla	Fla		1864	yes	2	By order Pro. Marshal
91	26	Robinson, Rosannah			dk	f	9	Fla	Fla		1864	no		
91	27	Robinson, Henrietta			dk	f	7	Fla	Fla		1864	no		
91	28	Robinson, Columbus			dk	f	5	Fla	Fla		1864	no		
91	29	Harrold, Kate	5	6	blue	f	30	Ireland	Fla		1864	yes	none	
91	30	Harold, Arthur			blue	f	1	Fla	Fla		1864	no	none	
91	31	Kinloch, Agnes	5	4	blue	f	26	Scotland	Fla		1864	yes	3 1/2	By order of Pro Marshal
91	32	Kinloch, Mary			blue	f	10	Fla	Fla		1864	no		Genl Scarnnon?
91	33	Kinloch, Jas			blue	f	8	Fla	Fla		1864	no		
91	34	Kinloch, Duncan			blue	f	7	Fla	Fla		1864	no		
91	35	Kinloch, Thos			blue	f	4	Fla	Fla		1864	no		
91	36	Kinloch, Eliza	4	3	blue	f	13	Fla	Fla		1864	no		
91	37	Bentoza, Walkien	5	10	blk	dk	30	Spain	Fla	never	1864	yes	none	Boot and shoe maker
91	38	Bentoza. Civility	5	0	blue	f	25	GA	Fla		1864	yes	none	
91	39	Ortagus, John	5	6	blk	dk	41	Fla	Fla	never		yes	1	Govt. Employee
91	40	Ortagus, Sarah	5	3	blk	dk	38	Fla	Fla			yes	none	
91	41	Ortagus, Mary	4	0	blk	dk	11	Fla	Fla			no	none	
91	42	Barry, Antonio	5	3	blk	dk	43	Fla	Fla	never		yes	none	
91	43	Zimanions, Jane	5	2	blk	dk	81	Fla	Fla			no	none	
91	44	Segue, Jane	5	0	blk	dk	14	Fla	Fla			no	none	
91	45	Andone?, Andreas	5	5	blk	dk	15	Fla	Fla	never		yes	1	Govt. Employee
91	46	Mixon, Nancy	5	4	blk	dk	65	S.C.	Fla		1848	yes	none	
91	47	Walker, Rachel	5	5	blk	dk	26	Fla	Fla			yes	none	
91	48	Walker, Mary			blk	dk	7	Fla	Fla			no	none	

"CENSUS" DEPARTMENT OF THE SOUTH - NOVEMBER, 1864

Pg	No	Name	Height Ft	Height In	Eyes	Com-plexion	Age	Where born or contraband	Last residence	Where registered for draft or former owner	Date into Department	Oath of Allgn	No of Ration	Remarks
92	1	Ellis, Harrold	5	0	blue	f	84	S.C.	Fla	never	1837	no	none	Cripple
92	2	Crosby, Angeline	5	2	blk	dk	17	Fla	Fla		1864	yes	none	
92	3	GAnus, Mahala	5	4	blk	dk	28	GA	Fla		1864	yes	none	
92	4	Gordon, Mary A.	5	1	blk	f	21	Fla	Fla		1863	yes	none	
92	5	Gordon, Thos. H.			blk	f	6	Fla	Fla	never	1863	yes	none	
92	6	Gordon, Lucy A.			blk	f	4	Fla	Fla		1863	yes	none	
92	7	Gordon, Emerline			blk	f	2	Fla	Fla		1863	yes	none	
92	8	Ortagus, Scilla	5	0	blk	f	21	Fla	Fla			yes	none	
92	9	Ortagus, Prudincia			blk	f	5	Fla	Fla			no	none	
92	10	Ortagus, Mary			blk	f	2	Fla	Fla			no	none	
92	11	Armstrong, Mary	5	5	blue	f	23	GA	Fla		1864	yes	none	
92	12	Armstrong, Sarah A.	4	6	blue	f	11	Fla	Fla			no	none	
92	13	Armstrong, Anne E.			blue	f	6	Fla	Fla			no	none	
92	14	Acosta, Geo. C.	5	11	blk	dk	56	Fla	Fla	never		yes	none	
92	15	Acosta, Geo. F.	5	6	blk	dk	14	Fla	Fla			no	none	
92	16	Pillasters, Raphile	5	8	blk	dk	29	Fla	Fla	never		yes	none	
92	17	Mantus, Anna M.	5	4	blk	dk	25	GA	Fla		1845	yes	none	Unemployed
92	18	Masters, E. R.			blk	dk	10	GA	Fla			no	none	
92	19	Masters, Raphile			blk	dk	6	Fla	Fla			no	none	
92	20	Masters, Walter			blk	dk	4	Fla	Fla			no	none	
92	21	Mickler, Mannala	5	4	blk	dk	48	Fla	Fla			no	none	
92	22	Mickler, Katey			blk	dk	8	Fla	Fla			no	none	
92	23	Cox, Wm.	5	8	blk	dk	43	S.C.	Fla	never	1845	yes	1	By order Pro. Marshal
92	24	Cox, Mary	5	5	blk	dk	43	Fla	Fla			no	1	By order Pro. Marshal

Pg	No	Name	Height Ft	Height In	Eyes	Complexion	Age	Where born or contraband	Last residence	Where registered for draft or former owner	Date into Department	Oath of Allgn	No of Ration	Remarks
93	25	Cox, Henry			blk	dk	4	Fla	Fla			no	none	
93	26	Wright, Martha	5	5	blk	dk	23	Fla	Fla			yes	none	
93	28	Wright, Edward	4	0	blk	dk	11	Fla	Fla			no	none	
93	29	Hall, Maria	5	5	blue	f	23	Fla	Fla			yes	none	
93	30	Hall, Matilda			blue	f	6	Fla	Fla			no	none	
93	31	Hall, John T.			blue	f	1	Fla	Fla			no	none	
93	32	Sims, Emma	5	0	blue	f	19	D. C.	Fla		1864	no	none	
93	33	Sims, Andrew			blue	f	1	D. C.	Fla		1864	no	none	
93	34	Kelly, Jas.	5	5	blue	f	50	Va.	Fla	never	1864	yes	none	Laborer
93	35	Kelly, Eliza	5	4	blue	f	40	GA	Fla		1864	yes	none	
93	36	Kelly, Maria	5	4	blue	f	20	Fla	Fla		1864	no	none	
93	37	Kelly, Emeline	5	5	blue	f	21	Fla	Fla		1864	no	none	
93	38	Kelly, Jas.	5	0	blue	f	19	Fla	Fla	never	1864	no	none	
93	39	Kelly, Henry	4	3	blue	f	17	Fla	Fla	never	1864	no	none	
93	40	Kelly, Hubbard	4	1	blue	f	14	Fla	Fla	never	1864	no	none	
93	41	Kelly, Mary	4	0	blue	f	11	Fla	Fla		1864	no	none	
93	42	Kelly, Washg			blue	f	5	Fla	Fla		1864	no	none	
93	43	Kelly, Marg[t]			blue	f	1	Fla	Fla		1864	no	none	
93	44	Johns, Isaac	6	2	dk	dk	44	Fla	Fla	never	1864	yes	none	Laborer
93	45	Johns, Nancy	5	5	dk	dk	40	Fla	Fla			yes	none	
93	46	Jones, Jas.	4	1	dk	dk	13	Fla	Fla			no	none	
93	47	Jones, Isaac	4	0	dk	dk	12	Fla	Fla			no	none	
93	48	Johns, Vestia			dk	dk	9	Fla	Fla			no	none	

Pg	No	Name	Height Ft	Height In	Eyes	Com-plexion	Age	Where born or contraband	Last residence	Where registered for draft or former owner	Date into Department	Oath of Allgn	No of Ration	Remarks
94	1	Jones, Elias B.			dk	dk	4	Florida	Fla	never		no	none	
94	2	Dean, Mary	5	0	dk	dk	45	S.C.	Fla		1864	yes	none	
94	3	Hawthorne, Wm. L.	5	6	blue	f	32	Ala	Fla	never	1862	yes	none	Laborer
94	4	Hawthorne, Sylvester	5	4	blue	f	25	Ala	Fla		1862	yes	none	
94	5	Hawthorne, Kesiah			blue	f	4	Ala	Fla		1862	no	none	
94	6	Falana. Bertha	5	4	dk	dk	34	Florida	Fla			yes	none	
94	7	Falana, Joseph	4	1	dk	dk	11	Florida	Fla			no	none	
94	8	Falana, Mary			dk	dk	10	Florida	Fla			no	none	
94	9	Falana, Henry			dk	dk	7	Florida	Fla			no	none	
94	10	Falana, Frances			dk	dk	6	Florida	Fla			no	none	
94	11	Sweat, Catharine	5	4	dk	dk	22	GA	Fla		1864	yes	none	
94	12	Sweat, Jas. J.			dk	dk	6	Florida	Fla			no	none	
94	13	Sweat, Elizabeth			dk	dk	4	Florida	Fla			no	none	
94	14	Cason, Catherine	5	0	blue	f	13	Fla	Fla			no	none	
94	15	Cason, Sarah	5	3	blue	f	18	Florida	Fla			no	none	
94	16	Nix, Susan	5	3	blue	f	35	S.C.	Fla		1844	yes	none	Old resident
94	17	Nix, Leonra	5	5	dk	dk	20	Fla	Fla			no	none	
94	18	Nix, Larener	5	3	blue	f	17	Fla	Fla			no	none	
94	19	Nix, Wm.			blue	f	9	Fla	Fla			no	none	
94	20	Nix, Charles			blue	f	7	Fla	Fla			no	none	
94	21	Nix, Penelope			blue	f	5	Fla	Fla			no	none	
94	22	Nix, Infant			blue	f	1	Fla	Fla			no	none	
94	23	West, Ann	5	4	dk	dk	56	Va.	Fla		1844	yes	none	
94	24	Vaught, Susan L.	3	9	dk	dk	11	Fla	Fla			no	none	

Pg	No	Name	Height Ft	Height In	Eyes	Com-plexion	Age	Where born or contraband	Last residence	Where registered for draft or former owner	Date into Department	Oath of Allgn	No of Ration	Remarks
95	25	Vaught, Florida			dk	dk	8	Fla	Fla			no	none	
95	26	Kernan, Martha	5	4	blue	f	31	Pen.	Fla		1849	yes	none	
95	27	Kernan, Mary			blue	f	9	Fla	Fla			no	none	
95	28	Phelan, Sarah A.	5	4	blue	f	44	Mass.	Fla		1849	yes	none	
95	29	Phelan, Anne			blue	f	8	S.C.	Fla		1857	no	none	
95	30	Mahoney, Mary	5	6	blue	f	22	Mass.	Fla		1857	yes	none	
95	31	Mahoney, Lula			blue	f	4	Fla	Fla			no	none	
95	32	Mahoney, Sarah			blue	f	3	Fla	Fla			no	none	
95	33	Woodland, Ruth	5	1	blue	f	25	GA	Fla		1864	yes	none	
95	34	Woodland, Mary			blue	f	6	Fla	Fla			no	none	
95	35	Woodland, Latte			blue	f	4	Fla	Fla			no	none	
95	36	Crosby, Julia A.	5	5	blue	f	51	S.C.	Fla		1864	yes	none	
95	37	St. Johns, Louisa	5	2	blk	f	22	NY	N Y		1864	no	none	Wife of Capt. St. Johns USA
95	38	Dean, Maggie	5	4	blue	f	20	Fla	Fla			yes	none	
95	39	Silcox, Isaac	5	0	dk	dk	17	Fla	Fla			yes	none	Government Employee
95	40	Silcox, Susan	5	2	blue	f	13	Fla	Fla			no	none	
95	41	Silcox, Frances	4	4	blue	f	12	Fla	Fla			no	none	
95	42	Silcox, Eliza	4	1	blue	f	10	Fla	Fla			no	none	
95	43	Silcox, Henry L.			blue	f	3	Fla	Fla			no	none	
95	44	Smith, Frances	5	5	dk	dk	64	S.C.	Fla		1864	yes	none	
95	45	Holleyman, Herman	5	7	blue	f	58	S.C.	Fla		1855	yes	none	Old Resident
95	46	Holleyman, Frances	5	5	blk	dk	24	Fla	Fla			no	none	
95	47	Holleyman, Beatrice			blk	dk	4	Fla	Fla			no	none	
95	48	Bailey, Richard T.	5	8	blue	f	38	S.C.	Fla		1854	yes	none	unemployed

Pg	No	Name	Height Ft	Height In	Eyes	Com-plexion	Age	Where born or contraband	Last residence	Where registered for draft or former owner	Date into Department	Oath of Allgn	No of Ration	Remarks
96	1	Bailey, Ellen	5	0	dk	dk	21	Fla	Fla			yes	none	
96	2	Mott, Rosannah	5	4	dk	dk	61	GA	Fla		1840	yes	none	
96	3	Mott, John	5	3	dk	dk	17	Fla	Fla	never		yes	none	Clerk in store
96	4	Morris, Mary Jane	5	3	blue	f	48	Fla	Fla			yes	none	
96	5	Holmes, David W.			blue	f	5	Fla	Fla			no	none	
96	6	Nillyers, Jas.	5	5	blue	f	45	GA	Fla	never	1864	yes	none	Laborer
96	7	Myers, Caroline	5	3	dk	dk	39	Fla	Fla			yes	none	
96	8	Myers, Jane	5	0	dk	dk	16	Fla	Fla			yes	none	
96	9	Myers, Eliza	4	10	dk	dk	14	Fla	Fla			no	none	
96	10	Myers, Caroline			dk	dk	6	Fla	Fla			no	none	
96	11	Myers, Wm. W.			dk	dk	4	Fla	Fla			no	none	
96	12	Myers, David			dk	dk	1	Fla	Fla			no	none	
96	13	Mullally, Sarah	5	5	dk	dk	35	GA	Fla		1864	yes	none	
96	14	Mullally, Wm.	4	5	blue	f	15	GA	Fla		1864	no	none	
96	15	Mullally, Gerraid	4	2	blue	f	12	GA	Fla		1864	no	none	
96	16	Mullally, Mary			blue	f	5	GA	Fla		1864	no	none	
96	17	Roberts, Lydia	5	5	dk	dk	52	S.C.	Fla		1845	yes	none	
96	18	O'Farrel, Martha A.	5	5	blue	f	31	GA	Fla		1860	yes	none	
96	19	O'Farrel, Jim			blue	f	5	Fla	Fla			no	none	
96	20	Howell, David R.	5	10	blue	f	26	Fla	Fla			yes	none	Shop Keeper
96	21	Howell, Lucinda	4	11	blue	f	20	Fla	Fla			yes	none	
96	22	Howell, Wm. H.			blue	f	3	Fla	Fla			no	none	
96	23	Howell, Harrison	5	9	blue	f	21	Fla	Fla			yes	none	Deserter from Reb. Army
96	24	Gillan, Edward	6	0	blue	f	23	Fla	Fla			yes	none	Deserter from Reb. Army

Pg	No	Name	Height		Eyes	Com-plexion	Age	Where born or contraband	Last residence	Where registered for draft or former owner	Date into Department	Oath of Allgn	No of Ration	Remarks
			Ft	In										
97	25	Anders, Geo. W.	5	9	dk	dk	45	GA	Fla	never	1855	yes	none	Laborer
97	26	Hogarth, A. B.	5	10	blue	f	41	S.C.	Fla	never	1848	yes	none	Very Deaf
97	27	Hogarth, Lydia	5	5	blue	f	29	GA	Fla		1848	yes	none	
97	28	Hogarth, Jas.			blue	f	9	Fla	Fla			no	none	
97	29	Hogarth, Milly			blue	f	5	Fla	Fla			no	none	
97	30	Pendarvis, Ann	5	5	dk	dk	25	Fla	Fla		1864	yes	none	
97	31	Sykes, Henry	5	8	dk	dk	35	GA	Fla	never	1864	yes	none	Butcher
97	32	Sykes, Eliza	5	3	dk	dk	32	GA	Fla		1864	yes	none	
97	33	Sykes, Henrietta			dk	dk	9	GA	Fla		1864	no	none	
97	34	Sykes, Jos.			dk	dk	9	GA	Fla		1864	no	none	
97	35	Sykes, David			dk	dk	7	GA	Fla		1864	no	none	
97	36	Brown, Eliza[th]	5	5	blue	f	23	GA	Fla		1861	yes	none	
97	37	Taylor, Mary	5	6	dk	dk	26	GA	Fla		1861	yes	none	
97	38	Hogarth, Jas. L.	5	4	blue	f	50	S.C.	Fla	never	1848	yes	none	Inspector of Market
97	39	Hogarth, Eliza[th]	5	2	blk	dk	47	S.C.	Fla		1848	yes	none	
97	40	Green, Susan	5	4	blk	dk	21	S.C.	Fla		1848	yes	none	
97	41	Green, Chas.			blk	dk	6	Fla	Fla		1848	no	none	
97	42	Berry, Adeline	5	0	dk	dk	19	Fla	Fla			no	none	
97	43	Stanly, Theodoria	5	0	dk	dk	22	Fla	Fla			yes	none	
97	44	Stanly, Martha			dk	dk	3	Fla	Fla			no	none	
97	45	Adams, Jane	5	5	dk	dk	24	GA	Fla		1864	yes	none	
97	46	Weeks, John P.	5	5	blue	f	41	NC	Fla		1864	yes	none	Unemployed
97	47	Weeks, Anne	5	3	dk	dk	30	Fla	Fla		1864	yes	none	
97	48	Prescott, Henry	5	0	dk	dk	14	Fla	Fla			yes	none	

Pg	No	Name	Height Ft	Height In	Eyes	Com-plexion	Age	Where born or contraband	Last residence	Where registered for draft or former owner	Date into Department	Oath of Allgn	No of Ration	Remarks
98	25	Callahan, Geo	5	3	blue	f	19	Ireland		never	1864	no	1	Govt. Employee
98	26	Peake, E. D.	5	10	dk	dk	28	N Y		never	1864	no	1	Govt. Employee
98	27	Sapple, Oliver	5	9	f	f	25	Me		never	1864	no	1	Govt. Employee
98	28	Chick, Leander	5	10	dk	dk	34	Me		never	1864	no	1	Govt. Employee
98	29	Nason, Allen	5	9	dk	dk	21	Me		never	1864	no	1	Govt. Employee
98	30	Hagen, Jas.	5	8	blue	f	32	Me		never	1864	no	1	Govt. Employee
98	31	Fitzgerald, Ed^wd	5	5	blue	f	21	Ireland		never	1864	no	1	Govt. Employee
98	32	Lynch, John	5	8	blue	f	20	Ireland		never	1864	no	1	Govt. Employee
98	33	McMan, Bernard	5	9	blue	f	23	Ireland		never	1864	no	1	Govt. Employee
98	34	Nies?Conrad	5	8	blue	f	23	N Y		18	1864	no	1	Govt. Employee
98	35	Wadkins, Ivan	5	1	blue	f	36	Contra		Brainy, E. H.			1	Govt. Employee
98	36	Newsom, Jos.	5	5	dk	dk	36	S.C.		never	1864	yes	none	
98	37	Newsom, Rebecca	5	3	dk	dk	26	N Y			1864	yes	none	
98	38	Newsom, Benj			dk	dk	9	S.C.			1864	no	none	
98	39	Taylor, Ephrain	6	0	dk	dk	50	N Y			1864	yes	none	
98	40	Taylor, Charlotte	5	2	dk	dk	23	N Y			1864	yes	none	
98	41	Mathews, Melthy	5	4	blue	f	40	S.C.			1864	yes	none	
98	42	Mathews, Martha			blue	f	8	Fla	Fla		1864	no	none	
98	43	Moore, Eliza	5	2	blue	f	23	GA	Fla		1864	yes	none	
98	44	Moore, Jas.			blue	f	4	GA			1864	no	none	
98	45	Nelson, Amey	5	1	dk	dk	20	Fla	Fla		1864	yes	none	
98	46	Soul?, Mary	5	0	dk	dk	70	GA	Fla			yes	1	By order Pro Marshall
98	47	Lowe, Mary	5	4	blue	f	22	Fla	Fla		1864	yes	none	
98	48	Lowe, Thos.			blue	f	5	Fla	Fla			no	none	

Pg	No	Name	Height Ft	Height In	Eyes	Com-plexion	Age	Where born or contraband	Last residence	Where registered for draft or former owner	Date into Department	Oath of Allgn	No of Ration	Remarks
99	1	Weeks, Mary E.	3	6	dk	dk	8	Fla	Fla			no	none	
99	2	Weeks, Marg[t]	3	3	dk	dk	6	Fla	Fla			no	none	
99	3	Hunter, Mary	5	3	dk	dk	28	Fla	Fla			yes	21/2	By order Pro Marshall
99	4	Hunter, Ellenor			dk	dk	9	Fla	Fla			no	none	
99	5	Hunter, Danl			dk	dk	6	Fla	Fla			no	none	
99	6	Wright, Elizabeth	5	5	blue	f	20	Fla	Fla			yes	none	
99	7	Falany, Hooster	5	5	dk	dk	35	Fla	Fla	never		yes	none	
99	8	Falany, Victoria	5	3	dk	dk	30	Fla	Fla			yes	none	
99	9	Falany, Emanual	4	8	dk	dk	11	Fla	Fla			no	none	
99	10	Falany, Chas					9	Fla	Fla			no	none	
99	11	Falany, Mary					8	Fla	Fla			no	none	
99	12	Falany, Victoria					5	Fla	Fla			no	none	
99	13	Falany, Frances					1	Fla	Fla			no	none	
99	14	Triay, Mary	5	0	dk	dk	17	Fla	Fla			no	none	
99	15	Cooper, Robinson	6	1	blue	f	31	GA	Fla	never	1864	yes	1	Govt. Employee
99	16	Wilkerson, Bryant	6	1	blue	f	29	GA	Fla		1864	yes	1	Govt. Employee
99	17	Wingate, Robert	5	10	dk	dk	20	Fla	Fla		1863	yes	1	Govt. Employee
99	18	Birney, Cason	5	11	dk	dk	25	Fla	Fla			yes	1	Govt. Employee
99	19	GArny?, Wm.	5	8	dk	dk	32	S.C.	Fla		1864	yes	1	Govt. Employee
99	20	Smith, Isaac	6	2	dk	dk	32	GA	Fla		1864	yes	1	Govt. Employee
99	21	Hagin, Wm.	5	11	dk	dk	24	Ireland	Fla		1864	no	1	Govt. Employee
99	22	Hewitt, John	5	10	dk	dk	35	S.C.	Fla		1864	yes	1	Govt. Employee
99	23	Duter, John	5	4	dk	dk	21	N J	Fla		1864	no	1	Govt. Employee
99	24	Saulsberry, Thos.	5	4	b	f	23	Ireland	Fla		1864	no	1	Govt. Employee

Pg	No	Name	Height Ft	Height In	Eyes	Complexion	Age	Where born or contraband	Last residence	Where registered for draft or former owner	Date into Department	Oath of Allgn	No of Ration	Remarks
100	1	Pons, Jno. M.	5	9	blue	dk	50	Fla	Fla	never	native	no	1	Prisoner in Guard House
100	2	Holmes, John	5	11	blue	f	52	Me	Fla	never	1844	no	1	Prisoner in Guard House
100	3	Sanchez, Morris	5	10	dk	dk	65	Fla	Fla	never	native	yes	1	Prisoner in Guard House
100	4	Sanders, Daul W.	5	6	blue	f	48	GA	Fla	never	1826	yes	1	Prisoner in Guard House
100	5	Prevat, Jonathan K.	6	0	blue	f	47	GA	Fla	never	1826	no	1	Prisoner in Guard House
100	6	McLeod, Geo.	5	7	blue	f	45	Scotland	Fla	never	1852	yes	1	Prisoner in Guard House
100	7	Doggett, S. Forbs	5	6	blue	f	28	Fla	Fla	never		no	1	Prisoner in Guard House
100	8	Brown, Simon S.	5	11	blue	f	42	GA	Fla	never	1842	yes	1	Prisoner in Guard House
100	9	Brown, Jno.	5	8	blue	f	17	Fla	Fla	never		yes	1	Prisoner in Guard House
100	10	Baya, Tario	5	7	blue	f	25	Fla	Fla	never		yes	1	Prisoner in Guard House
100	11	Nichols, John	5	6	blue	f	47	GA	Fla	never	1820	yes	1	Prisoner in Guard House
100	12	Ayers, Henry	5	6	blue	f	46	S.C.	Fla	never	1858	yes	1	Prisoner in Guard House
100	13	Crewshaw, Marco	6	0	blue	f	29	S.C.	Fla	never	1851	yes	1	Prisoner in Guard House
100	14	Stewart, Jas.	5	11	dk	dk	45	GA	Fla	never	1864	yes	1	Prisoner in Guard House
100	15	Brady, Jno.	5	8	dk	dk	25	Ireland	N Y	never	1864	yes	1	Prisoner in Guard House
100	16	Wingate, Jno	6	0	blue	f	19	Fla	Fla	never		yes	1	Prisoner in Guard House
100	17	Bram, Chas.	4	6	blk	blk	13	Contr		Plummer, Jas.				
100	18	Scott, Jos. W.	5	10	blue	f	51	N.B.		never	1859	no	1	Prisoner in Guard House
100	19	Callahan, Jno.	5	7	blue	f	28	Ireland	Mass.	never	1858	no	1	Prisoner in Guard House
100	20	Johnson, Curtis	5	11	dk	dk	17	Fla	Fla	never		no	1	Prisoner in Guard House
100	21	Miller, Adolph	5	5	blue	f	21	Prussia	La.	never	1864	no	1	Prisoner in Guard House
100	22	Moore, Henry	5	7	blue	f	27	Va.	Fla	never	1864	yes	1	Prisoner in Guard House
100	23	Fitzpatrick, Jos.	6	0	blue	f	54	Ireland	Fla	never	1863	yes	1	Prisoner in Guard House
100	24	Carpenter, Ora	5	5	blk	dk	46	VT.	VT.	never	1864	yes	1	Prisoner in Guard House

Pg	No	Name	Height Ft	Height In	Eyes	Complexion	Age	Where born or contraband	Last residence	Where registered for draft or former owner	Date into Department	Oath of Allgn	No of Ration	Remarks
101	25	Turner, Jas.	5	8	blue	dk	47	Fla	Fla	never	native	yes	1	Prisoner in Guard House
101	26	Moore, Alfred M.	5	11	blue	f	41	Fla	Fla	never	1856	yes	1	Prisoner in Guard House
101	27	Price, Henry	5	8	blue	dk	17	Fla	Fla	never		yes	1	Prisoner in Guard House
101	28	Clarke, Wm. D.	5	10	blue	f	35	Fla	Fla	never		yes	1	Prisoner in Guard House
101	29	Crews Newnan	5	11	blue	f	19	Fla	Fla	never		yes	1	Prisoner in Guard House
101	30	Smith, John	5	6	blue	f	21	GA	Fla	never	1864	yes	1	Prisoner in Guard House
101	31	Wilson, Murray	5	7	blue	f	22	Ireland	NY	never	1864	yes	1	Prisoner in Guard House
101	32	Drawdy, Cornelious	5	11	blue	f	26	GA	GA	never	1864	yes	1	Prisoner in Guard House
101	33	Drawdy, Luke	5	11	dk	dk	24	GA	GA	never	1864	yes	1	Prisoner in Guard House
101	34	Drawdy, Smith	5	11	dk	dk	21	GA	GA	never	1864	yes	1	Prisoner in Guard House
101	35	Long, Henry	5	10	blue	f	20	GA	Fla	never	1861	no	1	Prisoner in Guard House
101	36	Nicholas,Constantine	5	7	dk	dk	49	Greece	Fla	never	1856	yes	1	Prisoner in Guard House
101	37	Wilson, Caroline	5	4	Blue	f	35	NC	Fla		1843	yes	none	Boarding House Keeper
101	38	Wilson, Julia	5	3	Blue	f	16	Fla	Fla			yes	none	
101	39	Wilson, Grovenor			Blue	f	7	Fla	Fla			no	none	
101	40	Ingraham, Maggie	5	4	dk	dk	18	Fla	Fla			yes	none	
101	41	Hudnal, Eliza	5	0	dk	dk	43	GA	Fla		1834	yes	none	Boarding House Keeper
101	42	Hudnal, Ebner?	5	4	dk	dk	18	Fla	Fla			yes	none	
101	43	Hudnal, Henry	4	6	dk	dk	11	Fla	Fla			yes	none	
101	44	Hudnal, Serephena			dk	dk	8	Fla	Fla			no	none	
101	45	Hudnal, Emma			dk	dk	6	Fla	Fla			no	none	
101	46	Hudnal, Edward			dk	dk	3	Fla	Fla			no	none	
101	47	Shad, Mahten?	5	5	dk	dk	24	Fla	Fla			yes	none	
101	48	Shad, Fru?			dk	dk	7	Fla	Fla			no	none	

"CENSUS" DEPARTMENT OF THE SOUTH - NOVEMBER, 1864

Pg	No	Name	Height Ft	Height In	Eyes	Com-plexion	Age	Where born or contraband	Last residence	Where registered for draft or former owner	Date into Department	Oath of Allgn	No of Ration	Remarks
102	1	Lowe, Mary					2	Fla	Fla				non	
102	2	Andrue, Antonio	5	5	blk	dk	15	Fla	Fla	never	1864	yes	1	Govt. Employee
102	3	Segwick, Wm	5	8	blk	f	46	NY	Fla	never	1864	yes	1	Govt. Employee
102	4	Sedgwick, Martha	5	2	blue	f	44	S.C.	Fla		186_	no		
102	5	Sedgwick, Lizzie	5	3	blue	f	18	Fla	Fla		1864	no		
102	6	Sedgwick, Frank			blue	f	6	Fla	Fla		1864	no		
102	7	Sedgwick, Lucy			blue	f	3	Fla	Fla		1864	no		
102	8	Prevatt, Elizabeth	5	5	blue	f	66	S.C.	Fla		1864	no		
102	9	Holleyman,Herman	5	6	blue	f	58	S.C.	Fla		1855	yes	non	
102	10	Holleyman, Fany	5	4	blue	f	24	Fla	Fla			yes		
102	11	Holleyman, Beatrice					4	Fla	Fla			no		
102	12	McDowell, Geo.W.	5	9	dk	dk	20	Fla	Fla	never		yes	1	Govt. Employee
102	13	Moore, J. W.	6	0	dk	dk	24	Fla	Fla	never		yes	1	Govt. Employee
102	14	Ross, John E.	5	8	dk	dk	24	GA	Fla	never	1864	yes	1	Govt. Employee
102	15	Griffith, Peter?	6	0	blue	f	32	GA	Fla	never		yes	1	Govt. Employee
102	16	Harris, John W.	5	7	blue	f	17	Fla	Fla	never		yes	1	Govt. Employee
102	17	Williams, Albert	5	0	blue	f	18	Fla	Fla	never		yes	1	Govt. Employee
102	18	Braddock, J. D.	5	0	blue	f	18	Fla	Fla	never		yes	1	Govt. Employee
102	19	Fluin, Jas.	5	9	blue	f	21	Fla	Fla	never		yes	1	Govt. Employee
102	20	Higginbotham, Jas.	5	11	blue	f	42	Fla	Fla	never		yes	1	Govt. Employee
102	21	McNeil, Chas.	5	7	dk	dk	17	Fla	Fla	never		yes	1	Govt. Employee
102	22	Wells, Saml	5	6	dk	dk	26	Fla	Fla	never		yes	1	Govt. Employee
102	23	Wood, Warren	5	10	blue	f	23	Fla	Fla	never		yes	1	Govt. Employee
102	24	Maning, Jno.	5	10	blue	f	20	Fla	Fla	never		yes	1	Govt. Employee

Pg	No	Name	Height Ft	Height In	Eyes	Complexion	Age	Where born or contraband	Last residence	Where registered for draft or former owner	Date into Department	Oath of Allgn	No of Ration	Remarks
103	25	Wells, Isaac P.	5	9	blue	f	17	Ala.	Fla	never	1864	yes	1	Govt. Employee
103	26	Sapp, Wm.	4	2	blue	f	17	Fla	Fla	never		yes	1	Govt. Employee
103	27	Padgett, Steven	5	7	dk	dk	49	Fla	Fla	never		yes	1	Govt. Employee
103	28	Forrest, Jas.	5	6	dk	dk	49	Fla	Fla	never		yes	1	Govt. Employee
103	29	Manning, J. H.	5	11	dk	dk	34	S.C.	Fla	never	1864	yes	1	Govt. Employee
103	30	Craig,John R.	5	7	dk	dk	30	N J	Fla	never	1857	yes	1	Govt. Employee
103	31	Crane, Geo. W.	5	6	blue	f	25	N H	NY	in NY	1862	yes		Qr. Masters Clerk
103	32	Hyatt, Wm. H.	5	7	blue	f	34	N Y	NY	in NY	1862	yes		Qr. Masters Clerk
103	33	Bogat, Duncan	5	8	blue	f	22	N Y	NY	in NY	1862	yes		Qr. Masters Clerk
103	34	Ward, Jessee	5	6	blue	f	29	Mich.	NY	in NY	1863	yes		Harbor Master
103	35	Kelly, Danl	5	8	dk	dk	38	Ireland	Fla	never	1856	yes	1	Govt. Employee
103	36	Kenam, Peter	5	8	dk	dk	41	Ireland	Fla	never	1849	yes	1	Govt. Employee
103	37	LaCourse, Jos.	5	8	blue	f	47	Canada	Fla	never	1853	yes	1	Govt. Employee
103	38	Higgins, John	5	7	blue	f	49	Ireland	Fla	never	1854	yes	1	Govt. Employee
103	39	Morris, Jno.	5	11	blue	f	51	GA	Fla	never	1849	yes	1	Govt. Employee
103	40	Davidson, Wm.	6	0	dk	dk	42	Me.	Me.	never	1864	no	1	Govt. Employee
103	41	Falana, Emanuel	5	7	dk	dk	43	Fla	Fla	never		yes	1	Govt. Employee
103	42	Wilson, Geo.	5	7	blue	f	27	MD	S.C.	never	1864	yes	1	Govt. Employee
103	43	Falana, Ben	5	6	dk	dk	45	Fla	Fla	never		yes	1	Govt. Employee
103	44	Miller, Nath'	5	10	blue	f	48	NY	Fla	never	1850	yes	1	Govt. Employee
103	45	McNamara, J. S.	5	8	blue	f	47	MD	Fla	never	1856	yes	1	Govt. Employee
103	46	Crowley, John	5	6	dk	dk	30	Ireland	NY	never	1864	no	1	Govt. Employee
103	47	Lohman, Wm.	5	9	blue	f	42	Fla	NY	never		yes	1	Govt. Employee
103	48	Dingle, John	5	9	blue	f	31	Ten.	NY	never	1864	yes	1	Govt. Employee

Pg	No	Name	Height Ft	Height In	Eyes	Com-plexion	Age	Where born or contraband	Last residence	Where registered for draft or former owner	Date into Department	Oath of Allgn	No of Ration	Remarks
104	1	Powers, Thos.	5	9	blue	f	32	Ireland	Boston	never	1864	yes	1	Bakery for Govt.
104	2	Boldue, Frank	5	8	dk	dk	26	Canada	Fla	never	1863	no	1	Bakery for Govt.
104	3	Kenan, Jas	5	9	dk	dk	30	Ireland	DC	never	1864	yes	1	Bakery for Govt.
104	4	Maher, John	5	9	blue	f	46	Ireland	Mass	never	1864	yes	1	Bakery for Govt.
104	5	Finning, John	5	8	blue	f	19	Mass.	N.Haven	never	1864	no	1	Bakery for Govt. Dis[ch] Soldier
104	6	Miller, Bird	5	11	blue	f	40	Contr	Florida	Ferris, S. P.			1	Govt. Employee
104	7	Stevens, S. T.	5	9	blue	f	36	N Y C.	N Y C.	never	1864	no	1	Supt. U.S. Bakery
104	8	Cherry, Wm.	5	10	blue	f	30	Canada	Canada	never	1864	no		Govt. Employee
104	9	Long, George W.	5	6	blue	f	26	Fla	Fla	never	1864	yes	1	Govt. Employee
104	10	Jones, Robert	5	7	dk	dk	33	NJ	NYC	NYC	1864	no	1	Govt. Employee
104	11	Griffis, J. H.	5	8	dk	dk	38	Fla	Fla	never	1864	yes	1	Govt. Employee
104	12	GArdner, Jas.	5	8	blue	f	26	Fla	Fla	never	1864	yes	1	Govt. Employee
104	13	Warren, Jas C.	5	8	blue	f	31	Fla	Fla	never		yes	1	Govt. Employee
104	14	Woodland, Aquita	5	7	blue	f	39	Fla	Fla	never		yes	1	Govt. Employee
104	15	Thomey?, Solomen	5	8	blue	f	24	Fla	Fla	never		yes	1	Govt. Employee
104	16	McLeod, Peter	5	9	blue	f	37	S.C.	Fla	never	1864	yes	1	Govt. Employee
104	17	Silcox, Henry O.	5	10	blue	f	38	Fla	Fla	never	1864	yes	1	Govt. Employee
104	18	Mullen, M. A.	5	8	blue	f	26	Canada	Canada	never	1864		1	Govt. Employee
104	19	Johnson, Geo. C.	5	10	dk	dk	30	KY	Pen.	Pen.	1864	no		Chief Clk. CS
104	20	Hallett, John	5	9	blue	f	40	Mass.	Barnastable	Barnastable	1864	yes	1	Govt. Employee Has furnst? Substitute
104	21	Young, Adam	5	6	blue	f	30	Germany	Con.	never	1864	yes	1	Govt. Employee Dis[ch] soldier
104	22	Peck, Geo. A.	5	8	blue	f	37	Con.	Con.	Derby, Con.	1864	yes		Jeweller
104	23	McLin, S. B.	5	8	dk	dk	33	Ten.	Fla	never	1864	yes		Refugee
104	24	Carmicheal, I.G.?	6	0	dk	dk	35	GA	Fla	never	1864	yes		

Pg	No	Name	Height		Eyes	Com-plexion	Age	Where born or contraband	Last residence	Where registered for draft or former owner	Date into Department	Oath of Allgn	No of Ration	Remarks
			Ft	In										
105	1	Wells, Elmyra			grey	fair	19	Alabama	Duval Co		Sept.1864	no		Single daughter of Enock? Wells
105	2	Wells, Jas. S.					13	Fla	Duval Co		Sept.1864	no		Son of Enock? Wells
105	3	Wells, Nancy E.					11	Fla	Duval Co		Sept.1864	no		Daughter of Enock? Wells
105	4	Wells, Jacob W.					5	Fla	Duval Co		Sept.1864	no		Son of Enock? Wells
105	5	Wells, June					45	South Car	Duval Co		Sept.1864	no		Wife of Enock? Wells
105	6	Mumby, Maria L.					37	Rhode Island	Duval Co			no		Dumb, Mute
105	7	Mumby, Frank W.					9	New York	Duval Co			no		Son of Maria L. Mumby
105	8	Hendricks, Elizabeth					44	Maryland	Duval Co			yes		
105	9	Hendricks, Louisa G.					20	Fla	Duval Co			no		
105	10	Hendricks, Mary C.					16	Fla	Duval Co			no		
105	11	Hendricks, Virginia E.					14	Fla	Duval Co			no		
105	12	Hendricks, Thos. G.					10	Fla	Duval Co			no		
105	13	Hendricks, Chas. E.					7	Fla	Duval Co			no		
105	14	Hendricks, Emma					4	Fla	Duval Co			no		
105	15	Hendricks, Jas. H.					2	Fla	Duval Co			no		
105	16	Minuey, Philip	5	10	dk	dk	48	Fla	Duval Co			yes		
105	17	Minuey, Carmin					40	Fla	Duval Co			yes		
105	18	Minuey, Baneta					19	Fla	Duval Co			yes		
105	19	Minuey, Kate					15	Fla	Duval Co			no		
105	20	Minuey, John	4	11	bk	dk	16	Fla	Duval Co			no		
105	21	Minuey, Margaret					8	Fla	Duval Co			no		
105	22	Minuey, Jas. P.					5	Fla	Duval Co			no		
105	23	Minuey, Joseph W.					4	Fla	Duval Co			no		
105	24	Smith, Joseph P.	5	11	blue	fair	54	S.C.	Duval Co		Dec. 1862	yes		

Pg	No	Name	Height Ft	Height In	Eyes	Com-plexion	Age	Where born or contraband	Last residence	Where registered for draft or former owner	Date into Department	Oath of Allgn	No of Ration	Remarks
106	1	Smith, Elizabeth					32	Fla	Duval Co			no		
106	2	Smith, Jas. A.					13	Fla	Duval Co			no		
106	3	Smith, Mary J.					11	Fla	Duval Co			no		
106	4	Smith, Alabemy					8	Fla	Duval Co			no		
106	5	Smith, Raymond G.					4	Fla	Duval Co			no		
106	6	Hancocke, Blanch					52	Georgia	Duval Co					
106	7	Joiner, Robt	5	4	yellow	ck?	19	Fla	Duval Co		Mch. 1864	yes		
106	8	McLelleand, John	5	10	yellow	ck?	64	S.C.	Duval Co		Sept. 1864	yes		
106	9	McLelleand, Sarah					30	Georgia	Duval Co		Apl 1864	yes		
106	10	McLelleand, Hiram	5	10	blk	ck?	20	Georgia	Duval Co		Apl 1864	yes		
106	11	Forrest?, Jane?					17	Georgia	Duval Co		Sept. 1864	yes		
106	12	Forrest?, Delphina?					2	Fla	Duval Co		Sept. 1864	no		
106	13	Forrest?, Hiram					1	Fla	Duval Co		Sept. 1864	no		
106	14	Wilkinson, Wm.	5	11	blk	ck?	30	GA	Duval Co		Feb. 1864	yes		
106	15	Wilkinson, Cornilia					30	GA	Duval Co		Feb. 1864	no		
106	16	Wilkinson, Elisha					10	Fla	Duval Co		Feb. 1864	no		
106	17	Wilkinson, William G.					8	Fla	Duval Co					
106	18	Wilkinson,Margaret V					6	Fla	Duval Co					
106	19	Wilkinson, George E.					4	Fla	Duval Co					
106	20	Wilkinson,Rebecca J.					13	Fla	Duval Co					
106	21	Green, John?	5	6	grey	dk	28	GA	Duval Co		Sept. 1864	yes		Husband in Reb. Service
106	22	Green, Levy G.					7	Fla	Duval Co					
106	23	Green, Silatha					5	Fla	Duval Co					
106	24	Green, Leonara					3	Fla	Duval Co					

Pg	No	Name	Height Ft	Height In	Eyes	Complexion	Age	Where born or contraband	Last residence	Where registered for draft or former owner	Date into Department	Oath of Allgn	No of Ration	Remarks
107	1	McLellan, Charley					7	Fla	Duval Co					
107	2	McLellan,Lusara					3	Fla	Duval Co					
107	3	Philips, Albert G.	5	10	blue	fair	60	GA	Duval Co			yes		Has three sons in Rebel Army
107	4	Philips, Margaret A.			blue	fair	50	Fla	Duval Co			yes		
107	5	Philips, George W.	5	8	blue	fair	15	Fla	Duval Co			yes		
107	6	Philips, Albert G. Jr.					14	Fla	Duval Co			no		
107	7	Philips, Mary A. J.					11	Fla	Duval Co			no		
107	8	Philips, Henry B.					7	Fla	Duval Co			no		
107	9	Philips, Hardy H.	5	10	blue	fair	53	GA	Duval Co			no		
107	10	Philips, Rebecca					58	Gea	Duval Co			no		Dumb Mute Lives with A. G. Phillips
107	11	Philips, Joanna					12	Contraband	Duval Co	Turknette, George				Lives with A. G. Philips
107	12	Pringle, John	5	11	dk	dk	40	GA	Duval Co		Mch 1864	yes		Deserter from Rebel Army
107	13	Pringle, David	5	10	dk	dk	18	Fla	Duval Co		Mch 1864	yes		
107	14	Stone, Hester					44	GA	Duval Co		Feb. 1864	yes		
107	15	Coward, Sydney B.					21	GA	Duval Co		Oct. 1864	yes		
107	16	McLewell?John	6		blue	fair	53	GA	Duval Co		Nov. 1864	yes		
107	17	Manning?, John	5	11	dk	dk	31	N. C.	Duval Co		May 1864	yes	1	US Sub Dept.
107	18	Manning?, Phebe			dk	dk	31	GA	Duval Co			yes		
107	19	Manning?, Mary E.					13	Fla	Duval Co			no		
107	20	Manning?, Johnathan					6	Fla	Duval Co					
107	21	Marniney?, Jas.					3	Fla	Duval Co					
107	22	Marniney?, John					3	Fla	Duval Co					
107	23	Blunt, Jane					20	Fla	Duval Co			yes		
107	24	Blunt, Redding	5	10	dk	dk	21	Fla	Duval Co			yes		Deserter from Rebel Army

Pg	No	Name	Height Ft	Height In	Eyes	Com-plexion	Age	Where born or contraband	Last residence	Where registered for draft or former owner	Date into Department	Oath of Allgn	No of Ration	Remarks
108	1	Blunt, Sarah F.					4	Duval Co.	Duval Co			no		Daughter of Redding Blunt
108	2	Blunt, Julia					2	Duval Co.	Duval Co					
108	3	Ellis, Giles W.	5	10	dk	ck	33	GA	Duval Co		May 1864	yes	1	Q. M. Dept.
108	4	Ellis, Jas.	5	8	dk	ck	30	GA	Duval Co		May 1864	yes	1	Q. M. Dept.
108	5	Ellis, John	5	9	dk	ck	25	GA	Duval Co		May 1864	yes	1	Q. M. Dept.
108	6	Norman, James	5	4	dk	ck	21	GA	Duval Co		Augst. 1864	yes		
108	7	Norman, Elizabeth					21	GA	Duval Co		Augst. 1864	yes		
108	8	Norman, Candacy					2	Fla	Duval Co		Augst. 1864			
108	9	Manning, Joseph H.	6		dk	ck	34	S.C.	Duval Co		Augst. 1864	yes		
108	10	Manning, Kisirah			blue	fair	25	Fla	Duval Co		Augst. 1864			
108	11	Manning, Darling B.					4	Fla	Duval Co		Augst. 1864			
108	12	Manning, Joseph M.					2	Fla	Duval Co		Augst. 1864			
108	13	Manning, Wm.S.					1	Fla	Duval Co		Augst. 1864			
108	14	Padget, Andrew J.	5	11	blue	dk	40	GA	Duval Co		Augst. 1864	yes		
108	15	Gibbon, Robert C.	5	10	dk	dk	26	Fla	Duval Co		Mch. 1864	yes		
108	16	Gibbon, Samantha					22				July 1864	no		
108	17	Gibbon, Milliera					3							
108	18	Gibbon, Frances					1							
108	19	Birney, Jas.	5	8	grey	dk	45	GA			Feb. 1864	yes		
108	20	Birney, Elizabeth					44	Fla.			Oct. 1864	no		
108	21	Birney, Adaline					19	Fla.			Oct. 1864			
108	22	Birney, Arther					14	Fla.			Oct. 1864			
108	23	Birney, Jesse					12	Fla.			Oct. 1864			
108	24	Birney, Elizabeth					10	Fla.			Oct. 1864			

Pg	No	Name	Height Ft	Height In	Eyes	Com-plexion	Age	Where born or contraband	Last residence	Where registered for draft or former owner	Date into Department	Oath of Allgn	No of Ration	Remarks
109	1	Birney, Lulah					8	Fla	Duval Co		Oct. 1864	no		Daughter of Jas Birney
109	2	Briney, Marg					6	Fla	Duval Co		Oct. 1864	no		Daughter of Jas Birney
109	3	Briney, Jane					4	Fla	Duval Co		Oct. 1864	no		Daughter of Jas Birney
109	4	Briney, Frances					1	Fla	Duval Co		Oct. 1864	no		Daughter of Jas Birney
109	5	McLellan, Gena					22	Fla	Duval Co			yes		
109	6	Hartley, John F.	5	11	blue	fair	43	Fla	Duval Co			yes		
109	7	Hartley, Mary					42	Fla	Duval Co			no		
109	8	Hartley, Margaret					22	Fla	Duval Co			yes		
109	9	Hartley, Mary E.					20	Fla	Duval Co			yes		
109	10	Hartley, Frances					18	Fla	Duval Co			no		
109	11	Hartley, John J.					16	Fla	Duval Co			no		
109	12	Hartley, Charlotte					13	Fla	Duval Co			no		
109	13	Hartley, Sarah					10	Fla	Duval Co			no		
109	14	Hartley, Virginia					7	Fla	Duval Co			no		
109	15	Hartley, David					4	Fla	Duval Co			no		
109	16	Rowe, William	5	10	blk	dk	21	S.C.	Duval Co		Dec. 1863	yes		
109	17	Williams, Elbert	5	2	dk	dk	18	N. C.	Duval Co		July 1864	yes		
109	18	Mills, Jas. T.	5	8	grey	dk	37	S.C.	Duval Co		Sept. 1863	yes		
109	19	Mills, Preston					8	Fla	Duval Co			no		
109	20	Mills, Olive					6	Fla	Duval Co					
109	21	Mills, Mary J.					4	Fla	Duval Co					
109	22	Mills, Eliza					2	Fla	Duval Co					
109	23	Canforde, Chas. B.	5	4	dk	dk	33	Fla	Duval Co		Mch. 1864	yes		
109	24	Canforde, Neta					26	Fla	Duval Co			yes		

"CENSUS" DEPARTMENT OF THE SOUTH - NOVEMBER, 1864

Pg	No	Name	Height Ft	Height In	Eyes	Com-plexion	Age	Where born or contraband	Last residence	Where registered for draft or former owner	Date into Department	Oath of Allgn	No of Ration	Remarks
110	1	Plummer, W^{m}	5	6	blue	dk	38	Fla	Duval Co		Nov. 1863	yes		Deserter Rebel Army
110	2	Plummer, Jane					30	Fla	Duval Co		Nov. 1863	no		Wife of Wm. Plummer
110	3	Plummer, Joseph A.					14	Fla						Son of Wm. Plummer
110	4	Plummer, Mary A.					10	Fla						Daughter of Wm. Plummer
110	5	Plummer, Alvin					8	Fla						Son of Wm. Plummer
110	6	Plummer,Charlott					6	Fla						Daughter of Wm. Plummer
110	7	Plummer, Richard					4	Fla						Son of Wm. Plummer
110	8	Plummer, Kate					2	Fla						Daughter of Wm. Plummer
110	9	Plummer, Jane A.					1	Fla						Daughter of Wm. Plummer
110	10	Plummer, Andrea					29	Fla				yes		Widow: Husband Killed in Rebel Army
110	11	Plummer, Matilda					5	Fla						Daughter of Andrea Plummer
110	12	Plummer, Anna					4	Fla						Daughter of Andrea Plummer
110	13	Plummer, Florida					2	Fla						Daughter of Andrea Plummer
110	14	Plummer, Eliza J.					16	Fla				no		
110	15	Petty, Mary A.					32	Fla				no		Husband died in Rebel Service
110	16	Petty, George?	5	2	dk	dk	15	Fla						Son of Mary A. Petty
110	17	Petty, Sarah A.					12	Fla						Daughter of A. Petty
110	18	Petty, Joseph A.					6	Fla						Son of Mary A. Petty
110	19	Plummer, Robert	5	8	grey	dk	25	?			Jan. 1864	yes		Deserter from Rebel Army
110	20	Plummer, Suanna					22	Fla			July 1864	no		Wife of Robert Plummer
110	21	Plummer, James					2	Fla			July 1864	no		Son of Robert Plummer
110	22	Plummer, Charlott					55	Fla						Widow
110	23	Plummer, Nathaniel					16	Fla						Son of Charlott Plummer
110	24	Plummer, Suanna	5	2	grey	dk	21	Fla			Sept. 1864	yes		Deserter from Rebel Army

Pg	No	Name	Height		Eyes	Com-plexion	Age	Where born or contraband	Last residence	Where registered for draft or former owner	Date into Department	Oath of Allgn	No of Ration	Remarks
			Ft	In										
111	1	Picket, Geo.	5	10	blk	dk	22	Fla	Duval Co		Feby 1864	yes		Deserter from Rebel Army
111	2	Picket, Ceny? C.	5	10	blue	fair	20	Fla	Duval Co		Jany 1864	yes		Deserter from Rebel Army
111	3	Pickett, Joseph W.	5	7	blue	fair	18	Fla			Jany 1864	yes		Deserter from Rebel Army
111	4	Pickett, John W.	6		blue	fair	27	Fla			Jany 1864	yes		Deserter from Rebel Army
111	5	Pickett, Emma					18	Fla				no		Wife of John W. Pickett
111	6	Pickett, Wm. S.	6		dk	dk	24	Fla			Jany 1864	yes		Deserter from Rebel Army
111	7	Plummer, David					7	Fla						Orphan Boy
111	8	Ginnople, Geo	5	6	dk	dk	70	Fla				yes		
111	9	Burress, Joseph	5	8	blue	fair	33	GA			Aug. 1864	yes		Invalid
111	10	Burress, Elizes. A.					25	GA			Aug. 1864	yes		Wife of Joseph Burress
111	11	Burress, Elizabeth					11	GA			Aug. 1864			Daughter of Joseph Burress
111	12	Smith, Wm. H.	5	8	blue	dk	24	Fla	Duval County		Dec. 1864	yes		Deserter of Rebel Army
111	13	Burress, Wm. R.					9	Fla						Son of Joseph L. Burress
111	14	Burress, Henry					5	Fla						Son of Joseph L. Burress
111	15	Burress, Mary J.					4	Fla						Daughter of Joseph Burress
111	16	Jones, Elizabeth					42	GA			Aug. 1864	no		Widow
111	17	Jones, Leonard					14	GA			Aug. 1864	no		Son of Elizabeth Jones
111	18	Jones, Joseph					8	GA			Aug. 1864	no		Son of Elizabeth Jones
111	19	Jones, Matilda A.					2	Fla						Daughter of Elizabeth Jones
111	20	Jones, Henry					8	Fla						Orphan Boy
111	21	Green, Wm. T.	5	11	dk	dk	42	Fla			Apr 1864	yes		Deserter of Rebel Army
111	22	Green, Malissa					42	GA			Apr 1864	yes		Wife of W. T. Green
111	23	Green, Rebecca					10	Fla			Apr 1864			{Twins } Daughters of W.T.Green
111	24	Green, Elizabeth					10	Fla			Apr 1864			

Pg	No	Name	Height Ft	Height In	Eyes	Com-plexion	Age	Where born or contraband	Last residence	Where registered for draft or former owner	Date into Department	Oath of Allgn	No of Ration	Remarks
112	1	Green, Drucilla					8	Fla	Duval Co		April 1864			Daughter of W. T. Green
112	2	Green, Harriet					6	Fla	Duval Co					Daughter of W. T. Green
112	3	Green, Lupina					5	Fla	Duval Co					Daughter of W. T. Green
112	4	Wilkinson, Allen	4	10	grey	dk	15	Fla	Duval Co			no		Orphan Boy
112	5	DaCosta, Elizabeth					30	Fla	Duval Co			no		Widow
112	6	DaCosta, Edward					15	Fla	Duval Co					Son of Elizabeth DaCosta
112	7	DaCosta, Elizabeth					14	Fla	Duval Co					Daughter of Elizabeth Da Costa
112	8	DaCosta, Joseph					11	Fla	Duval Co					Son of Elizabeth DaCosta
112	9	DaCosta, Julia A.					8	Fla	Duval Co					Daughter of Elizabeth Da Costa
112	10	DaCosta, Turacy					3	Fla	Duval Co					Daughter of Elizabeth Da Costa
112	11	Webb, Thos. R.	5	7	blue	fair	35	N Y				yes		
112	12	Webb, Francis K.					24	N Y				no		Wife of Thos. R. Webb
112	13	Webb, Camis P.?					5	Fla						Son of Thos. R. Webb
112	14	Webb, Henry R.					2	Fla						Son of Thos. R. Webb
112	15	Jones, Wm A.			blue	fair	41	GA			March 1864	yes		
112	16	Jones, Emily C.					24	GA			March 1864	no		Wife of Wm. A. Jones
112	17	Kowel, Malinda					11	Fla						Orphan Girl
112	18	Jones, Lily					1	Fla						
112	19	Reid, Chas. S.	5	9	dk	dk	33	Fla			March 1864			Deserter from Rebel Army
112	20	Reid, Sarah					27	Fla						Wife of Chas. S. Reid
112	21	Reid, Mary E.					10	Fla						Daughter of Chas. S. Reid
112	22	Reid, Sarah S.					8	Fla						Daughter of Chas. S. Reid
112	23	Reid, Alice J.					6	Fla						Daughter of Chas. S. Reid
112	24	Reid, Chas. C.					4	Fla						Son of Chas. S. Reid

Pg	No	Name	Height Ft	Height In	Eyes	Com-plexion	Age	Where born or contraband	Last residence	Where registered for draft or former owner	Date into Department	Oath of Allgn	No of Ration	Remarks
113	1	Reid, Horace L.					2	Fla	Duval Co					Son of Chas. S. Reid
113	2	Reid, Roselle					1	Fla	Duval Co					Daughter of Chas. S. Reid
113	3	Pickering, Chas. M.	5	9	dk	dk	50	N Y				yes		
113	4	Pickering, Phebe					45	N Y						Wife of the above
113	5	Broson, John C.	5	4	blue	fair	31	Fla				yes		Deserter from Rebel Army
113	6	Broson, Matelda A.					30	Fla				no		Wife of the above
113	7	Broson, Elizabeth A.					9	Fla						Daughter of the above
113	8	Broson, John A.					7	Fla						Son of the above
113	9	Broson, Philomena					5	Fla						Daughter of the above
113	10	Broson, Frances J.					4	Fla						Daughter of the above
113	11	Broson, Sydney O.					3	Fla						Daughter of the above
113	12	Bowden, Nancy					56	Fla				yes		Widow
113	13	Bowden, Mary A.					21	Fla				no		Daughter of the above
113	14	Bowden, Henry	5	6	blue	fair	18	Fla				yes		Son of the above
113	15	Bowden, Lewis	5	2	blue	fair	15	Fla				yes		Son of the above
113	16	Bowden, Thos.					13	Fla						Son of the above
113	17	Bowden, Thos.	5	9	blue	dk	38	Fla				yes		Justice of the Peace 5th ..?
113	18	Bowden, Ellen A.					28	Fla				no		Wife of the above
113	19	Bowden, Virginia					9	Fla						Daughter of the above
113	20	Bowden, Thos. J.					8	Fla						Son of the above
113	21	Long, David	5	8	gry	dk	23	Fla			Aug. 1864	yes		Lost arm in Reb. Service
113	22	Long, Isbella					20	Fla			Aug. 1864	yes		Wife of the above
113	23	Long, David					3	Fla						Son of the above
113	24	Long, Thos.					1	Fla						Son of the above

Pg	No	Name	Height Ft	Height In	Eyes	Com-plexion	Age	Where born or contraband	Last residence	Where registered for draft or former owner	Date into Department	Oath of Allgn	No of Ration	Remarks
114	1	Bearden, Joshua					5	Fla	Duval Co					Orphan Boy
114	2	Wilson, Wm.	5	11	grey	dk	42	Fla	Duval Co		May 1864	yes		Deserter from Rebel Army
114	3	Wilson, Jas. M.	5	11	grey	dk	18	Fla	Duval Co		July 1864	yes		Deserter from Rebel Army
114	4	Conway, Chas.	5	4	grey	dk	17	Fla	Duval Co		July 1864	yes	1	Q. M. Dept.
114	5	Peterson, Andrew J.	5	4	blue	dk	17	Fla	Duval Co		July 1864	yes		
114	6	Warren,Thos. A.	5	11	blue	fair	43	Fla	Duval Co		Dec. 1862	yes		Deserter from Rebel Army
114	7	Warren, Leonora					35	Fla	Duval Co		Dec. 1862	no		Wife of the above
114	8	Warren, Frances L.					15	Fla	Duval Co		Dec. 1862	no		Daughter of the above
114	9	Warren, Carolin L.					12	Fla	Duval Co		Dec. 1862	no		Daughter of the above
114	10	Warren,John W.					9	Fla	Duval Co		Dec. 1862	no		Son of the above
114	11	Warren, Mary J.					7	Fla	Duval Co		Dec. 1862	no		Daughter of the above
114	12	Warren, Charlotte A.					5	Fla	Duval Co		Dec. 1862	no		Daughter of the above
114	13	Warren, Thos. J.					3	Fla	Duval Co		Dec. 1862	no		Son of the above
114	14	Warren, Eliza. A.					1	Fla	Duval Co		Dec. 1862	no		Daughter of the above
114	15	Gardner, Jane P.					53	Fla	Duval Co			no		Widow
114	16	Christopher, Wm. G.	5	8	dark	dark	51	Fla	Duval Co			yes		
114	17	Christopher,Elizabeth W.					28	Ala	Duval Co			no		Wife of the above
114	18	Christopher, Emaline L.?					7	Fla						Daughter of the above
114	19	Christopher,Ella G.					5	Fla						Daughter of the above
114	20	Christopher, Alice R.					3	Fla						Daughter of the above
114	21	Christopher, Wm.L.					1	Fla						Son of the above
114	22	Stone, Eliza					83	N.H.						
114	23	Walker, Rebecca					52	N.H.						
114	24	Hatila ?					14	Contraband		Christopher, W.G.				

Pg	No	Name	Height Ft	Height In	Eyes	Complexion	Age	Where born or contraband	Last residence	Where registered for draft or former owner	Date into Department	Oath of Allgn	No of Ration	Remarks
115	1	Walken, Moses					10	Contraband	Duval Co	Christopher, W.G.				
115	2	Walken, Leah					8	Contraband	Duval Co	Christopher, W.G.				
115	3	Stone, Patience					28	Contraband	Duval Co	Stone, Rebecca				
115	4	Stone, Henry					7	Contraband	Duval Co	Stone, Rebecca				
115	5	Stone, Ann					3	Contraband	Duval Co	Stone, Rebecca				
115	6	Wingate, John	5	8	blue	fair	75	Contraband	Duval Co					Has but one arm
115	7	Wingate, Rachael					70	Contraband	Duval Co					Wife of the above
115	8	Buckles, Rich[d]	5	10	blue	dk	38	Ala	Duval Co		Feb. 1864	yes		Deserter from Rebel Army
115	9	Buckles, Thursey R.					31	GA	Duval Co		Feb. 1864	no		Wife of the above
115	10	Buckles, Elihu					10	Fla	Duval Co		Feb. 1864			Son of the above
115	11	Buckles, Edward G.					8	Fla	Duval Co		Feb. 1864			Son of the above
115	12	Buckles, Mary H.					6	Fla	Duval Co		Feb. 1864			Daughter of the above
115	13	Buckles, Calvin					4	Fla	Duval Co		Feb. 1864			Son of the above
115	14	Buckles, Rich[d]					2	Fla	Duval Co		Feb. 1864			Son of the above
115	15	Spikes, Wm.	5	7	dk	dk	35	GA	Duval Co		Sept. 1864	yes		Deserter from Rebel Army
115	16	Spikes, Caroline					25	GA	Duval Co		Sept. 1864	no		Wife of the above
115	17	Spikes, Jane					4	GA	Duval Co		Sept. 1864			Daughter of the above
115	18	Flynn, Wm. B.	5	11	blue	fair	48	S. C.	Duval Co		Jan. 1864	Yes		
115	19	Flynn, Caroline					32	GA	Duval Co		Jan. 1864	Yes		Wife of the above
115	20	Flynn, Catharine R.					16	Fla	Duval Co		Jan. 1864			Daughter of the above
115	21	Flynn, Charles R.					14	Fla	Duval Co		Jan. 1864			Son of the above
115	22	Flynn, Mary A.					12	Fla	Duval Co		Jan. 1864			Daughter of the above
115	23	Flynn, Emma C.					8	Fla	Duval Co		Jan. 1864			Daughter of the above
115	24	Flynn, Elizabeth J.					6	Fla	Duval Co		Jan. 1864			Daughter of the above

Pg	No	Name	Height Ft	Height In	Eyes	Complexion	Age	Where born or contraband	Last residence	Where registered for draft or former owner	Date into Department	Oath of Allgn	No of Ration	Remarks
116	1	Flynn, Wm. J.					8	Fla	Duval Co		Jan. 1864			Son of Wm. B. Flynn
116	2	Flynn, Georgeann					4	Fla	Duval Co		Jan. 1864			Daughter of Wm. B. Flynn
116	3	Flynn, Calvin E.					1	Fla	Duval Co		Jan. 1864			Son of Wm. B. Flynn
116	4	Broward, John	6		dk	dk	43	Fla	Duval Co			yes		Formerly in Rebel Army
116	5	Broward, Adelle E.					35	GA	Duval Co			yes		Wife of above
116	6	Broward, Wm. F.			dk	dk	17	Fla	Duval Co			no		Son of above
116	7	Broward, Martha A.					15	Fla	Duval Co					Daughter of above
116	8	Broward, Charles E.					14	Fla	Duval Co					Son of above
116	9	Broward, John P.					11	Fla	Duval Co					Son of above
116	10	Broward, Emma					9	Fla	Duval Co					Daughter of above
116	11	Broward, Ellen					7	Fla	Duval Co					Daughter of above
116	12	Broward, Preston					5	Fla	Duval Co					Son of above
116	13	Broward, Albert					4	Fla	Duval Co					Son of above
116	14	Broward, Adelle					1	Fla	Duval Co					Daughter of above
116	15	Broward, Dicke					67	Contraband	Duval Co	Broward, John				This person remained with Mr.John Broward
116	16	Broward, Joseph					60	Contraband		Broward, John				This person remained with Mr.John Broward from choice
116	17	Broward, Phillis					21	Contraband	Duval Co	Broward, John				This person remained with Mr.John Broward from choice
116	18	Broward, Margaret					2	Contraband		Broward, John				This person remained with Mr.John Broward from choice
116	19	Shearhouse, Jas.	5	9	blk	dk	30	GA			Aug. 1864	yes		Deserted from Rebel Army
116	20	Shearhouse, Elizabeth					30	GA			Sept. 1864	yes		Wife of the above
116	21	Shearhouse,Joseph					7	GA			Sept. 1864			
116	22	Shearhouse, Emanul					6	Fla			Sept. 1864			
116	23	Shearhouse, Lucette					4	Fla			Sept. 1864			
116	24	Shearhouse, Margaret					2	Fla			Sept. 1864			

Pg	No	Name	Height Ft	Height In	Eyes	Com-plexion	Age	Where born or contraband	Last residence	Where registered for draft or former owner	Date into Department	Oath of Allgn	No of Ration	Remarks
117	1	Nuffes?, Elizabeth					66	Fla	Duval Co			no		
117	2	Flynn, Susan					21	S.C.	Duval Co			yes		Husband at Hilton Head
117	3	Townsend, Chas.	5	7	grey	dark	30	GA	Duval Co		May 1864	yes		Employed by Parsons
117	4	Townsend, Rebecca J.					25	S.C.	Duval Co		Aug. 1864	no		Wife of above
117	5	Townsend, Melvin					7	Fla	Duval Co		Aug. 1864			Son of above
117	6	Townsend, Symantha					5	Fla	Duval Co		Aug. 1864			Daughter of above
117	7	Townsend, Calvin					3	Fla	Duval Co		Aug. 1864			Son of above
117	8	Townsend, Jesse					1	Fla	Duval Co		Aug. 1864			Son of above
117	9	Flynn, Joseph	6		olive	light	34	S.C.	Duval Co		Sept. 1863	yes		Deserter from Confed. Army
117	10	Flynn, Adaline					25	Fla	Duval Co			yes		Wife of above
117	11	Flynn, Eliza					4	Fla	Duval Co					Daughter of above
117	12	Flynn, Emily A.					3	Fla	Duval Co					Daughter of above
117	13	Flynn, Symintha					1	Fla	Duval Co					Daughter of above
117	14	Harroll, John	5	10	olive	light	67	GA	Duval Co			yes		
117	15	Harroll, Eliza					57	GA	Duval Co			no		Wife of John Harroll
117	16	Harroll, Henry	5	9	grey	dk	18	Fla	Duval Co			no		Son of John Harroll
117	17	Harroll, George					16	Fla	Duval Co			no		Son of John Harroll
117	18	Harroll, Arvilla					13	Fla	Duval Co			no		Daughter of John Harroll
117	19	Hartley, Michael H.	5	7	grey	dk	33	Fla	Duval Co			yes		Deserter
117	20	Hartley, Ella A.					31	Fla	Duval Co			no		Wife of above
117	21	Ponce, Isadore B.	5	5	dk	dk	18	Fla	Duval Co			yes		Discharged from Confed Serv
117	22	Ponce, Emma					25	Contraband		Hartley, Michael H				
117	23	Ponce, Benj.					6	Contraband		Hartley, Michael H				
117	24	Ponce, George					5	Contraband		Hartley, Michael H				

Pg	No	Name	Height Ft	Height In	Eyes	Com-plexion	Age	Where born or contraband	Last residence	Where registered for draft or former owner	Date into Department	Oath of Allgn	No of Ration	Remarks
118	1	Ponce, Savina					3	Contraband		Hartley, Michael H				Remained with Michael Hartley from choice
118	2	Ponce, Elizabeth					1	Contraband		Hartley, Michael H				
118	3	Hartley, Roderick	6		blue	fair	38	Fla			Sept. 1863	yes		Deserter from Confed. Service
118	4	Hartley, Elizabeth					36	Fla				no		Wife of above
118	5	Hartley, Eliza A.					15	Fla						Daughter of above
118	6	Hartley, Francis M.					13	Fla						Daughter of above
118	7	Hartley, Chas. F.					11	Fla						Son of above
118	8	Hartley, Mary E.					9	Fla						Daughter of above
118	9	Hartley, Roderick B.					7	Fla						Son of above
118	10	Hartley, Calvin S.					6	Fla						Son of above
118	11	Hartley, John A.					4	Fla						Son of above
118	12	Hartley, Ellen					2	Fla						Daughter of above
118	13	Hartley, Wm. E.					1	Fla						Son of above
118	14	Masters, Joseph P.	6		blk	dk	40	Fla			Dec. 1863	yes		Deserter from Confederate Service
118	15	Masters, Melinda					38	Fla						Wife of above
118	16	Masters, Peter					13	Fla						Son of above
118	17	Masters, Mary F.					7	Fla						Daughter of above
118	18	Dean, John	6		grey	dk	48	S.C.			Aug. 1864	Yes		
118	19	Dean, Jane S.					37	Fla			Oct. 1864	no		Wife of above
118	20	Dean, Jesse A.	5	2	dk	dk	22	Fla			Aug. 1864	Yes		Son of above
118	21	Dean, Eliza L.					19	Fla			Oct. 1864	no		Daughter of above
118	22	Dean, Mary E.					17	Fla			Oct. 1864	no		Daughter of above
118	23	Dean, Jas. S. H.					16	Fla			Oct. 1864	no		Son of above
118	24	Dean, Sarah A.					14	Fla			Oct. 1864	no		Daughter of above

Pg	No	Name	Height Ft	Height In	Eyes	Com-plexion	Age	Where born or contraband	Last residence	Where registered for draft or former owner	Date into Department	Oath of Allgn	No of Ration	Remarks
119	1	Silcox, David U.					10	Fla	Duval Co		Aug. 1864			Son of David Silcox
119	2	Silcox, Rachael					8	Fla	Duval Co		Aug. 1864			Daughter of David Silcox
119	3	Silcox, Ann					6	Fla	Duval Co		Aug. 1864			Daughter of David Silcox
119	4	Silcox, Elizabeth					4	Fla	Duval Co		Aug. 1864			Daughter of David Silcox
119	5	Silcox, Emmeretta					2	Fla	Duval Co		Aug. 1864			Daughter of David Silcox
119	6	Silcox, Infant						Fla	Duval Co		Aug. 1864			Daughter of David Silcox
119	7	Silcox, Wm.	5	10	blue	fair	38	Fla	Duval Co		Jan. 1864	Yes		Deserter from Confed Service
119	8	Mathews, Wm. E.	5	8	blue	fair	36	S.C.	Duval Co		May 1864	Yes		Deserter from Confederate Service
119	9	Mathews,Wealltry A.					37	S.C.	Duval Co		June 1864	Yes		Wife of above
119	10	Mathews, Martha E.					7	S.C.	Duval Co		June 1864			Daughter of above
119	11	Livingston, Elvin	6		blue	fair	35	S.C.	Duval Co		Feb. 1864	Yes		Deserter from Confed Service
119	12	Livingston, Eliza J.					32	GA	Duval Co		Sept. 1864	no		Wife of above
119	13	Livingston, Suanna					10	Fla	Duval Co		Sept. 1864			Daughter of above
119	14	Livingston, Louisa					8	Fla	Duval Co		Sept. 1864			Daughter of above
119	15	Livingston, Henrietta					6	Fla	Duval Co		Sept. 1864			Daughter of above
119	16	Livingston, Virginia					4	Fla	Duval Co		Sept. 1864			Daughter of above
119	17	James, Mary A.					49	Fla	Duval Co			Yes		Widow
119	18	James, Julia					18	Fla	Duval Co			Yes		Daughter of above
119	19	James, Isaac					16	Fla	Duval Co			Yes		Son of above
119	20	Janes, Frances					13	Fla	Duval Co			no		Daughter of above
119	21	Flynn, Eliza J.					21	Fla	Duval Co			Yes		Husband died in Confed. Service
119	22	Flynn, Jas. B.					4	Fla	Duval Co					Son of above
119	23	Flynn, Catharine P.					2	Fla	Duval Co					Daughter of above
119	24	Williams,Willoughten J.	5	4	grey	dk	21	GA	Duval Co		May 1864	yes		Deserter from Confed Service

Pg	No	Name	Height Ft	Height In	Eyes	Com-plexion	Age	Where born or contraband	Last residence	Where registered for draft or former owner	Date into Department	Oath of Allgn	No of Ration	Remarks
120	1	Dean, Joshua I.					12	Fla	Duval Co		Oct. 1864			Son of John Dean
120	2	Dean, John A.					10	Fla	Duval Co		Oct. 1864			Son of John Dean
120	3	Bowders, John	5	11	dk	dk	74	Fla	Duval Co			no		
120	4	Osteen, Jas.	5	4	grey	dk	30	GA	Duval Co		Jan. 1864	yes		Deserter from Confed Service
120	5	Osteen, Julia A.					20	Fla	Duval Co		Jan. 1864	yes		Wife of above
120	6	Osteen, Wm. E.					2	Fla	Duval Co		Jan. 1864	yes		Son of above
120	7	Hogan, Zackariah S.	6		dk	dk	40	Fla	Duval Co			yes		Engaged in Rafting
120	8	Hogan, Mary					28	Fla	Duval Co			no		Wife of above
120	9	Summerall, Jos. E.	5	10			55	Fla	Duval Co			yes		
120	10	Summerall,Catharine					44	Colored	Duval Co					
120	11	Summerall, Saura					21	Colored	Duval Co					
120	12	Summerall, Wm.					19	Colored	Duval Co					
120	13	Summerall,Anderson					16	Colored	Duval Co					
120	14	Summerall, Aura					15	Colored	Duval Co					
120	15	Summerall, Ary					14	Colored	Duval Co					
120	16	Summerall,Catharine					13	Colored	Duval Co					
120	17	Summerall, Edward					8	Colored	Duval Co					
120	18	Summerall, Latitia					7	Colored	Duval Co					
120	19	Summerall, Eliza					5	Colored	Duval Co					
120	20	Summerall, Lewis					3	Colored	Duval Co					
120	21	Silcox, David	5	10	blue	fair	36	Fla	Duval Co		May 1864	yes		Deserter from Confed. Service
120	22	Silcox, Keseah					36	GA	Duval Co		Aug. 1864	yes		Wife of above
120	23	Silcox, Sarah A.					15	Fla	Duval Co		Aug. 1864	no		Daughter of above
120	24	Silcox, Laura					12	Fla	Duval Co		Aug. 1864			Daughter of above

Pg	No	Name	Height Ft	Height In	Eyes	Complexion	Age	Where born or contraband	Last residence	Where registered for draft or former owner	Date into Department	Oath of Allgn	No of Ration	Remarks
121	1	Chestnut, Wm.					14	Fla	Duval Co		July 1864	no		
121	2	Chestnut, Geo.					10	Fla	Duval Co					
121	3	Chestnut, Luraine					8	Fla	Duval Co					
121	4	Chestnut, Jesse					6	Fla	Duval Co					
121	5	Chestnut, Emily					3	Fla	Duval Co					
121	6	Chestnur, Daniel					2	Fla	Duval Co					
121	7	Acosta, Jas. E.	5	7	blk	dk	36	Fla	Duval Co		July 1863	yes		
121	8	Acosta, Elizabeth					28	Fla	Duval Co		July 1863	no		
121	9	Acosta, Eliza E.					10	Fla	Duval Co					
121	10	Acosta, Victoria					8	Fla	Duval Co					
121	11	Acosta, Georgiana					6	Fla	Duval Co					
121	12	Acosta, Florida A.					4	Fla	Duval Co					
121	13	Acosta, Mary J.					2	Fla	Duval Co					
121	14	Acosta, Infant					"?	Fla	Duval Co					
121	15	Hagin, Josiah	6		blk	dk	47	Fla	Duval Co			yes		
121	16	Hagin, Catharine J.					36	GA	Duval Co			no		
121	17	Hagin, Thos. J.	5	11	blk	dk	17	Fla	Duval Co			no		
121	18	Hagin, Mary E.					15	Fla	Duval Co					
121	19	Hagin, Catharine J.					13	Fla	Duval Co					
121	20	Hagin, Laving L.					8	Fla	Duval Co					
121	21	Hagin, Josiah M.					5	Fla	Duval Co					
121	22	Hall, Loyd	5	8	blue	fair	26	S.C.	Duval Co		Feb. 1864	yes		
121	23	Hall, Sarah					21	S.C.	Duval Co		June 1864	yes		
121	24	Hall, Enos J.					4	Fla	Duval Co					

Pg	No	Name	Height Ft	Height In	Eyes	Com-plexion	Age	Where born or contraband	Last residence	Where registered for draft or former owner	Date into Department	Oath of Allgn	No of Ration	Remarks
122	1	Hall, Ensly	5	9	blue	dk	35	S.C.	Duval Co		Feb. 1864	yes		
122	2	Hall, Susan					31	Fla	Duval Co			no		
122	3	Hall, Hugh					9	Fla	Duval Co					
122	4	Hall, Elijah					8	Fla	Duval Co					
122	5	Hall, Henry P.					6	Fla	Duval Co					
122	6	Hall, Benj. F.					3	Fla	Duval Co					
122	7	Hall, Lydney					1	Fla	Duval Co					
122	8	Hardenbrock, Jas.	5	9	grey	dk	53	N. Y.	Duval Co		Sept. 1864	yes		
122	9	Hardenbrock, Helena					41	N. C.	Duval Co			no		
122	10	Hardenbrock, Mary					13	Fla	Duval Co					
122	11	Hardenbrock, Moses					9	Fla	Duval Co					
122	12	Hardenbrock, David					5	Fla	Duval Co					
122	13	Hardenbrock, Jefferson					2	Fla	Duval Co					
122	14	Sparkman, Alfred L.	5	11	blue	dk	39	Fla	Duval Co		Feb. 1864	yes		
122	15	Sparkman, Nancy					31	Fla	Duval Co			yes		
122	16	Sparkman, Elizabeth					13	Fla	Duval Co					
122	17	Sparkman, Levi					10	Fla	Duval Co					
122	18	Sparkman, Kisiah					8	Fla	Duval Co					
122	19	Rosier, Rebeca					55	GA	Duval Co		Aug. 1864	yes		
122	20	Rosier, Luke	5		blue	dk	20	GA	Duval Co		March. 1864	yes		
122	21	Rosier, Julia					15	GA	Duval Co		Aug. 1864	yes		
122	22	Rosier, Anna					12	GA	Duval Co		Aug. 1864			
122	23	Rosier, Henry					10	GA	Duval Co					
122	24	Acosta, George L.	5	8	blk	dk	37	Fla	Duval Co			yes		

Pg	No	Name	Height Ft	Height In	Eyes	Complexion	Age	Where born or contraband	Last residence	Where registered for draft or former owner	Date into Department	Oath of Allgn	No of Ration	Remarks
123	1	McCamy?, Abigail	5	4	blue	fair	53	GA	Fla	never	1848	no	none	
123	2	Ryals, Louis	6	0	blk	dk	45	GA	Fla		1848	yes	none	Hunter and Farmer
123	3	Ryals, Catharine	5	4	blk	dk	40	GA	Fla		1848	no	none	
123	4	Ryals, Lewis	5	3	blk	dk	16	GA	Fla	never	1848	yes	none	
123	5	Ryals, Mary A.	5	2	blk	dk	14	GA	Fla			no	none	
123	6	Ryals, Cath[rn]			blk	dk	8	GA	Fla			no	none	
123	7	Ryals, Wm.			blk	dk	4	GA	Fla			no	none	
123	8	Ryals, Mary			blk	dk	2	GA	Fla			no	none	
123	9	Henly, Wm.	5	5	Blue	f	54	VA	Fla	never	1835	yes	none	Farmer
123	10	Henly, Emeline	5	3	blue	f	45	S.C.	Fla		1835	no	none	
123	11	Henly, Zach	4	8	blue	f	14	Fla	Fla	never		no	none	
123	12	Henly, Laura			blue	f	7	Fla	Fla			no	none	
123	13	Henly, Andrew			blue	f	5	Fla	Fla			no	none	
123	14	Henly, Emma			blue	f	3	Fla	Fla			no	none	
123	15	Henly, Alice			blue	f	1	Fla	Fla			no	none	
123	16	Roberts, Bethel	5	9	blue	f	30	Fla	Fla			yes	none	Working for Parsons: getting Ranger Timber
123	17	Roberts, Marg[t]	5	6	blue	f	24	Fla	Fla			yes	none	
123	18	Roberts, Jack			blue	f	6	Fla	Fla			no	none	
123	19	Roberts, Bethel			blue	f	3	Fla	Fla			no	none	
123	20	Roberts, Cornelion			blue	f	1	Fla	Fla			no	none	
123	21	Houston, Thomas	5	9	blue	f	70	GA	Fla		1854	no	none	Farmer
123	22	Houston, Asia	5	4	blue	f	60	Fla	Fla		1854	no	none	
123	23	Houston, Wm.	5	8	blue	f	44	Fla	Fla		1854	no	1	Govt. Employee at the Bar
123	24	Houston, Bayard	5	8	blue	f	33	Fla	Fla		1854	no	1	Govt. Employee at the Bar

Pg	No	Name	Height Ft	Height In	Eyes	Com-plexion	Age	Where born or contraband	Last residence	Where registered for draft or former owner	Date into Department	Oath of Allgn	No of Ration	Remarks
124	25	Houston, Jos.	5	10	blue	f	19	GA	Fla	never	1854	yes	1	Govt. Employee
124	26	Houston, Eveline	5	4	blue	f	34	GA	Fla		1854	no	none	
124	27	Houston, Marg[t]	5	4	blue	f	30	GA	Fla		1854	no	none	
124	28	Houston, Mary	5	4	blue	f	21	GA	Fla		1854	no	none	
124	29	Houston, Eliza[th]	5	4	blue	f	24	GA	Fla		1854	no	none	
124	30	Brown, Chas.	5	10	dk	dk	48	Wales	Fla	never	1835	yes	1	Govt. Employee (Pilot)
124	31	Brown, Jos[hine]	5	4	dk	dk	45	Fla	Fla			yes	none	
124	32	Brown, Mary	5	5	dk	dk	25	Fla	Fla			yes	none	
124	33	Brown, Augustus	5	4	dk	dk	21	Fla	Fla			yes	none	
124	34	Brown, Frances	5	3	dk	dk	18	Fla	Fla			yes	none	
124	35	Brown, Louisa	5	4	dk	dk	16	Fla	Fla			yes	none	
124	36	Brown, John	4	9	dk	dk	14	Fla	Fla			no	none	
124	37	Brown, Abigail	4	6	dk	dk	12	Fla	Fla			no	none	
124	38	Brown, Josephine			dk	dk	10	Fla	Fla			no	none	
124	39	Brown, Charley			dk	dk	8	Fla	Fla			no	none	
124	40	Brown, Harry			dk	dk	6	Fla	Fla			no	none	
124	41	Brown, Napoleon			dk	dk	4	Fla	Fla			no	none	
124	42	Brown, Geo.			dk	dk	2	Fla	Fla			no	none	
124	43	Lama, Wm.	5	5	dk	dk	50	France	Fla		1835	yes	1	Pilot on U S. Sh.?Hale
124	44	Lama, Aneka	5	4	dk	dk	45	Fla	Fla			yes	none	
124	45	Lama, Mary	5	4	dk	dk	21	Fla	Fla			yes	none	
124	46	Lama, Frank	5	2	dk	dk	15	Fla	Fla			no	none	
124	47	Lama, Meleria	4	9	dk	dk	13	Fla	Fla			no	none	
124	48	Lama, Rosa	4	4	dk	dk	11	Fla	Fla			no	none	

Pg	No	Name	Height Ft	Height In	Eyes	Com-plexion	Age	Where born or contraband	Last residence	Where registered for draft or former owner	Date into Department	Oath of Allgn	No of Ration	Remarks
125	1	Geiger, Elizer L.					10	Fla	Duval Co					
125	2	Geiger, Wm. A.					13	Fla	Duval Co					
125	3	Geiger, Henry A.					8	Fla	Duval Co					
125	4	Geiger, Elenor					6	Fla	Duval Co					
125	5	Geiger, Mary A.					4	Fla	Duval Co					
125	6	Geiger, John L.					2	Fla	Duval Co					
125	7	Hartley, Jas. N.	5	10	blue	fair	38	Fla	Duval Co		Oct. 1863	yes		
125	8	Hartley, Toracy J.					29	Fla	Duval Co					
125	9	Hartley, Anna M.					12	Fla	Duval Co					
125	10	Hartley, Thos. E.					9	Fla	Duval Co					
125	11	Hartley, Archibald A.					4	Fla	Duval Co					
125	12	Hartley, Jas. L.					1	Fla	Duval Co					
125	13	Hagan,Thos. J.					16	Fla	Duval Co					
125	14	Cone, James					67	Fla	Duval Co			yes		
125	15	Cone, Zylpha					26	Fla	Duval Co			yes		
125	16	Cone, Elizabeth					22	Fla	Duval Co			yes		
125	17	Cone, Jas. B. C.					17	Fla	Duval Co			no		
125	18	Cone, Georgianna					15	Fla	Duval Co					
125	19	Cone, Union N. F.					12	Fla	Duval Co					
125	20	Cone, Arabella					8	Fla	Duval Co					
125	21	McGuaig, Wm. C.	5	10	grey	dk	50	Fla	Duval Co			yes		
125	22	McGuaig, Matilda					33	Fla	Duval Co			no		
125	23	McGuaig, Nancy E.					19	Fla	Duval Co					
125	24	McGuaig, Caroline					16	Fla	Duval Co					

Pg	No	Name	Height Ft	Height In	Eyes	Com-plexion	Age	Where born or contraband	Last residence	Where registered for draft or former owner	Date into Department	Oath of Allgn	No of Ration	Remarks
126	1	Curry, Wm.	5	4	Blue	fair	18	Fla	Duval Co			yes		
126	2	Stone, David	6				65	S. C.	Duval Co			yes		
126	3	Stone, Edy					75	N.C.	Duval Co			no		
126	4	Dew, Mary					25	S. C.	Duval Co			no		
126	5	Wingate, William					14	Fla	Duval Co					
126	6	Wingate, Edy					12	Fla	Duval Co					
126	7	Wingate, Mary A.					9	Fla	Duval Co					
126	8	Wingate, Elizabeth					6	Fla	Duval Co					
126	9	Lane, Edward	5	10	grey	dk	47	GA	St. Johns Co.		Aug. 1864	yes		
126	10	Lane, Daniel	5	5	grey	dk	35	GA	St. Johns Co.		May 1864	yes		
126	11	Lane, Priscella					26	GA	St. Johns Co.		May 1864	no		
126	12	Lane, Nancy					13	GA	St. Johns Co.		May 1864	no		
126	13	Lane, Absalum					10	GA	St. Johns Co.		May 1864	no		
126	14	Lane, Susan					8	GA	St. Johns Co.		May 1864	no		
126	15	Lane, Mary					4	GA	St. Johns Co.		May 1864	no		
126	16	Hartley, Caroline					35	Fla	Duval Co			no		
126	17	Ford, James M.					6	Fla	Duval Co					
126	18	Ann, Alfred					3	Fla	Duval Co					
126	19	Cooper, Mary					26	Fla	Duval Co		August /64	yes		
126	20	Cooper, Angula					9	Fla	Duval Co					
126	21	Cooper, William					2	Fla	Duval Co					
126	22	Geiger, John R.	5	8	blue	fair	43	Fla	Duval Co			yes		
126	23	Geiger, SarahFrancis					33	Fla	Duval Co					
126	24	Geiger, Jane? F.					16	Fla	Duval Co					

Pg	No	Name	Height Ft	Height In	Eyes	Com-plexion	Age	Where born or contraband	Last residence	Where registered for draft or former owner	Date into Department	Oath of Allgn	No of Ration	Remarks
127	1	Acosta, Bengna M.					35	Cuba	Duval Co			no		
127	2	Acosta, Dommgo					11	Fla	Duval Co					
127	3	Acosta, Christia					9	Fla	Duval Co					
127	4	Acosta, Patrick					7	Fla	Duval Co					
127	5	Acosta, Eugenia					3	Fla	Duval Co					
127	6	Sparkman,Josephine					28	Fla	Duval Co			yes		
127	7	Sparkman, Daniel					10	Fla	Duval Co					
127	8	Sparkman, Sarah E.					2	Fla	Duval Co					
127	9	Hartley, Ann M.					34	N. Y.	Duval Co			yes		
127	10	Hartley, George N.					15	Fla	Duval Co					
127	11	Hartley, Emanuel P.					8	Fla	Duval Co					
127	12	Hartley, Robt L.					6	Fla	Duval Co					
127	13	Hartley, Fredrick L.					3	Fla	Duval Co					
127	14	Hartley, Laura					14	Fla	Duval Co					
127	15	Hartley,Bartholomew					12	Fla	Duval Co					
127	16	Hartley, Milton					9	Fla	Duval Co					
127	17	Hartley, Sarah					7	Fla	Duval Co					
127	18	Hartley, Rosalia					4	Fla	Duval Co					
127	19	Hartley, Ellen					2	Fla	Duval Co					
127	20	Hartley, Wm. F.	5	10	grey	dk	45	Fla	Duval Co			yes		
127	21	Hartley, Susan E.					32	Fla	Duval Co					
127	22	Hartley, Jas. A.					11	Fla	Duval Co					
127	23	Hartley, John Wm.					9	Fla	Duval Co					
127	24	Hartley, Dan[l]					8	Fla	Duval Co					

Pg	No	Name	Height		Eyes	Com-plexion	Age	Where born or contraband	Last residence	Where registered for draft or former owner	Date into Department	Oath of Allgn	No of Ration	Remarks
			Ft	In										
128	1	Hartley, Mary A.					5	Fla	Duval Co					
128	2	Hartley, Virginia A.					1	Fla	Duval Co					
128	3	GArdner, George	5	8	dk	dk	30	Fla	Duval Co		Aug. 1864	yes		
128	4	GArdner, Elizer A.					50	Fla	Duval Co			no		
128	5	GArdner, Thos. L.					8	Fla	Duval Co					
128	6	GArdner, Sarah A.					48	S. C.	Duval Co			yes		
128	7	Hagan, Anthony	4	10	dk	dk	17	Fla	Duval Co			no		
128	8	GArdner, Francis					11	Fla	Duval Co					
128	9	Sparkman,Josephine					26	Fla	Duval Co					
128	10	Sparkman, Sarah E.					3	Fla	Duval Co					
128	11	Sparkman, Daniel					10	Fla	Duval Co					
128	12	Ford, William	5	5	dk	dk	40	Fla	Duval Co		July 1864	yes		
128	13	Ford, Emily					30	Fla	Duval Co		July 1864	yes		
128	14	Ford, Thos. R.					10	Fla	Duval Co					
128	15	Ford, Wm H.					8	Fla	Duval Co					
128	16	Hartley, Emaline					1	Fla	Duval Co					Twins
128	17	Hartley, Adaline					1	Fla	Duval Co					
128	18	Hartley, Nathaniel					65	Fla	Duval Co			no		Partially Blind
128	19	Hartley, Catharine					21	Fla	Duval Co			no		
128	20	Hartley, Mary J.					50	Fla	Duval Co			no		
128	21	Hartley, Victoria					18	Fla	Duval Co			no		
128	22	Hartley, Calvin					6	Fla	Duval Co					
128	23	Hartley, Elizer. J.					3	Fla	Duval Co					
128	24	Plumer, Lucinda					23	Fla	Duval Co					

Pg	No	Name	Height Ft	Height In	Eyes	Com-plexion	Age	Where born or contraband	Last residence	Where registered for draft or former owner	Date into Department	Oath of Allgn	No of Ration	Remarks
129	1	Pacetti, Charles					1	Fla	St. Johns					
129	2	Hernandez, Deigo					74	Fla	St. Johns			yes		Blind
129	3	Pacetti, Jane					34	Fla	St. Johns					
129	4	Pacetti, Mary					10	Fla	St. Johns					
129	5	Pacetti, Francis					8	Fla	St. Johns					
129	6	Pacetti, Andrew					6	Fla	St. Johns					
129	7	Pacetti, Eliza					5	Fla	St. Johns					
129	8	Pacetti, Virginia					3	Fla	St. Johns					
129	9	Pacetti, Rosa L.					1	Fla	St. Johns					
129	10	Canova, Raphile	5	6	blk	dk	44	Fla	St. Johns			yes		
129	11	Canova, Susan					45	Fla	St. Johns			yes		
129	12	Canova, Laura					16	Fla	St. Johns			yes		
129	13	Canova, Raphile					11	Fla	St. Johns					Twins
129	14	Canova, Margaret					11	Fla	St. Johns					
129	15	Canova, Philip					9	Fla	St. Johns					
129	16	Canova, Matthew					4	Fla	St. Johns					
129	17	Weedman, Philip	5	9	blk	dk	63	Fla	St. Johns			yes		
129	18	Weedman, Eliza					55	Fla	St. Johns			yes		
129	19	Weedman,Alexander	5	11	grey	dk	18	Fla	St. Johns			yes		
129	20	Young, Mary					26	GA	St. Johns					
129	21	Young, Cornelia					5	Fla	St. Johns					
129	22	Young, Mary L.					2	Fla	St. Johns					
129	23	Brooker, Jas.	6		blue	Lt	47	GA	St. Johns		Aug.1864?	yes		
129	24	Tyler, Hugh	6		blue	Lt	56	S. C.	St. Johns			yes		

Pg	No	Name	Height Ft	Height In	Eyes	Com-plexion	Age	Where born or contraband	Last residence	Where registered for draft or former owner	Date into Department	Oath of Allgn	No of Ration	Remarks
130	1	Saunders, Henrietta					4	Fla	Duval Co					
130	2	Saunders, Wm. G.					2	Fla	Duval Co					
130	3	Hartley, Wm.	5	8	blue	dk	41	Fla	Duval Co			yes		
130	4	Hartley, Mary J.					36	Fla	Duval Co			yes		
130	5	Hartley, Jas. S.					14	Fla	Duval Co					
130	6	Hartley, Andrew					12	Fla	Duval Co					
130	7	Hartley, Ellen					10	Fla	Duval Co					
130	8	Hartley, Rudolph					8	Fla	Duval Co					
130	9	Hartley, Sarah					6	Fla	Duval Co					
130	10	Stucky, Pinckney					45	Fla	St. Johns					
130	11	Benet, Richard					65	Fla	St. Johns					
130	12	Benet, Hannah					50	Fla	St. Johns					
130	13	Tanlor?, Jas.	5	9	blue	dk	29	Fla	St. Johns		Sept. 1864	yes		
130	14	Tanlor?, Margaret					30	GA	St. Johns		Sept. 1864	yes		
130	15	Smith, Ann					35	Fla	St. Johns		Sept. 1864	yes		
130	16	Smith, Robert					8	Fla	St. Johns					
130	17	Smith, Julia					6	Fla	St. Johns					
130	18	Pacetti,, Antonio					34	Fla	St. Johns			yes		
130	19	Pacetti, William					12	Fla	St. Johns					
130	20	Pacetti, Lewis					9	Fla	St. Johns					
130	21	Pacetti, John					8	Fla	St. Johns					
130	22	Pacetti, Mary					7	Fla	St. Johns					
130	23	Pacetti, George					5	Fla	St. Johns					
130	24	Pacetti, Dennis					3	Fla	St. Johns					

Pg	No	Name	Height Ft	Height In	Eyes	Com-plexion	Age	Where born or contraband	Last residence	Where registered for draft or former owner	Date into Department	Oath of Allgn	No of Ration	Remarks
131	1	Mickler, Robert					8	Fla	St. Johns Co.					
131	2	Labata, Agatha					38	Fla	St. Johns Co.					
131	3	Labata, Frances					9	Fla	St. Johns Co.					
131	4	Labata, Mary					7	Fla	St. Johns Co.					
131	5	Labata, Susan					5	Fla	St. Johns Co.					
131	6	Labata, Christianna					3	Fla	St. Johns Co.					
131	7	Autagus, Enassu	5	6	blk	dk	37	Fla	St. Johns Co.			yes		
131	8	Autagus, Mainy A.					35	Fla	St. Johns Co.					
131	9	Autagus, Mary M.					12	Fla	St. Johns Co.					
131	10	Autagus, Antonio					10	Fla	St. Johns					
131	11	Autagus, Enafser?					9	Fla	St. Johns Co.					
131	12	Autagus, Wm.					7	Fla	St. Johns Co.					
131	13	Autagus,Matilda					5	Fla	St. Johns Co.					
131	14	Autagus, Erany?					4	Fla	St. Johns Co.					
131	15	Autagus, Josephine					2	Fla	St. Johns Co.					
131	16	Powers, Alx?	5	7	dk	dk	53	GA	St. Johns Co.			yes		
131	17	Powers, Mary					43	Fla	St. Johns Co.			no		
131	18	Powers, Benjamin	5	10	grey	dk	23	Fla	St. Johns Co.			yes		
131	19	Powers, Harriet					19	Fla	St. Johns Co.					
131	20	Powers, Jane M.					16	Fla	St. Johns Co.					
131	21	Powers, Alexander					13	Fla	St. Johns Co.					
131	22	Powers, Jas. A.					11	Fla	St. Johns Co.					
131	23	Powers, Hester A.					10	Fla	St. Johns Co.					
131	24	Powers, Susan A.					8	Fla	St. Johns Co.					

Pg	No	Name	Height Ft	Height In	Eyes	Com-plexion	Age	Where born or contraband	Last residence	Where registered for draft or former owner	Date into Department	Oath of Allgn	No of Ration	Remarks
132	1	McGurig?, Tabitham					15	Fla	Duval Co					
132	2	McGurig?, Chimpele					13	Fla	Duval Co					
132	3	McGurig?, Elizer M.					9	Fla	Duval Co					
132	4	McGurig?, John E.					7	Fla	Duval Co					
132	5	McGurig?, Macinda					3	Fla	Duval Co					
132	6	Carleton, McKeen	5	6	dk	dk	39	GA	Duval Co		Feb. 1864	yes		
132	7	Hersey?, Wm. .	6	3	blue	fair	34	GA	Duval Co		Feb. 1864	yes		
132	8	Cubbage?, Edward L.	5	7	grey	dk	47	S. C.	Duval Co			yes		
132	9	Cubbage?,Naome J.					43	S. C.	Duval Co			no		
132	10	Cubbage?, Rosa C.					19	S. C.	Duval Co			yes		
132	11	Cubbage?, Ann E.					17	S. C.	Duval Co			no		
132	12	Cubbage?, Mary A.					15	GA	Duval Co					
132	13	Cubbage?,George H.					12	Fla	Duval Co					
132	14	Cubbage?, Lezzie E.					6	Fla	Duval Co					
132	15	Adams, John F.	5	7	blue	dk	36	S. C.	Duval Co			yes		
132	16	Adams, Jane A.					24	Fla	Duval Co			yes		
132	17	Adams, Elizer E.					12	Fla	Duval Co					
132	18	Adams, Charles F.					9	Fla						
132	19	Adams, Marth J.					6	Fla						
132	20	Adams, Jane C.					4	Fla						
132	21	Adams, Albert F.					2	Fla						
132	22	Mickler, Robt. D.	5	9	black	dark	40	Fla				yes		
132	23	Mickler, Ruth					17	Fla						
132	24	Mickler, Lewis					10	Fla						

Pg	No	Name	Height		Eyes	Com-plexion	Age	Where born or contraband	Last residence	Where registered for draft or former owner	Date into Department	Oath of Allgn	No of Ration	Remarks
			Ft	In										
133	1	Strickland, Aaron	4	8	blue	fair	24	Georgia	Duval Co		Dec. 1863	yes		
133	2	Strickland, Julia A.					20	Fla	Duval Co		Aug. 1864	yes		
133	3	Strickland, James					3	Fla	Duval Co		Aug. 1864			
133	4	Strickland, Hester A.					1	Fla	Duval Co		Aug. 1864			
133	5	Waldrow, Michael B.	5	8	grey	dk	30	GA	Duval Co		April 1864	yes		
133	6	Waldrow, Martha A.					24	Fla	Duval Co		Sept. 1864	yes		
133	7	Waldrow, Sarah E.					7	Fla	Duval Co		Sept. 1864			
133	8	Waldrow, Martha A.					5	Fla	Duval Co		Sept. 1864			
133	9	Waldrow, David M.					4	Fla	Duval Co		Sept. 1864			
133	10	Waldrow, William W.					1	Fla	Duval Co		Sept. 1864			
133	11	Lutas, Frednck	5	8	blue	dk	38	Germany	Duval Co			yes		
133	12	Lutas, Frances					37	Fla	Duval Co					
133	13	Lutas, Mary					15	Fla	Duval Co					
133	14	Lutas, Henry					10	Fla	Duval Co					
133	15	Lutas, Leonora					7	Fla	Duval Co					
133	16	Lutas, Mariah					6	Fla	Duval Co					
133	17	Lutas, William					1	Fla	Duval Co					
133	18	Turner, Rachel					40	Fla	Duval Co			yes		
133	19	Turner, Jas. B.					18	Fla	Duval Co			yes		
133	20	Turner, Jane					16	Fla	Duval Co					
133	21	Turner, Martha A.					10	Fla	Duval Co					
133	22	Turner, John W.					4	Fla	Duval Co					
133	23	Booth, Wm. J.	5	7	dk	dk	37	Georgia	Duval Co		Feb. 1864	yes		
133	24	Booth, Susannah					34	Fla	Duval Co		Feb. 1864	no		

"CENSUS" DEPARTMENT OF THE SOUTH - NOVEMBER, 1864

Pg	No	Name	Height Ft	Height In	Eyes	Com-plexion	Age	Where born or contraband	Last residence	Where registered for draft or former owner	Date into Department	Oath of Allgn	No of Ration	Remarks
134	1	Booth, Andrew J.					12	Fla	St. Johns Co.		Feb. 1864			
134	2	Booth, Chas. M.					10	Fla	St. Johns Co.		Feb. 1864			
134	3	Booth, Martha E.					9	Fla	St. Johns Co.		Feb. 1864			
134	4	Booth, Rebecca J.					7	Fla	St. Johns Co.		Feb. 1864			
134	5	Booth, Wm. B.					5	Fla	St. Johns Co.		Feb. 1864			
134	6	Booth, Hugh					4	Fla	St. Johns Co.		Feb. 1864			
134	7	Booth, Jas. N.					2	Fla	St. Johns Co.		Feb. 1864			
134	8	McKee, Martha					39	Fla	Duval Co		June 1864	yes		
134	9	McKee, Benjamin	5	2	grey	dk	47	Fla	Duval Co		June 1864	yes	1	Courier
134	10	McKee, Georgian					15	Fla	Duval Co		June 1864			
134	11	McKee, Gideon					11	Fla	Duval Co		June 1864			
134	12	McKee, Melvin E.					9	Fla	Duval Co		June 1864			
134	13	Cooper, Isham	5	10	blue	fair	47	GA	Duval Co		May 1864	yes	1	Courier
134	14	Cooper, Mary A.					31	GA	Duval Co		May 1864	yes		
134	15	Cooper, Nancy P.					9	Fla	Duval Co		May 1864			
134	16	Cooper, James H.					7	Fla	Duval Co		May 1864			
134	17	Cooper, Roann					5	Fla	Duval Co		May 1864			
134	18	Cooper, John B.					3	Fla	Duval Co		May 1864			
134	19	Brown, Yekile	5	9	dk	dk	45	S. C.	Duval Co			yes		
134	20	Brown, Hannah					48	GA	Duval Co			yes		
134	21	Brown, Jas. C.					13	Fla	Duval Co					
134	22	Brown, Ellen S.					11	Fla	Duval Co					
134	23	Brown, Florida R.					7	Fla	Duval Co					
134	24	Saunders, Elizabeth					24	Fla	Duval Co					

Pg	No	Name	Height		Eyes	Com-plexion	Age	Where born or contraband	Last residence	Where registered for draft or former owner	Date into Department	Oath of Allgn	No of Ration	Remarks
			Ft	In										
135	1	Lee, Levi					14	Fla	St. Johns					
135	2	Lee, Babe					12	Fla	St. Johns					
135	3	Lee, Harriet					10	Fla	St. Johns					
135	4	Lee, Susan					8	Fla	St. Johns					
135	5	Weedman, Theresa					16	Fla	St. Johns					
135	6	Weedman, Rosa					14	Fla	St. Johns					
135	7	Weedman, Nelly					13	Fla	St. Johns					
135	8	Weedman, America					11	Fla	St. Johns					
135	9	Ashton, Wm.	5	6	grey	dk	37	Fla	St. Johns			yes		
135	10	Ashton, Mary					38	Fla	St. Johns			yes		
135	11	Ashton, John					12	Fla	St. Johns					
135	12	Ashton, Philip					10	Fla	St. Johns					
135	13	Ashton, Burton					8	Fla	St. Johns					
135	14	Ashton, Wm.					6	Fla	St. Johns					
135	15	Ashton, George					3	Fla	St. Johns					
135	16	Ashton, Infant					1	Fla	St. Johns					
135	17	Cooler, George	5	4	blue	dk	30	Fla	St. Johns			yes		
135	18	Cooler, Virginia					29	Fla	St. Johns			yes		
135	19	Lambias, Jerome	5	6	dk	dk	44	Fla	St. Johns			yes		
135	20	Solana?, Kite?	5	6	dk	dk	48	Fla	St. Johns			yes		
135	21	Solana?, Leoncia					44	Fla	St. Johns			yes		
135	22	Solana?, Marg[t].					22	Fla	St. Johns					
135	23	Solana?, Philip	5	6	dk	dk	21	Fla	St. Johns			yes		
135	24	Solana?, Virginia					18	Fla	St. Johns					

"CENSUS" DEPARTMENT OF THE SOUTH - NOVEMBER, 1864

Pg	No	Name	Height Ft	Height In	Eyes	Com-plexion	Age	Where born or contraband	Last residence	Where registered for draft or former owner	Date into Department	Oath of Allgn	No of Ration	Remarks
136	1	Tyler, Syntha Ann					36	GA	St. Johns			yes		
136	2	Tyler, Wm.	4	10	blue	dk	20	Fla	St. Johns		July 1863	yes		
136	3	Tyler, Mary					12	Fla	St. Johns					
136	4	Tyler, Alfred					10	Fla	St. Johns					
136	5	Tyler, Elizabeth					8	Fla	St. Johns					
136	6	Tyler, Eliza					5	Fla	St. Johns					
136	7	Tyler, Louis					2	Fla	St. Johns					
136	8	Tyler, Lenirue					1	Fla	St. Johns					
136	9	Bennett, Wm.	5	8	blue	fr	25	GA	St. Johns		April 1864	yes		
136	10	Bennett, Martha					20	Fla	St. Johns		Aug. 1864			
136	11	Bennett, Elizabeth					4	Fla	St. Johns					
136	12	Rosier, Henry	4		blue	fr	20	GA	St. Johns		March 1864	yes		
136	13	Rosier, Sarah					18	Fla	St. Johns		Aug. 1864			
136	14	Rosier, Levi					1	Fla	St. Johns					
136	15	Sykes, Owen	6	2	blue	fr	32	Fla	St. Johns		April 1864	yes		
136	16	O'Quinn, J. B.	5	5	grey	dk	37	GA	St. Johns		May 1864	yes		
136	17	Sykes, Henry	6		blue	fr	16	Fla	St. Johns		Sept. 1864	yes		
136	18	O'Quinn, Mary					28	GA	St. Johns					
136	19	O'Quinn, Mary L.					9	GA	St. Johns					
136	20	O'Quinn, Elizah D.					7	GA	St. Johns					
136	21	O'Quinn, Jas. W.					4	GA	St. Johns					
136	22	O'Quinn, Wm. S.					1	GA	St. Johns					
136	23	Lee, Jacob	5	4	grey	dk	52	GA	St. Johns			yes		
136	24	Lee, Martha					30	GA	St. Johns			yes		

Pg	No	Name	Height		Eyes	Com-plexion	Age	Where born or contraband	Last residence	Where registered for draft or former owner	Date into Department	Oath of Allgn	No of Ration	Remarks
			Ft	In										
137	1	Solana, Caytena					16	Fla	St. Johns					
137	2	Solana, Rosalia					13	Fla	St. Johns					
137	3	Solana, Alexander					10	Fla	St. Johns					
137	4	Solana, Emanders					9	Fla	St. Johns					
137	5	Solana, Kate					8	Fla	St. Johns					
137	6	Solana, Ellen					6	Fla	St. Johns					
137	7	Jones, John	5	8	grey	dk	42	GA	St. Johns			yes		
137	8	Jones, Susan					22	Fla	St. Johns					
137	9	Jones, Bryant					6	Fla	St. Johns					
137	10	Jones, Margaret J.					1	Fla	St. Johns					
137	11	Taylor, Wm.	5	10	grey	dk	52	GA	St. Johns			yes		
137	12	Taylor, Delilah					51	GA	St. Johns			yes		
137	13	Taylor, Nancy					17	GA	St. Johns					
137	14	Taylor, Matilda					14	GA	St. Johns					
137	15	Taylor, Martha E.					12	GA	St. Johns					
137	16	Taylor, Eliza A.					10	GA	St. Johns					
137	17	Bowen, Mary					16	GA	St. Johns			yes		
137	18	Bowen, Tabitha					8	GA	St. Johns					
137	19	Wipper, Lydia					26	GA	St. Johns					
137	20	Wipper, Jas. B.					6	GA	St. Johns					
137	21	Wipper, Elmina					3	Fla	St. Johns					
137	22	Craft, Adaline					30	GA	St. Johns					
137	23	Craft, Martha					8	GA	St. Johns					
137	24	Craft, Mary L.					6	GA	St. Johns					

Pg	No	Name	Height Ft	Height In	Eyes	Com-plexion	Age	Where born or contraband	Last residence	Where registered for draft or former owner	Date into Department	Oath of Allgn	No of Ration	Remarks
138	1	Craft, Louisa					4	Fla	St. Johns					
138	2	Craft, Ellen					3	Fla	St. Johns					
138	3	GAvin, John E.	5	10	blk	dk	46	GA	St. Johns			yes		
138	4	GAvin, Nahale					35	GA	St. Johns			yes		
138	5	GAvin, John					14	GA	St. Johns					
138	6	GAvin, Elizabeth					12	GA	St. Johns					
138	7	GAvin, Henry					9	GA	St. Johns					
138	8	GAvin, Charles					4	Fla	St. Johns					
138	9	GAvin, Frederick					2	Fla	St. Johns					
138	10	Booth, Wm.	5	11	dk	dk	40	GA	St. Johns			yes		
138	11	Booth, Emily					33	GA	St. Johns			yes		
138	12	Booth, Julia					17	Fla	St. Johns					
138	13	Booth, Margaret					13	Fla	St. Johns					
138	14	Booth, James					10	Fla	St. Johns					
138	15	Booth, William					8	Fla	St. Johns					
138	16	Booth, Ellen Dor					5	Fla	St. Johns					
138	17	Booth, Theresa					3	Fla	St. Johns					
138	18	Booth, Mary					2	Fla	St. Johns					

Pg	No	Name	Height Ft	Height In	Eyes	Com-plexion	Age	Where born or contraband	Last residence	Where registered for draft or former owner	Date into Department	Oath of Allgn	No of Ration	Remarks
139	1	Stuckey, Chas. N.					14	Fla	St. Johns Co.					Orphan Boy
139	2	Stuckey, Welphena					12	Fla	St. Johns Co.					Orphan Girl
139	3	Masters, John P.	5	4	bk	dk	45	Fla	St. Johns Co.			yes		
139	4	Masters, Civility					35	Fla	St. Johns Co.					
139	5	Masters, Susan					12	Fla	St. Johns Co.					
139	6	Masters, John W.					10	Fla	St. Johns Co.					
139	7	Masters, Civility					8	Fla	St. Johns Co.					
139	8	Masters, Catharine					5	Fla	St. Johns Co.					
139	9	Masters, Elizer					2	Fla	St. Johns Co.					
139	10	Masters, Louisa					1	Fla	St. Johns Co.					
139	11	Masters, Cloe					50	contraband	St. Johns Co.	Masters, John P.				These people remain with Mr. Masters from choice
139	12	Masters, Josephine					10	contraband	St. Johns Co.	Masters, John P.				
139	13	Masters, Ellen					5	contraband	St. Johns Co.	Masters, John P.				
139	14	Hall, Ansley	5	6	dk	dk	35	S.C.	St. Johns Co.		Oct. 1863	yes		
139	15	Hall, Susan					30	Fla	St. Johns Co.					
139	16	Hall, Robt					10	Fla	St. Johns Co.					
139	17	Hall, Allosses?					8	Fla	St. Johns Co.					
139	18	Hall, Randolph					6	Fla	St. Johns Co.					
139	19	Hall, Benjn					4	Fla	St. Johns Co.					
139	20	Hall, Ausley					1	Fla	St. Johns Co.					
139	21	Carter, Levi	5	11	grey	dk	30	Fla	St. Johns Co.			yes		
139	22	Braden, Jas.					60	N Y	St. Johns Co.			no		
139	23	Braden, Mary A.					16	Fla	St. Johns Co.					
139	24	Braden, George					14	Fla	St. Johns Co.					

Pg	No	Name	Height Ft	Height In	Eyes	Com-plexion	Age	Where born or contraband	Last residence	Where registered for draft or former owner	Date into Department	Oath of Allgn	No of Ration	Remarks
140	1	Braden, Charlotte					10	Fla	St. Johns Co.					
140	2	Petty, Elijiah					65	Fla	St. Johns Co.			yes		
140	3	Petty, Mary					36	Fla	St. Johns Co.			yes		
140	4	Colemen, Obediah	6		grey	dk	35	GA	St. Johns Co.		April 1864	yes		
140	5	Colemen, Sarah					28	GA	St. Johns Co.		Aug. 1864	no		
140	6	Colemen, Francis					16	Fla	St. Johns Co.		Aug. 1864			
140	7	Colemen, Martha					12	Fla	St. Johns Co.		Aug. 1864			
140	8	Colemen, Nancy					10	Fla	St. Johns Co.		Aug. 1864			
140	9	Colemen, Darling					8	Fla	St. Johns Co.		Aug. 1864			
140	10	Colemen, Samuel					6	Fla	St. Johns Co.		Aug. 1864			
140	11	Colemen, Elijah					4	Fla	St. Johns Co.		Aug. 1864			
140	12	Colemen, Ralph					2	Fla	St. Johns Co.		Aug. 1864			
140	13	Grey?, David					80	Colored	St. Johns Co.					
140	14	Grey?, Barbaret					50	Colored	St. Johns Co.					
140	15	Grey?, Julia					25	Colored	St. Johns Co.					
140	16	Grey?, George					10	Colored	St. Johns Co.					
140	17	Grey?, Sophia					8	Colored	St. Johns Co.					
140	18	Grey?, Lewis					6	Colored	St. Johns Co.					
140	19	Mickler, Henry					18	contraband	St. Johns Co.	Mickler, R. D.				
140	20	Sykes, Rich L.	6		blue	dk	35	N. C.	St. Johns Co.		Sept. 1864	yes		
140	21	Glysson, Wm. R.	5	10	blue	dk	34	GA	St. Johns Co.		Sept. 1864	yes		
140	22	McGoorin, John	5	5	grey	dk	52	Ireland	St. Johns Co.		Aug. 1864	yes		
140	23	Prescott, Moses	5	11	blue	fair	52	S.C.	St. Johns Co.		June 1864	yes		
140	24	Prescott, Miley C.					46	GA	St. Johns Co.					

Pg	No	Name	Height Ft	Height In	Eyes	Com-plexion	Age	Where born or contraband	Last residence	Where registered for draft or former owner	Date into Department	Oath of Allgn	No of Ration	Remarks
141	1	Griffiths, Jas.	6	0	black	fair	40	GA	Fla	never	1859	yes	none	Unemployed
141	2	Griffiths, Elizabeth	5	4	dark	dark	22	Fla	Fla			yes	none	
141	3	Griffiths, Wm.	4	0	blue	fair	10	Fla	Fla			no	none	
141	4	Griffiths, Mary			blue	fair	8	Fla	Fla			no	none	
141	5	Griffiths, Sarah			blue	fair	3	Fla	Fla			no	none	
141	6	Douglas, Lucinda	5	3	dark	fair	16	Fla	Fla			no	none	
141	7	Burney, Mark	5	10	blue	fair	36	Fla	Fla	never		yes	none	Laborer
141	8	Hogans, Robert	5	10	blue	fair	40	Fla	Fla	never		yes	none	Farmer
141	9	Suarez, Ellen	5	4	blue	fair	47	Fla	Fla	never		yes	none	
141	10	Suarez, Serephina	4	3	blue	fair	9	Fla	Fla			no	none	
141	11	Hogans, Mary	5	5	blue	fair	59	S.C.	Fla		1806?	no	none	
141	12	Brazile, Eliza	5	4	blue	fair	39	S.C.	Fla		1841	no	none	
141	13	Brazile, Ebenezer	4	5	blue	fair	14	Fla	Fla			no	none	
141	14	Brazile, Henry	4	3	blue	fair	10	Fla	Fla			no	none	
141	15	Brazile. Leanot	3	4	blue	fair	8	Fla	Fla			no	none	
141	16	Wilds, Charles	5	8	dark	dark	49	Fla	Fla	never		yes	none	Unemployed
141	17	Wilds, Priscilla	5	4	dark	dark	43	Fla	Fla			yes	none	
141	18	Wilds, Ansign	5	6	dark	dark	21	Fla	Fla	never		yes	none	unemployed
141	19	Wilds, Wm	5	4	dark	dark	18	Fla	Fla	never		yes	none	unemployed
141	20	Wilds, Ellen	5	0	dark	dark	16	Fla	Fla			no	none	
141	21	Wilds, Washington	4	5	dark	dark	12	Fla	Fla			no	none	
141	22	Wilds, Cabell			dark	dark	6	Fla	Fla			no	none	
141	23	Wilds, Napoleon			dark	dark	2	Fla	Fla			no	none	
141	24	Register, Aaron	5	10	blue	fair	31	N. C.	Fla	never		yes	none	Burning Tar

"CENSUS" DEPARTMENT OF THE SOUTH - NOVEMBER, 1864

Pg	No	Name	Height Ft	Height In	Eyes	Com-plexion	Age	Where born or contraband	Last residence	Where registered for draft or former owner	Date into Department	Oath of Allgn	No of Ration	Remarks
142	1	illegible			blue	fair	50	Fla	Fla	never		yes	none	Farmer
142	2	illegible			blue	fair	30	Fla	Fla	never		yes	none	Laborer on farm
142	3	Hy....?., Wm			blue	fair	28	Fla	Fla	never		yes	none	Laborer on farm
142	4	Rishard?, Dorata?	5	2?	dk	dk	40	Colored	Fla	free			none	Lives on farm
142	5	Burnham, Esman?	5	8?	dk	dk	18	Colored	Fla	free			none	Daughter of the above
142	6	Burnham, Alonzo	5	10	dk	dk	22	Colored	Fla	free			none	Son of the above
142	7	Burnham, Thos.	4	6	dk	dk	9	Colored	Fla	free			none	Son of the above
142	8	Burnham, Geo.			dk	dk	1	Colored	Fla	free			none	Son of the above
142	9	Palmer, David L.	5	8	blue	fair	70	N.Y.	Fla	never	1818	yes	none	Farmer
142	10	Palmer, Eliza	5	4	dk	dk	49	Fla	Fla			yes	none	
142	11	Hoey, Halstead H.	6	0	blue	fair	47	N.Y.	Fla	never	1848	yes	none	Lives with Mr. Palmer
142	12	Hoey, Abby	5	5	blue	fair	31	Fla	Fla			yes	none	Lives with Mr. Palmer
142	13	Holmes, Emma	5	3	blue	fair	29	Fla	Fla			yes	none	Lives with Mr. Palmer
142	14	Holmes, Abby	4	6	blue	fair	12	Fla	Fla			no	none	Lives with Mr. Palmer
142	15	Holmes, Eddie	4	2	blue	fair	9	Fla	Fla			no	none	Lives with Mr. Palmer
142	16	Holmes, Julia	3	3	blue	fair	7	Fla	Fla			no	none	Lives with Mr. Palmer
142	17	Holmes, Ida	2	3	blue	fair	3	Fla	Fla			no	none	Lives with Mr. Palmer
142	18	Holmes, George			blue	fair	1	Fla	Fla			no	none	Lives with Mr. Palmer
142	19	Wilson, Jas. Y.	5	9	blue	fair	31	Ireland	Fla	never	1856	yes	none	Unemployed
142	20	Wilson, Eliza	5	6	blue	fair	21	Fla	Fla			yes	none	
142	21	Boud?, Jas. W.	6	0	dk	dk	49	GA	Fla		1864	yes	none	Works for D. L. Palmer
142	22	Phil,,,?, Mary	illegible		blue	f	19	S.C.	Fla		1862	no	none	Governess in Mrs. Holmes' family
142	23	Sadler, Sam	illegible		blue	f	60	contraband	Fla	Sadler, Henry	1828		none	
142	24	Sadler, Sarah	illegible		blue	fair	50	contraband	Fla	Kelly, Wm			none	

Pg	No	Name	Height Ft	Height In	Eyes	Complexion	Age	Where born or contraband	Last residence	Where registered for draft or former owner	Date into Department	Oath of Allgn	No of Ration	Remarks
143	25	Register, Louisa	5	4	dk	dk	35	Fla	Fla			yes	none	
143	26	Register, Robert	5	4	dk	dk	8	Fla	Fla			yes	none	
143	27	Register, Laura			dk	dk	6	Fla	Fla			no	none	
143	28	Register,Beauregard			dk	dk	3	Fla	Fla			no	none	
143	29	Register, Aaron			dk	dk	1	Fla	Fla			no	none	
143	30	Palmer, Jim			blk	blk	8	contraband	Fla	Palmer, D. L.		no	none	
143	31	Palmer, John			blk	blk	7	contraband	Fla	Palmer, D. L.		no	none	
143	32	Holmes, Nelly			blk	blk	8	contraband	Fla	Holmes, Henry E.		no	none	
143	33	Mosely, Mary	5	4	dk	dk	40	Fla	Fla			yes	none	
143	34	Mosely, Mary A.	5	0	blue	f	14	Fla	Fla			yes	none	
143	35	Mosely, Andrew J.			blue	f	10	Fla	Fla			yes	none	
143	36	Mosely, Seaborn			blue	f	8	Fla	Fla			no	none	
143	37	Mosely, John			blue	f	1	Fla	Fla			no	none	
143	38	Barber, Celena	5	0	blue	f	30	Fla	Fla			yes	none	
143	39	Barber, John			blue	f	10	Fla	Fla			no	none	
143	40	Barber, Thos.			blue	f	8	Fla	Fla			no	none	
143	41	Barber, Nancy			blue	f	5	Fla	Fla			no	none	
143	42	Barber, Jefferson			blue	f	4	Fla	Fla			no	none	
143	43	Terrell, Reason	6	0	blue	dk	41	GA	Fla		1844	yes	none	
143	44	Terrell, Cinderella	5	5	blue	dk	39	GA	Fla		1844	yes	none	
143	45	Terrell, Andrew	5	0	blue	f	19	Fla	Fla			yes	none	
143	46	Terrell, Nathaniel	5	8	blue	f	17	Fla	Fla			yes	none	
143	47	Terrell, Melinda	4	4	blue	f	14	Fla	Fla			no	none	
143	48	Terrell, James			blue	f	12	Fla	Fla			no	none	

Pg	No	Name	Height Ft	Height In	Eyes	Com-plexion	Age	Where born or contraband	Last residence	Where registered for draft or former owner	Date into Department	Oath of Allgn	No of Ration	Remarks
144	1	Terrell, Aaron			blue	fair	10	Fla	Fla			no	none	
144	2	Terrell, Maggie			blue	fair	7	Fla	Fla			no	none	
144	3	Terrell, Rachel			blue	fair	4	Fla	Fla			no	none	
144	4	Roberts, Betsy	5	0	blk	dk	55	Fla	Fla			yes	none	Has drawn rations for self & family, but does not now
144	5	Roberts, Jackson	5	10	blk	dk	22	Fla	Fla	never		yes	none	
144	6	Roberts, Sallie	5	4	blk	dk	21	Fla	Fla			yes	none	
144	7	Roberts, Harrison	4	8	blk	dk	14	Fla	Fla			no	none	
144	8	Roberts, Louisa	4	4	blk	dk	12	Fla	Fla			no	none	
144	9	Roberts, Caroline	4	3	blk	dk	10	Fla	Fla			no	none	
144	10	Harris, Mary	5	4	blue	fair	35	Fla	Fla			yes	none	
144	11	Harris, John	5	8	blue	fair	17	Fla	Fla	never		yes	none	Did draw rations while in town, but does not now
144	12	Harris, Joe	4	5	blue	fair	12	Fla	Fla			no	none	
144	13	Harris, James	4	2	blue	fair	10	Fla	Fla			no	none	
144	14	Harris, Julia			blue	fair	8	Fla	Fla					
144	15	Harris, Thomas			blue	fair	6	Fla	Fla					
144	16	Harris, GAbriel			blue	fair	4	Fla	Fla					
144	17	Harris, Jasper			blue	fair	2	Fla	Fla					
144	18	Roberts, Dozier			blue	fair	4	Fla	Fla					Orphan Children
144	19	Roberts, Fletcher			blue	fair	3	Fla	Fla					Orphan Children
144	20	Vandigriff, David	5	8	blue	fair	39	N.J.	Fla	never	1844	yes	none	Fisherman by Permit from Dist.
144	21	Vandigriff, Louisa	5	4	dk	dk	40	Me.	Fla		1850	yes	none	Head Quarters
144	22	Cox, Hatch	5	6	dk	dk	40	N.C.	Fla	never	1850	yes	none	Fisherman by same authority
144	23	Bearden, Jane	5	3	blue	f	20	Fla	Fla			yes	none	
144	24	Grace, Joseph	6	0	blue	f	40	GA	Fla	never	1853	yes	none	Farmer

Pg	No	Name	Height Ft	Height In	Eyes	Complexion	Age	Where born or contraband	Last residence	Where registered for draft or former owner	Date into Department	Oath of Allgn	No of Ration	Remarks
145	1	Harris, Mary	5	3	blue	fair	40	GA	Fla		1847	yes	non	
145	2	Harris, Eli	5	3	blue	fair	12	Fla	Fla			no	non	
145	3	Harris, Mary			blue	fair	6	Fla	Fla			no	non	
145	4	Box, John S.	5	8	dk	dk	39	Fla	Fla	never		yes	none	Laborer
145	5	Box, Emeline	5	4	blue	fair	30	Fla	Fla			yes	non	
145	6	Box, Thos.			blue	fair	6							
145	7	Box, Jefferson			blue	fair	4							
145	8	Pomeroy, Asa	5	8	blue	fair	55	Me.	Fla	never		yes	1	Government Employee
145	9	Pomeroy, Lohere	5	0	dk	dk	40	Colored	Fla	free			1	Wife of above
145	10	Pomeroy, Benj.	5	6	dk	dk	20	Colored	Fla	free		yes	1	Govt Employee
145	11	Pomeroy, Catharine	4	6	dk	dk	17	Colored	Fla	free		no	1	
145	12	Pomeroy, Isadore	4	0	dk	dk	13	Colored	Fla	free		no	1	
145	13	Pomeroy, Louis			dk	dk	10	Colored	Fla	free		no	1	
145	14	Pomeroy, Alice			dk	dk	6	Colored	Fla	free		no	1	
145	15	Pomeroy, Eveline			dk	dk	2	Colored	Fla	free		no	1	
145	16	Sallas, Frances	5	4	dk	dk	20	Colored	Fla	free		no	1	
145	17	Wood, Jas. N.	6	2	dk	dk	57	N.H.	N.Y.	never	1864	no	1	Govt Employee
145	18	Van Nostrand, Jacob	5	8	dk	dk	27	N.Y.	N.Y.	never	1864	no	1	Govt Employee
145	19	Brackett, Wm.	6	0	dk	dk	25	Me.	Me.	never	1864	no	1	Govt Employee
145	20	Brackett, Peter	5	10	dk	dk	48	Me.	Me.	never	1864	no	1	Govt Employee
145	21	Battiff, David	5	10	blue	f	35	N.Y.	N.Y.	never	1864	no	1	Govt Employee
145	22	Nason, Alden	5	9	blue	f	21	Me.	Me.	never	1864	no	1	Govt Employee
145	23	Skinner, Olive C.	5	9	dk	dk	47	Me.	Fla	never	1858	yes	1	Govt Employee
145	24	Riley, Hugh	5	9	blue	f	22	Ireland	N.Y.	never	1864	yes	1	Govt Employee

Pg	No	Name	Height Ft	Height In	Eyes	Com-plexion	Age	Where born or contraband	Last residence	Where registered for draft or former owner	Date into Department	Oath of Allgn	No of Ration	Remarks
146	25	McManess, Jno.	5	7	blk	dk	37	Ireland	N.Y.	never	1864	yes	1	Govt Employee
146	26	McGrath, Ed[d]	5	8	blue	f	19	N. Y.	N.Y.	never	1864	no	1	Govt Employee
146	27	Corbett, Jno	5	6	dark	f	30	Ireland	N.Y.	never	1864	no	1	Govt Employee
146	28	Gibson, Jas.	5	7	blue	f	52	Eng[d]	N.J.	never	1864	yes	1	Govt Employee
146	29	Wood, Warren	5	10	blue	f	23	Fla	Fla	never		yes	1	Govt Employee
146	30	Wells, Sam[l] J.	5	10	blue	f	23	Ala	Fla	never	1845	yes	1	Govt Employee
146	31	Sanders, Rich[d]	5	5	dk	dk	17	Fla	Fla	never		yes	1	Govt Employee
146	32	Sallas, Rafile	5	4	dk	dk	18	Colored	Fla	free		yes	1	Govt Employee
146	33	Revels, John	5	10	blue	f	21	Fla	Fla	never		yes	1	Govt Employee
146	34	Roberts, Ryal	5	9	blue	f	45	GA	Fla	never	1844	yes	1	Govt Employee
146	35	Howard, Charles	5	6	blue	f	22	Me.	Me.	never	1864	no	1	Govt Employee
146	36	Savory, Jas.	5	8	blk	dk	30	Fla	Fla	never		yes	1	Govt Employee
146	37	Bennett, Henry E.	6	0	dk	f	39	GA	Fla	never	1855	yes	1	Govt Employee
146	38	Bennett, Martha	5	4	dk	dk	30	GA	Fla		1858	yes		
146	39	Bennett, Sarah			dk	dk	14	GA	Fla		1858	no		
146	40	Bennett, Andrew			dk	dk	12	GA	Fla		1858	no		
146	41	Bennett, Iris R.			dk	dk	10	GA	Fla		1858	no		
146	42	Bennett, George			dk	dk	6	Fla	Fla		1858	no		
146	43	Bennett, Sarah			dk	dk	4	Fla	Fla		1858	no		
146	44	Savory, Martha	5	4	blk	dk	25	Fla	Fla		1858	yes		
146	45	Savory, Jos.			blk	dk	8	Fla	Fla					
146	46	Savory, Jas.			blk	dk	4	Fla	Fla					
146	47	Sallas, Frank	4	0	blk	dk	55	Fla	Fla			yes		A cripple
146	48	Sallas, Catharine	5	4	blk	dk	60	Colored	Fla	Free		yes		Wife of the above

Pg	No	Name	Height		Eyes	Com-plexion	Age	Where born or contraband	Last residence	Where registered for draft or former owner	Date into Department	Oath of Allgn	No of Ration	Remarks
			Ft	In										
147	1	Sallas, Ed^{wd}	4	9	blk	dk	16	Colored	Fla	free	native	yes	none	
147	2	Christopher, Lizzie	5	4	blk	dk	25	Colored	Fla	free	native	yes	none	
147	3	Christopher,Angeline			blk	dk	8	Colored	Fla	free	native	no	none	
147	4	Christopher, Thos.			blk	dk	5	Colored	Fla	free	native	no	none	
147	5	Christopher, Anna			blk	dk	2	Colored	Fla	free	native	no	none	
147	6	Sallas, Louisa	4	3	blk	dk	11	Colored	Fla	free	native	no	none	
147	7	Wilbur, Chas. H.	5	10	blue	fair	40	N.Y.	Fla	never	1851	yes	none	Farmer
147	8	Wilbur, Louisa	5	4	blue	fair	38	Fla	Fla		native	yes	none	
147	9	Wilbur, John			blue	fair	9	Fla	Fla		native	no	none	
147	10	Rishard, Margaret	5	2	blue	fair	45	GA	Fla		1845	yes	none	Farms
147	11	Rishard, Clinton	5	6	blue	fair	17	Fla	Fla	never	native	yes	none	Her son clerks in town
147	12	Guthery, Aaron	5	10	blue	fair	23	GA	Fla		1854	yes	none	unemployed
147	13	Guthery, Lurena	5	3	dk	dk	34	Fla	Fla			yes	none	
147	14	Sanders, Sam	4	8	dk	dk	11	Fla	Fla	never		no	none	
147	15	Wood, Jas.	5	10	blue	f	36	Fla	Fla			yes	none	
147	16	Rishard, John	5	11	dk	dk	47	Colored	Fla	free	native	yes	1	Govt Employee
147	17	Rishard, Lucey	5	4	dk	dk	42	Colored	Fla	illegible	native	no	none	
147	18	Rishard, Adele	5	2	dk	dk	20	Colored	Fla	illegible	native	no	none	
147	19	Rishard, Francis	5	8	dk	dk	19	Colored	Fla	illegible	native	no	none	
147	20	Rishard, Mary	4	10	dk	dk	17	Colored	Fla	illegible	native	no	none	
147	21	Rishard, Ophelia	4	8	dk	dk	15	Colored	Fla	illegible	native	no	none	
147	22	Rishard, Fernando	4	0	dk	dk	13	Colored	Fla	illegible	native	no	none	
147	23	Rishard, Catharine	4	0	dk	dk	11	Colored	Fla	illegible	native	no	none	
147	24	Rishard, Leone			dk	dk	7	Colored	Fla	illegible	native	no	none	

Pg	No	Name	Height Ft	Height In	Eyes	Com-plexion	Age	Where born or contraband	Last residence	Where registered for draft or former owner	Date into Department	Oath of Allgn	No of Ration	Remarks
148	25	Rishard, Ella			dk	dk	5	Colored	Fla	free	native	no	none	
148	26	Hagins, Geo.	6	0	dk	dk	52	Colored	Fla		?	yes	none	
148	27	Hagins, Jas. C.	4	8	dk	dk	14	Colored	Fla		native	yes	none	
148	28	Hagins, Jno	4	6	dk	dk	12	Colored	Fla		native	no	none	
148	29	McIntire, Wm O.	5	8	blue	f	46	N.C.	Fla	never	1850	yes	none	farmer
148	30	McIntire, Julia C.	5	4	blk	dk	29	S.C.	Fla		1862	yes	none	
148	31	McIntire, Wm. H.	4	8	blue	f	13	Fla	Fla			no	none	
148	32	McIntire, Anthony			blue	f	6	Fla	Fla			no	none	
148	33	Wilkerson, GAsden	5	10	blue	f	25	Fla	Fla	never		yes	none	unemployed
148	34	Wilkerson, Martha	5	3	blue	f	25	Fla	Fla			no	none	
148	35	Wilkerson, Byant			blue	f	6	Fla	Fla			no	none	
148	36	Wilkerson, Celia			blue	f	2	Fla	Fla			no	none	
148	37	Jackson, Wm	5	10	blue	f	30	Fla	Fla			yes	none	unemployed
148	38	Jackson, Nancy	5	4	blue	f	22	Fla	Fla			no	none	
148	39	Wilkerson, Wm	5	11	blue	f	30	Fla	Fla			yes	none	unemployed
148	40	Wilkerson, Catharine	5	3	dk	dk	30	Fla	Fla			yes	none	
148	41	Wilkerson, Rebeca	4	9	dk	dk	13	Fla	Fla			no	none	
148	42	Wilkerson, Elisha			dk	dk	10	Fla	Fla			no	none	
148	43	Wilkerson, Wm			dk	dk	8	Fla	Fla			no	none	
148	44	Wilkerson, Margaret			dk	dk	6	Fla	Fla			no	none	
148	45	Wilkerson, Geo.			dk	dk	4	Fla	Fla			no	none	
148	46	Borea, Ozias	5	0	blue	f	16	Fla	Fla			no	none	
148	47	Borea, Maxey	5	6	blue	f	20	Fla	Fla			yes	none	
148	48	Johnson, Elizabeth	5	4	dk	dk	35	Fla	Fla			yes	none	

Pg	No	Name	Height Ft	Height In	Eyes	Com-plexion	Age	Where born or contraband	Last residence	Where registered for draft or former owner	Date into Department	Oath of Allgn	No of Ration	Remarks
149	1	McDowell, Geo.	5	10	dk	dk	35	Fla	Fla	never	native	yes	1	Govt Employee
149	2	Rop, John	5	10	dk	dk	24	GA	Fla	never	1864	yes	1	Govt Employee
149	3	Moore, John	6	0	dk	dk	24	GA	Fla	never	1848	yes	1	Govt Employee
149	4	McNeil, Chas	5	11	dk	dk	48	Fla	Fla	never		yes	1	Govt Employee
149	5	McNeil, Chas. J.	4	8	grey	dk	48	N.C.	Fla	never	1819	yes	none	A cripple
149	6	McNeil, Elizabetts	5	4	dk	dk	36	Colored	Fla	Free	native	no	none	Wife of the above
149	7	McNeil, Alvin	4	6	dk	dk	12	Colored	Fla	Free	native	no	none	
149	8	McNeil, Ellen			dk	dk	9	Colored	Fla	Free	native	no	none	
149	9	McNeil, Willie			dk	dk	6	Colored	Fla	Free	native	no	none	
149	10	McNeil, Anna			dk	dk	5	Colored	Fla	Free	native	no	none	
149	11	McNeil, Eliza			dk	dk	4	Colored	Fla	Free	native	no	none	
149	12	Elliot, Wm.	6	0	blue	f	69	Fla	Fla	never	native	no	none	Blind
149	13	Elliot, Henry	6	0	blue	f	37	Fla	Fla	never	native	yes	none	Lives on a farm
149	14	Braddock, Jos. D.	5	4	blue	f	18	Fla	Fla	never	native	yes	1	Govt Employee
149	15	Shields, Wm. H.	5	8	dk	dk	40	Ireland	Fla	never	1845	no	none	An alien-claims to be a British subject
149	16	King, Frank	5	9	blk	blk	53	Contr	Fla	Ledeirth, Thos.			1	Govt Employee
149	17	Bryan, Caesar	5	9	blk	blk	50	Contr	Fla	Bryan, Sarah			none	Works for Franklin Dibble
149	18	Morell, Wm.	5	11	blk	blk	21	Contr	Fla	Jones, John			none	Works for Franklin Dibble
149	19	Kelly, Valentine	6	0	blk	blk	27	Contr	Fla	Kelly, Jas.			none	Works for Franklin Dibble
149	20	Dibble, Franklin	6	0	dk	dk	44	N.Y.	Fla	never	1864	no	none	Manufacturing Tar
149	21	Taylor, Cornelia	5	4	dk	dk	54	Colored	Fla	free	native	no	none	Lives on her farm
149	22	Taylor, Pernal	5	4	dk	dk	15	Colored	Fla	free	native	no	none	
149	23	Taylor, Orin	4	10	dk	dk	13	Colored	Fla	free	native	no	none	
149	24	Bryan, Jake	5	4	dk	dk	45	Contr	Fla	Jones, John	native	no	none	

Pg	No	Name	Height Ft	Height In	Eyes	Com-plexion	Age	Where born or contraband	Last residence	Where registered for draft or former owner	Date into Department	Oath of Allgn	No of Ration	Remarks
150	25	Bryan, Nancy	5		blk	blk	10	Contr	Fla	Jones, John			none	
150	26	Bryan, John			blk	blk	8	Contr	Fla	Jones, John			none	
150	27	Taylor, Catharine	5	4	blk	blk	28	Colored	Fla	Free	native	no	none	Lives on her farm
150	28	Taylor, Ida			blk	blk	3	Colored	Fla	Free	native	no	none	
150	29	Taylor, Elmira			blk	blk	1	colored	Fla	Free	native	no	none	
150	30	Cronk, Alliberry	5	3	blk	blk	63	GA	Fla		1814	yes	none	Lives on her farm
150	31	Savory, Eliza	5	2	blk	blk	30	S.C.	Fla		1854	yes	none	
150	32	Algier, Elizabeth	5	5	blk	blk	55	GA	Fla		1814	yes	none	
150	33	Ferris, Sarah	5	4	blk	blk	56	Fla	Fla		native	yes	none	Lives on her farm
150	34	Ferris, Daviaus	5	10	blk	blk	15	Fla	Fla	never	native	yes	none	
150	35	Ferris, Stephen	5	10	blk	blk	29	Fla	Fla	never	native	yes	none	Farmer
150	36	Ferris, Ellen	5	4	blk	blk	25	Me	Fla		1856	yes	none	
150	37	Ferris, Jas. W.			blk	blk	4	Fla	Fla		native	no	none	
150	38	Ferris, Geo. C.			blk	blk	1	Fla	Fla		native	no	none	
150	39	Ferris, Isaac	5	0	blk	blk	80	Contr	Fla	Ferris, Sarah		no	none	All
150	40	Ferris, Adella	5	0	blk	blk	14	Contr	Fla	Ferris, Sarah		no	none	on Mrs. Ferris' farm
150	41	Ferris, Roland			blk	blk	9	Contr	Fla	Ferris, Sarah		no	none	
150	42	Ferris, Lavinia			blk	blk	10	Contr	Fla	Ferris, Sarah		no	none	
150	43	Ferris, Wm.			blk	blk	9	Contr	Fla	Ferris, Sarah		no	none	
150	44	Ferris, Susan			blk	blk	7	Contr	Fla	Ferris, Sarah		no	none	
150	45	McIntire, Eliza	5	0	blk	blk	50	Contr	Fla	McIntire, Wm. O.		no	none	
150	46	Pope, Jacob	5	10	dk	dk	60	N. C.	Fla	never	1840	yes	none	Lives on a farm
150	47	Pope, Nancy	5	4	dk	dk	48	Fla	Fla	never		no	none	
150	48	Pope, Jacob	4	6	dk	dk	18	Fla	Fla	never		no	none	

Pg	No	Name	Height Ft	Height In	Eyes	Complexion	Age	Where born or contraband	Last residence	Where registered for draft or former owner	Date into Department	Oath of Allgn	No of Ration	Remarks
151	1	Pope, Jas.	4	10	dk	dk	15	Fla	Fla	never	native	no	none	
151	2	Pope, Ann			dk	dk	10	Fla	Fla		native	no	none	
151	3	Pope, Geo. K.			dk	dk	8	Fla	Fla		native	no	none	
151	4	Higginbotham, Jas.	5	11	blue	fair	42	Fla	Fla	never	native	yes	none	Lives on his farm
151	5	Higginbotham, Eliz[th]	5	6	blue	fair	33	Fla	Fla		native	no	none	
151	6	Higginbotham, Virginia	4	8	blue	fair	12	Fla	Fla		native	no	none	
151	7	Higginbotham, Amenthy			blue	fair	9	Fla	Fla		native	no	none	
151	8	Higginbotham, Napoleon			blue	fair	8	Fla	Fla		native	no	none	
151	9	Higginbotham, Assian			blue	fair	5	Fla	Fla		native	no	none	
151	10	Higginbotham, Wm.			blue	fair	4	Fla	Fla		native	no	none	
151	11	Higginbotham, Simon			blue	fair	2	Fla	Fla		native	no	none	
151	12	Flinn, Jas.	5	11	dk	dk	21	Fla	Fla	never	native	no	none	Lives on Farm with Higginbotham
151	13	Flinn, Julia	5	4	blue	f	17	Fla	Fla		native	no	none	
151	14	Lofton, Wiley	5	10	dk	dk	51	Colored	Fla	free	native	no	none	Carpenter
151	15	Flinn, Joseph	4	8	dk	dk	12	Fla	Fla	never	native	no	none	
151	16	Falany, Peter	5	9	dk	dk	52	Fla	Fla	never	native	yes	none	Farmer
151	17	Falany, Sarah	5	4	blue	f	30	Fla	Fla		native	no	none	
151	18	Falany, Emanuel			blue	f	7	Fla	Fla		native	no	none	
151	19	Falany, Peter			blue	f	5	Fla	Fla		native	no	none	
151	20	Falany, Mary			blue	f	2	Fla	Fla		native	no	none	
151	21	Dukes, Wm	5	8	blue	f	44	Alabama	Fla	never	1848	yes	none	Farming with Peter Falany
151	22	Dukes, Ferribee	5	4	dark	f	35	Fla	Fla		native	no	none	
151	23	Dukes, Charles			dark	f	8	Fla	Fla		native	no	none	
151	24	Dukes, Isaac			dark	f	5	Fla	Fla		native	no	none	

Pg	No	Name	Height Ft	Height In	Eyes	Com-plexion	Age	Where born or contraband	Last residence	Where registered for draft or former owner	Date into Department	Oath of Allgn	No of Ration	Remarks
152	25	Bacon, Henrietta	4	6	dk	dk	17	Fla	Fla		native	no	none	
152	26	Bacon, Mahala	4	3	dk	dk	15	Fla	Fla		native	no	none	
152	27	Bacon, Eureline			dk	dk	8	Fla	Fla		native	no	none	
152	28	Bacon, Nimrod			dk	dk	6	Fla	Fla		native	no	none	
152	29	Wilkerson, Jos.	5	8	blue	f	65	Fla	Fla	never	native	yes	none	Very infirmed? lives with Tanner
152	30	Tanner, David	6	0	grey	dk	43	GA	Fla	never	1840	yes	none	Getting Ranging timber
152	31	Tanner, Harriet	5	4	blue	f	29	GA	Fla		1845	yes	none	
152	32	Tanner, Elizabeth	4	6	blue	f	12	Fla	Fla		native	no	none	
152	33	Tanner, Eliza			blue	f	10	Fla	Fla		native	no	none	
152	34	Tanner, Cornelia			blue	f	8	Fla	Fla		native	no	none	
152	35	Tanner, Mary			blue	f	6	Fla	Fla		native	no	none	
152	36	Tanner, Robert			blue	f	4	Fla	Fla		native	no	none	
152	37	Hammond, Sarah	5	2	dk	dk	27	GA	Fla		1858	no	none	
152	38	Hammond,Columbus			blue	f	5	Fla	Fla		native	no	none	
152	39	Hammond, Sarah A.			blue	f	3	Fla	Fla		native	no	none	
152	40	Hammond, Mary A.			blue	f	3	Fla	Fla		native	no	none	
152	41	Ivey, Wm.	5	9	dk	dk	28	GA	GA	never	1864	yes	none	Laborer
152	42	Ivey, Mary	5	4	dk	dk	20	GA	GA		1864	no	none	
152	43	Townsend, Charles	6	0	blue	f	35	Fla	Fla	never	native	yes	none	Getting Ranging timber
152	44	Townsend, Rebecca	5	4	blue	f	27	Fla	Fla		native	yes	yes	
152	45	Townsend, Melvin	4		blue	f	6	Fla	Fla		native	no	yes	
152	46	Townsend, Amenthy			blue	f	4	Fla	Fla		native	no	yes	
152	47	Townsend, Calvin			blue	f	2	Fla	Fla		native	no	yes	
152	48	Townsend, Jessee			blue	f	1	Fla	Fla		native	no	yes	

Pg	No	Name	Height Ft	Height In	Eyes	Complexion	Age	Where born or contraband	Last residence	Where registered for draft or former owner	Date into Department	Oath of Allgn	No of Ration	Remarks
153	1	Grien, Jas.	6	0	blue	fair	45	GA	Fla	never	1864	yes	none	Lives on a farm
153	2	Grien, Emeline	5	3	blk	dk	25	GA	Fla		1864	yes	none	
153	3	Grien, Jackson			blk	dk	9	GA	Fla		1864	no	none	
153	4	Grien, Mary			blk	dk	7	GA	Fla		1864	no	none	
153	5	Grien, Elisha			blk	dk	5	GA	Fla		1864	no	none	
153	6	Grien, Hester			blk	dk	1	GA	Fla		1864	no	none	
153	7	Furman, Walter	5	8	blk	dk	50	N.Y.	Fla		1840	yes	none	Lives on a farm
153	8	Furman, Eliz^{bth}	5	4	blk	dk	40	Fla	Fla			no	none	
153	9	Furman, Jos.	4	8	blue	fair	15	Fla	Fla			no	none	
153	10	Furman, Jno.	4	6	blue	fair	12	Fla	Fla			no	none	
153	11	Furman, Walter			blue	fair	10	Fla	Fla			no	none	
153	12	Hogans, Jno. R.	5	10	blue	fair	45	Fla	Fla			yes	none	Farmer
153	13	Hogans, Alice	5	4	blue	fair	29	Fla	Fla			no	none	
153	14	Bawzile, Jno	5	4	blue	fair	17	Fla	Fla			no	none	
153	15	Parsons, Amanda?	6	2	grey	dk	54	N.H.	Fla		1839	yes	none	Getting Ranging Timber
153	16	Parsons, Betsy	5	8	blue	f	52	N.H.	Fla		1845	no	none	
153	17	Loyd, Jno.	6	0	blue	f	37	GA	Fla		1858	yes	none	Working for Parsons
153	18	Cook, Ben	5	10	blk	blk	30	Contr	Fla	Jones, John			none	Working for Parsons
153	19	Green, Isaa	5	11	blk	blk	40	Contr	Fla	Hathison?, Alex			none	Working for Parsons
153	20	Potter, Ottawa	5	10	blk	blk	55	Contr	Fla	June, Dr.			none	Working for Parsons
153	21	Brown, Nelson	5	9	blk	blk	50	Contr	Fla	Braddock, A.			none	Working for Parsons
153	22	Clinton, Susan	5	4	blue	f	25	Fla	Fla			yes	none	
153	23	Davis, Jno.	6	0	blue	f	39	GA	Fla	never	1859	yes	none	
153	24	Sams, Julia	5	3	blue	f	48	Fla	Fla			yes	none	

"CENSUS" DEPARTMENT OF THE SOUTH - NOVEMBER, 1864

Pg	No	Name	Height Ft	Height In	Eyes	Com-plexion	Age	Where born or contraband	Last residence	Where registered for draft or former owner	Date into Department	Oath of Allgn	No of Ration	Remarks
154	25	Bowden, Mriah	5	11	blue	dk	42	Florida	Fla	never	native	yes	none	Lives on his farm
154	26	Bowden, Sary A.	5	5	blue	dk	38	Florida	Fla	never	native	no	none	
154	27	Bowden, Zack[y]	5	8	blue	dk	17	Florida	Fla	never	native	yes	none	
154	28	Bowden, Mercy	5	2	blue	dk	19	Florida	Fla		native	no	none	
154	29	Bowden, Uriah	4	5	dk	dk	13	Florida	Fla		native	no	none	
154	30	Bowden, John			dk	dk	10	Florida	Fla		native	no	none	
154	31	Bowden, Anna M.			dk	dk	7	Florida	Fla		native	no	none	
154	32	Bowden, Sarah			dk	dk	5	Florida	Fla		native	no	none	
154	33	Bowden, Belle			dk	dk	3	Florida	Fla		native	no	none	
154	34	Silcox, Jas.	6	0	blue	fair	40	Florida	Fla	never	native	yes	none	Works for Parsons
154	35	Silcox, Adeline	5	4	blue	fair	30	Florida	Fla		native	yes	none	
154	36	Silcox, May			blue	fair	11	Florida	Fla		native	no	none	
154	37	Silcox, Wade			blue	fair	9	Florida	Fla		native	no	none	
154	38	Silcox, Francis			blue	fair	6	Florida	Fla		native	no	none	
154	39	Silcox, Laura			blue	fair	3	Florida	Fla		native	no	none	
154	40	Silcox, Daniel			blue	fair	5	Florida	Fla		native	no	none	
154	41	Roberts, Conner	5	10	dk	dk	26	Florida	Fla	never	native	no	none	Unemployed
154	42	Roberts, Mary	5	4	grey	dk	20	Florida	Fla		native	yes	none	
154	43	Roberts, Jno.			grey	dk	1	Florida	Fla		native	no	none	
154	44	Lowe, Archard	5	10	dk	dk	26	Florida	Fla	never	native	yes	none	
154	45	Lowe, Mary A.	5	3	dk	dk	22	Florida	Fla		native	yes	none	
154	46	Lowe, Thos.			dk	dk	5	Florida	Fla		native	no	none	
154	47	Lowe, Henry			dk	dk	5	Florida	Fla		native	no	none	
154	48	Lowe, Anna			dk	dk	3	Florida	Fla		native	no	none	

Pg	No	Name	Height Ft	Height In	Eyes	Com-plexion	Age	Where born or contraband	Last residence	Where registered for draft or former owner	Date into Department	Oath of Allgn	No of Ration	Remarks
155	1	West, Wm.	6	0	blue	f	36	Fla	Fla	never		yes	none	Getting out Timber
155	2	West, Eliza	5	6	blue	f	22	Fla	Fla			yes	none	
155	3	West, Mary			blue	f	3	Fla	Fla			no	none	
155	4	West, Wm.			blue	fair	1	Fla	Fla			no	none	
155	5	West, Robert	6	0	blue	f	32	Fla	Fla	never		yes	none	
155	6	West, Betsy A.	5	4	blue	f	37	Fla	Fla			yes	none	
155	7	West, Joshua			blue	f	4	Fla	Fla			no	none	
155	8	West, Sarah			blue	f	2	Fla	Fla			no	none	
155	9	Jordon, Amanda	5	3	blue	f	20	Fla	Fla			yes	none	
155	10	Roberts, Cornelious	5	10	dk	dk	34	Fla	Fla	never		yes	none	
155	11	Roberts, Matilda	5	4	blue	f	31	Fla	Fla			yes	none	
155	12	Roberts, Mary	4	5	dk	dk	12	Fla	Fla			no	none	
155	13	Roberts, Margaret			dk	dk	6	Fla	Fla			no	none	
155	14	Roberts, John			dk	dk	4	Fla	Fla			no	none	
155	15	Roberts, Betsy			dk	dk	1	Fla	Fla			no	none	
155	16	Adams. Ezekiel	5	7	dk	dk	40	Gr?	Fla		1844	yes	none	Oysterman
155	17	Adams. Marg[t]	5	4	dk	dk	35	Gr?	Fla		1844	yes	none	
155	18	Adams, Willoughby	5	8	dk	dk	18	Fla	Fla	never		yes	none	
155	19	Adams, Wright	5	6	dk	dk	16	Fla	Fla	never		yes	none	
155	20	Adams, Didima	4	10	dk	dk	13	Fla	Fla			no	none	
155	21	Adams, Martha			dk	dk	5	Fla	Fla			no	none	
155	22	Adams, Elihue			dk	dk	2	Fla	Fla			no	none	
155	23	Adams, John Q.			dk	dk	1	Fla	Fla			no	none	
155	24	McCormick, John B.	5	8	dk	dk	45	S.C.	Fla	never	1855	yes	none	Oysterman

"CENSUS" DEPARTMENT OF THE SOUTH - NOVEMBER, 1864

Pg	No	Name	Height Ft	Height In	Eyes	Com-plexion	Age	Where born or contraband	Last residence	Where registered for draft or former owner	Date into Department	Oath of Align	No of Ration	Remarks
156	25	McCormick,Thompson	4	5	dk	dk	21	S.C.	Fla	never	1855	no	none	
156	26	McCormick, Steven	4	6	dk	dk	18	S.C.	Fla		1855	no	none	
156	27	McCormick, Thos.			dk	dk	10	Fla	Fla			no	none	
156	28	McCormick,Martha			dk	dk	8	Fla	Fla			no	none	
156	29	McCormick, Richard			dk	dk	6	Fla	Fla			no	none	
156	30	Danford, Isaac	5	7	dk	dk	28	Fla	Fla	never		yes	none	Fisherman
156	31	Danford, Mary	5	3	blue	f	14	Fla	Fla			no	none	
156	32	Breadalbano,Greyor	5	10	grey	dk	38	Fla	Fla			yes	none	Lives on his farm
156	33	Danford, Beckey?	5	6	blue	dk	52	S.C.	Fla		1852	yes	none	
156	34	Danford, Ruth	5	3	blue	dk	20	S.C.	Fla		1852	no	none	
156	35	Ellison, Jno.	5	11	blue	f	33	GA	Fla	never	1851	yes	none	Lives on his farm
156	36	Ellison, Madison	5	4	blue	f	22	GA	Fla		1851	yes	none	
156	37	Ellison, Eliza			blue	f	4	GA	Fla			no	none	
156	38	Oliver, Shepard	5	10	blue	f	33	GA	Fla	never	1859	yes	none	Lives on his farm
156	39	Oliver, Agnes	5	4	blue	f	33	GA	Fla		1859	no	none	
156	40	Oliver, Mary			blue	f	8	Fla	Fla			no	none	
156	41	Geracke, Henry	5	8	blue	f	46	Prussia	Fla	never	1860	yes	none	GArdener below town
156	42	McDowell, Jno.	5	11	dk	dk	47	Pen.	Fla	never	1839	yes	none	Farmer
156	43	McDowell, Mary A.	5	9	blue	dk	40	Fla	Fla			yes	none	
156	44	McDowell, Jas.	5	9	blue	dk	18	Fla	Fla			yes	none	
156	45	McDowell, Sarah	5	4	blue	dk	16	Fla	Fla			no	none	
156	46	McDowell, Louisa	4	8	blue	dk	12	Fla	Fla			no	none	
156	47	McDowell, John			blue	dk	9	Fla	Fla			no	none	
156	48	McDowell, Martha			blue	dk	7	Fla	Fla			no	none	

Pg	No	Name	Height Ft	Height In	Eyes	Com-plexion	Age	Where born or contraband	Last residence	Where registered for draft or former owner	Date into Department	Oath of Allgn	No of Ration	Remarks
157	1	McDowell, Marg[t]			blue	f	5	Fla	Fla			no	none	
157	2	McDowell, Anna			blue	f	2	Fla	Fla			no	none	
157	3	McDowell, Wm. H.			blue	f	1	Fla	Fla			no	none	
157	4	Wheaton, Cyrus	5	10	blue	f	26	Contraband	Fla	Suarez, Thos.		no	none	Working for Chas McNiel
157	5	McNeil, Cumbo	5	2	blue	f	60	Contraband	Fla	McNeil, Chas.		no	none	
157	6	Sammies, Toby	5	10	blue	f	90	Contraband	Fla	Sammis, J. S.		no	none	Blind
157	7	Turner, Ben	5	7	blue	dk	38	Fla	Fla	never		yes	none	
157	8	Turner, Sarah	5	4	blue	f	32	Fla	Fla			no	none	
157	9	Turner, GAbriel			blue	f	7	Fla	Fla			no	none	
157	10	Turner, Angeline			blue	f	7	Fla	Fla			no	none	
157	11	Turner, Jesse			blue	f	5	Fla	Fla			no	none	
157	12	Turner, Edward			blue	f	3	Fla	Fla			no	none	
157	13	Turner, Serener			blue	f	1	Fla	Fla			no	none	
157	14	Turner, Sarah	5	4	blue	f	21	Fla	Fla			no	none	
157	15	Mitchel, Wm.	5	6	blue	f	47	Md.	Fla	never	1837	yes	none	
157	16	Mitchel,Eliz[th]	5	4	dk	dk	35	free	Fla	colored		no	none	Free born
157	17	Mitchel, Jos.			dk	dk	16	free	Fla	colored		no	none	Free born
157	18	Mitchel, Wm.			dk	dk	12	free	Fla	colored		no	none	Free born
157	19	Mitchel, Ed[d]			dk	dk	9	free	Fla	colored		no	none	Free born
157	20	Mitchel, Elmira			dk	dk	7	free	Fla	colored		no	none	Free born
157	21	Mitchel, Rosa[l]			dk	dk	5	free	Fla	colored		no	none	
157	22	Mitchel, John	5	9	dk	dk	63	Pen.	Fla	never	1837	yes	none	
157	23	Adams, Geo. W.	5	9	dk	dk	36	Fla	Fla	never		yes	none	
157	24	Adams, Frances	5	3	blue	f	26	Fla	Fla			yes	none	

Pg	No	Name	Height Ft	Height In	Eyes	Com-plexion	Age	Where born or contraband	Last residence	Where registered for draft or former owner	Date into Department	Oath of Allgn	No of Ration	Remarks
158	25	Adams, Mary E.			blue	f	22	Fla	Fla			no	none	
158	26	Adams, Jos.			blue	f	8	Fla	Fla			no	none	
158	27	Adams, Josephine			blue	f	4	Fla	Fla			no	none	
158	28	Hammond, Wm.	5	9	dk	dk	36	Fla	Fla	never		yes	none	Lives on a farm
158	29	Hammond, Isabella	5	4	blac	f	30	Fla	Fla			yes	none	
158	30	Hammond, Martha			blac	f	6	Fla	Fla			no	none	
158	31	Hammond, Maria			blac	f	4	Fla	Fla			no	none	
158	32	Hammond, Cornelia			blac	f	2	Fla	Fla			no	none	
158	33	Hammond, William			blac	f	1	Fla	Fla			no	none	
158	34	David, Francis	5	0	blac	f	16	Fla	Fla			no	none	
158	35	Baker, Edward	5	8	blac	f	75	GA	Fla		1859	no	none	Completely paralyzed- an object of charity. Very poor
158	36	Baker, Anna	5	0	blac	f	18	GA	Fla		1859	no	none	
158	37	Webb, Andrew	5	10	blac	f	34	Ark.	Fla	never	1860	yes	none	
158	38	Webb, Julia	5	4	blac	f	32	GA	Fla		1859?	yes	none	
158	39	Baker, Jennet					10	Contraband	Fla	Baker, Edw[d]			none	
158	40	Lord, Jas.	6	0	blac	f	64	Me	Fla	never	1834	yes	none	Wood cutter and farmer
158	41	Lord, Caroline	5	4	blac	f	49	Fla	Fla			no	none	
158	42	Lord, Jno.	5	5	blac	f	18	Fla	Fla	never		yes	none	
158	43	Lord, Susan	5	3	blac	f	16	Fla	Fla			no	none	
158	44	Lord, Caroline	4	3	blac	f	11	Fla	Fla			no	none	
158	45	Lord, Elizabeth			blac	f	6	Fla	Fla			no	none	
158	46	Sykes, William	5	8	blac	f	55	GA	Fla	never	1864	yes	none	Laborer
158	47	Summers, Sam	5	6	blue	dk	52	N.J.	Fla	never	1836	yes	none	Farmer
158	48	Summers, Sam?			blue	dk	6	Fla	Fla			no	none	

Pg	No	Name	Height Ft	Height In	Eyes	Com-plexion	Age	Where born or contraband	Last residence	Where registered for draft or former owner	Date into Department	Oath of Allgn	No of Ration	Remarks
159	1	Street, Martha					23	GA	Duval Co		Jan. 1864	yes		
159	2	Street, Altamon	6		grey	dk	22	GA	Duval Co		Oct. 1863	yes		
159	3	Roberts, John F.	5	10	yellow	dk	47	GA	Duval Co			yes		Deserter from Rebel Army
159	4	Roberts, Amelia A.					32	Fla	Duval Co			no		Wife of John Roberts
159	5	Roberts, Miley					11	Fla	Duval Co					Daughter of John Roberts
159	6	Roberts, Mark					10	Fla	Duval Co					Son of John Roberts
159	7	Roberts, John W.					8	Fla	Duval Co					Son of John Roberts
159	8	Roberts, Royal B.					6	Fla	Duval Co					Son of John Roberts
159	9	Roberts, Louisa					4	Fla	Duval Co					Daughter of John Roberts
159	10	Roberts, Eliza					2	Fla	Duval Co					Daughter of John Roberts
159	11	Hagin, John	5	5	blk	dk	23	Fla	Duval Co		Sept. 1863	yes		
159	12	Black, Alex	6	5	blk	dk	20	Fla	Duval Co		Sept. 1862	yes		
159	13	Black, Louisa					46	Fla	Duval Co			no		
159	14	Black, Francis	6	5	blk	dk	24	Fla	Duval Co		Sept. 1862	yes		
159	15	Black, Jno. W.	6	5	blk	dk	28	Fla	Duval Co		Sept. 1862	yes		
159	16	Black, Jas. S.	5	5	blk	dk	22	GA	Duval Co		Sept. 1862	yes		
159	17	Black, Washington					15	GA	Duval Co			no		Twins
159	18	Black, Coneto					15	Fla	Duval Co			no		
159	19	Guthriz, John	5	7	blk	dk	22	GA	Duval Co		Dec. 1863	yes		
159	20	Guthriz, Elizabeth					19	GA	Duval Co		Jan. 1864	yes		
159	21	Guthriz, John E.					3	Fla	Duval Co					
159	22	Guthriz, Wm. W.					1	Fla	Duval Co					
159	23	Petty, Mary H.					47	Fla	Duval Co			yes		
159	24	Petty, Ellen C.					20	Fla	Duval Co			yes		

Pg	No	Name	Height Ft	Height In	Eyes	Com-plexion	Age	Where born or contraband	Last residence	Where registered for draft or former owner	Date into Department	Oath of Allgn	No of Ration	Remarks
160	1	Petty, Joshua J.					17	Fla	Duval Co			no		
160	2	Petty, Mary A.					15	Fla	Duval Co					
160	3	Petty, John W.					10	Fla	Duval Co					
160	4	Crews, Frak					14	Fla	Duval Co					Orphan
160	5	Hartley, Michael	5	7	blue	fair	44	Fla	Duval Co			yes		
160	6	Hartley, Cicilian					23	Fla	Duval Co					
160	7	Hartley, Zachariah					14	Fla	Duval Co					
160	8	Hartley, Albert					13	Fla	Duval Co					
160	9	Hartley, Leonard					8	Fla	Duval Co					
160	10	Hartley, Calvin					6	Fla	Duval Co					
160	11	Hartley, Michael N.					2	Fla	Duval Co					
160	12	Hartley, Mary E.					1	Fla	Duval Co					
160	13	Guthriz, Ruth					25	GA	Duval Co		Aug. 1864	yes		
160	14	Guthriz, Soltie A.					4	Fla	Duval Co					
160	15	Guthriz, Samuel					63	S.C.	Duval Co		Aug. 1864	yes		
160	16	Guthriz, Nancy					64	S.C.	Duval Co		Aug. 1864	yes		
160	17	Guthriz, David	5	7	grey	dk	22	GA	Duval Co					Insane
160	18	Morse, Eliza					23	GA	Duval Co		Feb. 1864	yes		
160	19	Morse, Jas. S.					4	Fla	Duval Co		Feb. 1864			
160	20	Morse, Wm.	5	9	blue	fair	28	GA	Duval Co		Feb. 1864	yes		
160	21	Padget, Thos.					14	GA	Duval Co		Feb. 1864	yes		
160	22	Chestnut, Jas.	6	9	blue	dk	37	GA	Duval Co		June 1864	yes		
160	23	Chestnut, Elizabeth					32	Fla	Duval Co		July 1864	yes		
160	24	Chestnut, Eliza J.					15	Fla	Duval Co		July 1864	no		

Pg	No	Name	Height Ft	Height In	Eyes	Com-plexion	Age	Where born or contraband	Last residence	Where registered for draft or former owner	Date into Department	Oath of Allgn	No of Ration	Remarks
161	1	Lama, Mniker?			dk	dk	7	Fla	Fla		native	no	none	
161	2	Lama, Frank			dk	dk	5	Fla	Fla		native	no	none	
161	3	Lama, Jas.			dk	dk	3	Fla	Fla		native	no	none	
161	4	Grace, Thos.	6	5	blue	f	36	GA	Fla	never	1854	yes	none	Fisherman
161	5	Grace, Sidney	5	4	blue	f	26	GA	Fla		1854	yes	none	
161	6	Grace, Frances			blue	f	3	Fla	Fla			no	none	
161	7	Clark, Jno	5	10	blue	f	47	Italy	Fla	never	1835	yes	1	Govt Employee (Pilot)
161	8	Mason, Chas.	5	9	blue	f	24	Eng[d]	Fla	never	1859	yes	1	Govt Employee (Pilot)
161	9	Misham?, Ephrain	6	0	blue	f	26	Fla	Fla	never		yes	none	Unemployed
161	10	Neale?. Antonio	6	0	blue	f	18	Fla	Fla	never		yes	none	Unemployed
161	11	Minor, Frank	5	8	blue	f	18	Fla	Fla			yes	none	Unemployed
161	12	Hogans, Wash[gton]	5	10	blue	f	35	Fla	Fla			yes	none	Fisherman
161	13	Hogans, Adeline	5	4	blue	f	40	Fla	Fla			yes	none	
161	14	Hogans, Louis	4	3	blue	f	12	Fla	Fla			no	none	
161	15	Hogans, Mary			blue	f	10	Fla	Fla			no	none	
161	16	Duanny, N.			dk	dk	22	Fla	Fla			no	none	Cripple
161	17	Daniels, John	5	8	blue	f	40	Fla	Fla			yes	none	GArdner
161	18	Daniels, Hoosapha	5	4	dk	dk	22	Fla	Fla			no	none	
161	19	Daniels, Mary			dk	dk	6	Fla	Fla			no	none	
161	20	Daniels, Jno.			dk	dk	4	Fla	Fla			no	none	
161	21	Amow, Steve	5	8	dk	dk	50	Fla	Fla			yes	none	Oysterman
161	22	Amow, Frances	5	4	dk	dk	47	Fla	Fla			no	none	
161	23	Amow, John	5	5	dk	dk	16	Fla	Fla			no	none	
161	24	Amow, Stephen	5	6	dk	dk	14	Fla	Fla			no	none	

Pg	No	Name	Height		Eyes	Com-plexion	Age	Where born or contraband	Last residence	Where registered for draft or former owner	Date into Department	Oath of Allgn	No of Ration	Remarks
			Ft	In										
162	25	Amow, Francis			dk	dk	10	Fla	Fla			no	none	
162	26	Amow, Lewis			dk	dk	8	Fla	Fla			no	none	
162	27	Amow, Anna			dk	dk	8	Fla	Fla			no	none	
162	28	Amow, Clara			dk	dk	1	Fla	Fla			no	none	
162	29	Floyed, Jas.	6	0	dk	dk	28	Fla	Fla	never		yes	none	Fisherman and GArdner
162	30	Floyed, Rosa	5	4	dk	dk	25	Fla	Fla			no	none	
162	31	Floyed, Clara	5	5	dk	dk	48	Fla	Fla			no	none	
162	32	Floyed, Francis	5	6	dk	dk	20	Fla	Fla			yes	none	
162	33	Floyed, Raphile	5	4	dk	dk	16	Fla	Fla			yes	none	
162	34	Floyed, Magdalene	5	3	dk	dk	22	Fla	Fla			no	none	
162	35	Floyd, Raphila	5	3	dk	dk	23	Fla	Fla			no	none	
162	36	Floyd, Elizabeth			dk	dk	4	Fla	Fla			no	none	
162	37	Floyd, Jos.	5	8	dk	dk	30	Fla	Fla			yes	none	Farmer
162	38	Floyd, Mary	5	4	dk	dk	29	Fla	Fla			no	none	
162	39	Floyd, Charles			dk	dk	10	Fla	Fla			no	none	
162	40	Floyd, Frances			dk	dk	8	Fla	Fla			no	none	
162	41	Floyd, America			dk	dk	6	Fla	Fla			no	none	
162	42	Floyd, Isabella			dk	dk	4	Fla	Fla			no	none	
162	43	Floyd, Ella			dk	dk	2	Fla	Fla			no	none	
162	44	Floyd, Brevard			dk	dk	1	Fla	Fla			no	none	
162	45	Braddock, Oscar	5	7	blue	dk	40	Fla	Fla	never		yes	none	
162	46	Braddock, Ann	5	4	blue	f	32	Fla	Fla			yes	none	
162	47	Braddock, W^{m}.	4	8	blue	f	13	Fla	Fla			no	none	
162	48	Braddock, Jas			blue	f	11	Fla	Fla				none	

Pg	No	Name	Height Ft	Height In	Eyes	Com-plexion	Age	Where born or contraband	Last residence	Where registered for draft or former owner	Date into Department	Oath of Allgn	No of Ration	Remarks
163	1	Braddock, Oscar			blue	f	9	Fla	Fla			no	none	
163	2	Braddock, Mary			blue	f	7	Fla	Fla			no	none	
163	3	Braddock, Christiana			blue	f	5	Fla	Fla			no	none	
163	4	Braddock, Eugenia			blue	f	2	Fla	Fla			no	none	
163	5	Mickler, Jas	5	8	blue	f	35	Fla	Fla	never	native	yes	none	Lives on his farm
163	6	Mickler, Theresa	5	4	blue	f	32	Fla	Fla			no	none	
163	7	Mickler, Robert	4	8	blue	f	13	Fla	Fla			no	none	
163	8	Mickler, Weldman	4	6	blue	f	11	Fla	Fla			no	none	
163	9	Mickler, Walter			blue	f	7	Fla	Fla			no	none	
163	10	Mickler, Menence			blue	f	5	Fla	Fla			no	none	
163	11	Mickler, Thos. J.			blue	f	3	Fla	Fla			no	none	
163	12	Mickler, Bill			blk	blk	11	Contraband		Mickler, James				Lives with James Mickler who is a farmer
163	13	Mickler, Frank			blk	blk	10	Contraband		Mickler, James				
163	14	Mickler, Lovey			blk	blk	7	Contraband		Mickler, James				
163	15	Mickler, Peter			blk	blk	6	Contraband		Mickler, James				
163	16	Mickler, Phillis			blk	blk	5	Contraband		Mickler, James				
163	17	Mickler, Mary			blk	blk	3	Contraband		Mickler, James				
163	18	Mickler, Lavinia			blk	blk	14	Contraband		Mickler, James				
163	19	Mickler, Jane			blk	blk	45	Contraband		Mickler, James				
163	20	Meale, Venancis	6	0	dk	dk	49	Fla	Fla	never		yes	none	Farmer
163	21	Meale, Ann	5	4	blue	f	35	Fla	Fla			no	none	
163	22	Meale, Antonio	5	4	blue	f	17	Fla	Fla			no	none	
163	23	Meale, Ann	5	2	blue	f	15	Fla	Fla			no	none	
163	24	Meale, Sallano?	4	8	blue	f	13	Fla	Fla			no	none	

Pg	No	Name	Height Ft	Height In	Eyes	Com-plexion	Age	Where born or contraband	Last residence	Where registered for draft or former owner	Date into Department	Oath of Allgn	No of Ration	Remarks
164	25	Meale, Emanuel	4	4	blue	f	11	Fla	Fla			no	none	
164	26	Meale, Mary			blue	f	9	Fla	Fla			no	none	
164	27	Meale, Lewis			blue	f	7	Fla	Fla			no	none	
164	28	Meale, Edw[d]			blue	f	5	Fla	Fla			no	none	
164	29	Meale, Wallace?			blue	f	4	Fla	Fla			no	none	
164	30	Meale, Venancis			blue	f	3	Fla	Fla			no	none	
164	31	Meale, Rosa			blue	f	2	Fla	Fla			no	none	
164	32	Meale, Morgan			blue	f	1	Fla	Fla			no	none	
164	33	Alverez, Antonio	5	10	dk	dk	70	Fla	Fla			yes	none	Farmer
164	34	Alverez, Anneker?	5	4	dk	dk	60	Fla	Fla			no	none	
164	35	Alverez, Raphila	5	4	dk	dk	35	Fla	Fla			no	none	
164	36	Andrue, Frank	5	0	dk	dk	25	Fla	Fla			yes	none	
164	37	Andrue, Lathier	5	0	dk	dk	20	Fla	Fla			no	none	
164	38	Andrue, Mary			dk	dk	2	Fla	Fla			no	none	
164	39	Andrue, Michael	5	0	dk	dk	75	Fla	Fla			yes	none	
164	40	Andrue, Maria	5	0	dk	dk	75	Fla	Fla			no	none	
164	41	Baya, Florence	5	10	dk	dk	38	Fla	Fla			yes	none	
164	42	Baya, Mary	5	4	dk	dk	26	Fla	Fla			no	none	
164	43	Baya, Ellen			dk	dk	8	Fla	Fla			no	none	
164	44	Baya, Jos			dk	dk	6	Fla	Fla			no	none	
164	45	Baya, Rosa			dk	dk	4	Fla	Fla			no	none	
164	46	Baya, Louisa			dk	dk	4	Fla	Fla			no	none	
164	47	Baya, John			dk	dk	1	Fla	Fla			no	none	
164	48	Williams, Frank	5	5	dk	dk	54	Fla	Fla			no	none	Unemployed

Pg	No	Name	Height Ft	Height In	Eyes	Com-plexion	Age	Where born or contraband	Last residence	Where registered for draft or former owner	Date into Department	Oath of Allgn	No of Ration	Remarks
165	1	Ponce, Antonio	5	4	dk	dk	70	Fla	Fla	never		yes	none	Lives on his farm
165	2	Ponce, Sally	5	2	dk	dk	60	Fla	Fla			no	none	
165	3	Ponce, James	5	8	dk	dk	22	Fla	Fla	never		yes	none	
165	4	Ponce, Florida	5	2	dk	dk	18	Fla	Fla			no	none	
165	5	Rowell, David	6	0	blue	dk	46	GA	Fla	never	1864	yes	none	
165	6	Rowell, Sally	5	4	blue	dk	34	GA	Fla	never	1864	no	none	
165	7	Rowell, Betsy	5	2	blue	dk	30	GA	Fla	never	1864	no	none	
165	8	Rowell, Nancy	5	0	blue	dk	28	GA	Fla		1864	no	none	
165	9	Rowell, Charles	4	8	blue	dk	15	GA	Fla		1864	no	none	
165	10	Rowell, Thos.	4	6	blue	dk	15	GA	Fla	never	1864	no	none	
165	11	Rowell, Sally	4	4	blue	dk	14	GA	Fla		1864	no	none	
165	12	Rowell, Jane	4	2	blue	dk	13	GA	Fla		1864	no	none	
165	13	Rowell, Molly	4	0	blue	dk	12	GA	Fla		1864	no	none	
165	14	Rowell, John	4	0	dk	dk	11	GA	Fla		1864	no	none	
165	15	Rowell, Wash[ton]			dk	dk	10	GA	Fla		1864	no	none	
165	16	Rowell, Napoleon			dk	dk	9	GA	Fla		1864	no	none	
165	17	Rowell, W[m]			dk	dk	7	GA	Fla		1864	no	none	
165	18	Rowell, Archard			dk	dk	6	GA	Fla		1864	no	none	
165	19	Dickerson, W[m]	5	10	blue	f	40	GA	Fla	never	1853	yes	none	Farmer
165	20	Dickerson, Eliz[th]	5	4	blue	f	35	GA	Fla		1853	no	none	
165	21	Dickerson, Eley	5	3	blue	f	18	GA	Fla		1853	no	none	
165	22	Dickerson,Ainenthy?	4	5	blue	f	13	GA	Fla		1853	no	none	
165	23	Dickerson, W[m]	4	0	blue	f	11	Fla	Fla		1853	no	none	
165	24	Dickerson, Henrietta			blue	f	6	Fla	Fla		1853	no	none	

"CENSUS" DEPARTMENT OF THE SOUTH - NOVEMBER, 1864

Pg	No	Name	Height Ft	Height In	Eyes	Com-plexion	Age	Where born or contraband	Last residence	Where registered for draft or former owner	Date into Department	Oath of Allgn	No of Ration	Remarks
166	25	Dickerson, Mary			blue	f	6	Fla	Fla			no	none	
166	26	Dickerson, John			blue	f	3	Fla	Fla			no	none	
166	27	Dickerson, Sally			blue	f	1	Fla	Fla			no	none	
166	28	Floyd, Stephen	5	0	dk	dk	24	Fla	Fla	never		yes	none	Unemployed
166	29	Floyd, Dora	5	4	blue	f	28	Fla	Fla			no	none	
166	30	Floyd, John			blue	f	4	Fla	Fla			no	none	
166	31	Floyd, Ida			blue	f	1	Fla	Fla			no	none	
166	32	Dillon, Henry	5	5	blue	f	30	GA	Fla		1862	yes	none	Unemployed
166	33	Dillon, Eliza	5	4	blue	f	25	Fla	Fla			no	none	
166	34	Dillon, Wash^g			blue	f	8	Fla	Fla			no	none	
166	35	Dillon, Willy			blue	f	6	Fla	Fla			no	none	
166	36	Dillon, Nelly			blue	f	2	Fla	Fla			no	none	
166	37	Amow, Margaret	5	4	dk	dk	90	Fla	Fla			no	none	
166	38	Jones, Wash^ton L.	5	9	blue	fair	41	S C	Fla	never	1857	yes	none	
166	39	Jones, Sarah	5	4	blue	fair	36	S C	Fla		1857	yes	none	
166	40	Jones, Lenah			blue	fair	10	Fla	Fla		1857	no	none	
166	41	Jones, Oleander			blue	fair	8	Fla	Fla		1857	no	none	
166	42	Stone, W^m	5	9	blue	fair	42	GA	Fla	never	1849	yes	none	Laborer
166	43	Stone, Eliza	5	4	blue	fair	48	GA	Fla		1849	no	none	
166	44	Stone, David	5	8	blue	fair	20	GA	Fla	never	1849	yes	none	
166	45	Stone, Ann	5	4	blue	fair	18	Fla	Fla			no	none	
166	46	Stone, Piety	5	2	blue	fair	16	Fla	Fla			no	none	
166	47	Stone, Peter	5	0	blue	fair	14	Fla	Fla			no	none	
166	48	Stone, W^m	4	10	blue	fair	12	Fla	Fla			no	none	

Pg	No	Name	Height Ft	Height In	Eyes	Com-plexion	Age	Where born or contraband	Last residence	Where registered for draft or former owner	Date into Department	Oath of Allgn	No of Ration	Remarks
167	1	Fatio, Lawrence	5	8	dk	dk	90	Fla	Fla	never	native	yes	none	Old resident formerly a Pilot
167	2	Fatio, Frances	5	4	dk	dk	52	Fla	Fla		native	no	none	
167	3	Fatio, Adeline	5	4	dk	dk	22	Fla	Fla		native	no	none	
167	4	Fatio, Antonio	5	6	dk	dk	20	Fla	Fla	never	native	no	none	
167	5	Fatio, Susan	5	4	dk	dk	18	Fla	Fla		native	no	none	
167	6	Fatio, Kate	5	0	dk	dk	15	Fla	Fla		native	no	none	
167	7	Brown, Ellenor	5	4	dk	dk	35	GA	Fla		1853	yes	none	This family are in object poverty,
167	8	Brown, Jane	5	0	dk	dk	13	GA	Fla		1853	yes	none	and are truly objects of charity
167	9	Brown, Martha	4	8	dk	dk	11	Fla	Fla		native	no	none	
167	10	Brown, Thos			dk	dk	9	Fla	Fla		native	no	none	
167	11	Brown, Jas			dk	dk	7	Fla	Fla		native	no	none	
167	12	Brown, Luke?			dk	dk	5	Fla	Fla		native	no	none	
167	13	Knowls, Jno	5	6	blue	fair	26	Fla	Fla		native	yes	none	Refugee squatted in the woods
167	14	Knowls, Frances	5	4	blue	fair	22	Fla	Fla		native	no	none	
167	15	Knowls, Robert			blue	fair	4	Fla	Fla		native	no	none	
167	16	Knowls, Frances			blue	fair	2	Fla	Fla		native	no	none	
167	17	Knowls, Emannel	5	6	blue	fair	28	Fla	Fla		native	yes	none	
167	18	Green, John	6	0	blue	fair	25	Fla	Fla		native	yes	none	Farmer
167	19	Green, Sarah	5	2	blue	fair	26	Fla	Fla		native	no	none	
167	20	Green, Oliver			blue	fair	3	Fla	Fla		native	no	none	
167	21	Wingate, Jos	6	0	blue	fair	23	Fla	Fla		native	yes	none	Lives with Green
167	22	Lee, Simeon	5	8	blue	fair	48	GA	Fla		1840	yes	none	Squatted in the woods & unemployed
167	23	Lee, Elizth	5	4	blue	fair	52	GA	Fla		1840	yes	none	
167	24	Lee, Simeon	4	2	blue	fair	14	Fla	Fla		1840	no	none	

Pg	No	Name	Height Ft	Height In	Eyes	Complexion	Age	Where born or contraband	Last residence	Where registered for draft or former owner	Date into Department	Oath of Allgn	No of Ration	Remarks
168	25	Hudnal, Gro	5	8	dk	dk	53	Fla	Fla	never	native	yes	none	Farmer
168	26	Hudnal, Rebecca	5	4	dk	dk	46	Fla	Fla		native	no	none	
168	27	Hudnal, Hannah			dk	dk	20	Fla	Fla		native	no	none	
168	28	Hudnal, Sam	5	6	dk	dk	18	Fla	Fla	never	native	no	none	
168	29	Hudnal, W^{m}	4	9	dk	dk	12	Fla	Fla	never	native	no	none	
168	30	Hudnal, Mary			dk	dk	8	Fla	Fla		native	no	none	
168	31	Wilkerson, Wm	5	10	blue	f	32	Fla	Fla	never	native	yes	1	Govt Employee
168	32	Wilkerson, Kesiah	5	4	blue	f	22	Fla	Fla		native	no	none	
168	33	Bennett, Richard	5	7	dk	dk	30	Fla	Fla	never	native	yes	1	Govt Employee
168	34	Bennett, Mary J.	5	4	blue	f	20	Fla	Fla		native	yes	none	
168	35	Gratham?, Elijah	6	1	blue	f	32	GA	Fla	never	1846?	yes	1	Govt Employee
168	36	Grantham, Nancy	5	4	blue	f	22	GA	Fla		1846?	yes	none	
168	37	Sapp, Jas.	5	10	blue	f	40	GA	Fla	never	1844	yes	none	Farmer
168	38	Sapp, Margaret	5	4	blue	f	33	GA	Fla	never	1844	yes	none	
168	39	Sapp, Mary J.	5	3	blue	f	18	Fla	Fla		native	yes	none	
168	40	Sapp, Billy			blue	f	10	Fla	Fla		native	no	none	
168	41	Sapp, Henry			blue	f	6	Fla	Fla		native	no	none	
168	42	Sapp, Anna			blue	f	4	Fla	Fla		native	no	none	
168	43	Pendarvis?, Edith	5	4	blue	f	59	S C	Fla		1830	yes	none	
168	44	Gunter, Hester	5	4	blue	f	25	Fla	Fla		native	yes	none	
168	45	Gunter, Catherine	5	4	blue	f	3	Fla	Fla		native	no	none	
168	46	Sherehouse, Moses	6	1	dk	dk	24	GA	Fla	never	1842	yes	1	Govt Employee
168	47	Sherehouse, Hetty	5	4	blue	f	27	Fla	Fla		native	yes	none	
168	48	Sherehouse, Geo			blue	f	5	Fla	Fla		native	no	none	

Pg	No	Name	Height Ft	Height In	Eyes	Com-plexion	Age	Where born or contraband	Last residence	Where registered for draft or former owner	Date into Department	Oath of Allgn	No of Ration	Remarks
169	1	Stratton, Nathaniel	5	8	blue	fair	35	N York	Fla	never	1836	yes	none	Farmer
169	2	Stratton, Nancy	5	5	blue	fair	28	Fla	Fla		native	no	none	
169	3	Stratton, Jno			blue	fair	6	Fla	Fla		native	no	none	
169	4	Stratton, Jas			blue	fair	4	Fla	Fla		native	no	none	
169	5	Stratton, Saml	5	7	blue	fair	32	N Y	Fla	never	1836	yes	none	Farmer
169	6	Hudnal, Jas.	5	8	blue	fair	28	Pen	Fla	never	1859	yes	none	Farmer
169	7	Hudnal, Lucy	5	4	blue	fair	29	S C	Fla		1856	yes	none	
169	8	Hudnal, Jas.	4	8	blue	fair	11	Fla	Fla		native	no	none	
169	9	Hudnal, Jno.			blue	fair	4	Fla	Fla		native	no	none	
169	10	Walden, Jesse	5	6	dark	dark	46	Fla	Fla	never	native	yes	none	Farmer
169	11	Walden, Mary	5	4	dark	dark	34	Fla	Fla		native	yes	none	
169	12	Walden, Jno.	4	7	dark	dark	14	Fla	Fla		native	no	none	
169	13	Walden, Sarah			dark	dark	10	Fla	Fla		native	no	none	
169	14	Walden, Mary			dark	dark	7	Fla	Fla		native	no	none	
169	15	Walden, Jepe			dark	dark	4	Fla	Fla		native	no	none	
169	16	Walden, Michael			dark	dark	1	Fla	Fla		native	no	none	
169	17	Drawdy, Mary	5	4	blue	fair	60	S C	Fla		1864	yes	none	
169	18	Drawdy, Hez^{kh}	5	7	blue	fair	18	GA	Fla	never	1864	yes	none	
169	19	Drawdy, Geo.	5	5	blue	fair	20	GA	Fla	never	1864	yes	none	Intends to farm
169	20	Warren, Josiah	5	5	blue	fair	20	GA	Fla	never	1864	yes	none	Intends to farm
169	21	Dias, Jno.	5	10	blue	fair	52	GA	Fla	never	1839	yes	none	Intends to farm

"CENSUS" DEPARTMENT OF THE SOUTH - NOVEMBER, 1864

Pg	No	Name	Height Ft	Height In	Eyes	Com-plexion	Age	Where born or contraband	Last residence	Where registered for draft or former owner	Date into Department	Oath of Allgn	No of Ration	Remarks
170	1	Andreu, Antonio	5	6	brwn	light	30	St. Augustine	St. Augustine		old resident	yes	31/2	Self, wife & 3 Children by order of Post Comdr.Mander?
170	2	Andreu, Elisabeth	5	5	blue	light	26	St. Augustine	St. Augustine		old resident	yes		
170	3	Andreu, Mary J.					7	St. Augustine	St. Augustine		old resident	no		
170	4	Andreu, Louisa					5	St. Augustine	St. Augustine		old resident	no		
170	5	Andreu, Edward					1	St. Augustine	St. Augustine		old resident	no		
170	6	Andrew, William	5	10 1/4	hazel	medium	42	St. Augustine	St. Augustine		old resident	yes		
170	7	Andrew, Delnora					15	St. Augustine	St. Augustine		old resident	no		
170	8	Andrew, Frances					13	St. Augustine	St. Augustine		old resident	no		
170	9	Andrew, Jane					10	St. Augustine	St. Augustine		old resident	no		
170	10	Andrew, Michael					8	St. Augustine	St. Augustine		old resident	no		
170	11	Andrew, Minniu					5	Mayport	St. Augustine		old resident	no		
170	12	Acosta, Isador					10		St. Augustine		old resident	no		
170	13	Andrew, Antonio	5	1 2/4	hazel	dark	51	St. Augustine	St. Augustine		old resident	yes	1	By order Post Comdr.
170	14	Andrew, Levilinia	5	1/4	hazel	dark	41	St. Augustine	St. Augustine		old resident	yes		
170	15	Andrew, Antonia Jr.	5	4 1/4	hazel	dark	17	St. Augustine	St. Augustine		old resident	yes		
170	16	Andrew, William					14	St. Augustine	St. Augustine		old resident	no		
170	17	Andrew, Joseph					8	St. Augustine	St. Augustine		old resident	no		
170	18	Andrew, Lewis					6	St. Augustine	St. Augustine		old resident	no		
170	19	Andrew, Frances					2	St. Augustine	St. Augustine		old resident	no		
170	20	Andrew, Mary					12	St. Augustine	St. Augustine		old resident	no		
170	21	Andrew, Margrett					10	St. Augustine	St. Augustine		old resident	no		
170	22	Andrew, Emanuel P.	5	3 1/4	hazel	medium	47	St. Augustine	St. Augustine		old resident	yes		
170	23	Andrew, GAbina	5	3 3/4	hazel	medium	44	St. Augustine	St. Augustine		old resident	yes		
170	24	Andrew, Mary	4	10 3/4	hazel	medium	18	St. Augustine	St. Augustine		old resident	yes		

Pg	No	Name	Height		Eyes	Com-plexion	Age	Where born or contraband	Last residence	Where registered for draft or former owner	Date into Department	Oath of Allgn	No of Ration	Remarks
			Ft	In										
171	25	Andrew, Robert					12	St. Augustine	St. Augustine		old resident	no		
171	26	Andrew, Josephine					10	St. Augustine	St. Augustine		old resident	no		
171	27	Andrew, Frances					9	St. Augustine	St. Augustine		old resident	no		
171	28	Andrew, George					3	St. Augustine	St. Augustine		old resident	no		
171	29	Andrew, Melonie					9/12	St. Augustine	St. Augustine		old resident	no		
171	30	Andrew, Christinia					29	Baltimore	St. Augustine		June 22/1864	yes		
171	31	Allen, Darius	5	5 1/2	hazel	medium	58	Bristol, R.I.	St. Augustine		old resident	yes		
171	32	Allen, Mary	5	1 1/2	hazel	light	52	Fernandina	St. Augustine		old resident	yes		
171	33	Allen, Martha	5	2 3/4	hazel	light	24	St. Augustine	St. Augustine		old resident	yes		
171	34	Allen, Daniel	5	8	grey	light	21	St. Johns Co.	St. Augustine		Feb.3^{d}1864	yes		Deserter from 2nd Florida Cavarly, Feb.3^{d},1864
171	35	Allen, Annie	4	11	hazel	light	18	St. Augustine	St. Augustine		old resident	yes		
171	36	Allen, Edward					14	St. Augustine	St. Augustine		old resident	no		
171	37	Allen, Julia					3	St. Augustine	St. Augustine		old resident	no		
171	38	Andrew, Mary	4	11 1/2	hazel	medium	63	St. Augustine	St. Augustine		old resident	yes	1	By order Post Comdr.
171	39	Andrew, Matiniu	5	1	hazel	light	27	St. Augustine	St. Augustine		old resident	yes		
171	40	Arnu, James	5	8 1/2	hazel	light	43	St. Augustine	St. Augustine		old resident	yes		
171	41	Arnu, Francis	5	8	hazel	light	46	St. Augustine	St. Augustine		old resident	yes		
171	42	Arnu, Agatha	4	11 1/4	blue	light	35	St. Augustine	St. Augustine		old resident	yes		
171	43	Arnu, Peter					13	St. Augustine	St. Augustine		old resident	no		
171	44	Arnu, Anna					10	St. Augustine	St. Augustine		old resident	no		
171	45	Arnu, Mary					7	St. Augustine	St. Augustine		old resident	no		
171	46	Arnu, Debnada					4	St. Augustine	St. Augustine		old resident	no		
171	47	Andrew, John	5	8 1/4	blue	light	63	St. Augustine	St. Augustine		old resident	yes		
171	48	Andrew, Cathrine	5	3	hazel	light	26	St. Augustine	St. Augustine		old resident	yes		

"CENSUS" DEPARTMENT OF THE SOUTH - NOVEMBER, 1864

Pg	No	Name	Height Ft	Height In	Eyes	Com-plexion	Age	Where born or contraband	Last residence	Where registered for draft or former owner	Date into Department	Oath of Allgn	No of Ration	Remarks
172	1	Andrew, Mary	5	1 3/4	hazel	light	23	St. Augustine	St. Augustine		old resident	yes		
172	2	Andrew, Calatia	5	1 1/2	hazel	light	21	St. Augustine	St. Augustine		old resident	yes		
172	3	Andrew, Francis	5		hazel	light	15	St. Augustine	St. Augustine		old resident	yes		
172	4	Andrew, Agatha					50	St. Augustine	St. Augustine		old resident	no		
172	5	Allun, James W.	5	9	grey	light	29	St. Augustine	St. Augustine		old resident	yes		Post master at St. Augustine
172	6	Andrew, Mary	5	1 3/4	hazel	light	21	St. Augustine	St. Augustine		old resident	yes		
172	7	Andrew, Mary	4	11 3/4	hazel	fair	50	St. Augustine	St. Augustine		old resident	yes		
172	8	Andrew, Joseph	5	7 1/2	dark	dark	25	St. Augustine	Jacksonville		Feb. 1863	yes		
172	9	Andrew, Murthina	5	3	hazel	light	22	St. Augustine	St. Augustine		old resident	yes		
172	10	Andrew, Antonia					1 1/2	St. Augustine	St. Augustine			no		
172	11	Andrew, John	5	10	hazel	dark	46	St. Augustine			old resident	yes		
172	12	Andrew, Ephinuy?	5	1/4	hazel	dark	34	St. Augustine			old resident	yes		
172	13	Andrew, Mary					10	St. Augustine			old resident	no		
172	14	Andrew, Francis					8	St. Augustine			old resident	no		
172	15	Andrew, John					6	St. Augustine			old resident	no		
172	16	Andrew, Peter					3	St. Augustine			old resident	no		
172	17	Anbriel, Edmond S.					51	France			old resident			Catholic Priest at St. Augustine
172	18	Alysia ?, Mary					25				old resident			Nun in Convent at St. Augustine
172	19	Anderson, C. C. ?	5	3	blue	light	64	New Hampshire			old resident	yes		
172	20	Avice, Mary	5	2 1/2	blue	light	62	St. Augustine	St. Augustine		old resident	yes		
172	21	Avice, Alexander	5	6 1/2	hazel	light	32	St. Augustine	St. Augustine		old resident	yes		
172	22	Barnes, Francis					1	Volusia Co., Fla	St. Augustine		July 10/1864	no	1/2	By order Post Commander
172	23	Barns, Frances	5	3 1/2	blue	light	21	Macon, GA	St. Augustine		July 10/1864	yes	1	Husband in U. S. Service
172	24	Benet, Joseph	5	7	blue	light	60	St. Augustine			old resident	yes		
172	25	Benet, Mary	5	3 1/2			51	St. Augustine			old resident	yes		

Pg	No	Name	Height		Eyes	Com-plexion	Age	Where born or contraband	Last residence	Where registered for draft or former owner	Date into Department	Oath of Allgn	No of Ration	Remarks
			Ft	In										
173	26	Benet, Ansolom	5	2 1/2	hazel	dark	15	St. Augustine			old resident	yes		
173	27	Benet, Frances					17	St. Augustine			old resident	no		
173	28	Benet, Adcasio					13	St. Augustine			old resident	no		
173	29	Benet, Margrett					11	St. Augustine			old resident	no		
173	30	Benet, Agatha	5	5 1/4	grey	light	21	St. Augustine			old resident	yes		
173	31	Benet, Stephen					2	St. Augustine			old resident	no		
173	32	Benet, Mary					2m	St. Augustine			old resident	no		
173	33	Bruvo, Donato	6	1/4	hazel	light	49	St. Augustine	St. Augustine		old resident	yes		
173	34	Bruvo, Antonia	5	1	hazel	light	45	St. Augustine	St. Augustine		old resident	yes		
173	35	Bruvo, Donato, Jr.					10	St. Augustine	St. Augustine		old resident	no		
173	36	Bruvo, Stephen					6	St. Augustine	St. Augustine		old resident	no		
173	37	Bruvo, Josephine					4	St. Augustine	St. Augustine		old resident	no		
173	38	Bruvo, John					9m	St. Augustine	St. Augustine		old resident	no		
173	39	Baya, Avena					22	St. Augustine	St. Augustine		old resident	yes		
173	40	Baya, Rose					4	St. Augustine	St. Augustine		old resident	no		
173	41	Baya, Joseph					1m	St. Augustine	St. Augustine		old resident	no		
173	42	Benet, Pedro	5	7 1/4	blue	light	66	St. Augustine	St. Augustine		old resident	yes		
173	43	Benet, Jane H.	5	3	hazel	fair	61	St. Augustine	St. Augustine		old resident	yes		
173	44	Benet, Isabell	4	1 3/4	hazel	light	26	St. Augustine	St. Augustine		old resident	yes		
173	45	Benet, Joseph R.	5	9 1/2	hazel	light	19	St. Augustine	St. Augustine		old resident	yes		
173	46	Beal, Jane	5	9 1/2	hazel	med.	71	St. Augustine	St. Augustine		old resident	yes	1	By order Post Commander
173	47	Brideir, Milinia	5	3 1/2	blue	light	46	France			old resident	yes		
173	48	Brideir, Mary C.	5	1 1/2	hazel	light	22	St. Augustine			old resident	yes		

"CENSUS" DEPARTMENT OF THE SOUTH - NOVEMBER, 1864

Pg	No	Name	Height Ft	Height In	Eyes	Com-plexion	Age	Where born or contraband	Last residence	Where registered for draft or former owner	Date into Department	Oath of Allgn	No of Ration	Remarks
174	1	Brideir, John					13	St. Augustine				no		
174	2	Brideir, Edwin					10	St. Augustine				no		
174	3	Britt, John	5	7	blue	fair	40	Ireland			old resident	yes		
174	4	Brinckerhoff, Isaac W	5	7 1/2	blue	light	43	New York	New York		March 9,1862	yes		Supt. Of Contrabands
174	5	Brinckerhoff, I. W. Jr.					37	New York	New York		May 1864	no		
174	6	Brinckerhoff, Cate C.					14	New York	New York		March 1864	no		
174	7	Brinckerhoff, Frank H					6	New York	New York		May 1864	no		
174	8	Brinckerhoff, Catherine					4	New York	New York		May 1864	no		
174	9	Brush, Mary	5		blue	light	33	St. Augustine	St. Augustine		old resident	yes		
174	10	Brush, Lewis					15	St. Augustine	St. Augustine		old resident	no		Children of Mrs. Brush
174	11	Brush, Edwin					11	St. Augustine	St. Augustine		old resident	no		
174	12	Bucurdy, Mrs.	4	11 1/2	hazel	light	60	France			old resident	yes	1	By order Post Commander
174	13	Biddlecom, Martha	5	4 1/2	hazel	light.	30	New York	St. Augustine		old resident	yes	1	By order Post Commander
174	14	Biddlecom, Anna					8	St. Augustine	St. Augustine			no	1/2	By order Post Commander
174	15	Biddlecom, Edward					4	St. Augustine	St. Augustine			no	1/2	By order Post Commander
174	16	Blunchard, Rubin	6	3/4	grey	light	54	Georgia	Volusia Co., FL		June 7,1864	yes	1	sick by order Post Commander
174	17	Blunchard, Nancy					49	Georgia	Orange Co Fla		June 8,1864	no	1	By order Post Commander
174	18	Blunchard, Elizabeth					18	Georgia	Orange Co Fla		June 8,1864	no		
174	19	Blunchard, Daniel	5	7	blue	light	16	Georgia	Orange Co Fla		June 8,1864	yes	1/2	By order Post Commander
174	20	Blunchard, Diantha					11	Georgia	Orange Co Fla		June 8,1864	no	1/2	By order Post Commander
174	21	Blunchard, Sylvania					9	Georgia	Orange Co Fla		June 8,1864	no	1/2	By order Post Commander
174	22	Balsan, Henry B.					58	Berlin, Prussia	St. Augustine		old resident	yes		
174	23	Balsan, Frances	5	3	blue	light	36	France	St. Augustine			yes		
174	24	Balsan, Fernaldo					25	Alabama	Beaufort, SC		April 1864	yes		
174	25	Balsan, Elisa	5	1/2	blue	light	19	St. Augustine	St. Augustine		old resident	yes		

Pg	No	Name	Height Ft	Height In	Eyes	Com-plexion	Age	Where born or contraband	Last residence	Where registered for draft or former owner	Date into Department	Oath of Allgn	No of Ration	Remarks
175	26	Balsan, Esadore					18	St. Augustine			old resident	no		
175	27	Balsan, Robert					14	St. Augustine			old resident	no		
175	28	Bias, Burbury	5	3/4	haze	fair	59	St. Augustine			old resident	yes		
175	29	Bruvo, Christobol	6	1	haze	light	57	St. Augustine	St. Augustine		old resident	yes		Merchant
175	30	Bruvo, Caprana	5	1/4	hazel	light	42	Fernandina	St. Augustine		old resident	yes		
175	31	Bruvo, Christopher					21	St. Augustine	GAinesville, FL		May 21,1864	no		on parole, citizen taken at Tampa bay by Genl Woodbury
175	32	Bruvo, Josephine	5	3 3/4	hazel	fair	19	St. Augustine	St. Augustine		old resident	yes		
175	33	Bravo, Alexander					13	St. Augustine	St. Augustine		old resident	no		Family of C. Bruvo
175	34	Bruvo, Mary L.					7	St. Augustine	St. Augustine		old resident	no		Family of C. Bruvo
175	35	Bruvo, Frances					5	St. Augustine	St. Augustine		old resident	no		Family of C. Bruvo
175	36	Bruvo, Manly					1 3/12	St. Augustine	St. Augustine		old resident	no		Family of C. Bruvo
175	37	Burt, George	5	8 3/4	grey	light	46	Vermont	St. Augustine		old resident	yes		Merchant
175	38	Burt, Charles					10	St. Augustine	St. Augustine		old resident	no		
175	39	Buffington, Samuel	5	8 3/4	hazel	fair	48	Milledgeville	St. Augustine		old resident	yes		Hotel Keeper
175	40	Buffington, Carri..?..					35	New York	St. Augustine			yes		
175	41	Bayan, Jane	5	1 1/4	hazel	light	71	St. Augustine	St. Augustine Fla		old resident	yes		
175	42	Colee, George	5	7 3/4	hazel	dark	58	England	St.Johns Co., Fl		old resident	yes		
175	43	Corbitt, Amos W.	6	1	hazel	fair	30	North Carolina	St. Augustine		old resident	yes	1	By order Post Commander
175	44	Corbitt, Manuela	5	1/4	hazel	light	25	St. Augustine	St. Augustine		old resident	yes	1	By order Post Commander
175	45	Corbitt, Millia					3	St. Augustine	St. Augustine		old resident	no	1/2	By order Post Commander
175	46	Cirbitt, Adam					1	St. Augustine	St. Augustine		old resident	no	1/2	By order Post Commander
175	47	Carr, Bourough E.	5	10	blue	light	52	New York	St. Augustine		old resident	yes		
175	48	Carr, John T.					18	New York	St. Augustine		old resident	no		

Pg	No	Name	Height Ft	Height In	Eyes	Com-plexion	Age	Where born or contraband	Last residence	Where registered for draft or former owner	Date into Department	Oath of Allgn	No of Ration	Remarks
176	1	Conova, Antonio	5	4 3/4	hazel	light	72	St. Augustine	St. Augustine		old resident	yes		
176	2	Conova, Margrett	4	11 1/2	hazel	light	70	St. Augustine	St. Augustine		old resident	yes		
176	3	Conova, Aleta					32	St. Augustine	St. Augustine		old resident	yes		
176	4	Conova, Lewis					10	St. Augustine	St. Augustine		old resident	no		
176	5	Conova, Antonia					4	St. Augustine	St. Augustine		old resident	no		
176	6	Capo, Rafrena	5	2 3/4	dark	dark	26	St. Augustine	St. Augustine		old resident	yes		
176	7	Capo, Mary					6	St. Augustine	St. Augustine		old resident	no		
176	8	Capo, Allice					4	St. Augustine	St. Augustine		old resident	no		
176	9	Capo, John	5	6	dark	dark	60	St. Augustine	St. Augustine		old resident	yes		
176	10	Capo, Mary	5	1 1/2	hazel	fair	56	St. Augustine	St. Augustine		old resident	yes		
176	11	Capo, Lewis					30	St. Augustine	St. Augustine		old resident	yes		Took oath at Hilton Head
176	12	Capo, Clauda					38	St. Augustine	St. Augustine		old resident	yes		
176	13	Capo, Martha	4	11 1/2	hazel	fair	20	St. Augustine	St. Augustine		old resident	yes		
176	14	Capo, Fernandina	5	5 1/4	hazel	med.	16	St. Augustine	St. Augustine		old resident	yes		
176	15	Capo, Betarlia A.					12	St. Augustine	St. Augustine		old resident	no		
176	16	Capo, Sarah	5	2	dark	med.	36	St. Augustine			old resident	yes		
176	17	Capo, William	5	6	blue	dark	80	St. Augustine			old resident	yes	1	By order Post Commander
176	18	Capo, Margrett	5	1/2	black	fair	80	St. Augustine			old resident	yes	1	By order Post Commander
176	19	Capo, Vanancio	5	6	hazel	dark	35	St. Augustine			old resident	yes		
176	20	Capo, Virginia	5		hazel	light	27	St. Augustine			old resident	yes		
176	21	Capo, John					9	St. Augustine			old resident	no		
176	22	Capo, Mary					7	St. Augustine			old resident	no		
176	23	Capo, Anna					5	St. Augustine			old resident	no		
176	24	Capo, Alexander					7 6/12	St. Augustine			old resident	no		
176	25	Copilin, Clarrisa	5	1 3/4	hazel	dark	68	St. Augustine			old resident	yes	1	By order of Post Commander

Pg	No	Name	Height Ft	Height In	Eyes	Complexion	Age	Where born or contraband	Last residence	Where registered for draft or former owner	Date into Department	Oath of Allgn	No of Ration	Remarks
177	26	Cararies, Frances	4	11 1/2	hazel	light	68	St. Augustine	St. Augustine		old resident	yes		
177	27	Capo, Joseph	5	8	hazel	light	35	St. Augustine	St. Augustine		old resident	yes		
177	28	Capo, Manualy					30	St. Augustine	St. Augustine		old resident	yes		
177	29	Capo, Joseph Jr.					9	St. Augustine	St. Augustine		old resident	no	1/2	By order Post Commander
177	30	Capo, John					5	St. Augustine	St. Augustine		old resident	no	1/2	By order of Post Commander
177	31	Capo, Lewis					3	St. Augustine	St. Augustine		old resident	no	1/2	By order of Post Commander
177	32	Capo, Fernando					6m	St. Augustine	St. Augustine		old resident	no		
177	33	Capo, John	5	6 1/2	black	dark	42	St. Augustine	Near Palatka		April 16,1864	yes		
177	34	Capo, Edwardo					39	St. Augustine	Near Palatka		June 1864	yes	1	
177	35	Capo, Dora					13	St. Augustine	Near Palatka		June 1864	no	1/2	By order Post Commander
177	36	Capo, Paul					10	St. Augustine	Near Palatka		June 1864	no	1/2	By order Post Commander
177	37	Capo, Phillip					8	St. Johns Co.	Near Palatka		June 1864	no	1/2	By order Post Commander
177	38	Capo, Elisabeth					4	St. Augustine	Near Palatka		June 1864	no	1/2	By order Post Commander
177	39	Capo, Anthony					2	St. Augustine	Near Palatka		June 1864	no	1/2	By order Post Commander
177	40	Capo, GAbriel	5	8 1/4	hazel	dark	46	St. Augustine	St. Augustine		old resident	yes		
177	41	Capo, Magdaline	5	3 1/4	grey	light	47	St. Augustine			old resident	yes		
177	42	Capo, William	5	6	hazel	light	18	St. Augustine			old resident	yes		
177	43	Capo, Margrett					17	St. Augustine			old resident	no		
177	44	Capo, Mary					16	St. Augustine			old resident	no		
177	45	Capo, Sarah					13	St. Augustine			old resident	no		
177	46	Capo, Frances					12	St. Augustine			old resident	no		
177	47	Capo, Joseph					10	St. Augustine			old resident	no		
177	48	Capellin, Sebena	5	5	grey	light	37	St. Augustine			old resident	yes		

"CENSUS" DEPARTMENT OF THE SOUTH - NOVEMBER, 1864

Pg	No	Name	Height Ft	Height In	Eyes	Complexion	Age	Where born or contraband	Last residence	Where registered for draft or former owner	Date into Department	Oath of Allgn	No of Ration	Remarks
178	1	Capellin, Mary					23	St. Augustine			old resident	no		
178	2	Capellin, Martha					4	St. Augustine			old resident	no		
178	3	Capellin, Ramon L.					2	St. Augustine			old resident	no		
178	4	Conant, Cate C.					30	Vermont	Vermont		Feb. 1863	no		School Teacher from Vermont
178	5	Campbell, Jacob	5	8	grey	fair	44	Georgia	Hilton Head		Aug. 31/1864	yes	1	By order Post Commander
178	6	Campbell, Mary J.	5	4	blue	fair	28	Camden Co., GA	Hilton Head		Aug. 31/1864	yes	1	By order Post Commander
178	7	Campbell, Martha					11	Wane Co. GA	Hilton Head		Aug. 31/1864	no	1/2	By order Post Commander
178	8	Campbell, Margrett					9	Wane Co. GA	Hilton Head		Aug. 31/1864	no	1/2	By order Post Commander
178	9	Campbell, Jacob					4	Wane Co. GA	Hilton Head		Aug. 31/1864	no	1.2	By order Post Commander
178	10	Campbell, Mary L.					1	Wane Co. GA	Hilton Head		Aug. 31/1864	no	1/2	By order Post Commander
178	11	Colt, Leonora	5	6	grey	light	20	Cuba	St. Augustine		old resident	yes		
178	12	Colt, Julia	5	3	blue	light	17	Pottsfield, Mass	St. Augustine		old resident	yes		
178	13	Clark, Mary J.					18							Nun in the convent
178	14	Colt, Louisa	5	6	grey	light	15	Cuba			old resident	yes		
178	15	Conova, Martin	5	9 1/2	hazel	dark	74	St. Augustine	St. Augustine		old resident	yes	1	By order Post Commander
178	16	Conova, John C.	6	3/4	hazel	dark	46	St. Augustine	St. Augustine		old resident	yes		
178	17	Conova, Antonio	5	2	hazel	dark	41	St. Augustine	St. Augustine		old resident	yes		
178	18	Conova, Mary	5	5	hazel	light	19	St. Augustine	St. Augustine		old resident	yes		
178	19	Conova, Cara	5	4	hazel	light	17	St. Augustine	St. Augustine		old resident	yes		
178	20	Conova, Anastatia					14	St. Augustine	St. Augustine		old resident	no		
178	21	Conova, Frances					10	St. Augustine	St. Augustine		old resident	no		
178	22	Conova, Christina					8	St. Augustine	St. Augustine		old resident	no		
178	23	Conova, Louisa					4	St. Augustine	St. Augustine		old resident	no		
178	24	Conova, John					1	St. Augustine	St. Augustine		old resident	no		
178	25	Cooper, Victoria	5	5	hazel	light	24	St. Augustine	St. Augustine		old resident	yes	1	By order Post Commander

Pg	No	Name	Height		Eyes	Com-plexion	Age	Where born or contraband	Last residence	Where registered for draft or former owner	Date into Department	Oath of Allgn	No of Ration	Remarks
			Ft	In										
179	26	Campbell, John W.	5	6 1/2	brwn	light	43	Troy,New York	St. Augustine		old resident	yes		Exempt from military duty/physical disability
179	27	Campbell, Susannah	5		blue	light	28	Baltimore	St. Augustine		old resident	yes		
179	28	Campbell, Martha A.					10	Baltimore	St. Augustine		old resident	no		
179	29	Campbell, Mary E.					8	Baltimore	St. Augustine		old resident	no		
179	30	Campbell, John T.					5	Baltimore	St. Augustine		old resident	no		
179	31	Campbell, Neliu					3	St. Augustine	St. Augustine		old resident	no		
179	32	Campbell, Andrew					9m	St. Augustine	St. Augustine		old resident	no		
179	33	Chamberlin, C. P.					31	New York	New York		1863			U.S. Dist. Attorney
179	34	Capellia, Cathrine	5	1 1/4	hazel	blue	62	St. Augustine	St. Augustine		old resident	yes	1	By order Post Commander
179	35	Cbar, George	5	4 3/4	hazel	light	78	St. Augustine	St. Augustine		old resident	yes	1	By order Post Commander
179	36	Carareis, Margarett	5	3 1/4	hazel	light	31	St. Augustine	St. Augustine		old resident	yes		
179	37	Carareis, John					7	St. Augustine	St. Augustine		old resident	no		
179	38	Crosby, James	5	6	blue	light	29	Brooklyn, NY	St. Augustine		old resident	yes		Has the use of only one arm
179	39	Desedo, Blinn					25	St. Augustine	St. Augustine		old resident	yes		
179	40	Doise, Mary					69	St. Augustine	Fernandina		old resident	no	1	By order Post Commander
179	41	Doise, Francis					27	St. Augustine	Fernandina		old resident	no	1	By order Post Commander
179	42	Doise, Ella					14	Jacksonville	Fernandina		old resident	no	1	By order Post Commander
179	43	Darling, Mary	5		hazel	light	60	St. Augustine			old resident	yes	1	By order Post Commander
179	44	Darling, Ann	5	3 1/4	grey	light	30	St. Augustine			old resident	yes	1	By order Post Commander
179	45	Dregzor, Jorden					23	McIntosh,Co., GA	Hilton Head		1863	yes		Took oath at Hilton Head
179	46	Dregzor, Amelia					19	McIntosh,Co., GA	Hilton Head		1863	yes		Took oath at Hilton Head
179	47	Dunn, John					30	Ireland	Fernandina		old resident			Took oath of Neutrality
179	48	Dunn,Cato					26	Ireland	Fernandina		old resident	yes		

Pg	No	Name	Height Ft	Height In	Eyes	Complexion	Age	Where born or contraband	Last residence	Where registered for draft or former owner	Date into Department	Oath of Allgn	No of Ration	Remarks
180	1	Dunn, John J.					5	Fernandina			old resident	no		
180	2	Dunn, Margrett					3	Fernandina			old resident	no		
180	3	Dunn Isabell					1/12	St. Augustine			old resident	no		
180	4	Dumas, Peter B.	5	10	hazel	light	75	France	St. Augustine		old resident	yes		
180	5	Dumas, Rose	5		hazel	light	68	St. Domingo	St. Augustine		old resident	yes		
180	6	Dumas, Estellia	5		black	light	42	St. Augustine	St. Augustine		old resident	yes		
180	7	Drury, Hannah S.	5	6 1/2	grey	light	49	Newport RI	St. Augustine		old resident	yes		
180	8	Dowling, Mathew	5	10 1/4	blue	dark	36	Wane Co. GA	Volusia Co., Fla		Oct.20,1864	yes		Deserter from Starke Co. Feb. 1864
180	9	Dolph, Margrett					33	Nassau Co., GA	St. Johns Co., Fla		April1864	yes		
180	10	Dolph, Athony					9	Jacksonville	St. Johns Co., Fla		April1864	no		
180	11	Dolph, Mary					7	Jacksonville	St. Johns Co., Fla		April1864	no		
180	12	Dolph, Isabell					5	Jacksonville	St. Johns Co., Fla		April1864	no		
180	13	Dunham, David R.	5	6	blue	light	70	New York	St. Augustine		old resident	yes		
180	14	Dunham, Mary M.	5	5	grey	light	48	St. Augustine	St. Augustine		old resident	yes		
180	15	Dunham, Mary S.	5		grey	light	24	St. Augustine	St. Augustine		old resident	yes		
180	16	Dunham, Frances	5	10 1/2	grey	light	17	St. Augustine	St. Augustine		old resident	yes		
180	17	Dunham, Elisa J.					14	St. Augustine	St. Augustine		old resident	no		
180	18	Davis, William J.	5	10	hazel	dark	34	North Carolina	Jacksonville		Jan.15,1863	yes		
180	19	Davis, Mary A.	5	2	grey	light	27	Duval Co., Fl.			old resident	yes		
180	20	Davis, John A.					9	Duval Co., Fl.			old resident	no		
180	21	Davis, Louisa A.					7	Duval Co., Fl.			old resident	no		
180	22	Davis, Clora					60	Bladen Co. No Ca			old resident	yes	1	By order Post Commander/Took the oath in Jacksonville
180	23	Dummett, Mortimer	4	10 1/2	hazel	light	54	West India	St. Augustine		old resident	yes		
180	24	Duncan, George	5	11	dark	light	45	Baltimore MD	Fernandina			yes		
180	25	Duncan, Jane	4	7 1/2	dark	dark	24	St. Augustine				yes		

Pg	No	Name	Height Ft	Height In	Eyes	Complexion	Age	Where born or contraband	Last residence	Where registered for draft or former owner	Date into Department	Oath of Allgn	No of Ration	Remarks
181	26	Duncan,Mary					16	Baltimore	Fernandina			no		
181	27	Duncan, David					14	Baltimore	Fernandina			no		
181	28	Duncan, William					12	Baltimore	Fernandina			no		
181	29	Duncan, Sally					10	Baltimore	Fernandina			no		
181	30	Duncan, John					8	Virginia	Fernandina			no		
181	31	Duncan, Virginia					6	Virginia	Fernandina			no		
181	32	Eaton, Sarah A.					37	Maine	Beaufort, SC		May, 1864	no		
181	33	Evans, Elisabeth	5	8 1/2	dark	light	30	Hamilton Co., Fla	Marion Co., Fla		July13, 1864	yes	21/2	By order post commander
181	34	Evans, Franklin					7	Tampa Bay			July13, 1864	no		
181	35	Evans, Sarah					4	Jacksonville			July13, 1864	no		
181	36	Evans, William					26	England			Jan. 1864			Clerk in Commissary Department
181	37	Falany, Thomas	5	5 1/2	hazel	light	25	St. Augustine	St. Augustine		old resident	yes		
181	38	Falany, Thomaser	5	1/2	hazel	light	27	St. Augustine	St. Augustine		old resident	yes		
181	39	Falany, Drucilla					5	St. Augustine	St. Augustine		old resident	no		
181	40	Falany, Fernando					3	St. Augustine	St. Augustine		old resident	no		
181	41	Falany,Patronia					56	St. Augustine	St. Augustine		old resident	yes		
181	42	Falany, Mary					21	St. Augustine	St. Augustine		old resident	yes	1	By order post commander
181	43	Fereira, Francis	5		black	light	49	St. Augustine			Dec.25,1863	yes		
181	44	Fereira, Paula	5	2 1/2	brwn	light	38	St. Augustine			Dec.25,1863	yes		
181	45	Fereira, Josephine					12	St. Augustine			Dec.25,1863	no		
181	46	Fereira, Francis					10	St. Augustine			Dec.25,1863	no		
181	47	Fereira, John					6	St. Augustine			Dec.25,1863	no		
181	48	Fereira, Eugenia					3	St. Augustine			Dec.25,1863	no		

"CENSUS" DEPARTMENT OF THE SOUTH - NOVEMBER, 1864

Pg	No	Name	Height Ft	Height In	Eyes	Com-plexion	Age	Where born or contraband	Last residence	Where registered for draft or former owner	Date into Department	Oath of Allgn	No of Ration	Remarks
182	1	Foster, Godfrey	5	3 3/4	blue	light	50	Germany	St. Augustine		old resident	yes		
182	2	Foster, Catherine	4	11 1/4	blue	fair	55	France	St. Augustine		old resident	yes		
182	3	Foster, Sarah	4	11	blue	light	17	St. Augustine	St. Augustine		old resident	yes		
182	4	Foster, George					14	St. Augustine	St. Augustine		old resident	no		
182	5	Foster, Flora					11	St. Augustine	St. Augustine		old resident	no		
182	6	Foster, Benjamin					7	St. Augustine	St. Augustine		old resident	no		
182	7	Foster, Andy					5	St. Augustine	St. Augustine		old resident	no		
182	8	Foster, Thomas S.					51	New Jersey	Philadelphia		Nov. 1863	no		
182	9	Foster, Mary S.					44	Philadelphia	Philadelphia		Nov. 1863	no		
182	10	Foster, Annie					9	Philadelphia	Philadelphia		Nov. 1863	no		
182	11	Fereira, Joseph	5	4	grey	light	45	St. Augustine			Jan.12, 1864	yes		
182	12	Fereira, Louisa	5		dark	light	41	St. Augustine	St. Johns Co.,Fla		Jan.12, 1864	yes		
182	13	Fereira, Millie	5		hazel	light	16	St. Augustine	St. Johns Co.,Fla		Jan.12, 1864	yes		
182	14	Fereira, Catherine					13	Pensacola, Fla	St. Johns Co.,Fla		Jan.12, 1864	no		
182	15	Fereira, Josephine					10	Pensacola, Fla	St. Johns Co.,Fla		Jan.12, 1864	no		
182	16	Fereira, Millia					9	Pensacola, Fla	St. Johns Co.,Fla		Jan.12, 1864	no		
182	17	Fereira, Mary S.					5	Pensacola, Fla	St. Johns Co.,Fla		Jan.12, 1864	no		
182	18	Fereira, Lewis					2	Picolata, Fla	St. Johns Co.,Fla		Jan.12, 1864	no		
182	19	Falany, Antonia	5	4	hazel	light	50	Mayport, Fla			old resident	yes		
182	20	Falany, James	5	8 1/2	hazel	light	49	St. Augustine	St. Augustine		old resident	yes		
182	21	Falany, Antonia					12	St. Augustine			old resident	no		
182	22	Falany, Mary					10	St. Augustine			old resident	no	1/2	By order post commander
182	23	Falany, Felhimania					5	St. Augustine			old resident	no	1/2	By order post commander
182	24	Falany, James					14	St. Augustine			old resident	no	1/2	By order post commander
182	25	Genover, Ann	5	1/2	hazel	light	49	St. Augustine	St. Augustine		old resident	yes	1	By order post commander

Pg	No	Name	Height Ft	Height In	Eyes	Complexion	Age	Where born or contraband	Last residence	Where registered for draft or former owner	Date into Department	Oath of Allgn	No of Ration	Remarks
183	26	Fatio, Louisa	5	2	blue	light	66	St. Augustine	St. Augustine		old resident	yes		
183	27	Fatio, Sophia	5	5 1/2	hazel	light	40	Fernandina	St. Augustine		old resident	yes		
183	28	Delk, William S.					50	Georgia	Orange County		May, 1864	yes		
183	29	Genover, Mary	5	2 1/2	blue	fair	18	St. Augustine	St. Augustine		old resident	yes		
183	30	Genover, Naston					14	St. Augustine	St. Augustine		old resident	no		
183	31	Genover, Dora					12	St. Augustine	St. Augustine		old resident	no	1/2	By order Post Commander
183	32	Genover, Monica					23	St. Augustine	St. Augustine		old resident	yes	1/2	By order Post Commander
183	33	Genover, Ann					3	St. Augustine	St. Augustine		old resident	no	1/2	By order Post Commander
183	34	Gomas, Phillip	6		hazel	light	55	St. Augustine	St. Augustine		old resident	yes		
183	35	Gomas, Mary	5	1 1/4	hazel	light	46	St. Augustine	St. Augustine		old resident	yes		
183	36	Gomas, John	5		hazel	light	16	St. Augustine	St. Augustine		old resident	yes		
183	37	Gomas, Mary L.					13	St. Augustine	St. Augustine		old resident	no		
183	38	Gomas, Catherine					10	St. Augustine	St. Augustine		old resident	no		
183	39	Gomas, Christina					8	St. Augustine	St. Augustine		old resident	no		
183	40	Gomas, GAbriel					6	St. Augustine	St. Augustine		old resident	no		
183	41	GAtlin, John	6		brwn	fair	37	Georgia	Putnam Co., Fla		Dec.14, 1863	yes		Deserter from McCormicks Batery
183	42	GAtlin, Ellen					33	Georgia	Putnam Co., Fla		March 1864	no		
183	43	GAtlin, Ezekeil					12	Georgia	Putnam Co., Fla		March 1864	no		
183	44	GAtlin, Ashbury					11	Putnam Co. FL	Putnam Co., Fla		March 1864	no		
183	45	GAtlin, John					10	Putnam Co. FL	Putnam Co., Fla		March 1864	no		
183	46	GAtlin, Charlotte					7	Putnam Co. FL	Putnam Co., Fla		March 1864	no		
183	47	GAtlin, Sarah E.					5	Putnam Co. FL	Putnam Co., Fla		March 1864	no		
183	48	GAtlin, William					1m	Putnam Co. FL	Putnam Co., Fla		March 1864	no		

"CENSUS" DEPARTMENT OF THE SOUTH - NOVEMBER, 1864

Pg	No	Name	Height Ft	Height In	Eyes	Complexion	Age	Where born or contraband	Last residence	Where registered for draft or former owner	Date into Department	Oath of Allgn	No of Ration	Remarks
184	1	Gilbert, Jane					43	Manderin	Duval Co., Fla		Sept 18,1863	no	1	By order Post Commander
184	2	Gilbert, Catherine					21	Manderin, Fla	Duval Co., Fla		Sept 18,1863	no		
184	3	Gilbert, John	5	6	brwn	dark	17	Manderin, Fla	Duval Co., Fla		Sept 18,1863	yes	1/2	By order Post Commander
184	4	Gilbert, Richard					13	Manderin, Fla	Duval Co., Fla		Sept 18,1863	no	1/2	By order Post Commander
184	5	Gilbert, Abner					11	Manderin, Fla	Duval Co., Fla		Sept 18,1863	no	1/2	By order Post Commander
184	6	Gilbert, Aldonia					8	Manderin, Fla	Duval Co., Fla		Sept 18,1863	no	1/2	By order Post Commander
184	7	Gilbert, Simmion					5	Manderin, Fla	Duval Co., Fla		Sept 18,1863	no	1/2	By order Post Commander
184	8	Gilbert, James					2	Manderin, Fla	Duval Co., Fla		Sept 18,1863	no	1/2	By order Post Commander
184	9	Green, Isaac					58	Georgia	Putnam Co., Fla		Sept 24,1864	yes	1	Took the oath in Jacksonville by
184	10	Green, Celia					28	Georgia	Putnam Co., Fla		Sept 24,1864	yes	1	order Post Commander
184	11	Green, Jessie					14	Clay Co., Fla	Putnam Co., Fla		Sept 24,1864	yes		
184	12	Green, Louisa					11	Clay Co., Fla	Putnam Co., Fla		Sept 24,1864	no		
184	13	Green, Elisia					9	Clay Co., Fla	Putnam Co., Fla		Sept 24,1864	no	1/2	By order Post Commander
184	14	Green, William D.					8	Putnam Co., Fla	Putnam Co., Fla		Sept 24,1864	no	1/2	By order Post Commander
184	15	Green, Mathew					4	Putnam Co., Fla	Putnam Co., Fla		Sept 24,1864	no	1/2	By order Post Commander
184	16	GArey, Maria F.	5	2	hazel	fair	76	St. Augustine	St. Augustine		old resident	yes		
184	17	GArey, Elisabeth	5	4 1/2	grey	fair	35	St. Augustine	St. Augustine		old resident	yes		
184	18	GArey, Melia					15	New Orleans	New Orleans		old resident	no		
184	19	GArdner, Margrett					56	St. Augustine	Duval Co., Fla		Oct. 1864	yes		
184	20	GArdner, Matilda					27	Ware Co. GA	Jacksonville		March/64	yes	1	By order Post Commander
184	21	GArdner, Richard					3	Duval Co., Fla.	Jacksonville		March/64	no	1/2	By order Post Commander
184	22	GArdner, Elisabeth					56	Maine	Maine		Winter 1846	no	1/2	By order Post Commander
184	23	GArdner, Millie					8	Maine			old resident	no		
184	24	Greenough, George					28	State of NY			Nov. 1864	no		Lately discharged from 4th NH Vols.
184	25	Greenough, Anna					27	Ireland	Mass.		Oct. 1858	yes		

Pg	No	Name	Height Ft	Height In	Eyes	Complexion	Age	Where born or contraband	Last residence	Where registered for draft or former owner	Date into Department	Oath of Allgn	No of Ration	Remarks
185	26	Gonztless, Frances	5	1/2	hazel	light	64	St. Augustine	St. Augustine		old resident	yes		
185	27	Greely, Gorham					62		Maine		Aug. 1864			Methodist minister from Maine
185	28	Greely, Harriet B.					58		Maine		Oct. 1864			
185	29	Giessman, A.					30	Germany			old resident	yes		trader at this post
185	30	Hanham, James R.	5	5	blue	light	87	England	St. Augustine		old resident	yes		
185	31	Hermandiz, Mary					37	St. Augustine			old resident	yes		
185	32	Hale, Christopher					38	England				no		lately discharged from Vol. Service
185	33	Hab, Louisa					23	Cuba			old resident	no		
185	34	Hernandis, Ramon	5	6 1/2	hazel	light	36	St. Augustine	St. Augustine		old resident	yes		
185	35	Hernandis, Angeline	4	3	hazel	light	28	St. Augustine	St. Augustine		old resident	yes		
185	36	Hernandis, Lewis					12	St. Augustine	St. Augustine		old resident	no		
185	37	Hernandis, Eugene					10	St. Augustine	St. Augustine		old resident	no		
185	38	Herlbert, Ann	5	2 1/2	hazel	fair	75	North Carolina	St. Augustine		old resident	yes		
185	39	Hartly, George	5	7 1/4	blue	light	41	Duval Co., Fla.	Duval Co., Fla		June 3, 1863	yes		
185	40	Hartly, Catherine	5	1/2	grey	light	24	Duval Co., Fla.	Duval Co., Fla		June 3, 1863	yes	1	By order post commander
185	41	Hartly, George W.					5	Duval Co., Fla.	Duval Co., Fla		June 3, 1863	no	1/2	By order post commander
185	42	Hartly, Raphale					3	Duval Co., Fla.	Duval Co., Fla		June 3, 1863	no	1/2	By order post commander
185	43	Hartly, Sarah A.					6m	St. Augustine			resident	no		
185	44	Hernandis, Joseph	5	6 1/2	black	dark	30	St. Augustine			old resident	yes		deserter from Rebel Service
185	45	Hernandis, Mercilla					25	St. Augustine	Jacksonville Fla			no		
185	46	Hernandis, Joseph Jr					8	St. Augustine	Jacksonville Fla			no		
185	47	Hernandis, Hubert					5	St. Augustine	Jacksonville Fla			no		
185	48	Hernandis, Macatha					3	JacksonvilleFla	Jacksonville Fla			no		

Pg	No	Name	Height Ft	Height In	Eyes	Com-plexion	Age	Where born or contraband	Last residence	Where registered for draft or former owner	Date into Department	Oath of Allgn	No of Ration	Remarks
186	1	Hudnell, Agnatha	5	2	black	fair	19	St. Augustine			old resident	yes		
186	2	Hudness, Louisa					6m	St. Augustine			old resident	no		
186	3	Hernandes, Gertrude					15	St. Augustine			old resident	yes		
186	4	Hagen, William	5	4	hazel	light	54	Duval Co., Fla.	Duval Co., Fla		May 29,1863	yes		
186	5	Hagen, Sarah	5	1/2	grey	light	46	South Carolina	Duval Co., Fla		May 29,1863	yes		
186	6	Hagen, Joseph	5	6	blue	light	26	Duval Co., Fla.	Duval Co., Fla		May, 1863	yes		
186	7	Hagen, Eliza A.	4	11 1/2	hazel	light	16	Duval Co., Fla.	Duval Co., Fla		May, 1863	yes		
186	8	Hagen, William					12	Duval Co., Fla.	Duval Co., Fla		May, 1863	no		
186	9	Hagen, Richard					12	Duval Co., Fla.	Duval Co., Fla		May, 1863	no		
186	10	Hagen, Edward					10	Duval Co., Fla.	Duval Co., Fla		May, 1863	no		
186	11	Hagen, John					7	Duval Co., Fla.	Duval Co., Fla		May, 1863	no		
186	12	Hagen, Mary G					4	Duval Co., Fla.	Duval Co., Fla		May, 1863	no		
186	13	Hermanies, Andrew	5	7 3/4	hazel	light	46	St. Augustine	St. Augustine		old resident	yes		
186	14	Hermanies,Catherine	5	1 3/4	hazel	light	45	St. Augustine	St. Augustine		old resident	yes		
186	15	Hermanies, Ralph	5	8 1/2	black	dark	20	St. Augustine	St. Augustine		old resident	yes		
186	16	Hermanies, Antonio	5	1 3/4	hazel	light	19	St. Augustine	St. Augustine		old resident	yes		
186	17	Hermanies, Mary	4	11 3/4	hazel	light	18	St. Augustine	St. Augustine		old resident	yes		
186	18	Hermanies, Edward					8	St. Augustine	St. Augustine		old resident	no		
186	19	Harris, Mary M.					29	New York	New York		1863	no		School Teacher from New York
186	20	Hunter, Mary E					19	Madison Co., Fla	Madison Co., Fla		March 1864	yes		
186	21	Hunter, Edward	5	10	grey	?	30	Charleston, SC	Madison Co., Fla		Feb. 1864	yes		
186	22	Hunter, John					6m	St. Augustine				no		
186	23	Hernandis, Mary E.					60	St. Augustine			old resident	yes		
186	24	Hara, Michael O.					33	Ireland	Orange Co Fla		June 1864			Took oath of Neutrality
186	25	Henry, John	5	1/4	hazel	light	22	St. Augustine			old resident	yes		

Pg	No	Name	Height Ft	Height In	Eyes	Com-plexion	Age	Where born or contraband	Last residence	Where registered for draft or former owner	Date into Department	Oath of Allgn	No of Ration	Remarks
187	26	Henry, William	4	10 3/4	hazel	light	18	St. Augustine	St. Augustine		old resident	yes		
187	27	Henry, B_?__					10	St. Augustine			old resident	yes		
187	28	Hernandiz, Mary M.					28	St. Augustine			old resident	yes		
187	29	Hayman, Jasper H.	5	8	grey	dark	34	Georgia	Volusia Co., Fla		May 3, 1864	yes		
187	30	Hayman, Martha E.	5	2 1/2	blue	light	?8	South Carolina	Volusia Co., Fla		May 3, 1864	yes		
187	31	Hayman, Justin					?	Volusia Co.	Volusia Co., Fla		May 3, 1864	no		
187	32	Hayman, Mary E.					8	Volusia Co.	Volusia Co., Fla		May 3, 1864	no		
187	33	Hayman, Allice					6	Volusia Co.	Volusia Co., Fla		May 3, 1864	no		
187	34	Hernandiz, Domingo					47	St. Augustine			old resident	yes	1	By order post commander
187	35	Hernandiz, Urania					20	St. Augustine			old resident	yes	1	By order post commander
187	36	Hemmingway, Mary					23	St. Augustine			old resident	yes	1	By order post commander
187	37	Hemmingway,MaryA					3	St. Augustine			old resident	no		
187	38	Iler, George					40	England			old resident			Took the oath of neutrality
187	39	Irvin, Fanny					18	St. Augustine			old resident	yes		
187	40	Jenks, Hannah P.	5	2 1/4	hazel	light	36	Indiana			old resident	yes		
187	41	Ivanosky, Julia	5		hazel	fair	19	St. Augustine			old resident	yes		
187	42	Ivanosky, Alexander	5	8 3/4	hazel	light	22	Palatka, Fla	Palatka, Fla		old resident	yes		
187	43	Ivanosky, Alenander					4m	St. Augustine	St. Augustine			no		
187	44	Jones, William B.	5	5 1/4	blue	light	37	Ridgefield, CT.	Orange Co Fla		Oct.15, 1864	yes		
187	45	Jones, Jane	5		dark	dark	30	Brooklyn, NY	Orange Co Fla		Oct.15, 1864	yes		
187	46	Jones, Andrew R.					3	Orange Co	Orange Co Fla		Oct.15, 1864	no		
187	47	Keogh, Michael W.	5	7	grey	light	27	New York	Augusta, GA		June 2, 1863	yes		
187	48	Keogh, Eliza	5	2	hazel	light	48	Ireland	Augusta, GA		June 2, 1863	yes		Has the use of only one arm

Pg	No	Name	Height Ft	Height In	Eyes	Com-plexion	Age	Where born or contraband	Last residence	Where registered for draft or former owner	Date into Department	Oath of Allgn	No of Ration	Remarks
188	1	Lopez, _?alota					35	St. Augustine		Old Resident		no	1	By order post commander
188	2	Lopez, Manula					3	St. Augustine				no		
188	3	Lopez, Ignatio	5	8	blue	dark	47	St. Augustine	St. Augustine		old resident	yes		
188	4	Lopez, Margritt	4	11 1/2	blue	light	42	St. Augustine	St. Augustine		old resident	yes	1	By order post commander
188	5	Lopez, Caroline	5	2 1/4	blue	light	17	St. Augustine	St. Augustine		old resident	yes		
188	6	Lopez, Leonora					12	St. Augustine	St. Augustine		old resident	no	1/2	By order post commander
188	7	Lopez, Mary					6	St. Augustine	St. Augustine		old resident	no	1/2	By order post commander
188	8	Lopez, Andrew	5	9	black	dark	49	Fernandina	St. Augustine		old resident	yes		
188	9	Lopez, Mary	5	3	hazel	dark	46	St. Augustine	St. Augustine		old resident	yes		
188	10	Lopez, Jane					16	St. Augustine			old resident	no		
188	11	Lopez, Edward					13	St. Augustine			old resident	no		
188	12	Lopez, Francis					11	St. Augustine			old resident	no		
188	13	Lopez, Lewis					6	St. Augustine			old resident	no		
188	14	Lopez, Bartola					63	St. Augustine			old resident	yes		
188	15	Long, GAbriel W.	6		grey	light	46	North Carolina	Putnam Co.		March 6/1864	yes		
188	16	Long, Elisabeth A.					46	North Carolina	Putnam Co.		May 28/1864	no		
188	17	Long, Sarah C.					22	North Carolina	Putnam Co.		May 28/1864	no		
188	18	Long, George W.	6		blue	light	19	Wilmington	Putnam Co., Fla		May 30/1864	yes		
188	19	Long, John G.	5	10	blue	light	17	Wilmington	Putnam Co., Fla		May 30/1864	yes		
188	20	Long, William J.	5	7	blue	light	15	Georgia	Putnam Co., Fla		May 30/1864	yes		
188	21	Long, Stephen B.			blue	light	13	Georgia	Putnam Co., Fla		May 30/1864	no		
188	22	Long, Elizabeth E.			blue	light	11	Marion Co. FL	Putnam Co., Fla		May 30/1864	no		
188	23	Long, Rinallia S.					8	Putnam Co. FL	Putnam Co., Fla		May 30/1864	no		
188	24	Long, Thomas C.					4	Putnam Co. FL	Putnam Co., Fla		May 30/1864	no		
188	25	Lane, Mary Ann	5	4	dark	fair	24	Georgia	Georgia		Aug. 1864	yes		

Pg	No	Name	Height Ft	Height In	Eyes	Com-plexion	Age	Where born or contraband	Last residence	Where registered for draft or former owner	Date into Department	Oath of Allgn	No of Ration	Remarks
189	26	Leonardy, Antonio	5	1/2	grey	light	?	St. Augustine			old resident	yes		
189	27	Leonardy, Rose	4	11 1/2	black	light	18	St. Augustine	St. Augustine		old resident	yes	1	By order post commander
189	28	Leornady, Maria	5	2 1/2			14	St. Augustine	St. Augustine		old resident	yes		
189	29	Leonardy, Carapina					?	St. Augustine	St. Augustine		old resident	no		
189	30	Leonardy, Catherine					?	St. Augustine	St. Augustine		old resident	no	1/2	By order post commander
189	31	Leonardy, Lewis					?	St. Augustine	St. Augustine		old resident	no	1/2	By order post commander
189	32	Leonardy, Matios					45	St. Augustine			old resident	yes		
189	33	Leonardy, Jennie					24	St. Augustine			old resident	yes		
189	34	Leonardy, Fanny					21	St. Augustine			old resident	yes		
189	35	Leonardy, Catherine					20	St. Augustine			old resident	yes		
189	36	Leonardy, Delia					18	St. Augustine			old resident	yes		
189	37	Leonardy, Matias					16	St. Augustine			old resident	yes		
189	38	Leonardy, Fernands					12	St. Augustine			old resident	no		
189	39	Leonardy, Cabenia	5	2 1/2	blue	light	50	St. Augustine	St. Augustine		old resident	yes		
189	40	Leonardy, George	5	7 1/4	hazel	light	18	St. Augustine	St. Augustine		old resident	yes		
189	41	Lincoln, Charles D.					29		Fernandina		old resident	yes		
189	42	Lopez, Antonio	5	6 3/4	hazel	dark	45	St. Augustine			old resident	yes		
189	43	Lopez, Mary	5	3 1/4	hazel	dark	49	St. Augustine			old resident	yes		
189	44	Lopez, Celestine	5	4 3/4	hazel	dark	15	St. Augustine			old resident	yes		
189	45	Lopez, Joseph					14	St. Augustine			old resident	no		
189	46	Lopez, Emanuel					12	St. Augustine			old resident	no		
189	47	Lopez, Jerome					10	St. Augustine			old resident	no		
189	48	Lopez, James					7	St. Augustine			old resident	no		

Pg	No	Name	Height Ft	Height In	Eyes	Com-plexion	Age	Where born or contraband	Last residence	Where registered for draft or former owner	Date into Department	Oath of Allgn	No of Ration	Remarks
190	1	Lopez, Mary					5	St. Augustine			old resident	no		
190	2	Lieb, Thomas K.					26	Philadelphia	Hilton Head		1862	yes		
190	3	Mombo, Elisa					38							Nun in the convent
190	4	Masters, Bartola	5	6	hazel	?	67	St. Augustine	St. Johns Co., Fla		Jan. 16/1864	yes		
190	5	Masters, Margrett	5	2	dark	dark	61	St. Augustine	St. Johns Co., Fla		Jan. 11/1864	yes		
190	6	Murry, Raphila	5	1	hazel	light	60	St. Augustine			old resident	yes	1	By order post commander
190	7	Michler, James A.	6	1/4	blue	light	42	St. Marys, GA	St. Augustine		old resident	yes		
190	8	Michler, Mary A.	5		hazel	light	32	St. Augustine	St. Augustine		old resident	yes		
190	9	Michler, Mathew					14	St. Augustine			old resident	no		
190	10	Michler, Paul					12	St. Augustine			old resident	no		
190	11	Mather, Sarah A.	5	6	blue	light	43	NorthHampton, Mass	St. Augustine		old resident	yes		
190	12	Medecis, Emanuel	5	71/4	blue	light	47	St. Augustine			old resident	yes		
190	13	Medecis, Antonia	5	3/4	hazel	light	40	St. Augustine			old resident	yes		
190	14	Medecis, Antonia	5	3/4	hazel	light	18	St. Augustine			old resident	yes		
190	15	Medecis, Elizabeth					12	St. Augustine			old resident	no		
190	16	Medecis, Emanuel					10	St. Augustine			old resident	no		
190	17	Medecis, Edmond					7	St. Augustine			old resident	no		
190	18	Medecis, Mary					4	St. Augustine			old resident	no		
190	19	Medecis, Ellouise					2	St. Augustine			old resident	no		
190	20	Michler, Ann M					72	St. Augustine			old resident	no	1	By order post commander
190	21	Masters, Bartolla C.	5	10 1/2	grey	dark	56	St. Augustine			old resident	yes		
190	22	Masters, Adaline	5	5 1/2	blue	light	41	St. Augustine			old resident	yes		
190	23	Masters, Sylvister					13	St. Augustine			old resident	no		
190	24	Masters, John					8	St. Augustine			old resident	no		
190	25	Masters, Mary L.					5	St. Augustine			old resident	no		

Pg	No	Name	Height Ft	Height In	Eyes	Com-plexion	Age	Where born or contraband	Last residence	Where registered for draft or former owner	Date into Department	Oath of Allgn	No of Ration	Remarks
191	26	Masters, Manley					1	St. Augustine			old resident			
191	27	Masters, Philamanie	4	10	dark	dark	24	St. Augustine			old resident	yes		
191	28	Masters, Raphil	5	7 1/2	grey	dark	30	St. Augustine			old resident	yes		
191	29	Masters, Anna	5	3	black	light	25	St. Augustine			old resident	yes		
191	30	Masters, Elizabeth					?	St. Augustine			old resident			
191	31	Masters, Raphil M.					6	St. Augustine			old resident			
191	32	Masters, Walter					4	St. Augustine			old resident			
191	33	Masters, Augustine	4	10	hazel	dark	67	St. Augustine			old resident	yes	1	By order post commander
191	34	Masters, Eveline	5		hazel	light	19	St. Augustine			old resident	yes	1	By order post commander
191	35	Masters, Peter	5	3 1/2	hazel	light	80	St. Augustine			old resident	yes		
191	36	Masters, Francis					74	St. Augustine			old resident			
191	37	Masters, Catherine					30	St. Augustine			old resident			
191	38	Masters, Susan					11	St. Augustine			old resident			
191	39	Masters, John S.	5	9 1/4	hazel	light	57	St. Augustine	St. Augustine		old resident	yes		
191	40	Masters, Mary M.	5		hazel	light	55	St. Augustine			old resident	yes		
191	41	Masters, Blaceda					19	St. Augustine			old resident			
191	42	Masters, Ucabia					15	St. Augustine			old resident			
191	43	Masters, Antonia					14	St. Augustine			old resident			
191	44	Mancey, Mary					79	St. Augustine			old resident	no	1	By order post commander
191	45	Mott, Jane					58	New York	New York		Feb. 1863	no		
191	46	McGraw, Robert	5	9 1/4	hazel	light	23	Union Co. SC	Duval Co., Fla		Dec. 7/1862	yes		
191	47	McGraw, Margrett	4	9 1/2	hazel	light	20	Duval Co.	Duval Co., Fla		Dec. 7/1862	yes		
191	48	McGraw, Richard					1	St. Augustine			born here	no		

Pg	No	Name	Height Ft	Height In	Eyes	Complexion	Age	Where born or contraband	Last residence	Where registered for draft or former owner	Date into Department	Oath of Allgn	No of Ration	Remarks
192	1	Machaelvain, Elizabeth					30	St. Augustine			old resident	no		
192	2	Machaelvain,Simion					6	St. Augustine			old resident	no		
192	3	Marine, Rosella	5	2	hazel	light	39	St. Augustine			old resident	yes		
192	4	Munson, Loranda	4	9 1/4	hazel	light	45	St. Augustine			old resident	yes	1	By order post commander
192	5	Munson, Minnie	5	2 3/4	blue	light	22	St. Augustine			old resident	yes	1	By order post commander
192	6	Munson, Jennie	5	4 3/4	blue	light	17	St. Augustine			old resident	yes		
192	7	Munson, Richard					14	St. Augustine			old resident	no		
192	8	Munson, Cato					12	St. Augustine			old resident	no	1/2	By order post commander
192	9	Munson, Antonio					9	St. Augustine			old resident	no	1/2	By order post commander
192	10	McKinney, James	5	4	blue	light	18	Crawford Co., Gea	Orange Co., Fla		July 3/1864	yes		
192	11	Manucey?, Joseph	5	1 1/2	blue	dark	73	St. Augustine			old resident	yes		
192	12	Manucey?, Emanuel					43	St. Augustine			old resident	yes		A Lunatic
192	13	Maranda, Carma	5	5	grey	dark	40	St. Augustine			old resident	yes	1	By order post commander
192	14	Maranda, Tliminia	5	2 3/4	blue	light	17	St. Augustine			old resident	yes	1/2	By order post commander
192	15	Maranda, Sycurgus					14	St. Augustine			old resident	no	1/2	By order post commander
192	16	Maranda, Frances					10	St. Augustine			old resident	no	1/2	By order post commander
192	17	Maranda, Delphine					6	St. Augustine			old resident	no	1/2	By order post commander
192	18	Matison, Cato					12	St. Augustine			old resident	no		
192	19	Masters, Matilda	4	9 3/4	hazel	dark	59	St. Augustine			old resident	yes	1	By order post commander
192	20	Masters, Demecia					17	St. Augustine			old resident	no		
192	21	Masters, Antonio					13	St. Augustine			old resident	no	1/2	By order post commander
192	22	McFarland, Josephine					19	St. Augustine			old resident	yes	1	By order post commander
192	23	McFarland, Frances E.					1	St. Augustine			old resident	no		
192	24	Masters, Jane	5	2 1/2	grey	light	24	St. Augustine			old resident	yes	1	By order post commander
192	25	Masters, Mary L.					6	St. Augustine			old resident	yes	1/2	By order post commander

Pg	No	Name	Height Ft	Height In	Eyes	Com-plexion	Age	Where born or contraband	Last residence	Where registered for draft or former owner	Date into Department	Oath of Allgn	No of Ration	Remarks
193	26	Masters, Antonio					4 3/12	St. Augustine			old resident	no	1/2	By order post commander
193	27	Manly, Herbert	5	10 1/2	hazel	light	32	Massachusetts			old resident	yes		
193	28	McClenden, James	5	9 3/4	blue	fair	45	Georgia	Manderine Fla		Sept. 7,1863	yes		
193	29	McClenden, Hester					25	Duval Co.	Manderine Fla		Sept. 7,1863	no	1	By order post commander
193	30	McClenden,Virginia R.					7	Duval Co.	Manderine Fla		Sept. 7,1863	no	1/2	By order post commander
193	31	McClenden,SavanahR.					4	Duval Co.	Manderine Fla		Sept. 7,1863	no		
193	32	Masters, Mercey	5	3 1/2	hazel	light	20	St. Augustine			old resident	yes		
193	33	Nelligan, Michael	5	5 1/4	hazel	light	55	Lyome, CT ?			old resident	yes		
193	34	Nelson, Thomas	5	11 1/2	blue	light	51	Irland			old resident	yes		
193	35	Nelson, Frances	5	3 1/2	hazel	light	37	St. Augustine			old resident	yes		
193	36	Nelson, Mary A.	5	3 3/4	hazel	light	17	St. Augustine			old resident	yes		
193	37	Nelson, Florentina	4	11 1/2	hazel	light	16	St. Augustine			old resident	yes		
193	38	Nelson, Josephine					14	St. Augustine			old resident	no		
193	39	Nelson, Eugenia					11	St. Augustine			old resident	no		
193	40	Nelson, Joseph					10	St. Augustine			old resident	no		
193	41	Nelson, Thomas					7	St. Augustine			old resident	no		
193	42	Nelson, Christina					6	St. Augustine			old resident	no		
193	43	Nelson, Anetia					4	St. Augustine			old resident	no		
193	44	Noda, Antonia	5	3 1/2	hazel	light	49	St. Augustine			old resident	yes		
193	45	Noda, Antonia	5		hazel	light	42	St. Augustine			old resident	yes		
193	46	Noda, Mary L.					12	St. Augustine			old resident	no		
193	47	Noda, Agatha					7	St. Augustine			old resident	no		
193	48	Noda, Catherine					5	St. Augustine			old resident	no		

Pg	No	Name	Height Ft	Height In	Eyes	Complexion	Age	Where born or contraband	Last residence	Where registered for draft or former owner	Date into Department	Oath of Align	No of Ration	Remarks
194	1	Noda, Josephine					3	St. Augustine			old resident	no		
194	2	Noda, Ramon					13	St. Augustine			old resident	no		
194	3	Noda, Emanuel					12	St. Augustine			old resident	no		
194	4	Noda, Antonio					9	St. Augustine			old resident	no		
194	5	Olivers, Bartolla	5	7 1/2	hazel	fair	64	St. Augustine			old resident	yes		
194	6	Ortagus, Mary					62	St. Augustine			old resident	no	1	By order post commander
194	7	Oliveras, Caroline	5	2	hazel	light	27	St. Augustine			old resident	yes		
194	8	Oliveras, Gonsilus					8	St. Augustine			old resident	no		
194	9	Oliveras, Earnest					6	St. Augustine			old resident	no		
194	10	Oliveras, Mary					4	St. Augustine			old resident	no		
194	11	Oliveras, Georgia					2	St. Augustine			old resident	no		
194	12	Palmer, Mary	4	11 1/2	hazel	light	19	St. Augustine			old resident	yes		
194	13	Parault, Ade	4	11	hazel	light	60	France			old resident	yes		
194	14	Preist, Granville C.	6	1/2	blue	light	25	Duval Co.	Putnam Co., Fla		May 30/1864	yes		
194	15	Preist, Hellen					21	North Carolina	Putnam Co., Fla		May 30/1864	no		
194	16	Preist, Angeline					2	Putnam Co.,F	Putnam Co., Fla		May 30/1864	no		
194	17	Perrit, Rebecca L.	5	5	hazel	light	39	Philidelphia, Pa			old resident	yes		
194	18	Pinkham, Agatha	4	10 1/4	hazel	light	55	St. Augustine			old resident	yes	1	By order post commander
194	19	Pinkham, Artonett	5	6 3/4	hazel	light	24	St. Augustine			old resident	yes		
194	20	Pinkham, Cato					14	St. Augustine			old resident	no	1/2	By order post commander
194	21	Pinkham, William					12	St. Augustine			old resident	no	1/2	By order post commander
194	22	Pinkham, Ruben C.					9	St. Augustine			old resident	no	1/2	By order post commander
194	23	Pinkham, Nancy	5	3 3/4	hazel	light	50	Hudson, NY			old resident	yes		
194	24	Pinkham, Sally A.	5	4	blue	fair	45	Hudson, NY			old resident	yes		
194	25	Pacettia, Bartolo	5	8 1/2	blue	fair	73	St. Augustine			old resident	yes		

Pg	No	Name	Height Ft	Height In	Eyes	Com-plexion	Age	Where born or contraband	Last residence	Where registered for draft or former owner	Date into Department	Oath of Allgn	No of Ration	Remarks
195	26	Pacettia, Joseph R.					55							
195	27	Pacettia, Mary R.	5				40	St. Augustine			old resident	yes		
195	28	Pacettia, Lewis					14	St. Augustine			old resident	no		
195	29	Pacettia, Catherine	4	11 1/2	hazel	dark	65	St. Augustine			old resident	yes	1	By order post Commander
195	30	Pacettia, Anna					21	St. Augustine			old resident		1	Sick, by order Post Commander
195	31	Pacettia, Catherine	5	2	hazel	light	19	St. Augustine			old resident	yes		
195	32	Pallicer, Antonio	5	11	blue	dark	55	Matanzas			old resident	yes		
195	33	Pallicer, Leonarda	5	1/2	hazel	fair	46	St. Augustine			old resident	yes		
195	34	Pallicer, Catherine					21	St. Augustine			old resident	?		
195	35	Pallicer, Frank					15	St. Augustine			old resident	no		
195	36	Pallicer, Mary					12	St. Augustine			old resident	no		
195	37	Pallicer, Margrett					11	St. Augustine			old resident	no		
195	38	Pallicer, Antonio					7	St. Augustine			old resident	no		
195	39	Ponce, James B.	5	4 3/4	brwn	dark	48	St. Augustine			old resident	yes		
195	40	Ponce, Germania	5		black	dark	34	St. Augustine			old resident	yes	1	By order post Commander
195	41	Ponce, Virginia					15	St. Augustine			old resident	no		
195	42	Ponce, Mary J.					13	St. Augustine			old resident	no		
195	43	Ponce, Alonzo					11	St. Augustine			old resident	no		
195	44	Ponce James					8	St. Augustine			old resident	no		
195	45	Ponce, Louisa					6	St. Augustine			old resident	no	1/2	By order post Commander
195	46	Ponce, Elizabeth					4	St. Augustine			old resident	no	1/2	By order post Commander
195	47	Ponce, Albina					9/12	St. Augustine			old resident	no		
195	48	Pacetta, Andrew	5	10 1/2	grey	fair	60	St. Augustine			old resident	yes		

"CENSUS" DEPARTMENT OF THE SOUTH - NOVEMBER, 1864

Pg	No	Name	Height Ft	Height In	Eyes	Com-plexion	Age	Where born or contraband	Last residence	Where registered for draft or former owner	Date into Department	Oath of Allgn	No of Ration	Remarks
196	1	Pacetta, Mary	5	2	hazel	fair	48	Fernandina			old resident	yes		
196	2	Pacetta, Mary	5	4	hazel	light	18	St. Augustine			old resident	yes		
196	3	Pallicer, Sildony	5	6	brwn	dark	31	St. Augustine	St. Johns Co., FL		Aug.14,1863	yes		
196	4	Pallicer, W-bana?	5		black	dark	28	St. Augustine	St. Johns Co., FL		Aug.17,1863	yes		
196	5	Pallicer, Charles H.					8	St. Augustine	St. Johns Co., Fl		Aug.17,1863	no		
196	6	Pallicer, Lewis					6	St. Augustine	St. Johns Co., Fl		Aug.17,1863	no		
196	7	Pappy, Josephine	4	10 1/2	hazel	light	78	St. Augustine			old resident	yes		
196	8	Ponce, Bartolo	5	6 1/2	hazel	dark	78	St. Augustine			old resident	yes		
196	9	Ponce, Antonia	5		hazel	dark	47	St. Augustine			old resident	yes		
196	10	Ponce, Fanny	5	1	hazel	light	21	St. Augustine			old resident	yes		
196	11	Ponce, Alonzo	5	3	hazel	light	16	St. Augustine			old resident	yes		
196	12	Ponce, Frances					12	St. Augustine			old resident	no		
196	13	Ponce, Lewardo					8	St. Augustine			old resident	no	1/2	By order post Commander
196	14	Ponce, Charles					4	St. Augustine			old resident	no	1/2	By order post Commander
196	15	Pacettia, GAbriel	5	5 1/4	blue	?	48	St. Augustine			old resident	yes		
196	16	Pacettia, Mary	5	1	hazel	light	40	Fernandina			old resident	yes		
196	17	Pacettia, GAbriel	5	1/2	hazel	light	17	St. Augustine			old resident	yes		
196	18	Pomar, Joseph E.	5	4 1/4	hazel	light	68	St. Augustine			old resident	yes		
196	19	Ponce, Margrett	5	2 1/4	hazel	light	69	St. Augustine			old resident	yes		
196	20	Ponce, Mary	5	2	hazel	light	57	St. Augustine			old resident	yes		
196	21	Pallicer, John	5	6	black	dark	42	St. Augustine			old resident	yes		
196	22	Pallicer, Teresia	5	5	grey	light	25	St.Mary's River, Gea			old resident	yes		
196	23	Pallicer, Sarah					5	St. Augustine			old resident			
196	24	Pallicer, Ellen					1	St. Augustine			old resident			
196	25	Pallicer, Margrett					7	St. Augustine			old resident			

Pg	No	Name	Height Ft	Height In	Eyes	Com-plexion	Age	Where born or contraband	Last residence	Where registered for draft or former owner	Date into Department	Oath of Allgn	No of Ration	Remarks
197	26	Pacetta, Barby	5	1 1/2	hazel	dark	76	St. Augustine			old resident	yes	1	By order post Commander
197	27	Pacetta, John S.	5	6 1/4	hazel	dark	56	St. Augustine			old resident	yes		
197	28	Pacetta, Tecla	5	3	blue	light	58	St. Augustine			old resident	yes		
197	29	Pacetta, C.	5	9 1/4	grey	dark	53	St. Augustine			old resident	yes		
197	30	Pacetta Hortenia	5		hazel	light	51	St. Augustine			old resident	yes		
197	31	Pacetta, Jane	5	5	hazel	light	23	St. Augustine			old resident	yes		
197	32	Pacetta, Leonarda	5	4 3/4	hazel	fair	16	St. Augustine			old resident	yes		
197	33	Pacetta, Stephen					14	St. Augustine			old resident	no		
197	34	Pacetta, Louisa					11	St. Augustine			old resident	no		
197	35	Pallicur, Andrew J.					31	St. Augustine			old resident	no		
197	36	Pallicur, Barby					27	St. Augustine			old resident	no		
197	37	Pallicur, Elizabeth	5	2	dark	dark	5	St. Augustine			old resident	yes		
197	38	Pallicur, Andrew J.					3	St. Augustine			old resident	no		
197	39	Pallicur, Edward					9/12	St. Augustine			old resident	no		
197	40	Pomar, Burnidina	4	11 1/2	hazel	fair	20	St. Augustine			old resident	yes		
197	41	Pomar, GAbriel	5	6 1/4	hazel	light	59	St. Augustine			old resident	yes		
197	42	Pomar, Mary	5	3 1/4	hazel	light	29	St. Augustine			old resident	yes		
197	43	Pomar, Jane	5	3	hazel	light	18	St. Augustine			old resident	yes		
197	44	Pomar, Antonio	5	1	hazel	light	15	St. Augustine			old resident	yes		
197	45	Pacetta, Mary	5	1	grey	light	26	St. Augustine	Lake City, Fla		July 22,1864	yes	1	By order post Commander
197	46	Pacetta, Mary S.					2 3/12	Lake City, Fla			July 22,1864	no	1/2	By order post Commander
197	47	Pomar, Antonio	5	5 1/2	hazel	dark	60	St. Augustine			old resident	yes		
197	48	Pomar, Mary	5	2 1/2	hazel	dark	48	St. Augustine			old resident	yes		

Pg	No	Name	Height Ft	Height In	Eyes	Com-plexion	Age	Where born or contraband	Last residence	Where registered for draft or former owner	Date into Department	Oath of Align	No of Ration	Remarks
198	1	Pomar, James	5	4	hazel	light	18	St. Augustine			old resident	yes		
198	2	Pomar, Mary	5	3 1/4	hazel	light	20	St. Augustine			old resident	yes		
198	3	Pomar, Antonia	5	1	hazel	light	24	St. Augustine			old resident	yes		
198	4	Pomar, Lorenzo	4	8 1/2	hazel	light	16	St. Augustine			old resident	yes		
198	5	Pomar, Bartola					13	St. Augustine			old resident	no		
198	6	Pomar, Antonio					6	St. Augustine			old resident	no		
198	7	Pomar, Celia					11	St. Augustine			old resident	no		
198	8	Pacetta, Domingo	5	4 1/2	hazel	dark	40	St. Augustine			old resident	yes		
198	9	Pacetta, Leanda	5	1 1/2	hazel	dark	36	St. Augustine			old resident	yes		
198	10	Pacetta, Mary C.					10	St. Augustine			old resident	no		
198	11	Pacetta, Ellen					6	St. Augustine			old resident	no		
198	12	Pacetta, Domingo					4	St. Augustine			old resident	no		
198	13	Pacetta, Albert					2	St. Augustine			old resident	no		
198	14	Pringle, Ann					35	Georgia	St. Johns Co., Fla		Feb. 1863	yes		
198	15	Pringle, Kisiah					8	Georgia	St. Johns Co., Fla		Feb. 1863	no		
198	16	Quigley, Jesse	5	7 1/2	hazel	fair	24	St. Augustine	St. Johns Co., Fla		April 26,1963	yes		
198	17	Quigley, Owen	5	4 1/2	blue	fair	53	Ireland	St. Johns Co., Fla		Feb. 7, 1863	yes		
198	18	Quigley, Hester A.	5	6	blue	fair	50	North Carolina	St. Johns Co., Fla		May 1863	yes		
198	19	Quigley, Mary A.	5	2 1/2	blue	fair	16	St. Johns Co.	St. Johns Co., Fla		May 1863	yes		
198	20	Quigley, John					9	St. Johns Co.	St. Johns Co., Fla		June 1862	no		
198	21	Quigley, Daniel					7	St. Johns Co.	St. Johns Co., Fla		June 1862	no		
198	22	Quigley, Susan					5	St. Johns Co.	St. Johns Co., Fla		June 1862	no		
198	23	Quigley, Hester A.					4	St. Johns Co.	St. Johns Co., Fla		June 1862	no		
198	24	Quigley, --?--					2	St. Augustine	St. Johns Co., Fla		June 1862	no		
198	25	Remington, --?--					54	Rhode Island	Rhode Island		March 1864	no		

Pg	No	Name	Height		Eyes	Com-plexion	Age	Where born or contraband	Last residence	Where registered for draft or former owner	Date into Department	Oath of Allgn	No of Ration	Remarks
			Ft	In										
199	26	Remington, Alsa					45	Rhode Island	Rhode Island		March 1864	no		
199	27	Remington, Fanny					18	Rhode Island	Rhode Island		March 1864	no		
199	28	Remington, Henry					20	Fall River, NY	Fall River, NY		Jan. 1864	no		
199	29	Ranty, Felix	5	6	hazel	dark	48	Fernandina			old resident	yes		
199	30	Ranty, Germania	5	4	hazel	light	42	St. Johns Bluff			old resident	yes		
199	31	Ranty, Jane					14	St. Augustine			old resident	no		
199	32	Ranty, Frances					10	St. Augustine			old resident	no		
199	33	Ranty, Joseph					8	St. Augustine			old resident	no		
199	34	Reyer, William	5	5 1/2	hazel	dark	37	Fernandina			old resident	yes		
199	35	Reyer, Mary	5	3	hazel	dark	32	St. Augustine			old resident	yes		
199	36	Reyer, Fanny					12	St. Augustine			old resident	no		
199	37	Reyer, Roselia					11	St. Augustine			old resident	no		
199	38	Reyer, Florida					9	St. Augustine			old resident	no		
199	39	Reyer, Josephine					5	St. Augustine			old resident	no		
199	40	Reyer, Anna					4	St. Augustine			old resident	no		
199	41	Reyer, Ellen					2m	St. Augustine			old resident	no		
199	42	Rogero, Edwin					8	St. Augustine			old resident	no		
199	43	Rose, Mary	5	2 1/2	hazel	light	47	St. Augustine			old resident	yes	1	By order post Commander
199	44	Rose, William					26	St. Augustine			old resident	no		
199	45	Rose, Mary E.	5	3/4	hazel	light	23	St. Augustine			old resident	yes	1	By order post Commander
199	46	Rose, Nettia B.	5		hazel	light	18	St. Augustine			old resident	yes	1	By order post Commander
199	47	Rose, Bartolo H.	5	3	grey	light	16	St. Augustine			old resident	yes		
199	48	Rose, Mary A.	5	1/4	hazel	light	14	St. Augustine			old resident	yes	1	By order post Commander

Pg	No	Name	Height Ft	Height In	Eyes	Com-plexion	Age	Where born or contraband	Last residence	Where registered for draft or former owner	Date into Department	Oath of Allgn	No of Ration	Remarks
200	1	Rose, Anna					12	St. Augustine			old resident	no		
200	2	Rose, Charles					9	St. Augustine			old resident	no		
200	3	Reyer, Mary	5		hazel	dark	75	St. Augustine			old resident	yes		
200	4	Reyer, Mary C.	5	1/4	hazel	med.	50	St. Augustine			old resident	yes		
200	5	Reyer, Roselia	5	2	dark	dark	40	St. Augustine			old resident	yes		
200	6	Reyer, Inocent	5	3 1/2	hazel	dark	29	St. Augustine			old resident	yes		
200	7	Reyer, Claudius	5	9 3/4	black	dark	45	Cuba	Madison Co., Fla		Oct. 2, 1863	yes		
200	8	Reyer, Elisabeth	5	4 1/2	hazel	dark	32	Madison Co., Fla	Madison Co., Fla		Oct. 2, 1863	yes		
200	9	Reyer, Anna					2	St. Augustine	St. Augustine			no		
200	10	Reyer, Mary					1	St. Augustine	St. Augustine			no		
200	11	Rogero, Albert D.	5	7 1/2	grey	light	52	St. Augustine			old resident	yes		
200	12	Rogero, Elogene	5	2 1/2	hazel	light	42	St. Augustine			old resident	yes		
200	13	Rogero, Annaclata	5	2 1/2	hazel	light	20	St. Augustine			old resident	yes		
200	14	Rogero, Ignatia	5	3 3/4	blue	light	19	St. Augustine			old resident	yes		
200	15	Rogero, Nine					15	St. Augustine			old resident	no		
200	16	Rogero, Delora					13	St. Augustine			old resident	no		
200	17	Rogero, Urtancia					11	St. Augustine			old resident	no		
200	18	Rogero, Phillip					8	St. Augustine			old resident	no		
200	19	Rogero, Albert					3	St. Augustine			old resident	no		
200	20	Rogero, Ann	5	2	grey	light	68	St. Augustine			old resident	yes	1	By order post Commander
200	21	Roper, William H.	5	7	blue	light	56	Graften Co. NH	Volusia Co., Fla		May 19, 1863	yes	1	By order post Commander
200	22	Reyer, John	5	5 3/4	hazel	dark	46	Fernandina			old resident	yes		
200	23	Reyer, Mary	5	3	hazel	light	37	St. Augustine			old resident	yes		
200	24	Reyer, Mary L.	4	10	hazel	light	16	St. Augustine			old resident	yes		
200	25	Reyer, Frances					9	St. Augustine			old resident	no		

Pg	No	Name	Height Ft	Height In	Eyes	Com-plexion	Age	Where born or contraband	Last residence	Where registered for draft or former owner	Date into Department	Oath of Allgn	No of Ration	Remarks
201	26	Reyer, Mercy					7	St. Augustine			old resident	no		
201	27	Reyer, Antonio					4	St. Augustine			old resident	no		
201	28	Reyer, Anna					3/12	St. Augustine			old resident	no		
201	29	Rogero, Nicholas	5	9 1/4	hazel	light	48	St. Augustine			old resident	yes	1	By order Post Commander
201	30	Rogero, Catherine	5	1/2	dark	?	34	St. Augustine			old resident	yes	1	By order Post Commander
201	31	Rogero, Ramon	5	4 1/2	dark	dark	78	St. Augustine			old resident	yes	1	By order Post Commander
201	32	Rogero, Ramon					15	St. Augustine			old resident	no	1/2	By order Post Commander
201	33	Rogero, Roake					13	St. Augustine			old resident	no	1/2	By order Post Commander
201	34	Rogero, Manuella					9	St. Augustine			old resident	no	1/2	By order Post Commander
201	35	Rogero, Anna					7	St. Augustine			old resident	no	1/2	By order Post Commander
201	36	Rogero, John					5	St. Augustine			old resident	no	1/2	By order Post Commander
201	37	Rogero, Vincent					3	St. Augustine			old resident	no	1/2	By order Post Commander
201	38	Rogero, James					1 8/12	St. Augustine			old resident	no	1/2	By order Post Commander
201	39	Stewart, Ulin	5	5 1/2	blue	light	60	Wayne Co. GA	Putnam Co., Fla		Nov. 7/1864	yes	1	By order Post Commander
201	40	Stewart, Franklin					20	Wayne Co. GA	Putnam Co., Fla			yes		Lives At Jacksonville, Fla
201	41	Stewart, Catherine	5	3	grey	light	18	Wayne Co. GA	Putnam Co., Fla		Nov. 7/1864	yes	1	Lives At Jacksonville, Fla
201	42	Stewart, James	5	4 1/2	grey	light	17	Wayne Co. GA	Putnam Co., Fla		Nov. 17/1864	yes	1/2	Lives At Jacksonville, Fla
201	43	Stewart, Mary E.					13	Pierce Co., GA	Putnam Co., Fla		Nov. 7/1864	no	1/2	Lives At Jacksonville, Fla
201	44	Stewart, Elias					8	Pierce Co., GA	Putnam Co., Fla		Nov. 7/1864	no	1/2	Lives At Jacksonville, Fla
201	45	Stewart, Newton					7	Pierce Co., GA	Putnam Co., Fla		Nov.7/1864	no	1/2	Lives At Jacksonville, Fla
201	46	Stewart, Issac					5	Pierce Co., GA	Putnam Co., Fla		Nov. 7/1864	no	1/2	Lives At Jacksonville, Fla
201	47	Simmons, Moses	6		blue	light	37	Scriven Co, GA	Marion Co., Fla		Oct. 10/1864	yes	1	By order Post Commander
201	48	Simmons, Sarah					24	Georgia	Marion Co., Fla		Sept. 1864	yes		

Pg	No	Name	Height Ft	Height In	Eyes	Complexion	Age	Where born or contraband	Last residence	Where registered for draft or former owner	Date into Department	Oath of Allgn	No of Ration	Remarks
202	1	Simmons, Enoch					3	Marion Co., Fla	Marion Co., FL		Sept. 1864	no	1/2	By order post Commander
202	2	Simmons, Sarah A.					2	Marion Co., Fla	Marion Co., FL		Sept. 1864	no	1/2	By order post Commander
202	3	Simes, Jane	5	3 3/4	grey	dark	23	St. Augustine			old resident	yes		
202	4	Simes, Henry	5	2 3/4	blue	light	23	St. Johns Co., Fla			April 1863	yes		
202	5	Simes, Genova					1	St. Augustine			old resident	no		
202	6	Strickland, Aaron	5	9	blue	light	33	Wane Co., Geo			Sept.25,1863	yes		Deserter from rebel service
202	7	Strickland, Mary	5	11	black	dark	17	Louns?Co. Geo			Jan. 26/1864	yes		
202	8	Strickland, Laura L.					13	Waine?Co, Geo			June 1869	no		
202	9	Strickland, Lewis N.					11	Waine?Co, Geo			June 1869	no		
202	10	Strickland, Mary J.					5	Waine?Co, Geo			June 1869	no		
202	12	Segue, Bartola	5	3 1/4	hazel	light	46	St. Augustine			St. Augustine	yes		
202	13	Segue, Margrett	5	1 3/4	hazel	light	33	St. Augustine			St. Augustine	yes		
202	14	Segue, Mary	4	11	hazel	light	16	St. Augustine			St. Augustine	yes		
202	15	Segue, Eveline					13	St. Augustine			St. Augustine	no		
202	16	Segue, Lorenzo					10	St. Augustine			St. Augustine	no		
202	17	Segue, Charles					9	St. Augustine			St. Augustine	no		
202	18	Segue, Eugene					4	St. Augustine			St. Augustine	no		
202	19	Segue, Rose					1	St. Augustine			St. Augustine	no		
202	20	Segue, John 2nd	5	5 3/4	hazel	dark	45	St. Augustine			St. Augustine	yes	1	Sick: By order Post Commander
202	21	Segue, Victoria	5	2	hazel	dark	38	St. Augustine			St. Augustine	yes		
202	22	Segue, Peter	4	10	hazel	dark	19	St. Augustine			St. Augustine	yes		
202	23	Segue, Agatha	4	11	hazel	dark	16	St. Augustine			St. Augustine	yes		
202	24	Segue, Jane					14	St. Augustine			St. Augustine	no		
202	25	Segue, Julia					12	St. Augustine			St. Augustine	no	1/2	By order Post Commander
202	26	Segue, Lewis					9	St. Augustine			St. Augustine	no	1/2	By order Post Commander

Pg	No	Name	Height		Eyes	Com-plexion	Age	Where born or contraband	Last residence	Where registered for draft or former owner	Date into Department	Oath of Allgn	No of Ration	Remarks
			Ft	In										
203	27	Segue, John	5	8	black	dark	50	St. Augustine			old resident	yes	2	Self and child: by order Post Commander
203	28	Segue, Jane	5	4	black	dark	43	St. Augustine			old resident	yes		
203	29	Segue, Celia					15	St. Augustine			old resident	yes		
203	30	Silus, Gomas	5	7	blue	dark	24	St. Augustine			old resident	yes		
203	31	Silus, Julia	5		dark	light	21	St. Augustine			old resident	yes	1	By order Post Commander
203	32	Silus, Matilda					2	St. Augustine			old resident	no		
203	33	Silus, George					7m	St. Augustine			old resident	no		
203	34	Sykes, James F.					33	North Carolina	Ochaway Co., Fla		May 1863	yes		
203	35	Sykes, Mary J.					31	St. Augustine	Ochaway Co., Fla		May 1863	yes		
203	36	Sykes, Mary A.					6	Ochaway Co.	Ochaway Co., Fla		May 1863	no		
203	37	Sykes, James W.					3	Achaway Co	Ochaway Co., Fla		May 1863	no		
203	38	Storm, William					13	Bronswick Co., Geo	Stonwich Co		April 1852	no		
203	39	Surtland, Mary A.					29	Saratoga Co., NY	Saratoga Co NY		Feb. 1863	no		
203	40	Surtland, Naomi					10	Saratoga Co., NY	Saratoga Co NY		Feb. 1863	no		
203	41	Surtland, Jennie					5	Saratoga Co., NY	Saratoga Co NY		Feb. 1863	no		
203	42	Surtland, Daniel B.					2	Saratoga Co., NY	Saratoga Co NY		Feb. 1863	no		
203	43	Sparkman, Mary					26	St. Augustine			old resident	yes	1	Husband in US Service: by order of Post Comdr
203	44	Sparkman, Charles					8	St. Augustine			old resident	no	1/2	By order post Commander
203	45	Sparkman, Julia					3	Jacksonville			old resident	no	1/2	By order post Commander
203	46	Silus, Dematrus	5	7 3/4	hazel	dark	60	Fernandina			old resident	yes		
203	47	Silus, Francis	5	1 1/4	hazel	dark	30	St. Augustine			old resident	yes		
203	48	Silus, Tatralena					12	St. Augustine			old resident	no	1/2	By order post Commander

Pg	No	Name	Height Ft	Height In	Eyes	Complexion	Age	Where born or contraband	Last residence	Where registered for draft or former owner	Date into Department	Oath of Allgn	No of Ration	Remarks
204	1	Silus, John					5	Mayport, Fla			old resident	no	1/2	By order post Commander
204	2	Silus, Glendora					4	St. Augustine			old resident	no	1/2	By order post Commander
204	3	Silus, Francis					2	St. Augustine			old resident	no	1/2	By order post Commander
204	4	Silus, Mary					13	St. Augustine			old resident	no	1/2	By order post Commander
204	5	Smith, Cornelia					38	North Pitcher, NY	North Pitcher NY		Nov. 1862	no		
204	6	Smith, Eliza J.					30	North Pitcher, NY	North Pitcher NY		Apr 1863	no		
204	7	Sancher, Antonia	5	4 1/4	hazel	light	37	St. Augustine			old resident	yes	1	By order Post Commander
204	8	Sancher, Christina	5	1 1/4	hazel	light	20	St. Augustine			old resident	yes	1	By order Post Commander
204	9	Sancher, Frances	5	10	hazel	dark	43	St. Augustine			old resident	yes		
204	10	Sancher, Julia	4	11 3/4	hazel	fair	48	St. Augustine			old resident	yes		
204	11	Sancher, Mary	5	3 3/4	hazel	light	22	St. Augustine			old resident	yes		
204	12	Sancher, Cathrine					15	St. Augustine			old resident	no		
204	13	Sancher, Emanuel					12	St. Augustine			old resident	no		
204	14	Sancher, John					8	St. Augustine			old resident	no		
204	15	Strickland, Elisa					14	Duval Co., Fla	Duval Co., Fla		old resident	no		
204	16	Sureny, Anna	5	2 3/4	hazel	light	62	Charleston			old resident	yes		
204	17	Strickland, Maria					11	Duval Co., Fla	Duval Co., Fla		old resident	no		
204	18	Strickland, Mary					8	Duval Co., Fla	Duval Co., Fla		old resident	no	1/2	By order Post Commander
204	19	Simmons, Philip	5	9 1/2	blue	light	25	Duval Co., Fla	Orange Co., Fla		May19,1864	yes		
204	20	Simmons, Mary J.					30	Georgia	Orange Co., Fla		June 30,1864	no		
204	21	Simmons, Mecuyata					6	Orange Co., Fla	Orange Co., Fla		June 30,1864	no		
204	22	Simmons, John H.					3	Orange Co., Fla	Orange Co., Fla		June 30,1864	no		
204	23	Sancher, Florentina	5	3 3/4	hazel	light	39	St. Augustine			old resident	yes		
204	24	Striscka, Mary S.	5	3 1/2	blue	light	50	Baltimore			old resident	yes		
204	25	Striscka, Josephine	5	3 3/4	hazel	light	36	Baltimore			old resident	yes		

Pg	No	Name	Height		Eyes	Com-plexion	Age	Where born or contraband	Last residence	Where registered for draft or former owner	Date into Department	Oath of Allgn	No of Ration	Remarks
			Ft	In										
205	26	Smith, Christine	5	3/4	blue	light	46	Baltimore			old resident	yes		
205	27	Smith Lissie					22	Baltimore, MD			old resident	no		
205	28	Segue, Peter	5	6	hazel	light	36	St. Augustine			old resident	yes		
205	29	Segue, Mary	4	10 1/4	hazel	light	34	Duval Co., Fla			old resident	yes		
205	30	Segue, Joseph					14	St. Augustine			old resident	no		
205	31	Segue, Alexander					12	St. Augustine			old resident	no		
205	32	Segue, Peter					10	St. Augustine			old resident	no		
205	33	Segue, Lewis					7	St. Augustine			old resident	no		
205	34	Segue, Thomas					4	St. Augustine			old resident	no		
205	35	Segue, Mary F.					1	St. Augustine			old resident	no		
205	36	Segue, Jane Ann					10	St. Augustine			old resident	no		
205	37	Segue, Joseph					6	St. Augustine			old resident	no		
205	38	Sabaty, Antonia	5	1 1/2			70	St. Augustine			old resident	yes		
205	39	Triay, Cathrine					70	St. Augustine			old resident	no		
205	40	Triay, Peter	5	4 1/2	hazel	dark	63	St. Augustine			old resident	yes	1	By order post Commander
205	41	Triay, Jane	5	1 1/2	grey	light	57	St. Augustine			old resident	yes	1	By order post Commander
205	42	Triay, Cathrine	4	11 3/4	grey	light	23	St. Augustine			old resident	yes	1	By order post Commander
205	43	Triay, Phillip					12	St. Augustine			old resident	no	1/2	By order post Commander
205	44	Triay, Peter					1 1/2	St. Augustine			old resident	no	1/2	By order post Commander
205	45	Thynne, Isabella	5	2 3/4			36	St. Augustine			old resident	yes		
205	46	Thynne, Mary					12	St. Augustine			old resident	no		
205	47	Triay, Victorini	5	5 1/4	hazel	dark	51	St. Augustine			old resident	yes		
205	48	Triay, Lucinda	5	1	hazel	dark	46	St. Augustine			old resident	yes		

Pg	No	Name	Height Ft	Height In	Eyes	Complexion	Age	Where born or contraband	Last residence	Where registered for draft or former owner	Date into Department	Oath of Allgn	No of Ration	Remarks
206	1	Triay, Cindra	4	10 3/4	hazel	medium	16	St. Augustine			old resident	yes	1/2	By order post Commander
206	2	Triay, Micalena					15	St. Augustine			old resident	no	1/2	By order post Commander
206	3	Triay, Frances					13	St. Augustine			old resident	no	1/2	By order post Commander
206	4	Triay, Louisa					8	St. Augustine			old resident	no	1/2	By order post Commander
206	5	Thigpin, Mary A.	5	4 1/2	blue	light	28	Sumpter Dist., SC	Orange Co. F		July 11,1864	yes	1	Husband in US service: by order Post C
206	6	Thigpin, Cornelius					8	Volusia Co., Fla	Volusia Co., Fla		July 11,1864		1/2	By order post Commander
206	7	Thigpin, Valero					5	Volusia Co., Fla	Volusia Co., Fla		July 11,1864		1/2	By order post Commander
206	8	Thigpin, Grabella S.					2	Volusia Co., Fla	Volusia Co., Fla		July 11,1864		1/2	By order post Commander
206	9	Turner, Cerara					24	South Carolina	Volusia Co., Fla		May 28/1864	no	1 1/2	Husband killed in US service:by order Post Comd'g
206	10	Turner, Samuel					7	Hamilton Co., Fla	Volusia Co., Fla		May 28/1864	no		
206	11	Thomas, Deonvcia	5	1 1/2	hazel	light	28	St. Augustine			old resident	yes		
206	12	Thomas, Maria	4	11 3/4	hazel	light	20	St. Augustine			old resident	yes	1	By order Post Commander
206	13	Thomas, Agatha	4	11 3/4	hazel	light	26	St. Augustine			old resident	yes		
206	14	Thomas, Jane	5	1/4	hazel	light	14	St. Augustine			old resident	yes	1	By order Post Commander
206	15	Thigpin, Ozias	5	7 1/2	grey	light	30	Black Creek Fla	Orange Co., Fla		April 16/1864	yes		
206	16	Thigpin, Vyrous C.					22	Black Creek Fla	Orange Co., Fla		1864	yes		
206	17	Tomlinson, David R.	5	8 1/2	blue	light	33	New Haven,Conr	Leon Co., Fla		1863	yes		
206	18	Tomlinson, Martha	5	3	dark	light	26	New Haven,Conr	Leon Co., Fla		July 15/1864	yes		
206	19	Thomas, Charles	5	10	blue	light	45	Germany	Jacksonville		1862	yes		
206	20	Thomas, Julia C.	5	4	hazel	light	30	St. Augustine	Jacksonville		old resident	yes		
206	21	Thomas, Irena					9	St. Augustine	Jacksonville		1862	no		
206	22	Thomas, Annie					2	Monticellia	St. Augustine		1862	no		
206	23	Thomas, Charles W.					3m	St. Augustine	St. Augustine		born in St.A	no		
206	24	Triay, -?ard					50	Cuba			old resident			Took the oath of Neutrality
206	25	Triay, -?-					50	Cuba			old resident			

Pg	No	Name	Height Ft	Height In	Eyes	Com-plexion	Age	Where born or contraband	Last residence	Where registered for draft or former owner	Date into Department	Oath of Allgn	No of Ration	Remarks
207	1	Walton, Eunice					21	St. Augustine			old resident	yes		
207	2	Walton, Mary A.					16	St. Augustine			old resident	yes		
207	3	Walton, Eliza J.					13	St. Augustine			old resident	no		
207	4	Walton, Louisa M.					10	St. Augustine			old resident	no		
207	5	Walton Helen					7	St. Augustine			old resident	no		
207	6	Walton, William D.					5	St. Augustine			old resident	no		
207	7	Young, William					22	Germany	New Jersey		Dec. 1863	no		Clerk for Sutler 17th Conn. Vols.
207	8	Regnord, Victor C.					26							Catholic Priest
207	9	Strasbourgh, Magdaline					68	France						In convent
207	10	Groceski, Lawrence	5	8 1/2	hazel	dark	78	St. Augustine			old resident	yes		
207	11	Myers, Jerimiah					68	St. Augustine			old resident	no		
207	12	Anderson, Alexander					5	Contraband		Sanchez, Mrs	old resident		1/2	On recommendation Supt. Of Contrabands
207	13	Adams?, Venus					70	Contraband		Fairbanks, George	old resident			
207	14	Alonzo, Sarah					60	Contraband		Baya, William	old resident		1	On recommendation Supt. Of Contrabands
207	15	Allen, Nancy					50	Contraband	Volusia County	Baker, Jack	May 1864			
207	16	Allen, Clarissa					16?	Contraband	Volusia County	Baker, Jack	May 1864			
207	17	Allen, Annie					16?	Contraband	Volusia County	Baker, Jack	May 1864		1/2	On recommecdation Supt. Of Contrabands
207	18	Allen, Rose					29	Contraband	Volusia County	Baker, Jack	May 1864			
207	19	Allen, Amos					7	Contraband	Volusia County	Baker, Jack	May 1864		1/2	On recommendation Supt. Of Contrabands
207	20	Allen, Stephen					5	Contraband	Volusia County	Baker, Jack	May 1864		1/2	On recommendation Supt. Of Contrabands
207	21	Allen, Abram					6m	Contraband	Volusia County	Baker, Jack	May 1864			
207	22	Anderson, Mary					60	Contraband		Anderson, George	old resident			
207	23	Anderson, Elisabeth					50	Contraband		Andrew, John	old resident			
207	24	Anderson, Emanuel					7	Contraband		Andrew, John	old resident		1/2	On recommendation Supt. Of Contrabands
207	25	Anderson, Dora					16?	Contraband		Andrew, John	old resident		1/2	On recommendation Supt. Of Contrabands

Pg	No	Name	Height Ft	Height In	Eyes	Complexion	Age	Where born or contraband	Last residence	Where registered for draft or former owner	Date into Department	Oath of Allgn	No of Ration	Remarks
208	26	Triay, GAbriel					14	Cuba			old resident	no		
208	27	Triay, Edward					12	Cuba			old resident	no		
208	28	Triay, Josephine					9	St. Augustine			old resident	no		
208	29	Triay, Alfred					7	St. Augustine			old resident	no		
208	30	Usenia, Michael	5	6 1/2	hazel	dark	58	St. Augustine			old resident	yes		
208	31	Usenia, Jenovavar	5	3	hazel	dark	53	St. Augustine			old resident	yes		
208	32	Usenia, Mary	5	4 1/2	blue	light	26	St. Augustine			old resident	yes		
208	33	Usenia, Phillip	4	10	hazel	dark	17	St. Augustine			old resident	yes		
208	34	Usenia, Albert					13	St. Augustine			old resident	no		
208	35	Usenia, Joseph					9	St. Augustine			old resident	no		
208	36	Usenia, John	5	6 1/2	black	dark	49	Fernandina	St.Johns Co., Fla		Sept. 1864	yes		
208	37	Usenia, Elisabeth					12	St. Augustine	St.Johns Co., Fla		Sept. 1864	no		
208	38	Usenia, Agness	4	11	grey	light	22	St. Augustine	St. Augustine		old resident	yes		
208	39	Ugean, Lissie					22	St. Augustine						
208	40	Vileronga, Catherine	4	6	blue	dark	75	St. Augustine			old resident	yes	1	By order Post Commander
208	41	Weedman, Mary A.	5	5 1/2	grey	fair	59	St. Augustine			old resident	yes		
208	42	Weedman, Ellen	5	5	hazel	fair	54	St. Augustine			old resident	yes		
208	43	Weedman, Margrett	5	4	hazel	fair	49	St. Augustine			old resident	yes		
208	44	Verina, Julia					40	St. Augustine						
208	45	WhitBy, William					6	St. Augustine					1/2	By order Post Commander
208	46	Whitby, Joseph					4	St. Augustine					1/2	By order Post Commander
208	47	Walton, George W.	5	10	brwn	light	60	Onslow Co NC	Volusia Co., Fla		May 7/1863			
208	48	Walton, Mary A.					44	St. Augustine			old resident	no		

Pg	No	Name	Height Ft	Height In	Eyes	Com-plexion	Age	Where born or contraband	Last residence	Where registered for draft or former owner	Date into Department	Oath of Allgn	No of Ration	Remarks
209	26	Adams, Rose					45	Contraband		Bravo, Christol	old residence		1	On recommendation Supt. of Contrabands
209	27	Adams, Florida					7	Contraband		Bravo, Christol	old residence		1/2	On recommendation Supt. of Contrabands
209	28	Adams, Edward					8	Contraband		Bravo, Christol	old residence		1/2	On recommendation Supt. of Contrabands
209	29	Arthurton, Mary					9	Contraband		Bravo, Nativ?	old residence		1/2	On recommendation Supt. of Contrabands
209	30	Alveraz, Abby					50	Contraband		Alveraz	old residence		1/2	On recommendation Supt. of Contrabands
209	31	Ashton, Kate					22	Contraband		Triay, Peter	old residence			
209	32	Ashton, James					7	Contraband		Triay, Peter	old residence			
209	33	Anderson, Lena					6	Contraband		Anderson, Mrs.	old residence			
209	34	Baya, Emma					11	Contraband		Baya, Joseph	old residence		1/2	On recommendation Supt. of Contrabands
209	35	Bram, Hester					20	Contraband	Lanche County	Brown, Washington	Sept. 1864		1	On recommendation Supt. of Contrabands
209	36	Bram, Cilla					2	Contraband	Lanche County	Brown, Washington	Sept. 1864		1/2	On recommendation Supt. of Contrabands
209	37	Babb, Antonia					40	Contraband		Tacetty, Bartola	old residence			
209	38	Bronson, Mary A.					18?	Contraband	Talatha?	Bronson, Judge	Sept. 1864			
209	39	Bume?, Charles					90	Contraband		Camova, Antonio	old residence		1	On recommendation Supt. of Contrabands
209	40	Barbar, Mary J.					22	Contraband	Orange County	Barbar, Moses	June 1864		1	On recommendation Supt. of Contrabands
209	41	Barbar, Joseph					12	Contraband	Orange County	Barbar, Moses	June 1864		1	Employed by Quarter Master
209	42	Barbar, Mary					70	Contraband	Orange County	Barbar, Moses	June 1864		1	On recommendation Supt. of Contrabands
209	43	Burner, Louisa					21	Contraband		Philips, Capt.	old residence			
209	44	Bernardy, Rebecca					7	Contraband		Putnam, Major	old residence			
209	45	Bernardy, Samuel					12	Contraband		Putnam, Major	old residence			
209	46	Baya, Edward					13	Contraband		Baya, Joseph	old residence		1/2	On recommendation Supt. Of Contrabands
200	47	Baya, Lizzie					2	Contraband		Baya, Joseph	old residence			
209	48	Brown, Daniel					52	Contraband	Lochiway Co.	Brown, Washington	July 1864			

Pg	No	Name	Height Ft	Height In	Eyes	Com-plexion	Age	Where born or contraband	Last residence	Where registered for draft or former owner	Date into Department	Oath of Allgn	No of Ration	Remarks
210	1	Barbar, Ned					30	Contraband	Volusia County	Barbar, James	May 1864			
210	2	Baya, Mary					30	Contraband		Baya, Joseph	old residence			
210	3	Buffington, George					90	Contraband		Buffington, Samuel	old residence			
210	4	Buffington, Frank					45	Contraband		Buffington, Samuel	old residence			
210	5	Billy, Daddy					80	Contraband		Carr, John	old residence		1	On recommendation of Supt. of Contrabands
210	6	Bryant, Gena					29	Contraband		Smith, Buck	old residence		1	On recommendation of Supt. of Contrabands
210	7	Bryant, Liverna					3	Contraband		Smith, Buck	old residence			
210	8	Banks, Fanny					34	Contraband	Brevard County	Barbar, Moses	June 1864			
210	9	Banks, Alice					7	Contraband	Brevard County	Barbar, Moses	June 1864		1/2	On recommendation of Supt. of Contrabands
210	10	Banks, George					5	Contraband	Brevard County	Barbar, Moses	June 1864		1/2	On recommendation of Supt. of Contrabands
210	11	Banks, Cathrine					2	Contraband	Brevard County	Barbar, Moses	June 1864		1/2	On recommendation of Supt. of Contrabands
210	12	Cryer, Nancy					19	Contraband		Mickler, Daniel	old residence			
210	13	Caryall, Rosalea					4	Contraband		Mickler, Jacob	old residence			
210	14	Clark, Martha					25	Contraband		Mickler, Robert	old residence		1	On recommendation of Supt. of Contrabands
210	15	Clark, John					4	Contraband		Mickler, Robert	old residence		1/2	On recommendation of Supt. of Contrabands
210	16	Clark, Thomas					6	Contraband		Mickler, Robert	old residence		1/2	On recommendation of Supt. of Contrabands
210	17	Centre, Florida					20	Contraband		Always Free	old residence			
210	18	Centre, Annie					18	Contraband		Always Free	old residence			
210	19	Carr, Hager					30	Contraband		Carr, James	old residence			
210	20	Cook, Millia					50	Contraband	St. Johns County	Hamon, Charles	Nov. 1862			
210	21	Crocket, Wipey?					25	Contraband	Volusia County	Hamon, Charles	June 1864			
210	22	Crocket, Louisa					6m	Contraband	Volusia County	Hamon, Charles	June 1864			
210	23	Clark, Mary R.					70	Contraband			old residence			Freeborn
210	24	Cryer, Harriet					20	Contraband		Mickler, Daniel	old residence			
210	25	Cryer?, Joseph A.					1	Contraband		Mickler, Daniel	old residence			

Pg	No	Name	Height Ft	Height In	Eyes	Com-plexion	Age	Where born or contraband	Last residence	Where registered for draft or former owner	Date into Department	Oath of Allgn	No of Ration	Remarks
211	26	Clark, Millia					40	Contraband			old residence			Bought Free by her husband George D. Clark
211	27	Clark, Mary R.					60	Contraband		Mickler, Jacob	old residence			
211	28	Cryer, Joseph					55	Contraband		Mickler, Jacob	old residence			
211	29	Cryer, Charlotte					50	Contraband		Mickler, Jacob	old residence			
211	30	Cryer, Eve					14	Contraband		Mickler, Jacob	old residence			
211	31	Cryer, Rose					12	Contraband		Mickler, Jacob	old residence			
211	32	Cryer, Charles H.					4m	Contraband		Mickler, Jacob	old residence			
211	33	Doise, Jane					50	Contraband		Doise, Mrs.	old residence			
211	34	Delk, James					14	Contraband	Orange County	Delk, William S.	June 1864		1	On recommendation of Supt. of Contrabands
211	35	Dean, Maria					27	Contraband		Pappy, Joseph	old residence			
211	36	Dean, Elma					7	Contraband		Pappy, Joseph	old residence		1/2	On recommendation of Supt. of Contrabands
211	37	Dean, Fanny					3	Contraband		Pappy, Joseph	old residence		1/2	On recommendation of Supt. of Contrabands
211	38	Deias, Philip					80	Contraband		Deias, Antonio	old residence			
211	39	Delk, Judy					64	Contraband	Orange County	Delks, William S.	June 1864		1	On recommendation of Supt. of Contrabands
211	40	Delk, Abram					21	Contraband	Orange County	Delks, William S.	June 1864			
211	41	Delk, Hettie					28	Contraband	Orange County	Delks, William S.	June 1864		1	On recommendation of Supt. of Contrabands
211	42	Delk, Sarah					25	Contraband	Orange County	Delks, William S.	June 1864		1	On recommendation of Supt. of Contrabands
211	43	Delk, Harriet					24	Contraband	Orange County	Delks, William S.	June 1864		1	On recommendation of Supt. of Contrabands
211	44	Delk, Lucinda					16	Contraband	Orange County	Delks, William S.	June 1864		1	On recommendation of Supt. of Contrabands
211	45	Delk, Daniel					13	Contraband	Orange County	Delks, William S.	June 1864		1	On recommendation of Supt. of Contrabands
211	46	Delk, Millie					12	Contraband	Orange County	Delks, William S.	June 1864		1/2	On recommendation of Supt. of Contrabands
211	47	Delk, Nancy					12	Contraband	Orange County	Delks, William S.	June 1864		1/2	On recommendation of Supt. of Contrabands
211	48	Delk, Stepny?					9	Contraband	Orange County	Delks, William S.	June 1864		1/2	On recommendation of Supt. of Contrabands

Pg	No	Name	Height Ft	Height In	Eyes	Com-plexion	Age	Where born or contraband	Last residence	Where registered for draft or former owner	Date into Department	Oath of Allgn	No of Ration	Remarks
212	1	Delk, Samuel					6	Contraband	Orange County	Delk, William S.	June 1864		1/2	On recommendation of Supt. of Contrabands
212	2	Delk, Fredrick					4	Contraband	Orange County	Delk, William S.	June 1864		1/2	On recommendation of Supt. of Contrabands
212	3	Delk, Toby					5	Contraband	Orange County	Delk, William S.	June 1864		1/2	On recommendation of Supt. of Contrabands
212	4	Delk, Morgan					2	Contraband	Orange County	Delk, William S.	June 1864		1/2	On recommendation of Supt. of Contrabands
212	5	Delk, John					2 1/2	Contraband	Orange County	Delk, William S.	June 1864		1/2	On recommendation of Supt. of Contrabands
212	6	Dummitt, Mary					50	Contraband		Dummitt, Sarah	old resident		1	On recommendation of Supt. of Contrabands
212	7	Dummitt, Kate					40	Contraband		Dummitt, Sarah	old resident		1	On recommendation of Supt. of Contrabands
212	8	Dummitt, Sarah					8	Contraband		Dummitt, Sarah	old resident		1/2	On recommendation of Supt. of Contrabands
212	9	Dummitt, Margrett					8	Contraband		Dummitt, Sarah	old resident		1/2	On recommendation of Supt. of Contrabands
212	10	Dummitt, Frances					6	Contraband		Dummitt, Sarah	old resident		1/2	On recommendation of Supt. of Contrabands
212	11	Dummitt, Harry					4	Contraband		Dummitt, Sarah	old resident			
212	12	Delaney, Barrell					60	Contraband		Williams, William	old resident			
212	13	Delaney, Gena					50	Contraband		Pacetty, G.	old resident			
212	14	Delaney, Susan					13	Contraband		Pacetty, G.	old resident			
212	15	Delaney, Hannah					11	Contraband		Pacetty, G.	old resident			
212	16	Daniels, Catherine					30	Contraband	Lanche County	Brown, Washington	Sept. 1864			
212	17	Daniels, Daniel					40	Contraband	Lanche County	Brown, Washington	Sept. 1864			
212	18	Daniels, Henry					8	Contraband	Lanche County	Brown, Washington	Sept. 1864			
212	19	Daniels, Jock?					6	Contraband	Lanche County	Brown, Washington	Sept. 1864			
212	20	Daniels, Elizabeth					3	Contraband	Lanche County	Brown, Washington	Sept. 1864			
212	21	Dismake, Elethia					44	Contraband		Dismake, William	old resident			
212	22	Davenport, Peter					7	Contraband		Weedman, Mifer	old resident			
212	23	Erin, Laura					12	Contraband		Sanchy, James	old resident			
212	24	Ellis, Grace					21	Contraband		Sanchy, James	old resident		1	On recommendation of Supt. of Contrabands
212	25	Ellis, Nelson					40	Contraband		Sanchy, James	old resident			

Pg	No	Name	Height Ft	Height In	Eyes	Com-plexion	Age	Where born or contraband	Last residence	Where registered for draft or former owner	Date into Department	Oath of Allgn	No of Ration	Remarks
213	26	Eugene, Fortune					28	Contraband	St. Johns County	Dupont, Cornelius	July 1862			
213	27	Eugene, Edward					3/4	Contraband	St. Johns County	Dupont, Cornelius	old residence			
213	28	Erwin, Evelina					7	Contraband		Erwin, John	old residence			
213	29	Ellis, Grace					20	Contraband	GAinesville	Perry, Gov.	January 1864			
213	30	Floyd, Flora					70	Contraband		Michler, Antonio	old residence		1	On recommendation of Supt. of Contrabands
213	31	Fairbanks, Celia					60	Contraband		Fairbanks,George R.	old residence		1	On recommendation of Supt. of Contrabands
213	32	Furguson, Julia					45	Contraband	Lake Monroe	Watson, Eligah	May 1864			
213	33	Furguson, Laura					17	Contraband	Lake Monroe	Watson, Eligah	May 1864			
213	34	Furguson, Pompy					8	Contraband	Lake Monroe	Watson, Eligah	May 1864		1/2	On recommendation of Supt. of Contrabands
213	35	Furguson, Philip					5	Contraband	Lake Monroe	Watson, Eligah	May 1864		1/2	On recommendation of Supt. of Contrabands
213	36	Furguson, Anthony					5	Contraband	Lake Monroe	Watson, Eligah	May 1864		1/2	On recommendation of Supt. of Contrabands
213	37	Furguson, Adam					50	Contraband	BrevardCounty	Branning, George	July 1864			
213	38	Feelings, Aaron					40	Contraband		Dupont	old residence		1	On recommendation of Supt. of Contrabands
213	39	Feelings, Abby					40	Contraband		Albroy	old residence			
213	40	Feelings, Delphia					4	Contraband		Albroy	old residence			
213	41	Feelings, Mary					56	Contraband		Dupont	old residence			
213	42	Feelings, Andrew					56	Contraband		Dupont	old residence			
213	43	Feelings, Charlotte					30	Contraband		Dupont	old residence			
213	44	Fernandez, Ramona					44	Contraband		Dupont	old residence			Always Free
213	45	Floyd, Rena					45	Contraband	Mantanzas Bae	Dupont, Virgil	August 1862			
213	46	Floyd, Adams					13	Contraband	Mantanzas Bae	Dupont, Virgil	August 1862			
213	47	Graham, Emeline					10	Contraband		Triay, Mrs.	old residence			
213	48	Granger, Rebecca					14	Contraband		Triay, Mrs.	old residence			

Pg	No	Name	Height Ft	Height In	Eyes	Com-plexion	Age	Where born or contraband	Last residence	Where registered for draft or former owner	Date into Department	Oath of Allgn	No of Ration	Remarks
214	1	Green, Rose					36	Contraband	St. Johns County	Dupont, Cornelius	April 1864			
214	2	Green, Philip					4	Contraband	St. Johns County	Dupont, Cornelius	April 1862		1/2	On recommendation Supt. Of Contrabands
214	3	Green, Richard					9	Contraband	St. Johns County	Dupont, Cornelius	April 1862		1/2	On recommendation Supt. Of Contrabands
214	4	Green, Harry					1/2	Contraband			old residence			
214	5	Green, Phebe					70	Contraband	St. Johns County	Dupont, Cornelius	April 1862		1	On recommendation Supt. Of Contrabands
214	6	Glover, Hannah					45	Contraband	Palatka	Bronson, Grace	Aug. 1864			
214	7	Grover, Henry					50	Contraband	St. Marys	Creaton, Mrs.	Aug. 1864			
214	8	Gerry, Benajo					14	Contraband		Gerry, Elizabeth	old residence			
214	9	Goward, Sally					30	Contraband		Canovia, R. B.	old residence			
214	10	Groward, Michael					16	Contraband		Salany, Cate	old residence			
214	11	Groward, James					14	Contraband		Salany, Cate	old residence			
214	12	Groward, Handy					45	Contraband		Canovia, R. B.	old residence			
214	13	Granger, Frank					45	Contraband		Salany, Philip	old residence			
214	14	Granger, Maria					36	Contraband		Pacetty, Joseph	old residence			
214	15	Granger, Laura					15	Contraband		Pacetty, Joseph	old residence			
214	16	Granger, Heneretta					11	Contraband		Pacetty, Joseph	old residence			
214	17	Granger, John					8	Contraband		Pacetty, Joseph	old residence			
214	18	Granger, Mary L.					2	Contraband		Pacetty, Joseph	old residence			
214	19	Glover, Catherine					20	Contraband			old residence			Free born
214	20	Gibbs, George					80	Contraband		Gibbs, King	old residence		1	On recommendation Supt. Of Contrabands
214	21	Griffin, Rebecca					75	Contraband		Smith, Buck.	old residence			
214	22	Getters, Hyatt					40	Contraband		Riaire, Augustus	old residence			
214	23	Getters, Harriet					35	Contraband		Riaire, Augustus	old residence			
214	24	Getters, William					1/4	Contraband		Riaire, Augustus	old residence			
214	25	Grangers, Nicholas					28?	Contraband		Salany, Philip	old residence			
214	26	Grangers, Mary					27	Contraband		Triay, Philip	old residence			

Pg	No	Name	Height Ft	Height In	Eyes	Com-plexion	Age	Where born or contraband	Last residence	Where registered for draft or former owner	Date into Department	Oath of Allgn	No of Ration	Remarks
215	27	Granger, William					11	Contraband		Triay, Philip	old residence			
215	28	Granger, Rebecca					10	Contraband		Triay, Philip	old residence			
215	29	Granger, Julia					8	Contraband		Triay, Philip	old residence			
215	30	Granger, Jane					6	Contraband		Triay, Philip	old residence			
215	31	Hearns, Susan					60	Contraband	Enterprise	Hearn, Benj.	Jan. 1862			
215	32	Hearns, Richard					17	Contraband	Enterprise	Hearn, Benj.	Jan. 1862			
215	33	Hearns, Robert					12	Contraband	Enterprise	Hearn, Benj.	Jan. 1862			
215	34	Hearns, Catherine					9	Contraband	Enterprise	Hearn, Benj.	Jan. 1862			
215	35	Hearns, Ann					7	Contraband	Enterprise	Hearn, Benj.	Jan. 1862			
215	36	Huling, Victoria					28	Contraband		Canviro, Antonio	old residence			
215	37	Huling, William					43	Contraband		Carr	old residence			Priv. 33rd U. S. C. T.
215	38	Huling, Louisa					11	Contraband		Canviro, Antonio	old residence		1/2	On recommendation of Supt. of Contrabands
215	39	Huling, William					4	Contraband		Canviro, Antonio	old residence			
215	40	Henderson,Josephine					25	Contraband		Pacetty, Barbara	old residence			
215	41	Henderson, Alexander					5	Contraband		Pacetty, Barbara	old residence		1/2	On recommendation of Supt. of Contrabands
215	42	Henderson, Antonia					12	Contraband		Pacetty, Barbara	old residence			
215	43	Hayward, Amanda					60	Contraband	South Carolina	Bolden, James	Feb. 1864			
215	44	Hill, Leandra					40	Contraband		Alevaris, Patolo	old residence		1	On recommendation of Supt. of Contrabands
215	45	Hurlbutt, Maria					80	Contraband		Hurbrett, Daniel	old residence		1	On recommendation of Supt. of Contrabands
215	46	Hurlbutt, Samuel					90	Contraband		Hurbrett, Daniel	old residence		1	On recommendation of Supt. of Contrabands
215	47	Hull, Eletha					30	Contraband		Buffington,Samuel	old residence			
215	48	Hull, Clara					4	Contraband		Buffington,Samuel	old residence			

Pg	No	Name	Height Ft	Height In	Eyes	Com-plexion	Age	Where born or contraband	Last residence	Where registered for draft or former owner	Date into Department	Oath of Allgn	No of Ration	Remarks
216	1	Hills, Sarah					90	Contraband			old residence		1	Bought free by her husband,Charles Hills in 1852
216	2	Johnson, Maria					58	Contraband		Hanour?, Capt.	old residence		1	On recommendation Supt. Of Contrabands
216	3	Jenkins, Wiley					13	Contraband		Duil, Harriet	old residence			
216	4	Joseph, Philes					25	Contraband		Putnam, Judge	old residence			
216	5	Joseph, Frank					7	Contraband		Putnam, Judge	old residence			
216	6	Joseph, Elizabeth					3	Contraband		Putnam, Judge	old residence			
216	7	Jenkins, Matilda					15	Contraband	Jacksonville		Dec. 1862			Owner not known
216	8	Johnson, Harriet					28	Contraband		Michler, Jacob	old residence			
216	9	Johnson, Clara					11	Contraband		Michler, Jacob	old residence			
216	10	Johnson, Albert					8	Contraband		Michler, Jacob	old residence			
216	11	Johnson, Jerome					4	Contraband		Michler, Jacob	old residence			
216	12	Johnson, Mary E.					1	Contraband		Michler, Jacob	old residence			
216	13	Jackson, Medrith					85	Contraband	Milledgeville GA	Buffington, Samuel	Jan. 1862			
216	14	Jackson, Matilda					65	Contraband	Milledgeville GA	Buffington, Samuel	Jan. 1862			
216	15	Jenks, Willey					36	Contraband		Jenks, Edwin T.	old residence			
216	16	Jenks, Hattie					16	Contraband		Jenks, Edwin T.	old residence			
216	17	Jenks, Agnes					14	Contraband		Jenks, Edwin T.	old residence			
216	18	Jenks, Lewis					12	Contraband		Jenks, Edwin T.	old residence			
216	19	Jenks, Diannia					10	Contraband		Jenks, Edwin T.	old residence			
216	20	Jenks, John					6	Contraband		Jenks, Edwin T.	old residence			
216	21	Jober, George					47	Contraband	St. Johns County	Watson, Alexander	Dec. 24,1862			
216	22	Jober, Chloe					40	Contraband	St. Johns County	Dupont, Cornelius	April 1862			
216	23	Jober, Brown					7	Contraband	St. Johns County	Dupont, Cornelius	April 1862			
216	24	Jober, Washington					9	Contraband	St. Johns County	Dupont, Cornelius	April 1862			
216	25	Johnson, Amanda					47	Contraband	St. Johns County	Canviro, Antonio	old residence			
216	26	Jackson, Sally					?	Contraband	St. Johns County	Dupont, Cornelius	April 1862			

Pg	No	Name	Height Ft	Height In	Eyes	Com-plexion	Age	Where born or contraband	Last residence	Where registered for draft or former owner	Date into Department	Oath of Allgn	No of Ration	Remarks
217	27	Jackson, Ellen					16	Contraband	St. Johns County	Dupont, Cornelius	April 1862			
217	28	Jackson, Fanny					14	Contraband	St. Johns County	Dupont, Cornelius	April 1862		1/2	On recommendation of Supt. of Contrabands
217	29	Jackson, Abby					12	Contraband	St. Johns County	Dupont, Cornelius	April 1862		1/2	On recommendation of Supt. of Contrabands
217	30	Jackson, Jackson					8	Contraband	St. Johns County	Dupont, Cornelius	April 1862		1/2	On recommendation of Supt. of Contrabands
217	31	Jackson, Lebi					4	Contraband	St. Johns County	Dupont, Cornelius	April 1862		1/2	On recommendation of Supt. of Contrabands
217	32	Jackson, Charlotte					50	Contraband	St. Johns County	Floyd, John	Jan. 1862			
217	33	Jackson, Morris					7	Contraband	St. Johns County	Floyd, John	Jan. 1862		1/2	On recommendation of Supt. of Contrabands
217	34	Jackson, Cornelia					9	Contraband	St. Johns County	Floyd, John	Jan. 1862		1/2	On recommendation of Supt. of Contrabands
217	35	Jackson, Edward					5	Contraband	St. Johns County	Floyd, John	Jan. 1862			
217	36	Jackson, Mead					70	Contraband		Biah, Joseph	old residence		1	On recommendation of Supt. of Contrabands
217	37	Jenkins, Betsey					40	Contraband	Putnam County	Brannum, George	Aug. 1864			
217	38	Jenkins, Henry					18	Contraband	Putnam County	Brannum, George	Aug. 1864			
217	39	Jenkins, Wiley					16	Contraband	Putnam County	Brannum, George	Aug. 1864			
217	40	Jenkins, Lucy					22	Contraband	Putnam County	Brannum, George	Aug. 1864			
217	41	Jenkins, Abram					14	Contraband	Putnam County	Brannum, George	Aug. 1864			
217	42	Jenkins, Rebecca					12	Contraband	Putnam County	Brannum, George	Aug. 1864			
217	43	Jenkins, Prineas?					10	Contraband	Putnam County	Brannum, George	Aug. 1864		1/2	On recommendation of Supt. of Contrabands
217	44	Jenkins, Mack					8	Contraband	Putnam County	Brannum, George	Aug. 1864		1/2	On recommendation of Supt. of Contrabands
217	45	Jenkins, Cain					6	Contraband	Putnam County	Brannum, George	Aug. 1864		1/2	On recommendation of Supt. of Contrabands
217	46	Jenkins, Mary Ann					4	Contraband	Putnam County	Brannum, George	Aug. 1864			
217	47	Jenkins, Samuel					2	Contraband	Putnam County	Brannum, George	Aug. 1864			
217	48	Jenkins, Georgianna					1	Contraband	Putnam County	Brannum, George	Aug. 1864			

Pg	No	Name	Height Ft	Height In	Eyes	Com-plexion	Age	Where born or contraband	Last residence	Where registered for draft or former owner	Date into Department	Oath of Allgn	No of Ration	Remarks
218	1	Kelsey, Albert					14	Contraband	Beaufort	Rose, Sarah	May 1864			
218	2	King, Louisa					11	Contraband		Hanniun?, King	old residence			
218	3	King, Matilda					35	Contraband		Hanniun?, King	old residence			
218	4	King, William					5	Contraband		Hanniun?, King	old residence			
218	5	Lasine, Judy					60	Contraband		Calhoun, John C.	old residence			
218	6	Lasine, Nancy					3	Contraband		Calhoun, John C.	old residence		1/2	On recommendation of Supt. Of Contrabands
218	7	Lasine, Robert					8	Contraband		Calhoun, John C.	old residence		1/2	On recommendation of Supt. Of Contrabands
218	8	Lang, Jane					28	Contraband			old residence			Free born
218	9	Lang, Lucretia					18	Contraband			old residence			Free born
218	10	Lang, Sapha?					12	Contraband			old residence			Free born
218	11	Lang, Sophiah					7	Contraband			old residence			Free born
218	12	Lang, Mary					2	Contraband			old residence			Free born
218	13	Lang, Willie					1/2	Contraband			old residence			Free born
218	14	Lofton, Pink					70	Contraband		Lofton, William	old residence		1	On recommendation. of Supt. of Contrabands
218	15	Lopez, Ann M.					60	Contraband		Lopez, Domingo	old residence		1	On recommendation of Supt.of Contrabands
218	16	Lancaster, Tira					70	Contraband			old residence		1/2	Free born: on recommendation of Supt. of Contrabands
218	17	Lancaster, Wm					5	Contraband			old residence		1	Free born: on recommendation of Supt. of Contrabands
218	18	Lancaster, Mary					5	Contraband			old residence		1/2	Free born: on recommendation of Supt. of Contrabands
218	19	Lancaster, John					4	Contraband			old residence		1/2	Free born: on recommendation of Supt. of Contrabands
218	20	Lucas, Maria					40	Contraband		Anderson, George	old residence			
218	21	Lucas, Domingo					16	Contraband		Anderson, George	old residence			
218	22	Lucas, Mary					14	Contraband		Anderson, George	old residence			
218	23	Lucas, Levina					13	Contraband		Anderson, George	old residence			
218	24	Martin, Sarah					16	Contraband	Volusia County	Martin, James	May 1864			
218	25	Madison, ..mart?					64	Contraband		Madison, John	old residence			Set free by Master disceased ?11 years ago
218	26	Madison, Percillia					51	Contraband		Madison, John	old residence			

Pg	No	Name	Height Ft	Height In	Eyes	Complexion	Age	Where born or contraband	Last residence	Where registered for draft or former owner	Date into Department	Oath of Allgn	No of Ration	Remarks
219	27	Murry, Charlotte					40	Contraband		Gomez, Philip	old residence		1	On recommendation of Supt. Of Contrabands
219	28	Murry, Mary					18	Contraband		Gomez, Philip	old residence		1	On recommendation of Supt. Of Contrabands
219	29	Murry, Anna					2	Contraband		Gomez, Philip	old residence			
219	30	Mickler, Maria					90	Contraband		Michler, Jacob	old residence		1	On recommendation of Supt. Of Contrabands
219	31	Masters, Bartola					85	Contraband		Masters, Bartole	old residence		1	On recommendation of Supt. Of Contrabands
219	32	Mosby, John					88	Contraband			old residence		1	A long time free: recomm. of Supt.Of Contrabands
219	34	Mickler, Patty					75	Contraband		Michler, Jacob	old residence			
219	35	Martin, Lewis					30	Contraband		O'hario	old residence			
219	36	Martin, Rose					25	Contraband		Always Free	old residence			
219	37	Martin, Lewis H.					3/4	Contraband		Always Free	old residence			
219	38	Masters, Martha					22	Contraband		Fareria, Joseph	old residence			
219	39	Masters, Harriet					7	Contraband		Fareria, Joseph	old residence			
219	40	McGirt, Grace					38	Contraband		Fareria, Joseph	old residence			
219	41	McGirt, William					30	Contraband		Salany, Matea	old residence			
219	42	McGirt, Antonio					11	Contraband		Lopez, Domingo	old residence		1/2	On recommendation of Supt. Of Contrabands
219	43	McGirt, Alexander					3	Contraband		Lopez, Domingo	old residence		1/2	On recommendation of Supt. Of Contrabands
219	44	McHenny, Matilda					40	Contraband		Bennett, Peter	old residence			
219	45	McHenny, Frances					14	Contraband		Bennett, Peter	old residence			
219	46	Manuel, Jack					45	Contraband	St. Johns County	Floyd, John	Jan. 1864			
219	47	Martin, Fanny					40	Contraband	Volusia County	Martin, James	May 1864			
219	48	Martin, Sarah					15	Contraband	Volusia County	Martin, James	May 1864			

Pg	No	Name	Height Ft	Height In	Eyes	Com-plexion	Age	Where born or contraband	Last residence	Where registered for draft or former owner	Date into Department	Oath of Allgn	No of Ration	Remarks
220	1	Martin, Charles					17	Contraband	Volusia County	Martin, James	April 1864			
220	2	Martin, Eliza					20	Contraband	Volusia County	Martin, James	April 1864			
220	3	Martin, Jonas					10	Contraband	Volusia County	Martin, James	April 1864			
220	4	Maxwell, Louisa					35	Contraband	Orange County	Trowel	April 1862			
220	5	Martin, Mary					54	Contraband		Triay, Catherine	old residence			
220	6	Martin, Alex					15	Contraband		Triay, Catherine	old residence		1	On recommendation of Supt. Of Contrabands
220	7	Martin, Margrett					8	Contraband		Triay, Catherine	old residence		1/2	On recommendation of Supt. Of Contrabands
220	8	Martin, Stephen					12	Contraband		Triay, Catherine	old residence		1/2	On recommendation of Supt. Of Contrabands
220	9	Mitchell, Frances					28	Contraband	Old Residence	Sabaty, Antonio	old residence			
220	10	Mitchell, Sarah					60	Contraband		Sabaty, Antonio	old residence		1	On recommendation of Supt. Of Contrabands
220	11	Moses, Harriett					25	Contraband	Milledgeville	Buffington, Samuel	Dec. 1860			
220	12	Mickler, Patty					55	Contraband		Mickler, Robert	old residence			
220	13	McKinney, Mary					8	Contraband	Brevard County	Moses, Barbar	June 1864		1/2	On recommendation of Supt. Of Contrabands
220	14	Murry, James					14	Contraband			old residence			Free Born
220	15	McCollough, Judy					40	Contraband	St. Johns County	Hall, Dunham	Aug. 1862		1	On recommendation of Supt. Of Contrabands
220	16	Newman, John					64	Contraband		Canovia, Raphiel	old residence			
220	17	Newman, Orra					48	Contraband		Canovia, Raphiel	old residence		1	Cripple: On recommendation of Supt.Of Contrabands.
220	18	Newman, Patrick					11	Contraband		Canovia, Raphiel	old residence			
220	19	Natiel, John					52	Contraband		Canovia, Antonio	old residence			
220	20	Natiel, Rebecca					70	Contraband			old residence			Bought Free by daughter 5 years ago
220	21	Perpena, Isaac					52	Contraband			old residence			Always free
220	22	Parker, Eve					50	Contraband		Michler, Antonio	old residence			
220	23	Patterson, James					100	Contraband		Madison, John	old residence		1	On recommendation of Supt. Of Contrabands
220	24	Pappy, John					45	Contraband		Salany, Philip	old residence			
220	25	Pappy, Harriet					40	Contraband		Lambias, Antonio	old residence			
220	26	Pappy, Domingo					14	Contraband		Lambias, Antonio	old residence			

Pg	No	Name	Height Ft	Height In	Eyes	Com-plexion	Age	Where born or contraband	Last residence	Where registered for draft or former owner	Date into Department	Oath of Allgn	No of Ration	Remarks
221	27	Pappy, Alexander					11	Contraband		Lambias, Antonio	old residence			
221	28	Pappy, Jane					9	Contraband		Lambias, Antonio	old residence			
221	29	Perpenia, George					65	Contraband		Perpenia, George	old residence			
221	30	Purdum, Edward					45	Contraband		Harris, Ebenezer	old residence			
221	31	Purdum, Hester					40	Contraband		Dupont, Virgil	old residence			
221	32	Purdum, Julias					8	Contraband		Dupont, Virgil	old residence			
221	33	Petersons, Peggy					59	Contraband		Pomare, Joseph	old residence			
221	34	Petersons, John					58	Contraband		Sanchez, Maricea	old residence			
221	35	Peterson, Rose					54	Contraband		Sanchez, Maricea	old residence			
221	36	Perpenia, Teresa					45	Contraband		Sanchy, James	old residence			
221	37	Pacetty, Huldah					80	Contraband		Pacetty	old residence			
221	38	Pacetty, Nicholas					70	Contraband		Pacetty, Bartolo	old residence			
221	39	Pacetty, Antonio					69	Contraband		Parcetty, Bartolo	old residence			
221	40	Pappy, Rose					60	Contraband		Pappy, Joseph	old residence		1	On recommendation of Supt. Of Contrabands
221	41	Robinson, William					50	Contraband	Volusia County	Baker, Moses	May 1864			
221	42	Robinson, Elizabeth					20	Contraband	Volusia County	Baker, Moses	May 1864			
221	43	Robinson, Augustus					12	Contraband	Volusia County	Baker, Moses	May 1864			
221	44	Radicks, Henry					3	Contraband	Volusia County	Baker, Moses	old residence		1/2	On recommendation of Supt. Of Contrabands
221	45	Rial, Boatswain					95	Contraband	Smyrna	Dummit, Douglas	March 1862			
221	46	Radicks, Hannah					30	Contraband		Pappy, GArper	old residence		1	On recommendation of Supt. Of Contrabands
221	47	Radicks, Peter					40	Contraband		Pappy, GArper	old residence			
221	48	Radicks, Maria					14	Contraband		Pappy, GArper	old residence			

Pg	No	Name	Height Ft	Height In	Eyes	Com-plexion	Age	Where born or contraband	Last residence	Where registered for draft or former owner	Date into Department	Oath of Allgn	No of Ration	Remarks
222	1	Radicks, Josephine					8	Contraband		Reddeeks, Casper	old residence			
222	2	Radicks, Peter					3	Contraband		Reddeeks, Casper	old residence			
222	3	Sanchez, Tira					26	Contraband		Raias, Florence	old residence		?	On recommendation of Supt. Of Contrabands
222	4	Sanchez, Delia					5	Contraband		Raias, Florence	old residence		1/2	On recommendation of Supt. Of Contrabands
222	5	Sanchez, Lecia					3	Contraband		Raias, Florence	old residence		1/2	On recommendation of Supt. Of Contrabands
222	6	Sanchez, James					1	Contraband		Raias, Florence	old residence			
222	7	Simmons, Rose					60	Contraband		Putnam, Benjamin	old residence		1	On recommendation of Supt. Of Contrabands
222	8	Smith, Julius					89	Contraband		Smith, Buck	old residence		1	On recommendation of Supt. Of Contrabands
222	9	Sessions, Lydia					23	Contraband			old residence			
222	10	Sanchez, Amelia					21	Contraband		Arnowe, Frances	old residence			
222	11	Sanchez, Mary					5	Contraband		Arnowe, Frances	old residence		1/2	On recommendation of Supt. Of Contrabands
222	12	Sanchez, Sarah					2	Contraband		Arnowe, Frances	old residence			
222	13	Sanchez, Anna					24	Contraband		Arnowe, Paul	old residence			
222	14	Sanchez, Joseph					3/4	Contraband		Arnowe, Paul	old residence			
222	15	Sanchez, Mary					7	Contraband		Arnowe, Paul	old residence		1/2	On recommendation of Supt. Of Contrabands
222	16	Sanchez, Henry					4	Contraband		Arnowe, Paul	old residence			
222	17	Sanchez, Amelia					3	Contraband		Arnowe, Paul	old residence			
222	18	Smith, Dolly					55	Contraband	Green Cove Spring	Hamon, Charles	March 1864			
222	19	Spang, Matilda					70	Contraband		Raias, Mrs.	old residence			
222	20	Stark, Celia					70	Contraband	Volusia County	Stark, James	May 1864		1	On recommendation of Supt. Of Contrabands
222	21	Stark, Jackson					75	Contraband	Volusia County	Stark, James	May 1864			
222	22	Selell, Jane					45	Contraband			old residence			Free Born
222	23	Selell, Peter					56	Contraband		Salany, Domingo	old residence			
222	24	Selell, Harriett					19	Contraband			old residence			Free Born
222	25	Selell, Elizabeth					14	Contraband			old residence			Free Born
222	26	Selell, ...?...					11	Contraband			old residence			Free Born

Pg	No	Name	Height Ft	Height In	Eyes	Com-plexion	Age	Where born or contraband	Last residence	Where registered for draft or former owner	Date into Department	Oath of Allgn	No of Ration	Remarks
223	27	Shemtella?Henrietta					17	Contraband			old residence			Always Free
223	28	Shemtella?, Pheobe					50	Contraband		Dupont	old residence			Received Freedom papers of Dupont years ago.
223	29	Shemtella?, Charles					2 1/2	Contraband			old residence			Always Free
223	30	Saunders, Sykes					50	Contraband			old residence			Free Born
223	31	Saunders, Sally					85?	Contraband			old residence			
223	32	Stevens, Domingo					29	Contraband		Sapity, Domingo	old residence			
223	33	Sessions, Daniel					28	Contraband	Volusia County	Collison?, Weed	April 1863			
223	34	Sams, Mary					50	Contraband		Sapity, Domingo	old residence			
223	35	Sams, Mary					8	Contraband		Sapity, Domingo	old residence			
223	36	Sams, Domingo					40	Contraband		Sapity, Domingo	old residence			
223	37	Shanton, Antinett					30	Contraband			old residence			
223	38	Simmons, Edward					51	Contraband	St. Johns County	Palmer, Ned	Apirl 1862			Discharged from service of U. S.: sickness
223	39	Simmons, Sarah					48	Contraband	St. Johns County	Hall, Dunham	August 1862			
223	40	Smith, Jack					75	Contraband		Smith, Buck	old residence		1	On recommendation of Supt. Of Contrabands
223	41	Smith, Kate					40	Contraband		Smith, Buck	old residence		1	On recommendation of Supt. Of Contrabands
223	42	Stark, Benjamin					65	Contraband	Volusia County	Stark, James	May 1864			
223	43	Thomas, Delphy					25	Contraband		Carr, John	old residence			
223	44	Thomas, Julia					9	Contraband	South Carolina	Holmes	August 1864			
223	45	Thomas, Rose					30	Contraband		Fareria, Joseph	old residence			
223	46	Thomas, Frances					17	Contraband		Fareria, Joseph	old residence			
223	47	Thomas, James ..?..					12	Contraband		Always Free	old residence		1/2	On recommendation of Supt. Of Contrabands
223	48	Triay, Hozapha?					28	Contraband		Triay, Antonio	old residence			

"CENSUS" DEPARTMENT OF THE SOUTH - NOVEMBER, 1864

Pg	No	Name	Height Ft	Height In	Eyes	Com-plexion	Age	Where born or contraband	Last residence	Where registered for draft or former owner	Date into Department	Oath of Allgn	No of Ration	Remarks
224	1	Triay, Rosaleia					13	Contraband		Triay, Antonio	old residence			
224	2	Triay, Philicia					7	Contraband		Triay, Antonio	old residence			
224	3	Triay, Frank					5	Contraband		Triay, Antonio	old residence			
224	4	Triay, William					3	Contraband		Triay, Antonio	old residence			
224	5	Triay, Mary					2	Contraband		Triay, Antonio	old residence			
224	6	Thomas, Rebecca					30	Contraband		Sanchez, Simion	old residence			
224	7	Thomas, Alexander					10	Contraband		Sanchez, Simion	old residence			
224	8	Thomas, Elvira					8	Contraband		Sanchez, Simion	old residence			
224	9	Thomas, Nelia					6	Contraband		Sanchez, Simion	old residence			
224	10	Travise, Frank					50	Contraband		Pacetty, Joseph	old residence		1	On recommendation of Supt. Of Contrabands
224	11	Travise, Catharine					50	Contraband		Pacetty, Joseph	old residence			
224	12	Thomas, Patient					25	Contraband	Volusia County	Hart, William	March 1863			
224	13	Waters, Sarah					25	Contraband		Jenovara, Frank	old residence			
224	14	Waters, Patty					70	Contraband	St. Johns Co.	Pomara, William	Oct. 1864			
224	15	Waters, Mary J.					10	Contraband		Jenovara, Frank	old residence		1/2	On recommendation of Supt. Of Contrabands
224	16	Waters, Joseph					7	Contraband		Jenovara, Frank	old residence		1/2	On recommendation of Supt. Of Contrabands
224	17	Waters, Christina					5	Contraband		Jenovara, Frank	old residence		1/2	On recommendation of Supt. Of Contrabands
224	18	Waters, William					3	Contraband		Jenovara, Frank	old residence		1/2	On recommendation of Supt. Of Contrabands
224	19	Waters, Angelina					1	Contraband		Jenovara, Frank	old residence			
224	21	Weltres, Philis					65	Contraband		Bennett, Peter	old residence			
224	22	Weltres, Cedra					29	Contraband		Bennett, Peter	old residence			
224	23	Weltres, John					8	Contraband		Bennett, Peter	old residence		1/2	On recommendation of Supt. Of Contrabands
224	24	Weltres, Lizzie					2	Contraband		Bennett, Peter	old residence			
224	25	Weltres, Michael					4	Contraband		Bennett, Peter	old residence			
224	26	Wantley, Percillia					12	Contraband		Brooks, Nicholas	old residence		1/2	On recommendation of Supt. Of Contrabands
224	27	White, Catherine					70	Contraband		Qu....?..	old residence			

Pg	No	Name	Height Ft	Height In	Eyes	Com-plexion	Age	Where born or contraband	Last residence	Where registered for draft or former owner	Date into Department	Oath of Allgn	No of Ration	Remarks
225	28	White, Bimus					80	Contraband		Baya, Antonia	old residence		1	On recommendation of Supt. Of Contrabands
225	29	Williams, Matilda					80	Contraband		Williams, William	old residence			
225	30	Weedman, Harriet					50	Contraband		Canorio?, Susan	old residence			
225	31	Weedman, Lucy					24	Contraband		Weedman, Misses	old residence			
225	32	Weedman, Christina					12	Contraband		Canorio, Susan	old residence			
225	33	Whittaker, Rosetta					70	Contraband		Buffington,Samuel	old residence			
225	34	Williams, Betsey					50	Contraband		Bennett, Peter	old residence			
225	35	Williams, Thomas					45	Contraband		Salany, Matea	old residence			
225	36	Wilson, Emily					28	Contraband	St. Johns Co.	Henry, Charles	June 1863			
225	37	Williams, Mary					26	Contraband		Lopez, Domingo	old residence			
225	38	Williams, Vibenia					12	Contraband		Lopez, Domingo	old residence		1/2	On recommendation of Supt. Of Contrabands
225	39	Williams, William					7	Contraband		Lopez, Domingo	old residence		1/2	On recommendation of Supt. Of Contrabands
225	40	Williams, Charles					5	Contraband		Lopez, Domingo	old residence			
225	41	Williams, Martha					40	Contraband	Brevard County	Barbar, Moses	May 1864			
225	42	Williams, John					10	Contraband	Brevard County	Barbar, Moses	May 1864			
225	43	Williams, W_m H.					8	Contraband	Brevard County	Barbar, Moses	May 1864			
225	44	Williams, Lincoln					1/2	Contraband	Brevard County	Barbar, Moses	May 1864			
225	45	Warren, Caroline					50	Contraband		Coles, H.	old residence			
225	46	Warren, Isaac					60	Contraband		Coles, H.	old residence			
225	47	Warren, Florida					23	Contraband		Coles, H.	old residence			
225	48	Wilson, James					?	Contraband	Volusia County	Martin, James	May 1864			

Pg	No	Name	Height Ft	Height In	Eyes	Com-plexion	Age	Where born or contraband	Last residence	Where registered for draft or former owner	Date into Department	Oath of Allgn	No of Ration	Remarks
226	1	White, Louisa					40	Contraband	Volusia County	Baker, Jack	May 1864			
226	2	White, Caleff					16	Contraband	Volusia County	Baker, Jack	May 1864		1	On recommendation of Supt. Of Contrabands
226	3	White, George					10	Contraband	Volusia County	Baker, Jack	May 1864		1/2	On recommendation of Supt. Of Contrabands
226	4	White, Jerard					8	Contraband	Volusia County	Baker, Jack	May 1864		1/2	On recommendation of Supt. Of Contrabands
226	5	White, Henriatta					6	Contraband	Volusia County	Baker, Jack	May 1864		1/2	On recommendation of Supt. Of Contrabands
226	6	White, Samuel					4	Contraband	Volusia County	Baker, Jack	May 1864		1/2	On recommendation of Supt. Of Contrabands
226	7	White, Sarah					3	Contraband	Volusia County	Baker, Jack	May 1864			
226	8	White, Laura					1	Contraband	Volusia County	Baker, Jack	May 1864			
226	9	Wakeman, Levinia					6	Contraband			old residence			Free born
226	10	Wakeman, Sarah					8	Contraband			old residence			Free born
226	11	Wakeman, Joseph					1	Contraband			old residence			Free born
226	12	Williams, Delia					35	Contraband		Salany, Mrs.	old residence		1	On recommendation of Supt. Of Contrabands
226	13	Williams, Louisa					18	Contraband		Salany, Mrs.	old residence			
226	14	Williams, Cepra					4	Contraband		Salany, Mrs.	old residence			
226	15	Williams, Henry					1	Contraband		Salany, Mrs.	old residence			
226	16	Williams, Samuel					3	Contraband						Orphan child from Fernandina to Rebecca Griffins to support
226	17	Williams, Charles					4	Contraband						Orphan child from Fernandina to Rebecca Griffins to support
226	18	Walker, Ellen					13	Contraband		Smith, Buckingham	old residence			
226	19	Waley, Lewis					12	Contraband		Jenks, Hannah	old residence			
226	20	Wilson, George					3?	Contraband	Volusia County	Martin, James	May 1864		1/2	On recommendation of Supt. Of Contrabands
226	21	Young, Harriet					13	Contraband		Tomare, Joseph	old residence			
226	22	Wilson, Cornelius					5	Contraband	Volusia County	Martin, James	May 1864			
226	23	Ugean, Fortune					28	Contraband		Dupont, Cornelius	old residence			
226	24	Ugean, Edward					9m	Contraband			old residence			Free born
226	25	Vanhorn, Tena					16	Contraband	Matanzas bae?	Hemming, Col.	Sept. 1864			
226	26	Vanhorn, Primus?					25	Contraband	Matanzas bae?	Hemming, Col.	Sept. 1864			

Pg	No	Name	Height Ft	Height In	Eyes	Com-plexion	Age	Where born or contraband	Last residence	Where registered for draft or former owner	Date into Department	Oath of Allgn	No of Ration	Remarks
227	27	Adams, Hector					50	Contraband		Bravo, Christol	old residence			
227	28	Lang, Henriettia					14	Contraband			old residence			Free born
227	29	Mungan, Rose					60	Contraband		Feraria, Joseph	Jan. 1864			
227	30	Osborne, Maria					70	Contraband		Free	old residence		1	On recommendation of Supt of Contrabands
227	31	Osborne, Elizabeth					16	Contraband		Free	old residence		1	On recommendation of Supt of Contrabands
227	32	Reddecks, Hannah					40	Contraband		Pappy, GAsper	old residence		1	On recommendation of Supt of Contrabands
227	33	Smith, Mamary					80	Contraband		Smith, Buck	old residence			
227	34	Palm, Matilda					85	Contraband	St. Johns County	Feraria, Joseph	Jan. 1864			
227	35	Wilson, Emily					30	Contraband		Dupont, Abram	old residence			
227	36	Smith, Judy					80	Contraband		Smith, Burmingham	old residence			
227	37	Francis, March					60	Contraband		Tilenbar?	old residence			
227	38	Frances, Sophia					55	Contraband		Philips, John	old residence		1	On recommendation of Supt of Contrabands
227	39	Frances, Pierce					12	Contraband		Philips, John	old residence		1/2	On recommendation of Supt of Contrabands
227	40	Sanchez, Hester					90	Contraband		Sanchez, Venanchey	old residence		1	On recommendation of Supt of Contrabands
227	41	Lang, Mary Eliza					14	Contraband			old residence			Always Free
227	42	Wintley, Kate					28	Contraband		Long, Mathew	old residence			
227	43	Wintley, Sarah J.					4	Contraband		Long, Mathew	old residence		1/2	On recommendation of Supt of Contrabands
227	44	Wintley, Margrett					7	Contraband		Long, Mathew	old residence		1/2	On recommendation of Supt of Contrabands
227	45	Wintley, Frances					7	Contraband		Long, Mathew	old residence		1/2	On recommendation of Supt of Contrabands
227	46	Wintley, Harry					9	Contraband		Long, Mathew	old residence		1/2	On recommendation of Supt of Contrabands
227	47	Mungan, Mary					68	Contraband		Madison?, John	old residence		1	On recommendation of Supt. of Contrabands
227	48	Wallace, Mary					89	Contraband	Volusia County	Dupont, Virgil	June 1864		1	On recommendation of Supt of Contrabands

Pg	No	Name	Height Ft	Height In	Eyes	Com-plexion	Age	Where born or contraband	Last residence	Where registered for draft or former owner	Date into Department	Oath of Allgn	No of Ration	Remarks
228	1	Bennett, Cedra					28	Contraband		Bennett, Peter	old residence			
228	2	Bennett, John					9	Contraband		Bennett, Peter	old residence		1/2	On recommendation of Supt. Of Contrabands
228	3	Bennett, Michael					4	Contraband		Bennett, Peter	old residence		1/2	On recommendation of Supt. Of Contrabands
228	4	Bennett, Lizzie					2	Contraband		Bennett, Peter	old residence			
228	5	Fontinia, Philis					65	Contraband		Fontinia	old residence			
228	6	Holmes, David					53	Contraband		Duryier, Anthony	old residence			
228	7	Holmes, Letty					45	Contraband		Anderson, Mrs.	old residence			
228	8	Hills, Easter					35	Contraband		Carr, John	old residence			
228	9	Hernandez, Cedra					8	Contraband		Hernandez, James	old residence			
228	10	Harrison, Aaron					60	Contraband		Oliveras, Patolo	old residence			
228	11	Grey, Georgianara					20	Contraband	Nassau County	Walker, John	Nov. 1862			
228	12	Grey, Florida					5/12	Contraband	Nassau County	Walker, John	Nov. 1862			Free born
228	13	Kelly, Joseph					14	Contraband	Putnam County	Kelly, William	Aug. 1864			
228	14	Mallania, Joseph					51	Contraband		Perpina	old residence			
228	15	Jackson, Mary					33	Contraband		Pappy, GAsper	old residence			
228	16	Jackson, Hypolity					14	Contraband		Pappy, GAsper	old residence			
228	17	Joseph, Charles					60	Contraband		Salany, Philip	old residence			
228	18	Johnson, Matilda					10	Contraband		Henry, Nathaniel	old residence			
228	19	Johnson, Charles					7	Contraband		Henry, Nathaniel	old residence			
228	20	Masters, Friday					90	Contraband		Masters, Bartolo	old residence		1	On recommendation of Supt. Of Contrabands
228	21	Natiel, Philis					60	Contraband		Salany, Mrs.	old residence			
228	22	Natiel, Mary					38	Contraband		Salany, Mrs.	old residence			
228	23	Natiel, Philis					12	Contraband		Salany, Mrs.	old residence		1/2	On recommendation of Supt of Contrabands
228	24	Natiel, Frances					6	Contraband		Salany, Mrs.	old residence			
228	25	Natiel, John					?	Contraband		Salany, Mrs.	old residence			

Pg	No	Name	Height Ft	Height In	Eyes	Complexion	Age	Where born or contraband	Last residence	Where registered for draft or former owner	Date into Department	Oath of Allgn	No of Ration	Remarks
229	26	Natiel, Alecia					9	Contraband		Salany, Mrs.	old residence		1/2	On recommendation of Supt. Of Contrabands
229	27	Natiel, Francis					4	Contraband		Salany, Mrs.	old residence			
229	28	Natiel, Richard					80	Contraband		Salany, Mrs.	old residence			
229	29	Nicholas, Abram					65	Contraband			old residence			Free born
229	30	Ponce, Mary					12	Contraband		Ponce, Mrs.	old residence			
229	31	Rubia, Sydney					50	Contraband		Carr, John	old residence			
229	32	Sanchez, Alecia					25	Contraband		Knowe, Stephen R.	old residence			
229	33	Sanchez,Clementine					6	Contraband		Knowe, Stephen R.	old residence		1/2	On recommendation of Supt. Of Contrabands
229	34	Sanchez, Michael					3	Contraband		Knowe, Stephen R.	old residence			
229	35	Sanchez, Ann E.					5/12	Contraband		Knowe, Stephen R.	old residence			
229	36	Smith, Holgan					80	Contraband		Smith, Josiah	old residence		1	On recommendation of Supt. Of Contrabands
229	37	Salany, Jane					11	Contraband		Masters, Bartolo	old residence			
229	38	Salany, William					15	Contraband		Laurence, Paul	old residence			
229	39	Salany, Jane					51	Contraband		Masters, Bartolo	old residence			
229	40	Weedman, Peter					8	Contraband		Weedman, Misses	old residence			
229	41	Waters, William					30	Contraband		Masters, Patrolo	old residence			
229	42	Wills, Columbus					65	Contraband		Sanchez, James	old residence			
229	43	Lopez, Augustus					60	St. Augustine	St. Augustine		old residence		?	Ration by order of Post Commander
229	44	Lopez, Margrett					58	St. Augustine	St. Augustine		old residence		?	Ration by order of Post Commander
229	45	Lopez, Domingo					32	St. Augustine	St. Augustine		old residence		?	Ration by order of Post Commander
229	46	Turner, William					38	Florida	Volusia County		?			
229	47	Lopez, Patrolo	5	1	hazel	dark	55	St. Augustine	St. Augustine		old residence		?	Ration by order of Post Commander

EVERY NAME INDEX

(Excluding the Owners) Be aware, that many of the names are on the same page more than once.

EVERY NAME INDEX

(Excluding the Owners) Be aware, that many of the names are on the same page more than once.

EVERY NAME INDEX

(Excluding the Owners) Be aware, that many of the names are on the same page more than once.

EVERY NAME INDEX

(Excluding the Owners) Be aware, that many of the names are on the same page more than once.

EVERY NAME INDEX

(Excluding the Owners) Be aware, that many of the names are on the same page more than once.

EVERY NAME INDEX

(Excluding the Owners) Be aware, that many of the names are on the same page more than once.

EVERY NAME INDEX

(Excluding the Owners) Be aware, that many of the names are on the same page more than once.

EVERY NAME INDEX

(Excluding the Owners) Be aware, that many of the names are on the same page more than once.

EVERY NAME INDEX

(Excluding the Owners) Be aware, that many of the names are on the same page more than once.

EVERY NAME INDEX

(Excluding the Owners) Be aware, that many of the names are on the same page more than once.

EVERY NAME INDEX

(Excluding the Owners) Be aware, that many of the names are on the same page more than once.

EVERY NAME INDEX

(Excluding the Owners) Be aware, that many of the names are on the same page more than once.

EVERY NAME INDEX

(Excluding the Owners) Be aware, that many of the names are on the same page more than once.

EVERY NAME INDEX

(Excluding the Owners) Be aware, that many of the names are on the same page more than once.

EVERY NAME INDEX

(Excluding the Owners) Be aware, that many of the names are on the same page more than once.

EVERY NAME INDEX

(Excluding the Owners) Be aware, that many of the names are on the same page more than once.

EVERY NAME INDEX

(Excluding the Owners) Be aware, that many of the names are on the same page more than once.

EVERY NAME INDEX

(Excluding the Owners) Be aware, that many of the names are on the same page more than once.

EVERY NAME INDEX

(Excluding the Owners) Be aware, that many of the names are on the same page more than once.

EVERY NAME INDEX

(Excluding the Owners) Be aware, that many of the names are on the same page more than once.

EVERY NAME INDEX

(Excluding the Owners) Be aware, that many of the names are on the same page more than once.

EVERY NAME INDEX

(Excluding the Owners) Be aware, that many of the names are on the same page more than once.

EVERY NAME INDEX

(Excluding the Owners) Be aware, that many of the names are on the same page more than once.

EVERY NAME INDEX

(Excluding the Owners) Be aware, that many of the names are on the same page more than once.

EVERY NAME INDEX

(Excluding the Owners) Be aware, that many of the names are on the same page more than once.

EVERY NAME INDEX

(Excluding the Owners) Be aware, that many of the names are on the same page more than once.

EVERY NAME INDEX

(Excluding the Owners) Be aware, that many of the names are on the same page more than once.

EVERY NAME INDEX

(Excluding the Owners) Be aware, that many of the names are on the same page more than once.

EVERY NAME INDEX

(Excluding the Owners) Be aware, that many of the names are on the same page more than once.

EVERY NAME INDEX

(Excluding the Owners) Be aware, that many of the names are on the same page more than once.

EVERY NAME INDEX

(Excluding the Owners) Be aware, that many of the names are on the same page more than once.

EVERY NAME INDEX

(Excluding the Owners) Be aware, that many of the names are on the same page more than once.

EVERY NAME INDEX

(Excluding the Owners) Be aware, that many of the names are on the same page more than once.

EVERY NAME INDEX

(Excluding the Owners) Be aware, that many of the names are on the same page more than once.

EVERY NAME INDEX

(Excluding the Owners) Be aware, that many of the names are on the same page more than once.

INDEX OF OWNERS

Be aware, that many of the names are on the same page more than once.

INDEX OF OWNERS

Be aware, that many of the names are on the same page more than once.

INDEX OF OWNERS

Be aware, that many of the names are on the same page more than once.

INDEX OF OWNERS

Be aware, that many of the names are on the same page more than once.

INDEX OF OWNERS

Be aware, that many of the names are on the same page more than once.